Virtue Is Knowledge

Virtue Is Knowledge

The Moral Foundations of Socratic Political Philosophy

LORRAINE SMITH PANGLE

The University of Chicago Press
Chicago and London

Lorraine Smith Pangle is professor of government at the University of Texas at Austin, where she is also codirector of the Thomas Jefferson Center for the Study of Core Texts and Ideas. She is the author of three books, including, most recently, *The Political Philosophy of Benjamin Franklin*.

The University of Chicago Press, Chicago 60637
The University of Chicago Press, Ltd., London

Printed in the United States of America

23 22 21 20 19 18 17 16 15 14   1 2 3 4 5

ISBN-13: 978-0-226-13654-7 (cloth)
ISBN-13: 978-0-226-13668-4 (e-book)
DOI: 10.7208/chicago/9780226136684.001.0001

Library of Congress Cataloging-in-Publication Data

Pangle, Lorraine Smith, author.
Virtue is knowledge : the moral foundations of Socratic political philosophy / Lorraine Smith Pangle.
pages cm
Includes bibliographical references and index.
ISBN 978-0-226-13654-7 (cloth : alk. paper)—ISBN 978-0-226-13668-4 (e-book) 1. Socrates—Political and social views. 2. Plato. I. Title.
B317.P33 2014
184—dc23
2013040560

∞ This paper meets the requirements of ANSI/NISO Z39.48-1992 (Permanence of Paper).

For Heather

CONTENTS

ACKNOWLEDGMENTS

Work on this book was supported by fellowships from the United States National Endowment for the Humanities, the Social Sciences and Humanities Research Council of Canada, and the University of Texas College of Liberal Arts. A version of chapter 5 on *The Laws* was published as "Moral and Criminal Responsibility in Plato's *Laws*," *American Political Science Review*, 103:3 (August 2009), 456–73. For helpful comments on earlier drafts of the manuscript or of particular chapters, I am indebted to Peter Ahrensdorf, Timothy Burns, Susan Collins, Ariel Helfer, Thomas Pangle, Christina Tarnapoulsky, Aristide Tessitore, and several anonymous reviewers for the *APSR* and University of Chicago Press. Publication costs were defrayed in part by a generous subvention grant from the University of Texas.

INTRODUCTION

This book is a study of the moral foundations of Plato's political philosophy, pursued through an examination of his provocative claims about the relation of virtue to knowledge. Maintaining that the political art is "the art whose business it is to care for souls,"[1] Plato returns incessantly to the most fundamental of political questions, classically understood: What is the excellence or virtue of the human soul? Is it in our power to attain it? Is it teachable? What is the root cause of moral failing, and what is the just response to it? His apparent answers to these questions are as familiar as they are strange: virtue is knowledge; all virtue is ultimately one; anyone who grasps the goodness of virtue will choose to do what is just and will prefer to suffer rather than do injustice; vice is due to ignorance; the correct response to wrongdoing is education and not retributive punishment—and yet, despite all this, virtue may not be teachable after all. This book will trace Socrates' arguments for these claims and problems in the five dialogues that explore them most thoroughly, the *Apology*, the *Gorgias*, the *Protagoras*, the *Meno*, and the *Laws*, giving central attention to his arguments about the relation of virtue to knowledge. The claim that virtue is nothing but knowledge is paradoxical in the most radical sense, for not only does ordinary intuition tell us that we are free to follow or not follow the knowledge that we have, but intuition suggests that to the extent that we are imperfectly free, it is not ignorance but passion that constrains us and leads us astray. Despite the strangeness of this and all Socrates' paradoxes, it will be the contention of this book that there is a serious truth at the core of each of them, and especially at the core of his claim for knowledge, that has not been adequately appreciated.

In many ways the claim that virtue is knowledge is clearly rhetorical. Throughout Socrates' life, by making the claim in a simple and extreme form, he was able to present himself as a high-minded if naïve philosopher whose criticisms of the justice of all human law codes were both well-intended and politically so unrealistic as to be harmless. Thus he managed to protect himself even while giving potential students a glimpse of the radically unconventional nerve of his thought. At his trial in Plato's *Apology*, Socrates uses the claim to show the irrationality of punishing him, to portray himself as a moral hero who alone understands that virtue is the one thing that matters and who adheres to it more steadily even than Achilles, at great cost to himself, and to argue for his inestimable value to the city in his quest to find and to teach others the knowledge they all need in order to be good.

At a deeper level, the claim that virtue is knowledge works as a diagnostic and educational tool. Often, by appearing to take an excessively calculating view of virtue, Socrates succeeds in evoking the passionate resistance of even his most cynically hard-boiled interlocutors, thereby bringing to the surface for examination their commitments to a view of virtue that is nobly uncalculating, unselfish, and even unconstrained by what reason shows us to be good. In this way Plato's Socrates proceeds in dialogue after dialogue to show his interlocutors and all of us that our moral thought is both more deep-seated than we may think and also deeply confused. For his analyses implicitly argue that not only his Greek contemporaries but human beings everywhere are beset by a radical confusion about moral responsibility that is rooted in self-contradictory thoughts about the goodness of virtue. As we begin to examine our own opinions about virtue and moral responsibility under Plato's guidance, we see that Socrates' claims are misleading when taken at face value and yet turn out to have a strange power that is difficult to dismiss. Somehow virtue is indeed all about grasping clearly what is good and why it is good, and somehow this grasp, when truly solid, is efficacious. Somehow the unjust soul truly is unhealthy in a way that no one could wish to be and that calls more for compassion than for vengeance. Grappling with the claim that virtue is knowledge, then, is a first step towards clarity, inasmuch as it reveals the diverse and contradictory opinions that we thoughtlessly hold.

Third and finally, the Socratic paradoxes are an important part of Socrates' project of testing his own hypotheses about the inescapable power of the good as we perceive it in governing human choice, as well as about the character of the moral opinion underlying all law both human and divine. Compelling people to grapple with the strong claims he makes for knowledge of the good and to feel their force within their own souls helps him confirm his hypotheses about the structure of moral opinion and about the most important elements in it. In particular, he reveals again and again the copresence of beliefs that virtue is the greatest of goods and that virtue is at bottom a transcendence or sacrifice of what is good, and the difficulty of jettisoning either of these beliefs. It is an important part of Socrates' Delphic quest for wisdom to see how his companions change their views as a result of their encounter with his strange claims and with their own ambivalences and to see what else changes in them as their opinions evolve.

In order to unpack the most serious layers of Socratic argumentation, my method will be to proceed by means of a careful, systematic textual exegesis of the five dialogues, approaching each as a whole. For the *Meno* and the *Protagoras,* I provide a running commentary on the entire dialogue; for the other three dialogues I read more selectively but with constant attention to the drama of Socrates' encounter with his interlocutors, a drama that in each case illustrates and sheds crucial light on problems under discussion. By focusing on the question of how Plato's Socrates and Athenian Stranger are trying to elicit, challenge, and refine the views of their interlocutors, we can set ourselves on a path of reflection opened up by Plato and can profit from the education he offers without falling prey to the pitfalls of efforts to extract and distill once and for all what the true "doctrines" of Plato or Socrates were. These efforts, the mainstay of academic Plato studies, have yielded much fruit in the form of careful distinctions and reflections on the cogency or lack of cogency of many arguments. What they have failed to do is to distinguish with any clarity the "Socratic" from the "Platonic" teachings or to defend either as a rigorous and compelling whole. Thus, for example, Terence Irwin in his compendious *Plato's Ethics* exhaustively assembles arguments from the purportedly "early" dialogues to try to pin down Socrates' teachings on a wide array of psychological and ethical questions.[2] On point after point his evidence demonstrates genuine problems and refutes simplistic readings, but what we come away with is a Socrates who teaches that virtue is both necessary and sufficient for happiness, that virtue is wisdom, that wisdom is the whole of the human good, that virtue is nothing but an instrumental mean to secure one's own happiness, and that happiness is nothing other than the pleasure everyone wants: a radically incoherent Socrates who would have to have been astonishingly thoughtless about what happiness is and how it is secured. An opposite problem is exemplified in the interpretive approach of Thomas C. Brickhouse and Nicholas Smith. Attempting in *Plato's Socrates* to render a Socrates more coherent than Irwin's, they find themselves obliged to be endlessly "charitable" in giving more moderate, sensible glosses on those

Socratic statements that not only seem on their face unreasonable but that are contradicted by other Socratic statements. The result is a Socrates at once sensible and bland, who continually misstates his view for no evident reason.[3] There is no way around it: Plato's Socrates says strange, provocative, wildly unqualified, and contradictory things. Because the tensions arise not only between dialogues from allegedly different periods of Plato's life but within individual dialogues; because the most important paradoxical claims arise in so-called early, middle, and late dialogues; because the evidence for the dating is contested; and because Plato himself nowhere suggests that his views have changed or that the order of composition is a key to understanding his works, I think it best to leave the question of order of composition aside, and with it the question of the historical Socrates, and instead to turn to the closest possible reading of each work as a work of Plato's, seeking to understanding what his leading character is saying and doing in that drama and why his interlocutors are responding to him as they are.

As we explore in this way Socrates' arguments about the relation of virtue to knowledge, we see that his understanding of reason's power in the human soul is much more finely nuanced than first appears. In the process of making almost fantastic claims for the power of knowledge over passion, as for example the claim in the *Protagoras* that knowledge is the strongest of all things and can never be dragged around like a slave, Socrates points to many curious facts about the way thoughts and passions inform and influence one another in our efforts and our failures to act well. Many of the arguments for the Socratic thesis in fact involve explorations of the factors that make it exceedingly difficult for humans to be the rational creatures that Socrates at first sight seems to claim we are. We begin to see that in writing each dialogue Plato was admirably attuned to the complex causes of human action and the power of irrational passions and that he brings these factors to life in the dramas before us. Plato shows that these difficulties are intimately bound up with some of the best as well as some of the worst elements in human nature, and in particular with the elements that make us naturally political and social beings. Therefore, much more than most commentators, I argue that a key to Plato's analysis of the relation of virtue to knowledge is to be found in understanding the political dimensions of the relevant dialogues. Not only the obviously political *Gorgias* and *Laws* but also the epistemologically focused *Meno* and the argument from hedonism in the *Protagoras* require careful attention to the importance of the political passions and the distinction between civic and philosophic virtue in order to unravel their paradoxes and to distinguish the precise sense in which virtue may indeed be something like knowledge. When we do so, we see more fully the continuities between the dialogues as well as the gulf between Plato's own philosophic understanding of human excellence and moral responsibility and what he presents as universal and necessary features of the ordinary citizen's understanding; we see both his critique of this civic understanding and his reasons for avoiding a broadside attack upon it. This distinction in turn sheds light on many of the most prominent features of his political philosophy, including his skepticism about the possibility of popular enlightenment and his resulting preference for the small, rooted, communal polis of the *Laws* over the more cosmopolitan and liberal Athens. Yet, as we will see when we turn to the *Laws* in the final chapter, Plato also shows how it may be possible to weave elements of his own thought and spirit into an actual legal code—in his time or any time—so as to infuse a society with some degree of his own humanity and his sublime freedom from vindictiveness.[4]

Seven Ways to Understand the Thesis that Virtue Is Knowledge

Socrates' arguments for his thesis that virtue is knowledge are, as I have noted, astonishingly diverse. Therefore it may be helpful at the outset to provide an overview of the different arguments we find in Plato in support of this claim, which seem to include all the possible ways that it might be elaborated and defended, virtually all of them explicitly or implicitly made at some point by Socrates. The claims fall under two main headings: arguments for the supreme goodness of virtue, and arguments for the power of knowledge.

I. The Goodness of Virtue

The first component of the thesis that virtue is knowledge is an argument about the goodness of virtue. Virtue is in accordance with knowledge because virtue is supremely and invariably good. Seeing virtue for what it is means that one will choose it over any alternative if one is acting rationally. This argument has three basic variations, each of which has in turn two or more subtypes. The three basic variations may be classified as:

1) the *utilitarian* view that virtue is beneficial to the virtuous individual as the essential means to happiness;
2) the *eudaimonist* view that virtue is choiceworthy because it is the very essence of happiness; and

3) the *heroic* view that virtue is noble and as such is supremely choiceworthy, even if it often fails to bring happiness.

The utilitarian and eudaimonist positions each have, in turn, three subtypes: a conventionally *moral* version; a version original to Socrates, which I will call *hypermoral* and which claims or suggests that morality, more or less as it is conventionally understood, is not only binding on us but the only thing worthy of serious attention at all; and a *transmoral* version that defines virtue or human excellence in a way that leaves behind many of the elements of conventional morality, including beliefs about duties, obligations, and condign rewards and punishments. The heroic ethos has two possible subtypes, the moral and the hypermoral.[5] Let us examine each possible position in turn.

1) Utilitarian: virtue is the essential means to happiness

1a) Moral-utilitarian: Virtue is the widely recognized decency that is good for others and turns out to be good for the virtuous individual himself as well. Through its natural and predictable consequences, virtue brings us the mundane goods we want and need. Among these consequences may be the honors, pleasures, and material advantages that come from winning the love and trust of others. Thinking clearly about our real needs shows that obeying the laws and following the rules of conventional morality is the best policy.

1b) Hypermoral-utilitarian: Virtue, conventionally understood, ultimately guarantees all of the important good things that we want and need. By making us deserving of happiness, virtue and virtue alone assures that we will enjoy it. This claim would seem to depend in turn on the proposition that there is a divine providence with the power and justice to reward each according to his deserts. Corroborating the important connection of this view to claims about the divine, Plato characteristically presents it in mythical or quasi-mythical terms. Examples of such mythical presentations may be found in the *Apology*, the *Gorgias*, the *Meno*, and the *Laws*.

1c) Transmoral-utilitarian: In this view, virtue is the sum of those qualities that ensure one's ability to secure (within the limits of fortune) whatever is good for oneself. There is no gap between the demands of virtue and the requisites of happiness because virtue, correctly understood, is nothing other than a clear grasp of one's own good together with any other qualities needed to attain it. Callicles in the *Gorgias* and Meno in the *Meno* both at points assert this position, as do several of the sophists who posit that the human good consists in pleasure; Machiavelli will return to it, positing freedom and glory as the most important ends. But there is also a philosophic version of this position, which holds that virtue is the sum of good qualities of soul—such qualities as practical wisdom, self-control, courage, and even justice as simple law-abidingness—that are needed as instruments or to lay the foundations for the most successful and most pleasant philosophic life. It does not follow from this proposition that virtue guarantees happiness, since good fortune is needed as well. But it does follow that the dictates of virtue are always aligned with the individual's happiness, as they constitute the best humanly foreseeable means to attain it.

2) Eudaimonist: virtue is the essential core of happiness

2a) Moral-eudaimonist: The essence of virtue is a good condition of the soul whose presence or active exercise constitutes the core of human happiness, and this good condition is in fact the constellation of qualities generally recognized as virtues. This makes virtue the most valuable possession, and never worth sacrificing, though it is not the only thing that matters for happiness and thus is not a guarantee of happiness. Other things that may be considered necessary are health, simple pleasures or at least freedom from suffering, friends, the well-being of those one cares for, and perhaps most importantly, opportunities to exercise one's virtue in challenging and satisfying ways.

2b) Hypermoral-eudaimonist: The essence of virtue is the same good condition of the soul recognized by the moral-eudaimonist position, but now asserted to be both the necessary and sufficient cause of happiness because nothing else matters. Happiness needs nothing from fortune, not even opportunities to exercise virtue, because such opportunities are in fact always present. Socrates' occasional expressions of this view inspired the Cynic and later the Stoic philosophical schools.

2c) Transmoral-eudaimonist: The essence of virtue is a good condition of the soul, whose presence or active exercise constitutes the core of human happiness, but this excellence is not what conventional morality understands it to be. The most important version of this view would be the one sometimes suggested by Socrates: that true virtue is nothing but the bold intelligence of the philosopher, understood as the only virtue because it is the only quality that is truly, intrinsically, invariably good and admirable. It follows from the transmoral-eudaimonist position that virtue is essential for and never opposes one's happiness, but it does not follow that virtue guarantees happiness, for similar reasons to those given in 2a above.

All versions of the utilitarian and eudaimonist views have three corollaries.

Corollary 1: Virtue never demands the sacrifice of one's own greatest good (even if in the short run it appears to).

Corollary 2: Vice is pitiable. Vice may follow from ignorance or lack of self-control or lack of courage or all of these. But it is always pitiable.

Corollary 3: Moral indignation entails confusion. Gaining clarity on the first two corollaries and seeing vice for what it really is would eliminate the desire for retribution.

3) Heroic: Virtue is always good because supremely noble, even if it often fails to bring happiness

3a) Moral-heroic: Virtue is good because noble, but often bad for the one who chooses it. It is hence a tragic choice, which cries out for a divine recognition or compensation that the cosmos does not evidently provide. Many of the Homeric and tragic heroes of ancient Greece held this position; Socrates at least briefly takes this stance in the *Apology* when he speaks of the enormous sacrifices he has made for virtue.

3b) Hypermoral-heroic: Virtue is so noble that when seen correctly, nothing else matters. The wise man willingly pursues virtue single-mindedly, without regard for anything else and without any expectation of personal compensation in this life or the next for the inconsiderable things he gives up. Socrates takes this stance more prominently in the *Apology*.

II. The Power of Knowledge

The second component of the thesis that virtue is knowledge is an argument about the power of knowledge. Socrates seems at various times to argue that knowledge is the foundation for virtue in three different ways:

4) Knowledge is necessary but not sufficient for virtue.
5) Knowledge is sufficient for virtue, even if not necessary.
6) Knowledge is both necessary and sufficient for virtue.

4) Knowledge is necessary but not sufficient for virtue

The essence of human virtue is insight into the good, realized in practice. Such knowledge does not guarantee its own efficacy, either because no knowledge can be that powerful or because such knowledge as is available to human beings is necessarily so incomplete that other subrational qualities are needed in addition. These other qualities are not in themselves virtues, for such aspects of character as exist simply by nature or blind habit are as likely to result in harm as in benefit and are good only when brought under the guidance of knowledge. Thus virtue is knowledge in the somewhat loose sense that knowledge is its core and its only unqualifiedly good element. If virtue requires but is not strictly identical with knowledge, it follows that vice may be due either to ignorance or to weakness or lack of self-restraint. It also follows that the virtues differ in kind, each of the practical ones being woven out of knowledge and particular subrational qualities or inclinations that support the development and efficacy of that knowledge. Socrates seems to suggest the need for such subrational supplements to knowledge in his discussion of the guardians in the *Republic*, for example, who he says must have courage as well as intelligence, or in his metaphor of the ship captain in the *Laws*, who needs not only knowledge but immunity to seasickness if he is to rule the ship well.

What other qualities besides knowledge might virtue require? Some possible candidates are natural courage or spiritedness, tenacity or strength of soul, natural moderation or steadiness, a natural spirit of sympathy or generosity, a strong desire for one's own true good, or good habits. Different combinations of these qualities might be effective in different cases, so that, for example, the more desire one had for the good, the less courage one would need to overcome obstacles. Of the three possible claims about knowledge, this position is certainly closest to common sense. But Socrates routinely claims much more.

5) Knowledge is sufficient for virtue, even if not absolutely necessary

Socrates often argues that knowledge is perfectly efficacious, as in the *Protagoras* when he insists that knowledge cannot be dragged around like a slave. This claim is compatible with the view that at least some virtue exists simply by nature or through unreflective habit, which Socrates also suggests in the *Protagoras* and the *Meno*, for example, when he argues that virtue cannot be taught. But if knowledge when present guarantees good behavior, it follows that vice always involves ignorance or confusion.

6) Knowledge is both necessary and sufficient for virtue

Knowledge by itself always leads one to act in the best possible way in each situation, and hence vice is always due to ignorance or confusion. It follows that there is essentially only one virtue, knowledge, or a steady grasp of the truth that is of concern to us and especially of the truth about what is good and bad. However, this knowledge may have different ways of manifesting itself with respect to different objects. Thus knowledge of what is truly fearful and not fearful would be courage, and knowledge of what pleasures are truly worth having and not worth having would be moderation.

The great question that arises with the claim that knowledge is sufficient for virtue is: how can knowledge have such power? Do irrational desires and fears simply evaporate when the mind decides that resisting them is the most prudent thing to do? If they do not evaporate, is knowledge so powerful that it allows us to overcome them every time and act correctly, and if so, how does it do this? Or might it be that our ordinary fragmentary knowledge of the human good has no such power, but a comprehensive knowledge might have—a comprehensive knowledge of ourselves, of where we stand in the world, and of what is good and bad for us, not only at this moment but over the whole of our existence? Or might knowledge be sufficient in a different way, in the sense that the same subrational strength that is needed to assure its efficacy is needed to acquire knowledge in the first place, so that knowledge of the good, wherever it exists, will also be efficacious? Or again, might the knowledge in question include not only propositional knowledge but a kind of "knowing how" that includes knowing how to manage one's own passions? Might the knowledge that is virtue thus include both a comprehensive knowledge of oneself and what is good, together with the ability to "keep one's head" in the face of temptations and fears that threaten to loosen our grip upon what we know? If so, the knowledge in question might better be characterized as wisdom, and so we should consider as a final proposition:

7) Virtue is wisdom, as a trait of character both intellectual and practical

With this as a provisional hypothesis, then, let us turn to the *Apology*, attending closely to everything Socrates says about the goodness of virtue, the power of knowledge, and the character of wisdom as he leads us on a strange dance through all of the propositions above.

ONE

Education and Corruption: *Apology*

Socrates' argument that virtue is knowledge and vice is ignorance occurs in a number of Platonic dialogues, but perhaps the best place to begin our investigation of it is the *Apology*, the dialogue that stands as the traditional portal to the Platonic corpus and that takes as its central themes the philosophic life and the deadly conflict between philosophy and the classical city. Here, in his cross-examination of Meletus on the charge of corrupting the youth, Socrates argues that at least concerning the crime in question, no one who knew what he was doing would ever commit it voluntarily, as it invariably redounds to the harm of the perpetrator. He argues further that the proper remedy for one who has committed this crime involuntarily is instruction and not punishment. The question that this manner of presenting the virtue-is-knowledge thesis immediately raises is this: Why should a charge of corrupting the youth in a capital trial, in a crowded, hostile, noisy courtroom, provide the proper setting for Plato to introduce to us this fundamental and far-reaching theme of Socratic thought?

The Corruption Charge in Context

Socrates' cross-examination of Meletus, which constitutes his only direct rebuttal of the charges against him, is rapid, far-ranging, and highly compressed in its reasoning. It will be helpful, therefore, to consider how Socrates sets the stage for this surprisingly brief response to the charges against him before examining it in detail. In the version of his defense speech that Plato gives us, Socrates begins with a discussion of rhetoric. Socrates in some sense clearly has welcomed the opportunity the trial presents to make a major statement to the world about himself and what his philosophic activity is all about. But this occasion is a most dangerous one, for he must make his speech to an angry mob already predisposed to condemn him—a situation that not only any defense attorney but any citizen of even ordinary capacities would immediately recognize as calling for a careful selection of evidence and carefully constructed appeals to the better sentiments of the audience to counter the inflammatory rhetoric just deployed by the prosecution—at least if the defendant wishes to be acquitted. It is fitting, therefore, that this man who has spent his life constructing speeches should at the outset of his trial be reflecting deeply on the rhetorical demands of this situation, silently if not openly. But to our surprise, we find Plato's Socrates taking up the theme of rhetoric only to make a most implausible cascade of assertions and suggestions: He is an inept speaker who does not know how to put his thoughts in order; he is wholly ignorant of the proceedings of a law court and the manner of speech required there; he is indeed utterly naïve. For he tells the jury that "what you will hear will be spoken at random in the words that I happen upon, for I trust that the things I say are just" (17c1–3),[1] as if he is so trusting in the power of virtue to protect him, and so innocent of the ways of the world, as to believe that against clever accusers and violent passions one need only state the unadorned truth, in whatever words first come into one's head, and one is certain to find justice. For, he adds, it is the virtue of an orator simply to speak the truth without guile and of a judge to judge fairly without guile. Virtue is aligned perfectly, then, with truth, simplicity, and trust: Socrates evidently trusts that the jurors need only be reminded of their duty and they will do it, for he indicates that knowledge of his own duty is reason enough to do his, and he seems confident that one need only do it and all will come out well. At the outset, then, we have a strong statement on the power of truthfulness that looks somehow at once deadly serious and rather less than serious. Many commentators have observed the irony in these, as in other statements in the *Apology*.[2]

With this peculiar self-presentation, Socrates makes rhetoric a central theme of the *Apology*, not just his rhetoric on this day in court but his lifelong strategy for defending himself and his philosophic activity from a potentially hostile city, and perhaps vice versa. Socrates alludes to his ongoing preoccupation with defensive rhetoric when he tells his audience not to be surprised when they "hear me making my defense with the same speeches I am accustomed to speak both in the marketplace at the money-tables, where many of you have heard me, and elsewhere" (17c7–9). He will use not only the same manner of speech, but the very same arguments he has been making for years. Has he nothing specific to say in his defense? Or have all of his speeches perhaps in some sense been conceived with a view to his defense?[3] This dialogue contains recurring reflections on the aims and techniques of Socratic rhetoric as well as vivid examples of that rhetoric at work. Socrates' cross-examination of Meletus on the corruption charge is but one such example. As is often the case with Socratic rhetoric and is often complained of by Socratic interlocutors,[4] this cross-examination is in fact an egregiously slippery, incomplete, illogical defense of a thesis that is paradoxical and in need of much defense. Why does Socrates, a most careful thinker, engage so often in slipshod argumentation? How is his strange use of rhetoric in confronting Meletus connected to his strange claims about his rhetoric at the beginning of his speech? I would make this suggestion: the *Apology* truly is unusually frank in revealing the nerve of Socratic thought, but it is at the same time quite artfully deceptive. The framing Plato gives to the exposition of his virtue-is-knowledge thesis will help show that argument's potentially explosive power. In doing so, it may shed light on Socrates' curious rhetorical strategy, his underlying thought, and his complex intentions.

In the cross-examination of Meletus, Socrates addresses the charges on which Meletus, Anytus, and Lycon have indicted him, but this exchange is preceded by a long discussion of charges that no one but Socrates has brought into court on this day, the charges of the so-called old accusers, among whom Aristophanes figures prominently. These old accusers, Socrates says, got hold of many of the jurors from childhood, persuading them "that there is a certain Socrates, a wise man, a thinker on the things aloft, who has investigated all things under the earth, and who makes the weaker speech the stronger" (18b6–c1). This account is in itself not a charge of any crime at all but merely a description that might well have been made by an admirer. But it is dangerous, Socrates says, for this reason: not precisely he himself, nor precisely his first accusers, but their listeners "hold that those who investigate these things also do not believe in gods" (18c2–3). Students of natural science (among whom Socrates elsewhere quite openly includes himself, at least as a young man) were engaged in an effort to explain the world in terms of natural necessities that would admit of no exceptions;[5] such a project must either assume or prove the nonexistence of providential gods who at any time might, for example, intervene to spirit their favorites out of battle and make them reappear instantly in other places. For if there are no natural necessities, there can be no rigorous account of what must be, but only a description of what usually is or usually has been the case hitherto: there can be no science, but only history.

To assume that the world is governed by natural necessity, however, is an act of faith and not science, and to show in the case of every purported miracle that it has a wholly natural cause is a task that can never be completed and one that ultimately must assume what it sets out to prove.[6] At the opening of the *Phaedrus* Socrates remarks on this problem. Asked if he believes a certain miraculous tale, he indicates that he finds a natural explanation for the phenomenon more plausible, but he adds that he has no leisure to try to explain every purported miracle one by one, and that such a procedure would perhaps anyhow be "too clever." Instead, he says, he follows the injunction "know thyself," inscribed in the temple to Apollo at Delphi, and in particular he seeks to determine whether his unusual perspective on things is a monstrosity or whether his nature is in fact somehow divine (*Phaedrus* 229b–30a). In the *Apology*, Socrates similarly turns from a discussion of his purported investigations into the order and necessities of nature to an account of his obedience to what he presents as an injunction by the god at Delphi, and again what is at issue is self-knowledge, or more precisely, the relation between something Socrates already knows about himself and something he has yet to learn about the knowledge or the experience of others. As he tells the story in the *Apology*, his companion Chaerephon once asked the Delphic Oracle if there was anyone wiser than Socrates and the oracle said there was not; Socrates strangely interpreted this answer as an injunction to try to refute everyone who seemed to be wise in order to refute the oracle; yet the result was that Socrates confirmed the oracle's claim that no one was wiser and thereby came to a deeper knowledge of the significance of his own ignorance. Strangely, Socrates presents his attempt to refute the god and thereby to confirm what he does not know, and his attempt to confirm his wisdom and thereby vindicate the oracle, as one and the same quest. Could these be not two subsequent activities but a single project? In the accounts of both the *Phaedrus* and the *Apology*, Socrates combines apparent reverence for the god Apollo with an implicit or explicit challenge to the claims of purported revelations. Under both accounts, the second, "Delphic" investigation is perhaps not simply a new investigation but a new way of addressing the deepest concern that underlay the old investigation of natural phenomena—the desire to know where we stand in the cosmos and what the status is of the knowledge accessible to us as human beings. And at the heart of his new investigation as Socrates elaborates it in the *Apology* is an attempt to determine whether anyone knows what he is talking about when he makes claims about what is "noble and good" (*kalos kagathos*), an attempt that begins from Socrates' knowledge that he himself knows of no such thing (20a6–c2; 21d1–6). An investigation into the moral phenomena, not the physical beings, is perhaps the key to understanding the whole. But by the same token, the moral things that play such a central role in the *Apology* seem not to have been Socrates' first concern and may or may not ever have been the object of his deepest theoretical interest.

Socrates' story turns, then, on the question of what he and others know and do not know (*eidenai*) or have knowledge (*epistēmē*) of, and the question of whether he or others are wise (*sophos*) or have wisdom (*sophia*) or practical or active wisdom (*phronēsis*). There is, as we have suggested, a significant if subtle difference between knowledge and wisdom, the neglect of which has led to the widespread but erroneous notion that Socrates, in disavowing wisdom in the *Apology*, is claiming to know nothing whatsoever except the fact of his own ignorance. Socrates does explicitly profess to lack knowledge of a number of things, including the things under the earth and in the heavens (19c), the things in Hades (29b), and the fate of the soul after death (37b); but he does claim to know other things—for example, what would have happened if he had tried to be politically active (31d), what will happen if he accepts the punishment of exile, and that it will be bad (37b and d). In all these cases, Socrates uses the word *epistēmē* or its cognates: knowledge pertains to particular facts and particular skills.[7]

By contrast, Socrates uses the word *sophia* or wisdom in the *Apology* to characterize the understanding that Chaerephon and the oracle both attribute to Socrates himself and that he reluctantly comes to acknowledge he possesses, as well as for the sovereign understanding of human affairs that the leading statesmen were thought to possess but did not. Wisdom, then, is a higher-order capacity than ordinary knowledge. Its meaning is by no means merely theoretical as opposed to practical, as it tends to be in Aristotle's writings. By the same token, *phronēsis*, most often translated as "practical wisdom" or "prudence," is by no means merely practical in Plato: it ranges from a synonym for wisdom (*Apology* 22a) to the slightly more specific knowledge of how to live well that a wise person will place great value upon (29e; 36c). Plato's Socrates uses it and *sophia* as such close analogues, especially in the *Meno*, that I have chosen to translate *phronēsis* as "active wisdom." Neither here nor elsewhere does Plato's Socrates, any more than Xenophon's, suggest that anyone can have *sophia* without *phronēsis* or *phronēsis* without *sophia*. Socrates' choice of which term to use seems at least sometimes dictated by the proclivities of his interlocutor: he speaks especially of *sophia* with the sophist Protagoras, for example, and *phronēsis* with the future warrior Meno. In the *Apology*, Socrates denies that he is at all wise, either much or little (21b), and maintains that he has at best only "human wisdom" (20d), which perhaps is worth "little or nothing" (23a). Socrates deliberately provokes puzzlement about what he claims to know, but these statements are not contradictory if we attend to the difference between knowledge and comprehensive wisdom: he knows some things and not others, but wisdom he has only in a qualified, merely human form.[8]

Now within the context of his trial, Socrates' whole account of his old accusers and his Delphic quest is a digression, allegedly required because he claims he must combat old prejudices. The effect of the digression is of course to bring those prejudices more vividly to mind; it can help his defense only if he shows the old accusations to be baseless, which he by no means does. The tale he tells to explain how the old charge of natural science and the implied charge of atheism ever arose, the uncorroborated tale about Chaerephon and the Delphic Oracle, is circular in that it fails to explain how Socrates ever came to be reputed wise in the first place. For anyone who reads carefully, it in fact deepens rather than dispels the suspicion that he was indeed involved in studying natural science and may have been an atheist. But then, having blown all these suspicions in our faces and having made us wonder about the truth behind them, Socrates wafts them away. All the charges, old and new, he claims, are due to the humiliating refutations to which he has subjected Athens' reputedly wisest men and especially to his having inspired many of the young to imitate this irritating activity. In their anger, Socrates says, the examinees have charged him with corrupting the young. "And whenever someone asks them, 'By doing what and teaching what?' they have nothing to say, but are ignorant. So in order not to seem to be at a loss, they say the things that are ready at hand against all who philosophize: 'the things aloft and under the earth' and 'not believing in gods' and 'making the weaker speech the stronger'" (23d2–7). From among these men, Socrates now asserts, Meletus and Anytus and Lycon have arisen to prosecute him (23e). The old accusers have disappeared behind the new accusers; at the root of his troubles is not impiety at all but only Socrates' effect on the young.

When he turns to taking up the indictment of the new accusers, Socrates obliquely raises again the question of whether he really has had one set of accusers or two, as well as the question of which of the two charges against him is most important.

> So concerning the things about which my first accusers made their accusations, this is a sufficient defense speech before you. But against Meletus, the "good and patriotic" as he says, and the later accusers, I will try to speak next in my defense. Now again, just as if these were other accusers, let us take up in turn their sworn statement. It is something like this: "Socrates," it

> says, "does injustice by corrupting the youth and not believing in the gods in whom the city believes, but in other novel *daimonia*." The charge is of this sort. But let us examine each one of the parts of this charge. (24b3–c3)

Here Socrates echoes the language he used at 19b3–4, where he put the rumors and insinuations spread by the "first accusers" into the form of an imaginary indictment, saying, "Their sworn statement, just as though they were accusers, must be read." Now he takes up the charge of the new accusers "as if they were other accusers" and as if they cannot quite speak for themselves. Of course they can and they just have, but are they the same ones as before, or not? This question is related to Socrates' other strange maneuver in the passage just quoted. He highlights the corruption charge by putting it first, as if this were the real issue, while according to both Diogenes Laertius and Xenophon the actual indictment put impiety first.[9] In this way Socrates shifts attention to the legally less serious of the two offenses with which he is charged, for only impiety normally carried the death penalty. But he cannot be said to be sweeping the graver accusation under the rug; his whole spontaneous digression into the old accusers had the effect of spotlighting it as nothing in the accusers' speeches could have done.

About this curious shell game let me make the following suggestion. Careful attention to Socrates' argument will show a crucial difference between the two sets of accusers and will show that the issue of science and impiety was fundamental to the city's earlier hostility to Socrates and indeed its hostility to all philosophers. But if this is the case, why is Socrates making so much of the corruption charge at his trial? In a complicated way he seems to want both to call attention to and to divert attention away from his earlier scientific investigations, or to make some but only some of his listeners think more about them. This approach will leave a broad impression that it was only the Athenians' vanity and envy that got the innocent Socrates in trouble—he made the young respect him more than they respected their own fathers—while prompting his most serious listeners to ponder the relation between his scientific interests and his more recent cross-examinations of citizens and his involvement with the youth. At the same time, giving priority now to the corruption charge serves to indicate that while impiety is fundamental to the tension between philosophy and the city, it is not the crux of what has gotten Socrates into trouble now. The real problem in his life is the effect he has had on his students, most famously upon Critias and Alcibiades, both of whom betrayed the Athenian democracy, but also on the family of Plato, which with Critias was deeply implicated in the oligarchy known as the thirty tyrants. Why was

Socrates so involved with politically ambitious and well-connected youth? To begin to illuminate for us this most delicate issue of his relation to the young and especially to Plato, Socrates will confront the corruption issue in such a way as to reveal both the truth of the charge—we will see him making his subversive arguments first hand—and the deeper truth that he is the one real educator in Athens and that all the other Athenians are in a crucial sense the real corrupters. And somehow central to Socrates' activity both as corrupter and as benefactor to the young is this strange argument that virtue is knowledge and that the remedy for vice is not punishment but education.[10]

Socrates' First Refutation of the Corruption Charge (24c4–25c4)

Socrates opens his cross-examination of Meletus with a strange and strangely aggressive countercharge, addressed to the jury.

> Now he says that I do injustice in corrupting the youth. But I, men of Athens, say that Meletus does injustice, because he jests in a serious matter, lightly bringing human beings to trial, pretending to be serious and concerned about things not one of which he has ever cared about. That this is so, I will try to demonstrate to you as well. (24c4–9)

Now Meletus clearly is angry in good earnest, and Socrates has no evident grounds for charging him with jesting, a charge that is bound to alienate the jury. Yet he reiterates the charge in the course of his cross-examination, embellishes it with puns on Meletus' name (which resembles *meletē*, or care) and alludes to it again at the argument's close. If anyone is jesting, it is Socrates. What is his serious point? Meletus has devoted considerable passion but surprisingly little thought to the question of what education and corruption really are; his anger is thus not fully deserving of respect. It is the unruffled, detached, even ironic Socrates who has thought incessantly and profoundly all his life about these things. Socrates' contention is that Meletus and everyone he represents—virtually every citizen of every community—fails to think through to the bottom the things that he claims to be most serious about; he is hence a boaster in claiming to know and even in claiming to care deeply about them.

Socrates proceeds,

> "Now come here, Meletus, tell me: Is it not of utmost importance to you how the youth be as good as possible?"

> "It is."
>
> "Come, now, and tell these men, who makes them better? It is clear that you know, for you care. For having discovered, as you say, the one who corrupts them—me—you are summoning me before these men and accusing me. But the one who makes them better—come, tell them and reveal to them who it is.
>
> "Do you see, Meletus, that you are silent and have nothing to say? And indeed does it not seem to be shameful to you, and a sufficient proof of what I say, that you have not cared about any of this? But tell me, good man, who makes them better?" (24c9–d10)

Socrates' question is at first baffling to Meletus, as it might be to us and to any partisan of democracy. Who among us are the experts in moral education? We have none; it is the job of every parent to raise his or her own children to be good people; the premise of democracy is that virtually every parent is qualified for the task. The men in democratic Athens who claimed special expertise in education, the sophists, were regarded with popular suspicion. Their patrons were men like Callias, members of the oligarchically inclined elite, and although Socrates has distanced himself from the sophists in mentioning Callias' patronage of them at 20a, his question now suggests that he shares the sophists' and Callias' undemocratic assumptions.

Finally Meletus answers.

> "The laws."
>
> "But this is not what I am asking, best of men, but what human being it is who first knows this very thing, the laws." (24d11–e2)

Meletus' answer is less strange than it sounds to modern ears; it is in fact a sensible one in the context of the Greek polis, where laws assumed the robust task of governing all of life and shaping citizens' characters as well as preventing harm. Socrates himself approves such a role for the laws in Plato's *Crito* and *Republic*, as does the Athenian Stranger in the *Laws*.[11] Nor does Socrates suggest here that the answer is fundamentally wrong or that the laws of Athens are fundamentally flawed; to do so openly would be to show impiety as well as hostility to democracy, for the most basic Athenian laws were believed to be divinely inspired and the rest to reflect the will of the people in their rightful and sovereign assembly. Instead, Socrates asks a more cautious question: who is it that first, on the basis of a thorough knowledge of the law, is able to apply its wisdom in each case so as to make the people better and not worse? But the word "first" points to the question of what really is first: can it be the laws that are the ultimate basis of the knowledge needed to educate well, or must there not first be a wise lawgiver who knows the human soul and its needs and passions and variety of types so well as to be able to make the rules that will give guidance to a whole community? And if so, what divine or human being is it who has such knowledge?

Meletus proceeds to answer that *all* the Athenian citizens uphold and apply the law in such a way as to make the youth better.

> "These, Socrates, the jurors."
>
> "How do you mean, Meletus? Are these able to educate the young and do they make them better?"
>
> "Very much so."
>
> "All of them, or some and not others?"
>
> "All of them."
>
> "You speak well, by Hera, and you speak of a great abundance of benefactors. What then? Do the listeners make them better, or not?"
>
> "These too."
>
> "What about the councilmen?"
>
> "The councilmen too."
>
> "But then, Meletus, do those in the assembly, the assemblymen, corrupt the youth? Or do all those, too, make them better?"
>
> "Those too."
>
> "Then all, as it seems, of the Athenians make them noble and good except me, and I alone corrupt them. Is this what you are saying?"
>
> "Most vehemently I am saying this."
>
> "You have exposed in me (or charged me with) a great misfortune." (24e3–25a12)

We note in passing Socrates' paradoxical formulation in the last line, which foreshadows the radical argument he will soon make about moral responsibility, but he does not launch it yet. What he emphasizes here is his astonishment that so many people are able to benefit the young; in doing so, he goes further even than the sophists or than any traditional aristocrat would go in questioning the ability of most parents to confer real benefits on their own children. Protagoras, for example, says he assumes that most students will come to him both informed about and habituated to justice.[12] Aristotle, who tends to assimilate his moral outlook to that of the gentleman, does say that one must be brought up to love what is noble if one is to love it as an adult, implying that it takes a gentleman to raise a gentleman, and he says explicitly that the full flowering of virtue will be possible only for a few.[13] Yet he never suggests that the vast majority of parents and the laws that govern everyone are incapable of making ordinary people into decent, law-abiding citizens, nor would any Athenian aristocrat be likely to do so. Even Sparta, the classical city least willing to leave education in the hands of parents, assumed that good education required no special expertise but only a rigorous training that all Spartans recognized as good but that not all had the self-discipline to carry out. Socrates, however, argues that the knowledge of how to educate human beings is a rare possession indeed.

> "Now answer me. Does it seem to you to be this way with horses? That all human beings make them better, while one certain one is the corrupter? Or is it wholly the opposite of this, that one certain one is able to make them better, or a very few, those skilled in horsemanship, while the many, if they ever associate with and use horses, corrupt them? Is it not so, Meletus, both with horses and with all the other animals?
>
> "Of course it is in every way so, whether you and Anytus deny it or affirm it. For it would be a great happiness regarding the young, if one alone corrupts them and the rest benefit them. But in fact, Meletus, you have sufficiently displayed that you never yet gave any thought to the young, and you have shown clearly your own lack of care, for you have cared nothing about the things for which you summon me here." (25a12–c4)

In what ways does the education of human beings resemble the training of horses? Why does Socrates compare human education with a form of training in which trainer and trainee belong to different species? Are Socrates and Meletus in fact in any agreement at all about what it means to educate human beings and make them better? And why does Socrates put his charge against ordinary Athenians in such an extreme form? Horsemanship is indeed an art that only a very few experts possess in its full perfection—most of the arts have that character—but Socrates is surely exaggerating when he denies that ordinary farmers are capable of raising their own horses to be serviceable for ordinary purposes, and even more so when he suggests that any horse, once trained, stands to be harmed by the vast majority of riders of average ability. What is the purpose of this exaggeration?

To begin to tease apart the threads of Socrates' close-woven thought about education and corruption, let us look more carefully at the language he uses in this and the previous passage. One significant formulation comes at 24e9–10, which echoes an earlier observation: Where the patriotic citizen Meletus finds in the city what Socrates calls "a great abundance of benefactors," Socrates finds "a great abundance of human beings who suppose that they know something, but know little or nothing" (23c6–7). This echo and contrast are linked to a second. Socrates characterizes the power of benefiting the young that Meletus attributes to virtually everyone as the capacity to make them "noble and good" (*kalos kagathos*) and Meletus accepts this formulation (25a9–10). This is the third time in the dialogue that Socrates has used this term, an important term in Greek parlance that Socrates in the *Apology* seems to be giving an even more significant and precise sense. To the Greeks, the *kalos kagathos* was the gentleman, the man possessed of both virtue and refinement; to Meletus, every citizen is capable of being *kalos kagathos*. Socrates, while seeming to agree that the proper aim of education is to make human beings "noble and good," first uses the term to express doubt that anyone at all is capable of such a feat (20a6–b5). Then he uses the phrase to express the object of his own and others' ignorance after describing his first cross-examination of a fellow citizen: "probably neither of us knows anything noble and good, but he supposes he knows something when he does not know, while I, just as I do not know, do not even suppose that I do" (21d3–6), and he stresses that his conclusions from subsequent refutations have been precisely the same.[14] The abundance of people Meletus considers benefactors and Socrates considers corrupters are deficient in erroneously supposing themselves wise where they are ignorant about what is noble and good, or about the relation of the noble to the good. Socrates' famous knowledge of ignorance turns especially on this relation.

As we have seen, Socrates does not seriously claim to be ignorant of everything, nor does he claim that others are. The things that he acknowledges knowing include many things that are good—for example, he knows who the good craftsmen are—and many that are noble or beautiful (*kalos*)—for example, many of the swords and vases turned out by these same craftsmen (22d).[15] He knows likewise who the good horse trainers are. He even knows that it is possible to make a horse noble and good and he expresses no puzzlement as to what that means. Why should training humans to be noble and good be so much more problematic? Since his present references both to horse-training and to educating the young to be noble and good recall his previously recounted conversation with Callias about horses and sons, let us look more closely at that earlier passage.

> "Callias," I said, "if your two sons had been colts or calves, we would have been able to find and hire an overseer for them, who would make them noble and good in their appropriate virtue, and he would be one of those skilled in horsemanship or farming. But as it is, since they are human beings, what overseer do you have in mind to get for them? Who is knowledgeable in such virtue, that of human being and citizen? For I suppose you have considered it, since you have sons. Is there someone," I said, "or not?"
>
> "Quite so," he said.
>
> "Who," I said, "and where is he from, and for how much does he teach?"
>
> "Evenus," he said, "Socrates, from Paros; five minae."
>
> And I considered Evenus blessed, if he should truly have this art and teach at such a modest rate. I myself would be adorning myself and giving myself airs if I knew these things. But I do not know them, men of Athens. (20a6–c3)

Socrates is sure that he does not know the art of making human beings noble and good, which he equates with educating them in the excellence of both human being and citizen. By contrast, it seems a straightforward thing to make a horse noble and good, given the right nature. By a good horse we mean primarily a horse that is good for us; by a beautiful or noble horse we mean one whose form, movements, and habits are gracefully and perfectly suited to its function and needs. Even if we extend the meaning of a horse's goodness to include its own natural thriving, this seems to be adequately realized in the case of virtually all horses that are well trained and well used by their masters. There is an important aspect of human nobility that is precisely parallel to the speed, grace, and overflowing energy of a magnificent horse; this is an important aspect of human nobility or virtue that Socrates clearly recognizes in the way he connects virtue with happiness. But it is not the whole of human nobility. For a human being nobility seems to mean something both more problematic and more exalted than it does for a horse, and the perfection of the human being and that of the citizen do not seem to converge as neatly as do the nature and uses of a horse. As Socrates suggests with his recurring horse analogy, all civic education, all training of young men in their duty to serve their communities, has something crucial in common with the training of animals to serve their masters. Is what is good for the individual the same as what is good for the larger community? What is the relationship between moral excellence and habitual obedience? But if the virtue of the citizen can be more problematic than that of a horse, it can also be far more splendid. Human nobility at its peak seems to mean the heroic, freely chosen surrender of one's own good for the good of the community of which one is a citizen. Socrates suggests that his key insight has been a recognition of his own ignorance of how any education can bring human beings to a perfection that is both noble in what we think of as the highest sense—noble in the sense of entailing a complete overcoming or sacrifice of our self-interest, or in the sense of transcending all concern with the benefit of anyone or anything at all—and at the same time good in what we think of as the fullest sense—good as an end, without qualification, for the one who has it, in the way that happiness is.

Socrates goes on to call the wisdom claimed by Evenus "greater than human wisdom" (20e1) leaving unanswered the question whether such knowledge might still somehow be available through divine inspiration or whether it is just divine-sounding confusion (cf. 22b6–c6). He presents his quest as an attempt to discover whether anyone else might have the knowledge of the "noble and good" that he lacks. Now if Socrates began his quest already certain of his own ignorance of this, it would seem to be because he had already seen the contradictory character of the demands or hopes embodied in the very idea of the noble and good. Glaucon expresses most vividly the contradiction in his demand in the *Republic* that Socrates show that the just man who sacrifices his whole happiness to justice is precisely, in so doing, supremely happy (357a–62c).[16] But if the problem is a logical one, why does Socrates need to examine anyone else to know that others do not know of any such thing either? Or do his examinations have a different aim—for example, to see what people will do when shown their own ignorance? If their responses show that everyone can in principle be brought to share Socrates' characteristic ignorance, this might then increase his confidence in the ground on which the rest of his philosophizing stands.

Socrates' collision with Meletus is all about ignorance of this kind, ignorance that Socrates knows from the outset Meletus is beset by. Socrates is persuaded that civic education invariably entails a deep confusion and thus that the laws that purport to give it are flawed; Meletus thinks that such an education is simple and straightforward and that the vast majority of law-abiding citizens give it to their children in a satisfactory form already. Meletus and philosophy's other critics think that Socrates is taking the most promising youth and making some wicked (as Socrates was purported to make Alcibiades, for example) and ruining the rest for political careers, as Adeimantus puts it in the *Republic*. Socrates replies explicitly in the *Republic* and implicitly here that it is the city as it exists—inasmuch as it is not guided by philosophy—that is the corrupter of the best natures.

Through its clamorous, intoxicating praise and flattery, it induces them to serve its ignoble purposes and to subscribe to its confused view of human excellence (*Republic* 492a–c and 494b–e); through their ignorant handling of the young, the parents and the democratic assembly make them as corrupt and vicious as ill-used horses. It is a daring defense to turn the tables and the corruption charge on Meletus and the city, for Socrates makes it only at the cost of showing everyone whose eyes are open that his effect on his companions is indeed to subvert their respect for both their parents' authority and the legitimacy of their democratic government. It is a defense that cannot succeed before a court in Athens or anywhere, but only before the bar of subsequent thoughtful opinion. And at its core is a claim that virtue is, if not simply identical to, then at least impossible without a knowledge that is most difficult to attain.

Socrates' Second Refutation of the Corruption Charge (25c5–26b2)

In the second round of his cross-examination of Meletus, Socrates introduces even more radical arguments to show that if he ever has corrupted the young, he has done so involuntarily. In a limited and somewhat vulgar version, he thus introduces the corollary to the thesis that virtue is knowledge, namely that vice is involuntary. He opens with a simple question.

> "Tell us further, before Zeus, Meletus, whether it is better to live among citizens who are good or base? Good sir, answer. For surely I am asking nothing hard." (25c5–7)

Socrates' suggestion that the former is better is, as a generalization, perfectly sound. But when Meletus refuses to reply, Socrates rephrases his question in a way that actually points to a lacuna in his own argument.

> "Do not the base do some bad to those who are always closest to them, and the good some good?"
>
> "Very much so." (25c5–10)

Even if it were true that bad people invariably harm those who are always around them, what need is there to keep those one has harmed always around? Why not corrupt young people as Don Juan corrupted virgins, and then move on? Or why not try out a dangerous line of questioning on many young men—on promising young men at a time when they are most eager and open and impressionable—and then refuse to associate further with all who become worse as a result?[17]

But is it even true that people are invariably bad to those who have corrupted them? Socrates has disposed us to find this thought plausible by his reference to horses and horse trainers just before: vicious horses bite and kick indiscriminately and are hard for anyone to manage; no one would wish to have a vicious horse. But a comparison with dogs might have suggested a different possibility. Some people do intentionally breed vicious dogs, turning them on others and taking care not to get bitten themselves. Like breeders of vicious dogs, leaders of conspiracies often find corrupt or corruptible people they can profit from, and all the more do fellow dissidents and revolutionaries often show great loyalty in pursuit of a cause they all believe in. Socrates tacitly acknowledges a gap in his argument when he concedes a little later that those he has allegedly corrupted might "perhaps have a reason to come to my aid," although he still insists that their families would not (34b1–2). To be sure, his close associates would never have been so loyal if they did not consider Socrates their benefactor, but their loyalty is no proof that he has left their respect for the city's laws or their belief in its gods intact.

Socrates now asks another question that he again restates somewhat differently when Meletus refuses to answer, and again the new formulation points to a realm of unaddressed perplexities and problems.

> "Is there anyone, then, who wishes to be harmed by those he associates with, rather than benefited? Keep answering, good man. For the law orders you to answer. Is there anyone who wishes to be harmed?"
>
> "Of course not." (25d1–4)

This reply seems sensible enough with regard to the case at hand. Those who corrupt others surely seek some good for themselves and not any harm. But has Meletus conceded only this much? Socrates' last version of the question is completely general, and he expects and receives a negative answer. He then proceeds as if he has established as a universal principle that no one ever voluntarily does anything that he knows will bring any harm upon himself, or that everyone, to the extent that he acts knowingly, is what we have called an amoral utilitarian in his relations with others. If this looks like an unwarranted assumption, the more moderate and stronger claim implicit in this argument is that harming oneself is never anyone's *goal* in acting—so that even in inflicting self-punishment or committing suicide, Socrates might say, people seek redemption or an escape from unbearable suffering. This is an empirical claim that is not beyond questioning, although it certainly accords much more with common sense. But Socrates goes on to argue as if Meletus has agreed to something very different, that no one ever voluntarily does anything that he knows will bring him any harm whatsoever.

> "Come then, do you summon me here for corrupting the youth and making them more wicked voluntarily or involuntarily?"
>
> "Voluntarily, I say."
>
> "What is this, Meletus? Are you so much wiser at your age than I am at mine, that you know that the bad always do some bad to those who are closest to them, and the good do some good; whereas I have come into so much ignorance that I am even unaware of this, that if I ever do something wicked to any of my associates, I will risk getting something bad from him, so that I do so much bad voluntarily, as you assert? Of this I am not persuaded by you, Meletus, nor, do I suppose, is any other human being. But either I do not corrupt, or if I corrupt, I do it involuntarily, so that in both cases you lie. If I corrupt involuntarily, the law is not that you summon me here for such involuntary wrongs, but that you take me aside in private to teach and admonish me. For it is clear that if I learn, I will at least stop what I do involuntarily. But you avoided associating with me and teaching me and were not willing to do it, but instead you summoned me here, where the law is to summon those in need of punishment, not learning.
>
> "But in fact, men of Athens, what I was saying is already clear, that Meletus never cared about any of this, either much or little." (25d5–26b2)

Socrates sketches here three types of scenarios in criminal cases, of which he says only two are possibilities in his own. First, a defendant may be wholly innocent of the charges, in which case he should be acquitted and let go. Second, he may have inadvertently committed the alleged crime, in which case he should be instructed and admonished: a group of young political activists do not know they are required to get a permit before holding a rally in a public space; it is the job of a kindly policeman to point this out and give them a warning rather than a punitive fine—although both among us and in Athens the law is in fact less understanding than are its wisest enforcers. Third, a defendant may have committed on purpose a crime that is bad for him, knowing that his act was illegal and harmful to another but ignorant of its effect on himself. Socrates claims that only the first two possibilities are conceivable in his own case. He knows too much to be ignorant of the effects of corrupting his companions, so either he has not been corrupting them or he has been doing so inadvertently. He seems to imply that someone younger and less thoughtful than himself might do the third, deliberately harming others and unwittingly harming himself through a voluntary act. He reinforces the impression that people can voluntarily do such things at 37a5–6 when he insists that he has never voluntarily done injustice to anyone, implying again that some people do.[18] But perhaps it is best to say that such wrongs are "voluntary" only in a qualified sense, in the sense that the agent did intend to do the particular act when he did it, but not in the sense that he fully understood what he was doing. This qualification would bring Socrates' statements here into accord with his argument in the *Gorgias* that one who in seeking to benefit himself does what is in fact harmful to himself does not know what he is doing, so that his act too is really at the deepest level involuntary. The present analysis also leaves open at least in principle a fourth possibility: one might commit another type of crime that is not bad for oneself, but Socrates never acknowledges that there are any such crimes. He implies that the law distinguishes a class of involuntary harms that call for education from a class of acts that call for punishment, but he never specifies the contents of the latter class, nor does he comment on the justice of the city's response to them, if indeed he thinks they exist.[19]

How sound is Socrates' argument that only the first two possibilities are credible in his case? The phrasing at 25c underscores the fact that it is only a corrupted person's constant companions who are very likely to suffer at his hands; it also quietly concedes that even that is only a risk and not a certainty. But how could establishing a mere risk of harm prove that Socrates would never have done the deed? This argument is conclusive only on the absurd assumption that no sensible person would choose or even risk any harm to himself for any reason whatsoever. What the argument more seriously does is to highlight again the question of what Socrates' goal was in his allegedly subversive conversations with the young. To judge whether Socrates is likely to have deliberately carried on discussions with them that risked making them worse citizens, we would have to know what he hoped both he and his companions might gain, how grave he judged the dangers to each party and to the city to have been, and how he weighed all of these potential gains and losses against one another. Even if he knew that his conversations would potentially harm his interlocutors and bring some danger on himself and Athens, has Socrates shown that no possible gain for him—no possible discovery that he could make only through this activity—could outweigh the risks? But especially if he cared about any of his companions and had good reason to hope that his conversations might benefit them as well—if corruption in the city's eyes was in fact education in Socrates', if the danger of failure and true corruption could be minimized, and especially if the potential gain for his young friends was the escape from an unexamined life no better than a walking death—might not the prospect of mutual benefit justify considerable risk?

Socrates' proof that he could not have voluntarily corrupted the young thus is logically incomplete even on its own terms; when we consider that atheists and political subversives generally consider it a good thing to be such as they are and are often quite loyal to one another, it is a complete failure. Its effect on most of the jurors can be only to irritate or at best perplex them, as Socrates must know, for as he reminds them at this very moment, he is not a naïve man. But if the corruption defense does little or nothing to secure Socrates' acquittal, it is still useful in providing us with a window into his thoughts about law and corruption and his effect on the young.

Perhaps the most significant thing about this second argument against the corruption charge is the simple but ultimately subversive question it takes as its starting point. That question is whether the act of breaking the law, taken in itself and considered wholly apart from whether one is caught and punished, is good or bad for the citizen himself. Simple as this question is, parents and educators and political leaders almost always avoid raising it, focusing instead on the bad consequences of crime for society and the bad consequences for the criminal of being caught. When the sophists first began to raise it, they answered that for the most part crime is good for one who can get away with it, though bad according to conventional opinion, and that while law-abidingness always benefits some, it harms others, others who in their natures may be no worse and perhaps better. Their conclusion was, as Thrasymachus argues in the *Republic*, that law is merely a conspiracy of the strong against the weak, or as Callicles perhaps more perceptively argues in the *Gorgias*, of the weak and timid against the strong (*Republic* 338c ff., *Gorgias* 482c–86d; cf. *Republic* 358e–59b).

Socrates turns both arguments on their heads by insisting that crime is bad above all for the criminal himself. But this new argument, if more supportive of the listener's respect for virtue, proves ultimately just as subversive of respect for existing penal laws, by suggesting that their response to offenders is foolish. Here in the exchange with Meletus, Socrates makes a very limited case for this claim. Adapting himself to the shallow and vulgar understanding of the good prevalent in an Athenian courtroom (and perhaps in any courtroom), he speaks only of the way crime can endanger one's property or safety, not the way injustice corrupts the soul, as he does in the *Gorgias,* or the way justice constitutes the true health of the soul by ordering its different parts, as he does in the *Republic.* To be sure, he will address the listeners' concern with the good of their souls in the next digression. The shallow view of the human good that prevails in the courtroom is not the whole view of even the most vulgar citizens, but it does come close to being the whole view of the law. Socrates analyzes only the single crime of corrupting the youth without giving any hint about how broadly this analysis might apply. As he paints the scenario, there is no conflict of interest between citizen and city where corruption is concerned, although the offender mistakenly thinks that there is. Choosing what he considers best for himself, the offender in fact gives himself wicked associates and endless trouble. The law's response to this case, and the response of every fervent law enforcer like Meletus, is to call for punishment. Socrates pretends that the law of Athens in all such cases prescribes education rather than punishment, but this fiction only calls more attention to the truth: the law seeks to punish citizens who are already harming themselves and who do not understand that they are doing so; rather than seeking to enlighten them, it piles harm upon harm in a vindictive spirit. It is part of the bedrock of Socratic moral thought that such vindictiveness is not good. Does Socrates make any suggestion as to why the law supports it? The evidence in this terse passage is scarce, but his suggestion would seem to be that the law itself, like Meletus the prosecutor, fails to recognize the ways in which wrongdoers harm themselves; it treats every crime as a case in which the criminal is gaining at society's expense. As Socrates will show in the *Gorgias,* at the bottom of its harshness is the premise that criminals are getting away with something good and that punishment is needed to even the score. The law's implicit premise and thus its implicit teaching is the sophists' own premise: crime, if you can get away with it, pays. The laws are at the deepest level corrupting; they are the original and greatest sophists. This argument shows that Socrates does indeed undermine respect not just for parents and for Athenian democracy but for the basic presuppositions of law as it exists everywhere.

This Socratic teaching is based on ordinary insights that everyone has, however; Socrates differs only in being willing to follow ordinary insights through to their conclusions and to press forward to a resolution of the self-contradictions that ordinary moral thought is entangled in. To let a criminal get away with his crime is a terrible thing, the common view holds, and by this it means not that successfully carrying out a murder is a terrible thing (which of course it is) but that it is terrible for a murderer to escape suffering something dreadful in return, as if this would mean that the murderers would win and decent people would lose and all the world might turn murderers if we let this happen. Yet no good parent wants his child to be a criminal, and at the bottom of this wish seems to be the deep conviction (a conviction dismissed much too quickly by all the sophists, and even by many modern students of political philosophy) that being a criminal is intrinsically terrible. Ordinary moral opinion cannot make up its mind, however, whether acting virtuously is intrinsically choiceworthy, as the soul's admirable and eminently desirable perfection, or a sacrifice of one's own good that makes sense only if virtue is given a reward. Meletus has never thought any of this through; he has been strangely but by no means unusually careless about this whole constellation of questions regarding education and corruption and crime and moral responsibility. It is as if there were something in the ordinary view of moral responsibility that precisely does not want to probe too far. Meletus does not truly care about what he so vehemently claims to care about, and to that extent he is ridiculous.[20]

But why, in this dialogue that is very much about reasoned argument and passion and rhetoric, has Socrates made such incomplete and slippery arguments against Meletus, arguments that, when considered closely, only highlight his subversive activity? Part of the answer is that they do contribute to an overall impression of radical if naïve high-mindedness, especially among that part of his present and future audience that is not examining them closely. But perhaps the arguments' very defectiveness serves a constructive purpose as well. This little exchange, made in the most hostile encounter of Socrates' life, is an epitome of the more or less inadequate arguments he makes in all of his more or less friendly exchanges with more or less promising interlocutors.[21] In each case Socrates plants important ideas without giving them a fully cogent exposition. He leaves a great deal of work to the interlocutor or onlooker, who in the best case will note each gap in the argument and will either push Socrates to correct the argument's deficiencies or correct them himself when he goes off to think about what Socrates has said. Thus the student will take the germs of Socratic arguments and make them his own. But what about the less fortunate cases of interlocutors who lack the courage or determination to think their way through to a better understanding of moral responsibility? Socrates' incomplete argument may be a gift to those people as well, generally sparing them the corrosive experience of having their moral convictions demolished and replaced with nothing better. These interlocutors can go away saying to themselves, "Socrates tripped me up in the thrust and parry of argument, but he was just using tricky rhetoric; my position has not been refuted; shame on Socrates." If they are not honest and brave and determined enough to work their way through to the deepest, truly philosophic reasons for loving virtue, they can thus keep intact their inadequate reasons that rest on rewards and punishments; in very few cases will they be done any harm, though often they will be intensely irritated. For them, Socrates is the gadfly that bites without benefiting but also without harming; it is only for a few that Socratic stings are the spur to the profound wakefulness that ushers in a different and better life.

This distinction between the few and the many brings us back to another such distinction we noted earlier, Socrates' claim that virtually all riders corrupt the horses they ride, with the implication that virtually all parents corrupt their children. If it is true that the great majority of parents do not cultivate in their children the highest form of virtue, it may still be true that they give them in a reasonably complete form a virtue that is still valuable—law-based civic virtue, with its inner contradictions but with its generally good restraining effects. Socrates in fact seems to think that his own sons are capable only of so much. At the end of the dialogue he enjoins not those who voted to acquit him but those who voted to condemn him to educate and admonish his sons towards virtue. Ordinary citizens may be good enough educators for ordinary natures, but the claim that they harm those they deal with may still hold for the most gifted young. Likewise, Socratic education itself, if given in undiluted form, would be a corruption to most of the young; it is only a few that it truly benefits. And at the core of the explosiveness of Socratic education is his strange thesis, still inadequately defended or even explained, that virtue is knowledge.

Versions of the Socratic Thesis

In the *Apology*, Socrates' thought about the involuntariness of vice and the appropriateness of education rather than punishment as its remedy appears only in limited form, and only in the cross-examination of Meletus. The ultimate significance and applicability of this thought depends upon its premise regarding the goodness of virtue. Is virtue the necessary or even the necessary and sufficient condition for happiness, in such a way that the virtuous choice is in every situation the prudential choice? This question is a theme of sustained attention throughout the rest of the *Apology*. But strangely, though Socrates' answer seems invariably to be yes, he gives a bewildering array of reasons in support of his claims about the goodness and reach of virtue, which stand in evident tension both with the implicit assumptions of the argument Socrates has given Meletus and with one another. Probably the strangest and most troubling thing about the argument Socrates makes to Meletus is its assumption of the irrationality of harming oneself or even risking any harm to oneself, but he contradicts that assumption in a small way even in the immediate context and in a massive way as soon as the dialogue with Meletus is concluded. No sooner has he insisted that no one ever chooses willingly to harm or disadvantage oneself, than Socrates upbraids Meletus for his selfishness. Instead of indulging his animosity towards Socrates and seeking to do away with him, he says, Meletus should have taken on the disagreeable and time-consuming task of educating him. More dramatically, the impression Socrates gives of himself here as a narrowly calculating man who would never endanger his own safety is in sharp tension with the heroically public-spirited stance he assumes elsewhere in the *Apology* and especially in its second long digression, where he presents himself as the new Achilles, who gives no thought to death or danger as he pursues his just and divinely appointed mission (28b3–29a4; see also 21e3–22a1, 23c6–7, and 30c4–31c3). But even when he takes this heroic stance, he gives different reasons for doing so, the common thread being only his insistence that he understands better than his fellow Athenians the true importance of virtue. What exactly does Socrates claim to know that his fellow citizens grasp so incompletely? Let us trace Socrates' cascade of pronouncements about why virtue is always choiceworthy and try to distinguish the different claims he makes for it. If this exercise yields no definitive answers about Socrates' ultimate views, it will at least help us sharpen the questions we will need to take to his more elaborate expositions of the virtue-is-knowledge thesis in other dialogues.

First, Socrates raises and scornfully dismisses an imaginary Athenian's rebuke of him for following a pursuit that would put his life in danger. He replies, "You do not speak nobly, human being, if you suppose that a man who is of even a little benefit should take into account the danger of living or dying, but not rather consider this alone when he acts: whether he does just or unjust things, and the deeds of a good man or a bad" (28b5–9).[22] At 28d6–10 he restates and perhaps amends this: if a man stations himself somewhere or is stationed there by a ruler, "there he must stay and run the risk . . . and not take into account death or anything else compared to what is shameful." Is the shameful (*aischros*) quite the same as the unjust, or does Socrates now suggest that, besides virtue, reputation is a second if overlapping object of the wise man's solicitude? Immediately he reiterates that when ordered by the god to philosophize, it would be terrible to abandon his "post" out of fear of death or "any other thing whatever" (28d10–29a1). Is obedience to the god precisely the same as the just and the honorable? He does not say, nor does he explain why *all* other evils pale to utter insignificance in comparison with the evil of disobeying the god, but we scarcely notice this because of the bold scorn he voices for the one evil that virtually all of us fear the most, death.

So far Socrates appears to be taking the position that we have termed hypermoral-heroic, insisting that what is right or noble is the only thing worth serious attention and proclaiming a sublime indifference to all considerations of personal gain or loss. But the next statement brings his own good back into consideration. If he abandoned his post, he says,

> that would be terrible, and truly one would then justly haul me into the law court for not believing the gods to exist, disobeying the oracle and fearing death and supposing myself to be wise when I am not. For to fear death, men, is nothing else than to seem wise and not be so. For it is to seem to know what one does not know. No one knows if death does not turn out to be the greatest good for a human being, but people fear it as if they knew well that it is the greatest of evils. And how is this not reproachable ignorance, that of supposing one knows what one does not know? (29a1–b2)

All this is most impressive, but how exactly is the mere knowledge of our uncertainty of what happens after death supposed to dissolve the fear of losing everything? Can such indifference to death really be grounded in knowledge of ignorance, or, as Socrates hints, would it not require special knowledge, such as a certainty of divine favor? But Socrates insists that he is ignorant about the things in Hades and yet certain that "to do injustice and to disobey one's betters, both divine and human, is bad and shameful" (29b6–7). Here again we have a virtual restatement, and the new formulation again raises fresh questions. What is the relation between the bad and the shameful? Could an act be noble but bad, or shameful but good? What is the precise character of the badness of the things that Socrates says are worse than death, and of the goodness of the virtue that he values above all?

While Socrates continues in subsequent lines to characterize his own virtue as action in obedience to a divine commandment and to imply that its goodness arises from this commandment, what he says he has been commanded to do begins to change. He becomes now less a seeker than a teacher or preacher of virtue. At the same time, he presents virtue as less a series of actions than a possession, good for its possessor in a way that is independent of any god's command and ascertainable by unaided human reason.

> Best of men, you are Athenians, from a city that is greatest and most famous for its wisdom and strength; are you not ashamed to care that you may have as much money as possible, and reputation and honor, but you neither care nor give thought to active wisdom and truth and how your souls may be as good as possible? (29d7–e3)

This statement does not define active wisdom, knowledge of the truth, or the good condition of the soul, nor does it clarify their relationship. Neither does it explain whether each of these is good as a means or an end, and if as an end, whether as the core of happiness (the moral-eudaimonist position) or as happiness itself (the hypermoral-eudaimonist position). The statement is perhaps most naturally taken to mean that virtue is an end. But a few lines later Socrates suggests otherwise:

> I go around and do nothing but persuade you, both younger and older, not to care for bodies and money before, nor as intensely as, how your soul will be the best possible, saying, "Not from money does virtue come, but from virtue comes money and all of the other good things for human beings both privately and publicly." (30a7–b4)[23]

Now truth drops out and it is virtue alone that is the key to everything good. Or does virtue entail speaking the truth, or at least possessing it? At any rate, Socrates now suggests that the goods of the soul are valuable at least in significant part as means to the *other* good things that constitute happiness, as the moral-utilitarian position holds—and that the core of his whole activity is to teach just this.[24]

But again, if virtue is good chiefly or entirely as a foundation for other goods, does it guarantee the other good things or merely make them possible? If it guarantees them, is it through some intrinsic power of virtue that the other elements of happiness arise, or is it as a reward conferred by divine providence?[25] And if virtue does not guarantee the other good things, what else is required to secure them? Soon Socrates speaks to these questions, but again equivocally.

> Know well, that if you kill me, being such a man as I say, you will not harm me more than you yourselves. For Meletus or Anytus would not harm me at all—he would not be able to—for I suppose it is not sanctioned for a better man to be harmed by a worse. He might kill or banish or dishonor me. But while both he and another might suppose these things to be great evils, I do

> not suppose so, but much worse is to do what he does now, to attempt to kill a man unjustly. (30c6–d5)

Is Socrates saying that death and banishment and dishonor are not bad at all for the good man, or that they are bad but less so than the evil of doing great injustice? The first half of this statement seems to endorse what we have termed the hypermoral-utilitarian view of virtue, according to which virtue does not constitute but does guarantee the happiness of the virtuous man—perhaps through the agency of some protecting divinity, as the word "sanctioned" implies. But the second half of the statement moves in a different direction, suggesting that the virtuous man may indeed come to some harm, but that doing injustice is still worse, perhaps because, as he argues elsewhere, such deeds are the expression and the deepening of a terrible disorder in the soul. But if death and banishment and dishonor are bad at all, why does Socrates say it is not sanctioned for a worse man to harm a better, since surely these things often are inflicted by bad men on innocent ones? On the other hand, if death and banishment are really not bad for the good man, then what is so terrible about the unjust man's attempt to impose them upon him? Socrates—or perhaps rather the universal moral intuition that Socrates is capturing here—is incoherent on all these questions.

But lest we think that Socrates has slipped all the way from the most heroic to the most utilitarian view of virtue, he now reminds us of the enormous price his service to the god has cost him, the virtually "inhuman" way he has neglected his own affairs and endured seeing his family neglected, and the fact that he has not even accepted any pay in return for tirelessly exhorting his fellow citizens to care for virtue (31a7–c3). Thus he stakes out momentarily the moral-heroic position of a tragic hero, according to which the dictates of virtue are binding but are far from being a guarantee of happiness. But again, lest we think of the philosophic life as truly heroic, Socrates in a rapid reversal at 31c4 begins to present himself as eminently cautious and self-protective. It turns out that he has not, after all, been willing to run all risks for the sake of acting as virtue requires, nor has he acted as one who knows that death is nothing bad. He has abstained from political involvement and has refused to do anything to prevent many injustices, because to have intervened in Athenian politics, he claims, would inevitably have brought him to an early death. Compounding our puzzles, Socrates attributes this caution itself to a divine source, his daimonic voice, and he even calls its injunctions "all-noble" (31d6). Compounding them further, Socrates immediately gives examples of times when he *did* risk his life in political altercations with the city's authorities, now denying that he would ever yield anything unjust to anyone, even if the cost were immediate death (32a4–e1).

Can we make these pronouncements in any way consistent? Is Socrates saying that one can and should avoid any heroic opposition to injustice that is clearly futile, because then, as he observes, he would have died and been "of no use to you or myself" (31d8–e1)? But then why did Socrates commit acts of defiance that were almost certainly futile, such as his refusal to try as a group the generals from the battle of Arginusae or to take part in the arrest of Leon of Salamis (32a9–e1)? And why does he say that these deeds show "that I do not care about death, if it is not too crude to say so, in any way at all" (32d1–2)? And just to make certain that we do not try to save his position through some elaborate distinction between injustices one is obligated to oppose and injustices one has no responsibility to concern oneself with, Socrates concludes his litany of his own brave deeds with this astonishing admission of irresponsibility, momentarily seeming to align himself with the amoral-utilitarian view:

> Do you suppose, then, that I would have survived so many years, if I had taken part in public affairs and acted in a way worthy of a good man, coming to the aid of the just things and, as one should, regarding this as all-important? Far from it, men of Athens. (32e2–5)

In short, Socrates suggests both that a good man is careful about his own life and that he gives no thought to his own life; both that a good man acts prudently with a view to accomplishing some real good and that he thinks of nothing but what is just; both that he himself is a hero and that he has shirked the duty of a good man.

But the cascade of strange contradictions continues. At 34d1–35b8 it becomes evident that Socrates after all gives weight to reputation and not exclusively to virtue: he says it is especially his concern for the reputation both of Athens and of himself as a wise man that stops him from stooping to the shameless begging and pleading for his life that were common in Athenian criminal trials. Then he again connects his impressive integrity with what he claims is an outstandingly firm faith in the gods. To induce a juror to break his oath is to show that one doubts the gods' existence, he explains, but he has no such doubt: "I believe, men of Athens, as none of my accusers does" (35d6–7). But then is it only a hope for the afterlife that causes Socrates to rate the life of virtue better than one that seeks earthly advantage and neglects justice? By no means. At 36c3–d1 Socrates says he has brought each of his fellow citizens the greatest of benefits through his exhortations "not to care for any of his own things until he cares for himself, how he will be the best and most prudent possible, nor to care for the things of the city until he cares for the city itself, and so to care for the other things in the same way." The result, as he describes it, is not that through any heroic acts of self-denial his beneficiaries deserve to be rewarded with happiness by the gods, but rather that, he says, while others seem to make the city happy, "I do so" (36d9–e1). The virtue he has instilled in his fellow citizens is, in other words, good not because of its anticipated rewards but because it is itself the substance of happiness, here and now. Socrates thus aligns himself again with the hypermoral-eudaimonist position. And he does so even though in his prime example of the virtuous life, his own life, there has been no leisure to care for "his own things."

But is virtue alone really enough to make a life happy and worth having? Socrates immediately implicitly denies that it is, and at the same time implicitly retracts his earlier claim that he, as a good man, is beyond any danger of being harmed by a worse man (30c4–d1). He may be almost inhumanly unafraid of death, but he acknowledges that imprisonment and especially exile would be real evils for him, and that life as a wandering exile would be miserable.[26] For, Socrates says, the only way for him to obtain peace and security (real goods, evidently) would be to stop philosophizing, but "the unexamined life is not worth living" (37b5–38a6). With this last thought, in what seems to be Socrates' frankest speech in the *Apology* but one that he openly admits few of the jurors will find credible, he indicates that it is not after all justice or any other moral virtue that is the heart and soul of the happy life, but philosophy. Could it be only for those so happily absorbed with philosophy as Socrates is that the ordinary objects of human concern pale almost to insignificance and the goods of the soul are almost the only ones that matter? In his *Memorabilia* Xenophon gives us a beautiful portrait of the rare human type whose priorities are so ordered, a man who could live contentedly in ten thousand–fold poverty, who could face neglect or scorn by most of his fellow citizens and feel no bitterness, and who could find joy in the quality of his own thought, together with a tiny number of like-minded friends, or with none at all (see esp. *Memorabilia* 1.5; 1.6). Yet even then, the importance of mundane goods does not drop to zero: Socrates has long cared about staying alive and now cares a good deal about his reputation.

In his final speech to the jury after receiving the death sentence, Socrates returns to the question of what happens to the soul after death. He argues that whatever awaits him, it can be nothing bad. Without answering the many puzzles he has raised about the status of virtue, these last arguments, addressed to the jurors who voted to acquit him, at least lend an aura of seriousness to Socrates' claim that his virtue renders him immune to any serious harm at the hands of his accusers. Socrates casts a shadow of doubt over his final arguments, however, when he prefaces them with the remark that so long as the officials are occupied with court business, "nothing prevents our telling myths to one another" (39e4–5). He then reports this surprising turn of events: his divine sign, which all his life has frequently opposed him even in the smallest matters and has often stopped him in midsentence, has objected to nothing that he has done or said today. That suggests, Socrates says, that we are wrong in supposing death to be anything bad. On the other hand, since this same divine voice has often in the past opposed actions that would have endangered Socrates' life, a more sober conclusion might be that death for Socrates is not a bad thing now (cf. Xenophon *Apology* 1, 5–8). Yet Socrates proceeds to argue that death may well be a positive good. For death means either an end to all experience and perception or a migration of the soul from this place to another. But the former is like an endless sleep, and what is more pleasant than a deep and dreamless sleep? And the latter means joining all those who have died before, and what could be more interesting than to converse forever with the wisest of them? As Christopher Bruell points out, these arguments for the goodness of death are undercut by Socrates' earlier reports of the way he has spent his life pursuing and encouraging wakefulness (30e1–31a7; 38a2–6) and by his present remark that the future state will be especially happy because those living in it will no longer have to fear death (41c5–7).[27] Socrates does not deny that they will face judgment upon entering the next world, but he insists that a good man has nothing to fear from the true judges in Hades, in contrast to the false judges in trials such as his own. He strikes a slightly jarring note when he names among the judges in Hades Minos, the legendary Cretan king who was said to pass good laws for Crete but was also said to have exacted from the Athenians an annual tribute of seven youths and seven maidens and fed them to the Minotaur. Why should anyone, including Socrates, be so certain that the judges there, if such there are, are fair to everyone?[28] Or have Socrates' investigations somehow brought him a deep confidence on this point that he does not explain?

Socrates makes a more understandable argument that death is good, at least in his case and at least now, when he calls his death a release from troubles (41d4–5). But this statement, too, is in tension with another immediately adjoining it: Socrates has just given his most absolute statement of the protective power of virtue in asserting that "there is nothing bad for a good man, whether living or dead . . ." But in fact he calls this reassuring claim into question even before he has finished the sentence: ". . . and the gods are not without care for his troubles" (41d1–2). What troubles are these that the gods concern themselves with and that make Socrates' own life so burdensome that death is a welcome release, if there is nothing bad for a good man? Socrates leaves us to wonder as he goes off to a death that he now says may or may not be better than the lives his friendly jurors return to: "Which of us goes to a better thing is unclear to everyone except to the god" (42a3–5).[29] And with that he concludes the most famous defense speech in history.

What is strange about this series of arguments is the rapid succession of incompatible claims it makes, but what is perhaps even stranger is the way the arguments appear, to any but the most careful reading, as a seamless whole. Socrates presents himself as the quintessential moral man, rare in his intransigence but perfectly recognizable in every moral stance he takes. Only on close inspection is it evident that Socrates has left us with a fragmented view of himself, of his view of intelligent action, and of his thesis that virtue is knowledge. Might it be one of his chief and his most important introductory educational activities to bring us face to face with this array of contradictory opinions we each hold in our own minds, so that the *Apology* is the proper portal to the Platonic works above all because it arouses our moral intuitions and our admiration for morality in all its multiplicitous incoherence?

Let us sum up the main fault lines in Socrates' account, then, and offer a provisional hypothesis as to how he may resolve them in his own life. We have first the cautiously utilitarian and prudently self-protective Socrates. Especially in the exchange with Meletus, Socrates goes quite far in suggesting that his sole or at least his invariably predominant concern is the desire to avoid harm to himself. This is the same spirit he attributes to his *daimonion,* which never impels him forward, intervenes only to protect him from harm, and even limits his willingness to play the part of a good citizen. But Socrates also portrays himself as strangely indifferent to most of the usual objects of prudent concern, including property and status in the city and even survival itself. Something else in him that he also characterizes in divine terms, this time not as a daimonic voice but as a divine mission assigned to him by the god at Delphi, drives him to amazing neglect of these ordinary concerns. This side of Socrates bears a certain resemblance to the single-minded pursuit of glory of Achilles or the moral intransigence of the most serious devotee of justice. Socrates wraps himself in the garb of both, and in so doing appeals to a second universal moral intuition: virtue is an absolute adherence to what is right at all costs. Socrates characterizes the goal of this side of his virtue in complex terms: unlike the caution that drives his *daimonion*, this "Delphic" virtue is driven by an uncanny devotion to the truth, but also a strange kind of piety and a deep concern for the good of others. It is this heroic Socrates who gives up his "own things" to exhort his fellow citizens to virtue and who, in his proud refusal to pander to the jury's baser motives or to besmirch the name of Athens or of philosophy, is willing to give up his own life. Yet this form of virtue as well Socrates presents as resting on knowledge of what is intrinsically good or right, whether it is good for oneself or not.

If we take into account only these first two facets of Socrates' self-presentation, and especially if we take with utmost seriousness the heroic stance he assumes in the latter, we are left with an utterly schizophrenic account of the principles Socrates lived by. But there is a third aspect of his self-portrait that bridges these two: his claim that he is the one man in Athens who sees with perfect clarity that virtue *is* his own good, and who is good because he sees it. This claim is the most prominent strand of his self-presentation and the one most readers are likely to remember most powerfully. Here again Socrates captures an important moral intuition with the thought that virtue is of all things the best to possess and the one that wise people set their sights upon. Yet common opinion is again divided as to why virtue is so good. Is it because an excellent soul is so valuable that it eclipses all that fortune can add or take away (a thought that Socrates did much to promote and that became the seed of Stoicism, but still a thought for which he found the germ in ordinary opinion)? Is it because virtuous people generally prosper in this life, perhaps because their souls are so healthy, or perhaps because they are so prudent? Or is it because virtue, while costing us much in this life, wins us a divine reward in the next? This seemingly simple claim that virtue is good for us on inspection breaks into many, all supported by common opinion, and often voiced by the same person and in almost the same breath. Far from resolving these tensions, Socrates merely reproduces them in all their vivid profusion, but in doing so he at least helps us see them for what they are and thus perhaps sets us on the road to untangling them for ourselves.

Might these contradictions all be resolved in Socrates' own case by saying that his love of wisdom was the unifying principle that guided his whole adult life, a love so strong that it eclipsed everything else and that its object and the quest for it could fairly be characterized as "divine," so that his virtue was nothing but the active wisdom that guided him towards ever greater understanding? True, he presents his Delphic quest as an endlessly costly duty imposed on him from without. But if wisdom was the one good he cared about, then he was in fact indifferent to almost all the objects of ordinary concern, including all the external goods he calls "his own things," which his way of life forced him to neglect. True, he presents the quest as service not only to the god but to his fellow citizens. But if through examining others he stood not only to gain important knowledge for himself but also to make good friends, here is an erotic quest of which prudent reason could only approve. This understanding of the Delphic quest is suggested by Socrates' last mention of it, in the counter-penalty speech, where he openly acknowledges that his listeners may consider the Delphic Oracle story an example of his famous irony. Not only does he fail to deny this allegation, but he rather confirms it in the next and most famous lines of the whole speech, in which he gives an alternative, wholly human and wholly rational explanation for his cross-examinations:

> If I say that this is to disobey the god and that because of this it is impossible to keep quiet, you will not be persuaded by me, on the grounds that I am being ironic. And on the other hand, if I say that this even happens to be the greatest good for a human being—to make speeches every day about virtue and the other things about which you hear me conversing and examining both myself and others—and that the unexamined life is not worth living for a human being—you will be persuaded by me even less when I say these things. (37e5–38a6)

Could the commandment that Socrates considered himself bound at all costs to obey have been nothing other than the commandment of his own wisdom about the best way of life?

But what should we make of Socrates' equally emphatic claim to have been under the command of a divine voice, which often throughout his life ordered him, if not positively to act, then at least to refrain from acting, and which, unlike the strange story of the Delphic Oracle, was known to all his companions? Is this *daimonion* the more serious aspect of Socrates' belief in the divine? Socrates describes its interventions in the *Apology*, however, as if it were merely applying principles of caution in ways perfectly evident to human reason: it knows and Socrates knows that he cannot live his chosen life if he gets involved in politics (31c4–32a3). Just as Socrates attributes the wisdom of the poets both to nature and to inspiration and he attributes his lifelong activity both to Apollo's command and to his own insight that the unexamined life is not worth living, might the *daimonion* be equally well interpreted both as somehow divine and as the uncanny human wisdom that kept Socrates safe through a lifetime of dangerous activity?[30] Why, then, would it fall silent now and allow him to die? Or might it be that Socrates, seeing now in old age that he had little remaining time, growing troubles, and little prospect of continued intellectual progress, saw also that by provoking Athens into a rash execution that it would regret and making himself into a celebrated martyr, he could do much for the reputation of philosophy and the welfare of his philosophic friends? This choice, though it could never be easy, would have been less difficult if something in the investigations Socrates had already made convinced him that he had no good reason to fear vengeful judges in Hades, daring and even impious though his life of questioning had been. Might those investigations have been "divine" in the serious sense that their ultimate aim was to settle just this question of Hades, or of providence, or of whether the first causes of all things were or were not only natural necessities?[31]

Even if this is so, however, Socrates' life still seems divine in a different way. While most of us stumble through life, sometimes pursuing one thing and sometimes another, often judging one thing to be best and yet desiring something else more, Socrates seems to have had not only an uncanny wisdom but an uncanny ability to keep his focus on what he judged best and to do the difficult things that his judgment prescribed. If wisdom in his life had such sovereign power, why is wisdom in other lives so much less effective even where it exists? What is the connection between wisdom as Socrates understands it and virtue as it is normally understood? How can the human soul and the concerns of a healthy human being be such a unity that virtue may be said to be always good for us, and what are the unifying principles of that virtue? How far does Socrates take his critique of ordinary views of moral responsibility and ordinary law, and how might his arguments about moral responsibility and law be connected to his sublime freedom from fear of death and from possible punishment in the afterlife? Plato's *Apology* serves less to answer these questions than to send us into the rest of his corpus piqued with puzzlement and wonder.

TWO

The Critique of Retribution: *Gorgias*

The *Gorgias* is the story of Socrates' encounter with the celebrated teacher of rhetoric Gorgias of Leontini, his student Polus, and the otherwise unknown Athenian Callicles. This dialogue, which develops and refines the paradoxical claims for virtue that we found in the *Apology*, is closely linked to that work in many ways. As in the *Apology*, we find here an indictment and a defense of the Socratic way of life, with many reminders of how distant Socrates' outlook and priorities are from those of the common man, and with a similar proud insistence from Socrates that only his own moral principles hold up to scrutiny. As in the *Apology*, we meet with Socrates' companion Chaerephon, this time in person and not by hearsay. As there, sophistry becomes an important theme, especially the question of whether the sophists understand what they claim to know. Likewise rhetoric, an important theme of the *Apology*, becomes the central theme here, as Socrates gives sustained attention to its uses, abuses, power, and limits, commenting upon the difficulty of teaching a great mass of people anything important, especially in a short time. Finally, as in the *Apology*, we find Socrates propounding his thesis that virtue is knowledge and vice ignorance, and propounding it in more than one version: again we encounter both a utilitarian argument for virtue and a far more vivid and arresting hypermoral defense of virtue as a thing incomparably more precious than any other good. Focusing in the *Gorgias* on the virtue of justice, the virtue that has perhaps the most problematic relation to the agent's own good, Socrates claims as he does in most of the *Apology* that it is always best for us to be virtuous. In particular, he argues now that it is always better to suffer injustice than to do it, that injustice is rationally to be regarded with pity and not anger, that retributive punishment is irrational, that the true function of punishment is to improve the offender, and even that it is always better for offenders to be punished than to "get away" with their crimes.[1] Why is the thesis that virtue is knowledge again presented in such strange multiplicity, in such extreme terms, and in conjunction with a discussion of rhetoric? Our analysis will focus on Socrates' fascinating discussion with Polus on crime and punishment and responsibility, the central of the three conversations in this dialogue, but his briefer opening discussion with itinerant rhetoric teacher Gorgias sheds light on all of these questions as well.

Rhetoric, Knowledge, and Justice (447a1–461b2)

At the opening of the *Gorgias*, the little-known Socrates arrives at the house where the celebrated Gorgias has been holding forth and begins to question the rhetorician about his art. As he puts it, he wants to discover "what the power of the man's art is, and what it is that he professes and teaches" (447c1–3). It is not immediately clear what the crux is of Socrates' curiosity and puzzlement, but we soon get a clue when he restates his fundamental question: "Which of the beings does rhetoric happen to be about?" (449d1–2). When Gorgias replies that it is about speeches, Socrates is not satisfied. He divines that Gorgias considers himself a knower of something more serious and powerful than how to balance phrases and to make pretty similes. But is Gorgias such a knower? Is rhetoric based on any solid knowledge of important things, such as human nature, or the truth about justice? Or is it merely a skill at guessing how to produce certain gratifying effects, which Socrates will later call flattery and compare to such insinuating arts as cosmetics and pastry-making? Gorgias identifies his subject matter as "the greatest of human affairs . . . and the best" (451d7–8), by which he clearly means politics, and he calls himself a craftsman of that persuasion which brings its possessor freedom and rule (452d5–8). But Socrates wonders what Gorgias understands about the human soul and the reasons for the impressive sway that beautiful speeches can indeed have over it. What is at the root of this power to move men to extraordinary undertakings, and what is at the root of the love of freedom and power and also justice and nobility that great political speeches appeal to? And finally, what are the limits of this power, and does Gorgias in his professions offer an accurate assessment of what he is and is not able to teach and what his students will and will not be able to do?

Pressing Gorgias further so as to pin him down about his subject of expertise, Socrates gets him to acknowledge that his art is one that especially produces persuasion about "what is just and unjust" (454b7). But it soon becomes clear that Socrates has given more thought than Gorgias has to the relationship between Gorgias' highly intellectual, mildly disreputable, but undeniably potent art of persuasion and the demands of citizenship and justice. Socrates exposes Gorgias' thoughtlessness by provoking him into such a bold claim for the power of his art to persuade multitudes, without his needing to impart or even possess the relevant knowledge and against the advice of true experts who have it (454e4–9; 455d6–56c7; cf. 459a1–c2), that Gorgias feels compelled to add a proviso. This power should never be used unjustly, any more than any other competitive skill should be, and teachers of rhetoric should no more be blamed for their students' unjust use of their skills than should teachers of boxing. But clearly the power to make justice look unjust and injustice just is a more dangerous art than the art of boxing. Is Gorgias a teacher who irresponsibly equips unscrupulous politicians to manipulate assemblies' notions of justice for pernicious ends? Or does his art rest on a knowledge of and dedication to justice and a commitment to imparting that understanding to his students? Presented in effect with this question, Gorgias takes the less damaging alternative and affirms that he does know and teach justice; he agrees moreover that "one who has learned the just things" will be just (460b7). These concessions, however, involve him in a contradiction that Socrates immediately exposes: Gorgias claims that the art he confers on his students entails a full and efficacious knowledge of justice, and yet he maintains that some students of this art (not necessarily his own) act unjustly and that it is not their teachers' fault.

What has Socrates accomplished through this entrapment? Socrates is gentle in that he proves only that Gorgias has contradicted himself and not that he is unscrupulous, but the surrounding argument exposes in Gorgias' understanding two great flaws. He has not thought deeply enough about the passions and especially the concern for justice that he plays upon, and he overestimates the power of his own art of persuasion and of reason in general. By showing the first, Socrates lays the groundwork for the critique of rhetoric that soon follows.[2] Unlike medicine and gymnastics and the art of legislation, rhetoric is not a true art based on true knowledge of human nature and the natural human needs; it involves a certain knowledge of the passions, to be sure, but it is able to provide no comprehensive account of the proper ordering of the passions or the health of the soul, nor any method for achieving these. Rhetoric is an irresponsible art because it is a false art; true knowledge of the soul is at least a precondition if not a guarantee of doing real good. Curiously, however, Socrates' fundamental charge is not that rhetoric manipulates or exploits its subjects, but that it flatters and panders to them. Thus he suggests that rhetoric is less masterful or free than Gorgias and Polus imagine. This classification of rhetoric as flattery reminds us of Socrates' belittling account of sophistry in the *Republic,* where he compares the sophists in their political machinations to men who are rearing a great beast and have become skilled in interpreting its many moods and sounds and who call whatever delights it good and whatever vexes it bad (493a–c).

But how exactly does oratory tend to flatter its audience? As Stauffer suggests, "Gorgian rhetoric . . . tells people they can fulfill their desires with a good conscience; it . . . depends on nothing more than an acquaintance with human desires and a knack for telling people what they want to hear."[3] History is full of cynical uses of rhetoric to give coloring to unjust acts: consider, for example, Cleon's appeal to justice in encouraging the Athenians to indulge their anger against the Mytileneans in Thucydides.[4] But does rhetoric flatter only our lower desires, by reassuring us that they are just, or does it not equally flatter our commitment to justice, persuading us that we are nobler and more free of self-concern than we are? Such is the magic Shakespeare's Henry V spins in persuading his troops that they are indeed glad to be a happy few, fighting gloriously against the French horde at Agincourt. Such, likewise, is Gorgias' own work in inducing patients to submit to the physician's knife, by rousing in them a noble sense of their own courageous self-overcoming to win them to a course that is purely prudential. At an even deeper level, does the finest rhetoric not flatter us most of all, in appealing to the belief that we know what justice is and what it demands and in stifling any sense of doubt or felt need to question this—and in assuring us of our cosmic significance as supporters of high principles?

Gorgias well knows how important it is to assure an audience that what it wants is just; he knows how effective it is to appeal to men's wish to believe that they are in their heart of hearts noble and disinterested; he knows how useful it is to insist that they know exactly what justice is and demands; he knows further how easily each of these concerns may be satisfied and manipulated. But has he pondered the strange connection between these facts? Why, if it is so easy for people to justify whatever they want, do they nevertheless care so much about having a justification, and why, if they care so much about having a justification, are they so easily satisfied with such flimsy excuses as they often use to fob themselves off? This ambivalence about justice, a subject of endless investigation in Socratic dialectic, is exploited by Gorgias with little thought. In voicing his curiosity about "the power of the man's art" at the opening of the dialogue, Socrates is no doubt interested especially in what Gorgias really understands about the roots of that power in the human ambivalence towards justice and our susceptibility to self-deception. But instead of finding clarity about this problem, Socrates finds the ambivalence thoughtlessly present in Gorgias himself, who combines an easy cynicism about politics with a gentlemanly urbanity and a faith that his students will remain gentlemen, as well as a keen desire not to be thought a charlatan or an exploiter. If Gorgias understands neither his audience's concern with justice nor even his own, is he not the ultimate flatterer of both the masses and himself?

Socrates has also revealed a secondary but still significant flaw in Gorgias' understanding by eliciting his unqualified agreement that whoever "learns the just things" will be just (460b7). This agreement is all the more remarkable as it makes it impossible for Gorgias to save his position with the protest that while he is just and exhorts his students to be just, some of them only pretend to respect justice and others later fall away from it. Thus it seems likely that behind this tactical error is a pervasive overestimation of the power of reason. Indeed, Xenophon suggests in the *Anabasis* that this misjudgment was a crucial feature that separated Gorgias from Socrates. He tells the story of Proxenus, a student of Gorgias, who was good at leading gentlemen with appeals to their reason and nobility but lost his command through his inability to inspire fear in the common soldiers. By contrast, Xenophon himself, a student of Socrates, had no illusions about the need to use force and no hesitation about beating his own men when that was required: the student of Socrates and not the student of Gorgias understood the limits to the power of reasoned speech.[5] But what is Socrates' own claim that virtue is knowledge and that one who knows what is good will do it, if not a fantastic overestimation of the power of reason over passion, habit, laziness, and cowardice? Or could that doctrine in its simplistic extremism possibly be a page Socrates took from Gorgias' book, a deliberate adoption of Gorgias' error into a rhetorical stratagem that would cloak a radical Socratic thought in the garb of a harmlessly high-minded piece of naïveté? In the *Republic* Socrates hints that his doctrine of ideas is just such a stratagem, meant to conceal from the city his radical critique of its understanding and practice of justice and to persuade it that philosophy, far from having anything dangerous to teach, is absorbed in contemplating castles in the sky of another world (476d–80a). Could his claims about the perfect efficacy of knowledge serve the same purpose?

Whether in fact Socratic or Socratic-Platonic rhetoric owes this particular feature to Gorgias, the politically vulnerable Socrates clearly is interested in thinking about the potential as well as the limitations of Gorgias' art, and the humbled but not humiliated Gorgias is intensely interested in hearing what Socrates will have to say to Polus and Callicles. In those discussions Socrates will show him that the human concern for justice runs deeper than it seems to, even in men who appear liberated from its sway; in the first he will also sketch a new and more civically responsible use to which Gorgian rhetoric might be put. One agenda of the entire dialogue thus seems to be to explore the possibility of an alliance between Socrates and Gorgias that would make Gorgian rhetoric more thoughtful about the power of the human concern for justice, the danger of the city's suspicion of politically detached intellectuals, and the limits of the power of speech—all of which contribute to the vulnerability of men like Gorgias and Socrates—thus rendering Gorgias' rhetoric better suited to protect them and to make a positive contribution to society. It is in this context that Socrates makes his claim for the absolute superiority of justice to injustice, the involuntary character of vice, and the benefits of punishment for the one punished. Are these claims rhetorical or serious? I submit that they are in the highest degree both.

To call them serious is not to deny that Socrates' deepest thoughts in this dialogue about moral responsibility are obscure and difficult to extract. Not only are his claims about justice presented in extreme terms and in contradictory versions; not only does the whole discussion take place within a framing that reminds us of Socrates' need for a defensive rhetoric, which his hypermoral claims certainly provide; but, as we shall see, the arguments he employs at every step are tendentious and full of holes. And yet in the exchange with Polus and in the subsequent exchange with Callicles, Socrates shows something remarkable that by no means hangs upon any of his problematic arguments. He shows that the most characteristic act of imputing responsibility, the act of blaming and calling for punishment, is fraught with self-contradiction. He shows, in other words, that moral indignation is irrational, not merely in the biased and clouded judgments and rash actions it so often leads to, but in its essential assumptions about the character and status of the person against whom it is directed. When Socrates finishes his conversation with Polus, Callicles cannot believe that Socrates believes the astonishing things he has just said. But Socrates levels against him a challenge that is equally a challenge to all of us in our most important attributions of responsibility and our most important judgments about justice:

> Either refute [my friend philosophy] . . . by showing that doing injustice and not paying the just penalty when one does injustice are not the utmost of all evils; or else, if you leave this unrefuted—by the dog, the god of the

> Egyptians!—Callicles will not agree with you, Callicles, but will be dissonant his whole life. (482b2–6)

And Socrates makes good on his challenge. He proves that anger and its characteristic demand for retributive punishment rest on a profound confusion, regardless of how one ultimately judges the various versions of Socrates' thesis that virtue is knowledge and regardless of how the many puzzles of the dialogue are finally resolved.

Polus' Entry into the Dialogue (461b3–62b2)

Polus breaks into the dialogue twice, first in an unsuccessful attempt to shield Gorgias from the questioning of Socrates and his acolyte Chaerephon, and again in an angry rebuke to Socrates after the latter has caught Gorgias in self-contradiction. In both interventions we get a vivid glimpse of his character. Polus exhibits in the highest degree the constellation of passions and convictions that come into play when we hold ourselves and others morally responsible: pride, a belief in and love of our freedom of action, contentiousness, anger, envy, and a strong sense of the noble and the base. In terms of Platonic psychology, Polus, whose name means "colt," is *thumos* or spiritedness incarnate.

In the first intervention, Polus interprets Socrates' desire to question Gorgias as a desire not to learn something but to engage in a contest; he leaps in to defend his own teacher against the outsiders who seem both to pose a threat and to do so unfairly, since Gorgias is already tired. His answer to the Socratic "what is" question, rather ineptly posed by Chaerephon, is not to define the art of rhetoric but to praise it as the best and the noblest of all arts. For this alleged failure to answer the question asked, Socrates brushes him aside. In his second intervention, already hurt by Socrates' disrespect, Polus is so incensed by the apparent craziness of Socrates' conclusion that no true rhetorician even has the power to do injustice that he cannot keep his syntax straight (461a4–7, b4–c3). Intensely sensitive to pride and shame himself, Polus interprets Gorgias' acknowledgment that Gorgias teaches justice as an acknowledgment motivated by shame, although it is not clear that it was motivated by anything but cautious prudence. Polus himself is a teacher of rhetoric (and hence no doubt of all manner of rhetorical devices), but despite this, and despite the fact that he will soon identify the life of an unjust tyrant as the happy life, he is incensed at Socrates for the unfairness of his own tricky rhetoric.

Socrates, who has quickly taken the measure of Polus and who seems determined to cross him, insists on curtailing his freedom to hold forth at length: only if he confines himself to short answers will Socrates talk with him at all. Polus is outraged. "What's this? Will I not be allowed to say as much as I wish?" (461d8–9). But his curiosity to know what Socrates really means and the necessity of complying in order to get any answer from him compel Polus to give up the freedom his spiritedness craves in order to have something else that he desires more. And thus Socrates takes the first step towards curbing Polus' spiritedness and teaching him that the objects of its yearnings are perhaps after all not the most important elements of happiness. But the limited success Socrates will have in this endeavor is also foreshadowed in this first exchange, for in fact Socrates must appeal not merely to Polus' desire to know, but also to his pride in answering any sort of question as well as Gorgias can, before he can get Polus to acquiesce to his terms. Polus' spiritedness may be moderated, but it will not cease to rule him. Indeed, in the ensuing discussion of Socrates' classification of rhetoric, the "young and swift" Polus turns out to be so intent on defending his art's dignity and so impatient to hear Socrates praise it that Gorgias must intervene to slow the discussion down and find out what Socrates is really saying.

The Classification of Rhetoric (462b3–66a3)

Now that we have seen something of Polus' character, let us look more closely at his conversation with Socrates about the arts and flatteries, considering why this exceedingly spirited man might be so interested in what Socrates calls the sham art of rhetoric, and considering as well what further light Socrates' observations about rhetoric might shed on the peculiar dynamics of Polus' soul as one most intensely concerned with moral responsibility and most badly in need of Socratic correction. According to Socrates' schema, there are two true arts of caring for bodies, gymnastics and medicine, and two corresponding arts of caring for souls, legislation and justice. By making justice analogous to medicine, Socrates suggests that at least the chief part of justice is corrective and that in the best case a healthy soul would be no more in need of it than a healthy body would be in need of medicine. The perfective arts of legislation and gymnastics, on the other hand, would be needed by all, including the best, and are therefore higher than medicine. Here Socrates attributes to legislation the very highest purpose, as does the Athenian Stranger in the *Laws*. But is legislation truly capable of securing the perfection of the individual soul? Does actual legislation even aim at perfecting the soul in more than a partial way, and for the most part only insofar as its good condition is necessary for keeping the community well ordered and well defended? Thus Socrates' description of the arts in the *Gorgias* would seem to contain a certain flattery of its own, an indication perhaps of what the good orator should encourage political life to aspire to rather than an accurate description of what the political art is in fact able to accomplish.

"Slipping in" under each of the true arts Socrates places an impostor that aims at pleasure rather than at genuine well-being: cosmetics, which feigns the health that gymnastics truly produces; cookery, which gratifies the appetites instead of demanding the moderation and more painful purgings that medicine imposes; sophistry, which only pretends to seek the good of the soul, or which seeks a bogus good not informed by an adequate account of human nature and human happiness; and rhetoric, which provides a gratifying shadow of what justice truly accomplishes. But again, does sophistry really imitate or replace legislation? In book 6 of the *Republic* Socrates presents it as rather an impostor for philosophy. Might philosophy, as the true art corresponding to sophistry, be in fact the only art that adequately cares for souls, if only one or two at a time? And why is rhetoric paired with justice and not with legislation? Perhaps it is because rhetoric addresses especially the question of what justice demands; perhaps it is also because rhetoric, to the extent that it is or can become an art, is a corrective and not a perfective one. For just as cookery tends to flatter our desires but can be enlisted by the good doctor to restore depleted bodies to their optimal state, so rhetoric tends to flatter our belief in our own justice but can be enlisted by the wise soul-doctor to control the bad proclivities of unhealthy souls.

Now our observations on the spiritedness of the lover of rhetoric that we have before us call attention to the fact that Socrates' division of the sham arts is not simply a division between practices that pertain to the body and ones that pertain to the soul; it is also, following another common Socratic division, between practices that promote the pleasures of the desiring part of the soul (cosmetics and cookery) and those that gratify the spirited part (sophistry and rhetoric). In particular, deliberative rhetoric, which always becomes most important where governments are most free and therefore most dependent on public opinion, stirs and flatters the love of freedom, of power, of empire, and of ambitious public undertakings, magnifying their importance to our well-being and minimizing the need for self-restraint, prudent realism, and calm acceptance of necessity. Similarly, forensic rhetoric stirs and flatters jurors' moral indignation towards crime and criminals. In the revealing example of Polus' soul, the love of rhetoric seems especially to grow out of two closely related but not altogether compatible expressions of spiritedness: the love of autonomy understood as the capacity and license to do and say whatever one likes, with the dignity that such successful self-assertion seems to bring; and the love of nobility, which demands that one limit or set aside one's own desires and interests for the sake of something higher. The first alone might impel him to try to become a tyrant; the second restrains him from injustice. Rhetoric appeals to Polus' desire to dominate others, to beat the system, but also to a yearning for something splendid that a thuggish life cannot possibly give him. These two aspects of dignity that attract him are connected insofar as both appeal to a certain real or perceived freedom—the former to a freedom to pursue his self-interested desires and the latter to a freedom to choose what is right and leave self-concern behind. But what unifying principle can combine the love of self-assertion with the love of self-overcoming into one coherent way of life? Polus does not know, and it is one of the great charms and evils of rhetoric that it celebrates both sides of the love of freedom and dignity while obscuring the tension between them, shielding a man like Polus from the painful work of understanding and resolving this tension. This problem is perhaps the deepest reason why Socrates insists that the genuine art of caring for the human soul must be able to give a reasoned account of the soul's workings and its true thriving (465a2–6); it is also the contradiction on which Polus will impale himself as he struggles to refute Socrates' strange claims about moral responsibility.

Socrates' Utilitarian Account of Power and Justice (466a4–68e5)

In his first attempt to defend the dignity of rhetoric against Socrates' disparagement, Polus focuses on the self-interested meaning of freedom. Do the orators not enjoy the greatest power in the cities? he asks. "Do they not, just like the tyrants, kill whomever they wish and confiscate property and banish from the cities whomever it seems good to them?" (466b11–c2). Socrates responds with an argument that remains on the level of self-interest, a wholly pragmatic argument that the freedom to do as one likes is not after all nearly so important for one's own happiness as Polus supposes. Neither such orators nor tyrants have real power, Socrates insists. Far from enjoying a dignified freedom, they do not even do what they wish; they are the victims of their own blindness and folly, and for this they deserve pity. What is more, they are not even esteemed by any of the people who seem to admire them.[6] The discussion proceeds on the basis of self-interested premises that seem at first to be Polus' own, but Socrates' argument will in fact be so coldly calculating that it will spark strong resistance from Polus, thus flushing out the more hidden and nobler side of his love of freedom.

The culmination of this first argument will be Socrates' assertion of the power or primacy of the good for human action. "For we wish the good things, as you say, but what is neither good nor bad we do not wish, nor the bad things" (468c5–7).[7] This is a fundamental premise that Socrates elsewhere reiterates (e.g. *Meno* 77c–78b) and nowhere calls into question; he denies that anyone ever wishes what is bad because it is bad, but only because it is or seems good; he denies, in other words, the possibility of radical evil. On this basis he will draw far-reaching conclusions: that whenever one chooses what is bad in the belief that it is good, one is acting with a folly that is regrettable and pitiable; that all unjust acts are of such a character; and that as such they are not voluntary. Indeed, we may say that they are not even in the full sense the agent's own act. For we attribute full responsibility only to what people do intentionally, with understanding of the specific acts that they perform, the good they aim at in performing them, and the likelihood of achieving the one with the other. Socrates will argue that these conditions are met only in the case of good choices, and that we are not free to choose between good and bad ends in the way we imagine we are. Rather, as he will argue explicitly in the *Meno* and the *Protagoras*, to whatever extent we know the good, we necessarily follow it.

To see more precisely what Socrates is arguing here about human wishes or intentions and their relation to the good, let us trace the argument in detail. Socrates starts with a premise that he takes from Polus, the premise that power is something good for the one who has it (466b6–7). Socrates himself may well prefer to think of power as an ambiguous capacity that is good only in the hands of one who knows how to use it well, but since Polus is so certain it is an unqualified good, Socrates grants this premise and proceeds to show the paradoxical conclusion that must result. If power is good, it must be not the capacity to do whatever *seems* good at any moment, for this is often destructive. It must instead be the capacity to do what one *truly wishes*, namely, to secure what *is* good, for only on that basis is power a real and not an illusory good. But securing what is good requires intelligence (*nous*), which Socrates implicitly defines here as knowledge of what is beneficial and what is not. Polus grants that power, to be good, requires intelligence, and Socrates, to confirm his agreement, reiterates, "and power is, as you say, a good thing, but you too agree that doing what seems good without intelligence is a bad thing, don't you?" Polus answers, "I do" (466e–67a). With Polus' full support, Socrates thus introduces into the discussion the distinction between what seems good and what truly is good, the latter providing a standard by which actions may be measured. But this concession remains abstract, and indeed Polus scarcely feels the force of it: he is astonished when Socrates denies that in doing what seems good to them, tyrants and orators do what they truly wish. It seems obvious to him what anyone would do if he had a free hand in politics, and obvious that having a free hand would itself be a fine thing. In order to prove the critical importance of knowledge or intelligence for happiness and hence for the goodness of any power or freedom, Socrates must do more to shake Polus' complacency and to substantiate his strange claim that rhetoricians and tyrants have the least power in the cities and do virtually nothing of which they wish (466b9–10, d6–e2).[8]

The new argument that begins at 467c is a first attempt at doing this, by driving a sharper wedge between the particular things that at each moment seem good to do and the ultimate reasons we choose to do them. Socrates begins by asking, "Do human beings seem to you to wish what they do on each occasion, or that for the sake of which they do what they do?" (467c5–7). To lead Polus to the answer he wants, he gives examples of people taking drugs to get well and undergoing deadly risks to earn money. Polus agrees that people do these things for the sake of some further end. Socrates concludes, speaking at once very precisely and misleadingly, "So isn't it also this way concerning everything? If someone does something for the sake of something, he doesn't wish that which he does, but that for the sake of which he does it?" (467d6–e1). Without denying that actions are ever chosen for their own sakes, Socrates continues to speak only of actions that are intrinsically risky, unpleasant, or uninteresting and that are done for the sake of some good beyond themselves, as if all actions were merely instrumental in this way.

Socrates next establishes that "among the things that are," everything can be correctly classified as either good or bad or intermediate—and by implication, ranked by its degree of goodness or badness (467e1–3). Socrates would of course grant that a thing can be good in one way and bad in another, but he is insisting that each thing must on balance not only appear to us but actually be either good or bad or neither—at least for us to have, or to experience, or to do, under the circumstances in which we find ourselves. Moreover, he says that what we do, we do because it seems to us "better" to do it than not (468b, d). If the lesser of available goods is a relative evil and the lesser of available evils is a relative good, nothing is better to do than to abstain from except what is best, so that everyone must at every point do the one thing that seems to him to be best.[9] True, the correct perspective may be hard to ascertain. We may think it is best to do what brings us the greatest pleasure whereas in fact it is better to give primacy to what is beneficial; we may think it is best to do what is most beneficial for ourselves whereas in fact it is better to give primacy to what is beneficial for our families or our nations or other fellow human beings or to what is noble; but in every case we do what seems best and apply the standard that seems best to apply, and if it is not truly best, we have suffered from an error in judgment. Without yet making any claim about where considerations of justice fall in a correct evaluation of priorities, Socrates is building here a simple but powerful case for the overwhelming importance to our lives of correct judgment about what is good.

Socrates then gives examples of what he means by good things: "So, then, do you say that wisdom (*sophia*) and health and wealth and the other such things are good, and the opposites of these are bad?" he asks (467e4–6). E. R. Dodds calls this a merely "conventional" list, arguing that Socrates himself does not regard either health or wealth as necessarily good, and citing *Meno* 87e–88a in support of this claim.[10] Dodds has on his side the many passages in the *Apology* where we have already seen Socrates speaking as if virtue were the only thing that matters. On the other side are Socrates' comments in the *Gorgias* itself about the importance of health and the undesirability of suffering injustice (512a; 469c1; cf. *Crito* 47d–e). Is the present passage an insincere bow to convention, then, or an acknowledgment that other goods besides the inner condition of one's soul really are important? The list is at any rate not quite conventional, if also not quite Socratic. It resembles but does not duplicate the catalogue of good things Socrates cited earlier from a common drinking song: "Health is best, and second is to have become beautiful, and third . . . is to be wealthy without fraud" (451e3–5). When he quoted that song Socrates dropped a fourth good that the scholiast reports was part of the original song: to be in the prime of youth among friends. Now he also omits the qualification "without fraud," and substitutes wisdom for beauty, moving wisdom to first place. Nowhere in this passage is there any suggestion that the goods we naturally seek include honor, power, freedom, justice for our communities, or the friendship Socrates evidently placed great value upon.[11] Socrates' new list could thus be said to describe the good condition of soul, body, and external possessions, but from a peculiarly individual and amoral perspective, perhaps just the self-interested and morally skeptical but intellectual perspective of Polus.

Finally, Socrates draws his conclusion: what each person wishes for and acts for the sake of, when he acts, is "the same thing, the good" (468b).

Now in a sense it is obvious that everyone wants good things, but the twists of the argument leave us with a puzzle as to what he is saying the true object of wish is. Is he saying that we never wish for means but only for ends, as 467c implies? No, for he speaks of wishing to do actions that are means to further ends at 468c. Is he saying that what each person wishes for and aims at in all that one does is the true, objective good, however well or poorly one grasps it?[12] No, for he speaks of wishing for wealth at 467d, which surely does not turn out to be good for everyone who gets it. Is he really only saying that everyone wishes for whatever appears good to him, then?[13] No, for that would make nonsense of the claim that tyrants, in doing what seems best to them—and thereby in many cases successfully amassing wealth, slaves, armies, and dominions—still do "nothing" of what they wish (466e1). The argument makes sense only when we see that he is using the word "wishing" in three different ways, applying it loosely or conditionally to actions that people deliberately choose, more precisely to the specific ends people have in view when they act, and most precisely and unconditionally to the good that would truly satisfy them and therefore what they are groping towards even if they do not know its contents. For we wish for what seems good only because it seems to be what we wish for more fundamentally, the true good that will meet our needs and those of the people we care about and who make us happy.[14]

Socrates will soon go on to argue that justice is central to the true goods that make one happy, but so far the human good in its higher reaches is not evident in the argument. And when Socrates returns from general reflections on the good to the case of orators and tyrants, he adduces as motives for their acts only their concern for their own personal benefit (468d). Thus he continues to paint a picture of human life as both narrowly selfish and drably utilitarian. This section of the dialogue, from 466a4–68e5, proceeds as if virtue were nothing intrinsically good, activities such as contemplation were never chosen for their own sakes, and the concern for the welfare of others were nothing natural. It is an argument with which Hobbes could have no disagreement: human beings are selfish and not political beings by nature; the aim of political action is to secure private goods; sensible people are utterly practical and never trample on others without a good reason; since everyone is equally self-interested and no one is free to be otherwise, no one is to be blamed for being such. Hence, as Socrates will soon argue and Hobbes heartily agrees, retributive punishment is irrational.

How far do all of these features represent merely a concession to Polus' premises and how far do they reveal a genuine strain in Socratic thought?

The argument's sober practicality is certainly not foreign to Socrates. His central message to Polus here, as to so many interlocutors in both Plato's and Xenophon's writings, is that he should think harder about his own good. At the same time, if this amoral argument is a concession to Polus' own premises, it is only a concession to one part of his soul. It provokes intense resistance from something else in him, culminating in an outburst of incredulity, and it is hard to believe that Socrates did not anticipate this reaction. Why, then, does Socrates make his argument in the incomplete way that he does? In part his approach seems designed to provoke exactly the opposition it elicits, and thus to help Polus to feel and Gorgias to see the depth of the spirited passions that defy any simplistic, narrowly selfish, or amoral understanding of the human soul.

In part the argument also seems designed to help both Gorgias and us begin to reflect on moral responsibility by starting with the simplest case. If human beings' sole motive in all that we did were to secure one or a few basic ends, such as our own survival and security, as Socrates suggests both here and in the cross-examination of Meletus in the *Apology*, or our own pleasure, as he postulates in the *Protagoras*, then it would be undeniable that we are compelled by the good, our own good. We would not be responsible for limiting it for the benefit of anyone else, for the simple reason that we would not be free to. As everyone's motives would be the same and naturally determined, none could be blamed. Any rational judgments of individuals or acts as good or bad could be based only on the intelligence and skill with which they secured the naturally good things, and any deviation from that standard would be an unwilling mistake. Watching other people seeking their own security or pleasure, any rational person would regard them as one athlete regards another, with a desire to win the first prize but with a full acceptance of the fact that each is naturally and equally seeking it for himself. If this account were correct, a rational government would pass laws and impose penalties to ensure the best prospect of success for those in power and those whose support they needed, and no rational subject would be angry or surprised to find it doing so. Nor would the rulers be angry with lawbreakers any more than a sensible animal-trainer is angry with his charges when they fail to do his bidding. They would simply keep adjusting rewards and deterrents to get the results they wanted.

To think about moral responsibility this way is to see more clearly why Hobbes' brand of rationalism and the Hobbesean argument against retribution have met with so little success. It thus forces us to consider what else in the human soul must be taken into consideration if we are to have an adequate account of moral responsibility. Polus' reaction is thus most helpful in bringing to the fore what Socrates' first account of human motivation has left out. It helps us see why Hobbes' simple utilitarianism will always remain unconvincing, and why Socratic political philosophy took such a different direction, even when it made a similar argument about responsibility. This starting-point also invites us to ask, however, how much the basic picture of human beings as compelled by the good really changes even when we do take into account the full range of concerns and motives that full-blooded human beings have.

What, precisely, is at the bottom of Polus' resistance to Socrates' amoral, utilitarian analysis? Polus does not say; he is sullenly silent when Socrates asks whether tyrants do not kill and expel and confiscate the goods of others solely out of a wish to benefit themselves (468c2–8). But likely he is thinking that tyrants do these things not just for prudential reasons but because it is pleasant to push others around, or because it is satisfying to punish the guilty, or both. To be sure, these motives are in moral terms opposed, but they have something in common: both involve a pleasing sense of strength and dignity, to which Polus is deeply drawn; both are key expressions of human spiritedness. At this point Polus may or may not be aware of either a moral or a benevolent component in his attraction to punishing—that is, either a principled attachment to justice or a compassionate concern for the welfare of injustice's victims—but he is certainly aware that the power that Socrates insists is only a means to securing personal benefits is for him something much more deeply attractive. Perhaps it even seems the most desirable thing of all. And what he expresses so vividly is present in varying degrees in virtually all human beings: few have so little *thumos* as Socrates. Thus we see in Polus the passions that must be brought to the surface and addressed if human beings are ever to be convinced that the freedom to do as we please is not all-important and is not in itself even good. But as we proceed into the next and very different phase of the argument with Polus, we must keep in mind Socrates' demonstrative project in the drama unfolding here. Socrates is going to show Gorgias the deep passions that Gorgias has failed to take seriously enough, above all the passionate concern for justice. Thus he will point the way to a better, more thoughtful, more responsible rhetoric than Gorgias has used and taught hitherto. But the possibility must be considered that what Socrates will sketch in the rest of this dialogue is only a better rhetoric. His genuine view will remain difficult indeed to discern.

Socrates' Hypermoral Account of Justice and Power (468e6–70c3)

By suggesting that individuals are, in everything they do, merely pursuing their own pleasure and utility, Socrates elicits from Polus a vehement expression of his inchoate concern for something higher and more dignified that goes beyond these ends. To be sure, what first comes to sight—Polus' envy of the tyrant's freedom to inflict whatever harm he wishes on whomever he wishes—is hardly noble. But this envy is deeply entangled with other passions, especially pity for innocent victims and righteous indignation towards their tormenters, that entail a more moral and generous set of concerns. Polus envies those with the power to kill and imprison and confiscate the property of anyone they wish, but he assumes it is especially attractive to everyone to be able to do so justly (469a9–10). He pities those who are hurt unjustly, but not those who are hurt deservedly (469b3–7): clearly he feels a satisfaction at seeing the wicked punished that quenches any compassion he might otherwise feel at their suffering. But his wish to see the just protected and the unjust punished has become largely eclipsed by a countervailing wish, in the face of evidence that justice is not enforced in the world, to be one of the strong who triumph over others and not one of their victims.

Only by interrogating Polus' sense of what enviable freedom and dignity consist in can Socrates begin to build a case that the tyrant's happiness is incomplete and his apparent power illusory, for no one can doubt the tyrant's ability to secure for himself all the simpler objects of common desire. And yet the argument Socrates will make to prove the tyrant's weakness is as strange as his conclusion. For he now claims that those who do injustice are profoundly ignorant about matters of the greatest importance: they think that they are benefiting themselves at others' expense, whereas in reality they are harming themselves most of all. The upshot is an almost complete inversion of normal judgments about who is really enviable and who is pitiable. While Polus envies the doers of injustice and pities their victims, Socrates suggests that both the envy and the pity are in large degree misplaced, for he claims that doing injustice is the greatest of evils, far worse than suffering injustice. Although killing justly is not as bad as killing unjustly, Socrates says the one who kills justly is still not enviable: evidently he sees nothing noble and nothing naturally and properly pleasant in avenging injustice (469a9–b2). On the other hand, it is better to be killed unjustly than justly, since one who deserves death must have the worst of evils within him (469b3–9).

But the picture Socrates paints with his inversion of common judgments is not complete. While he is explicit about what is unenviable, what is pitiable, and what is the worst of evils, he is silent on what is enviable or the best of good things. If living unjustly is the worst of evils, it may or may not be the case that living justly is the greatest of goods, as the moral and hypermoral-eudaimonist positions hold. It may be merely the necessary precondition for the greatest good, as the moral utilitarian position holds. Likewise, Socrates is not quite clear here on whether injustice is the only evil that matters, as he suggests repeatedly in the *Apology*, or just one of many. True, by calling injustice the worst of evils he certainly implies that there are others, and by agreeing that the tyrant's victims are pitiable he suggests that one needs much more than justice to thrive. Yet his claim about the evil of being unjust is so extreme that it would seem to imply a vanishingly insignificant role for the goods of fortune by comparison. For if doing injustice is *always* worse than suffering it (and Socrates never qualifies this categorical assessment) then it would seem that no amount of misfortune could ever outweigh the evil of the smallest theft, such as stealing a paper clip. The Stoics would later draw the conclusion that the possession and loss of the so-called goods of fortune is then really a matter of indifference. An equally logical and perhaps more sensible conclusion is that Socrates cannot possibly mean what he says and is exaggerating to provoke Polus. But a third possibility is that what Socrates means by justice is something so fundamental for human well-being that no other evil can be worse than its absence and no other good can compensate for its loss. If it is hard to conceive of ordinary civic justice in this way, is there another understanding of justice that could make sense of this extreme claim? In Book 4 of the *Republic* Socrates equates justice with the good order in the soul, an order rooted in a wise assessment of what everything is worth, an order in which desires are in harmony with judgment and judgments are not distorted by fears and temptations. If few people would give such weight to "order in the soul," perhaps all would give it to sanity. Might we disagree with Socrates only in imagining that ordinary life is far more sane, resting on far better judgment about what things are and what they are worth, than Socrates thinks?

Since Socrates does not at this point throw any light on what the evil of injustice consists in, it is hard to know how close his extreme claim for the value of justice comes to a moral claim as normally understood. On the surface, at least, the argument now takes a sharp turn from the low selfishness of the previous section to the hypermoral praise of virtue we saw in the *Apology*. And yet Socrates' argument here, as in many parts of the *Apology*, remains or at least encourages Polus to remain focused on the question of what is good for oneself. The self-regarding element returns as he probes again the meaning of power, demonstrating to Polus that power is indeed not the bare ability to do things but the ability to secure what is "beneficial" (470a), and if he does not say "beneficial for oneself" it is clear that this is what Polus takes him to mean. If power were merely the ability to act at will, Socrates argues, any man in the agora with a knife under his cloak would have great power, for he, like Polus' admired tyrant, may indeed kill whomever he wishes. But the would-be assassin cannot kill without paying a penalty, as Polus protests, and according to Socrates neither can the tyrant, whose penalty is certain because it is already within him.

Envy, Pity, and Indignation (470c4–74b10)

If the low utilitarianism of Socrates' first critique of the tyrant elicits from Polus a strong statement of his concern with dignity, the hypermoralism of the following section now evokes an even more vehement expression of scorn for Socrates and frank admiration for unjust men whose criminal schemes are successful. To demonstrate that the unjust are by no means wretched, Polus raises the example of the tyrant Archelaus and his brutal and fratricidal accession to the throne of Macedonia. As more than one commentator has noted, Polus combines expressions of admiration and even envy for the tyrant with signs of compassion for his victims and a palpable indignation at the magnitude and brazenness of his crimes.[15] Again we must wonder, do we have here a lover of injustice, or a lover of justice? Is it possible that these two loves are not so far apart as we might think? Might they even grow from the same root? If the ruling passion in Polus' soul is a desire to act freely on a grand scale with impunity, and if his conviction is that such freedom is the substance of both dignity and happiness, we can well understand his attraction to tyranny and his envy of the successful tyrant. If, at the same time, his own lawless urges are held in check by some countervailing fear or habit or desire—a desire for respectability or self-respect, for example, or a desire to be deserving of some divine protection he scarcely admits to himself he hopes for—this restraint need not diminish and may even increase his estimation of the value of what his lawless alter ego has so palpably gotten away with, fueling his indignation (473b12–d2).

At the opposite pole from Archelaus and Polus is Socrates, who shows no indignation towards Archelaus and no desire for the kind of life he leads. So free is Socrates of the desire for dignity as Polus understands it—so little does he want the power to push people around or even the respect of ordinary people—that when Polus tells him, "even a child could refute you," Socrates replies that if one did, he would be grateful for the instruction (470c6–7). Reinforcing this reminder of Socrates' unusual perspective is his refusal to join the rest of the world in calling Archelaus happy, or even the Great King—for, he says, "I do not know how he stands in regard to education and justice" (470e6–7). Not only do these rulers' evident enjoyments fail to amount to happiness in Socrates' eyes but their openly tyrannical acts are no conclusive proof for him of their injustice. When Polus asks, in reply, "Is the whole of happiness in this?" Socrates answers, "As I say, at any rate, Polus. For I assert that the noble and good man and woman are happy; the unjust and base, wretched" (470e8–11). Socrates never explains what he means by the "noble and good" man and woman, although now, unlike in the *Apology*, he implies that he knows at least one who is such. Nor, as we have seen, does he define justice for Polus or explain exactly how it contributes to the happiness of the just individual. What he does do from this point on, however, is to drop any discussion of education, leaving the impression that he thinks that justice alone is the core of happiness.[16]

It is little wonder that Polus finds Socrates' claim incredible. Unable to follow his hints about his unconventional understanding of justice, Polus imagines that Socrates means by justice mere lawfulness, or the judicial punishments aimed to restore citizens to lawfulness, and how can bare lawfulness amount to happiness? But even if we apply the more sophisticated analysis of justice that Socrates has provided in his analyses of the arts and flatteries, according to which justice is the art that restores the good condition of the soul, justice seems to fall far short of constituting happiness. For according to that schema justice is merely an art that corrects the soul's bad condition as medicine does that of the body; it is left to another art, legislation (or perhaps philosophy or true education) to perfect the soul, as gymnastic perfects the body. Only if we think of justice in the comprehensive sense of the good order of a soul guided by wisdom does the strong claim Socrates makes for justice and the disappearance of education as an independent criterion of happiness make sense. For justice as the good order of the soul would necessarily include or presuppose an education resulting in wisdom, and the natural, unimpeded activity of a just or wholly excellent soul might fairly be called happiness. Why, then, does Socrates give Polus so little help in seeing this more positive and higher meaning of justice? Evidently it is because the first step towards becoming just in the full sense is to confront inner contradictions that Socrates' more starkly paradoxical formulations are best devised to elicit, and because all subsequent steps require the interlocutor's own active pursuit of the question of what virtue is. But perhaps Socrates stresses the corrective aspect of justice for another reason also. Perhaps the tidy division of labor between doctor and trainer in caring for the body is answered by no equivalent division of labor between doctors and educators of the soul. In equating happiness with justice and describing justice as a corrective art, perhaps Socrates is hinting that the true education and perfection of the soul *are* profoundly corrective or medicinal and to that extent painful, inasmuch as the soul is almost naturally unhealthy and in need not only of a one-time cure but of continual correction.

At any rate, Socrates freely acknowledges that his view of what produces happiness could scarcely be further from that of most human beings. Denying that he agrees with "any one of the things" Polus has said about Archelaus (471d8–9), he concedes that nevertheless, "concerning the things you are saying, all Athenians and foreigners, save a few, will assert the same things along with you, if you wish to provide witnesses against me to testify that what I'm saying isn't true" (472a2–5). His own student Isocrates, for example, would later express the majority view in stating approvingly that "faced with a choice to do or suffer evil, our ancestors chose to do it."[17] If the majority take Polus' side on all the points in contention, do they share his curious mixture of envy and indignation towards people who push other people around? The fundamental contentions that Polus makes here and that Socrates denies are, as they agree at 472d1–9, that "it is possible for the man who does injustice and is unjust to be blessed," that Archelaus is such a man, and that such a man to be happy must evade punishment. Socrates provides prominent examples of the myriad of people he says he could easily produce as witnesses for Polus' claims, if truth could be established by counting votes. As Stauffer points out, these examples also call attention to the piety of many who secretly or openly admire Archelaus and his ilk: piety does not stop this view of injustice and perhaps even presupposes it.[18]

Yet Socrates also says that all the witnesses Polus can produce will be "false witnesses" (472a1). His project will be to show in the paradigmatic and revealing case of Polus—and his claim is that he could in principle show with anyone—that alongside the admiration for tyrants that Polus proclaims and the many secretly share is another conviction that gives this admiration the lie. In calling Polus and everyone else false witnesses, he implies at the least that some attachment to justice is present in them alongside its opposite and that they are speaking falsely when they deny its presence. Is he arguing as well that the admiration for justice is actually deeper or stronger than the countervailing admiration for tyrants, even in people in whom it is scarcely in evidence at all? In other words, do we have in Polus, as an especially vivid exemplar of phenomena present in "nearly everyone," a fundamental love of self-assertion and freedom, overlaid by a shallower love of respectability from which he has not fully wrested himself free, although he thinks that he has? Or do we have at the deeper level a love of justice, which Polus disowns out of fear that justice is weak and the just are losers, and is it his inclination to go over to the dark side that is in fact superficial? Callicles thinks the former, but Socrates will prove that even Callicles has a much deeper love of justice than his conventionalist arguments would suggest.

If Socrates does not here spell out what he means in calling "false witnesses" those who deny that the "noble and good" man is happy, he does shed some light now on who the "noble and good" person might be, by illustrating two different ways of understanding what is noble or beautiful (*kalon*), and in fact these two meanings correspond to the two ways we might take the charge that the majority are false witnesses. At 472a7–b1 Socrates speaks of the beautiful votive offerings of Aristocrates, which were made at great cost to Aristocrates and which are both emblematic of his devotion to the gods and beautiful for all onlookers to behold. Socrates, however, does not call the offerings good or Aristocrates himself noble, and he mentions them only in the context of adducing men who share Polus' envy of tyrants. Soon after this, he says that the objects of dispute between Polus and himself "do not happen to be at all small but are pretty much the things that it is most noble to know about and most shameful to be ignorant of: and the chief of them is to be cognizant or ignorant of who is happy and who is not" (472c6–d1). The possession that Socrates himself prizes is a knowledge that is both noble and indisputably good, and although he may not know of anyone besides himself who possesses it without confusion, he does claim unequivocally in this dialogue to have it. Thus we have two possible accounts of the noble that point to two possible grounds for the attachment to justice of Polus and of everyone who is "on his side," one an intuition about what we owe to or can hope for from the gods who reward and punish, and the other an intuition about what we need to seek in order to be strong and whole.

Perhaps, then, in calling false witnesses all those who disagree with him about who is happy and who is enviable, Socrates means only that everyone who seems to envy tyrants is in fact attached to the noble in some sense, as Aristocrates doubtless is, for example. But his claim, which deserves to be considered carefully, is that everyone really agrees with *him*. If he is serious in his assertion that the universal clamor against him is that of false witnesses, he is suggesting that in those who seem to love pleasure, wealth, and power most, the love of justice is even more deep-seated and powerful, if also profoundly obscured. To the extent that the love of justice is rooted in a fear of shame or of punishment, or even in the deeper wish to deserve as reward good things that one cannot acquire for oneself, it can only be derivative from other desires. But to the extent that human beings all somehow divine that what matters most of all is not pleasure or wealth or even survival, but having a soul that is in good condition and living well according to a clear grasp of the truth, then they really are at bottom witnesses on Socrates' side. And in some way, not only Polus but everyone Socrates talks to is forced to acknowledge this, however undeveloped the intuition may be and however much curtailed by their observations about the weakness in the world of justice as conventionally understood.

Accompanying Socrates' claim to know the truth, and to know that everyone who denies it is speaking falsehood, is Socrates' insistence on the superiority of his method of proving his case dialectically, in contrast to the common method of addressing men in crowds and bringing forward witnesses to corroborate one's claims. He does not here explain why his method is better. If it is because his conversational approach can produce a witness who will not contradict himself, as he later suggests to Callicles all who do not refute him must do (482b2–6), then it fails with both Polus and Callicles: neither reaches an understanding of justice that is free from contradiction. We may even ask whether the dialectic Socrates uses with them is even true dialectic, for it is of the essence of true dialectic that it proceeds not only through conversation but also by means of clear distinctions and definitions, yet Socrates egregiously fails to define justice in this dialogue and to distinguish its true essence from the conformity to conventional and often irrational law that it is routinely confounded with. What Socrates will bring Polus to is not an agreement with his own wise, gentle contempt for the confused and disorderly souls of evildoers, but a strange and twisted imitation of that outlook. We must wonder, then, whether the rhetoric that achieves this result—the rhetoric Socrates is proposing to Gorgias as replacement for Gorgias' current, irresponsible rhetoric—is not likewise a mere imitation of true dialectic. If this rhetoric does not reveal to Polus the truth about justice, it may still reveal to Gorgias and to all perspicacious observers the true state of Polus' soul with regard to justice, which is important in itself. It may also reveal important things to Socrates that he can get at in no other way.

But when we look elsewhere for Socrates' more rigorous and more serious arguments about justice itself, we find that the flawed form of discourse that characterizes this dialogue is to a degree present in every Platonic dialogue. This form of incomplete argumentation is Plato's and apparently Socrates' preferred method of sparking the thought even of the most promising. Not only may the unpromising benefit from being given an escape hatch from Socrates' disturbing questions, but the most promising, it seems, must not only climb but build the riggings of a true account of justice if it is ever to become their own. If Socrates' one-person-at-a-time method is best, then, it is not in producing true agreement most of the time, but in opening the only possible path towards that agreement for those who accept Socrates' challenge.

Proof that Doing Injustice Is Worse than Suffering It (474c1–76a3)

After Polus has called in witnesses, as it were, and laughed at Socrates, and told vivid stories of the terrible things that victims of injustice suffer in contrast to those who get away with their crimes, an unflappable Socrates finally brings him to a standstill and persuades him to submit to cross-examination on the question of who is happier. He drives a simple wedge that begins to pry Polus' discordant views apart: Polus thinks that suffering injustice is worse than doing it but admits that he thinks doing it is more shameful (474c4–d2). Dodds sees this dichotomy as the key weakness that brings Polus down, but is it really fatal? Could Polus not say that the wise person perceives that the good and the noble point in different directions and that, while the noble is pleasing to behold and useful to others, it is not good for the one who does it and so is not chosen by one who is wise?[19] The precise problem that impales Polus is not that he separates what is noble and good for the doer but rather that, at one and the same time, he separates and fails to separate them. Specifically, he views the noble as detrimental for the doer but conventionally honored, and as somehow truly beneficial for the doer, all at the same time.

This confusion becomes evident as soon as Polus makes his initial distinction between the noble and the good. Socrates gets him to agree that he does not call things noble or beautiful "without looking off towards anything" (474d3–5). Instead, Socrates asks, starting with the case of physical objects,

> Socrates: "Don't you say that beautiful bodies are beautiful either in reference to the use, for this thing that each is useful for, or in reference to some

pleasure, if it makes those who look upon it rejoice in the looking? Do you have anything beyond these things to say about the beauty of the body?"

Polus: "No, I don't." (474d5–e1)

Generalizing his point about bodies, Socrates asks whether the same thing is not true of beautiful or noble shapes, colors, voices, music, laws, practices, and sciences, that they are all called such "on account of some pleasure or benefit or both" (474e1–75a2). Socrates secures Polus' agreement to the corollary that what is base or shameful must be painful, bad, or both, and hence that injustice, being more shameful than justice, must be so because it is more painful, more bad, or both. Since it is not more painful it also is not both; it thus must be worse—the very thing that Socrates set out to prove.

The great problem with this argument, as commentators have noted, is that it is silent on the crucial question of who the beneficiary of a noble action is.[20] It was a basic assertion of the sophists that nobility and baseness are merely conventional concepts, but they did not deny that so-called noble deeds could be beneficial and base ones harmful for society at large, or for the majority, or for those who hold power and can set the rules of justice that others feel obliged to honor.[21] Yet Socrates' whole argument hangs on the unstated and unproven assumption that to be noble, a deed must be either pleasant or beneficial for the one who does it. In order to grasp and evaluate Socrates' most serious claim about justice, Polus would need to press him on what makes good things good and how the good of others is related to the good of one who acts on their behalf. By failing to do so, Polus confirms that he is not a thoughtful man. Such carelessness would not normally be surprising in one who is so spirited and impetuous, but in this case the failure results in Polus' being forced to contradict his passionately held belief that the tyrant's life is enviable. Why does he only grow silent and sulky and not object, "Of course there is something good in noble acts, Socrates, but it is good only for others"? It must be because Socrates has tapped into a vein of profound ambivalence in his soul. Polus believes there is something noble about justice, and when forced to consider what he means by this thing that he calls "noble," he cannot say that it is just submission to the exploitative schemes of others. He sees in nobility something deeply desirable for the noble man himself, but he cannot say what it is.

When Polus balks and stops replying to Socrates' questions, Socrates urges him to "submit yourself in a high-born manner to the argument, as to a doctor, and answer" (475d6–7). Socrates suggests that what he is doing to Polus is painful but beneficial as surgery is, and that dialectics is the cure for his disordered mind and soul. But although Polus seems to acquiesce in the treatment, he is never really cured. Instead of becoming wise and moderate and free of self-contradiction as Socrates is, he will at best adopt a new outlook that is superficially closer to Socratic equanimity but if anything even more self-contradictory than the view with which he began. What goes wrong? Socratic medicine requires, it seems, not the passive acquiescence one gives a doctor but active engagement, questioning, and self-examination. What is this thing that I call noble that has such a hold on me?, Polus needs to ask. For whom is a noble act really good, and why? Can something that is simply good for others and bad for oneself be noble? Does society have a right to demand it? Why do we all sense and society claim when it makes its demands that in the final analysis it is not demanding something bad for us, perhaps because virtue will be rewarded but perhaps simply because it is best to be the kind of person society is calling on us to become? And how can these two very different inklings of why virtue is good for me fit together? If it is the best of all things for me, can it really need and deserve a reward, and if it needs a reward, can it really be best?[22] Socrates does not make clear his own answers to these questions but merely sets Polus' feet on the path to pursuing them if he will. But he gives us an important clue about his own views. While the sophists were united in separating the noble from the good and considering the noble as merely conventional, Socrates everywhere insists and nowhere in Plato or Xenophon denies that whatever is truly noble is also good (even if it is only a subset of the good): this insistence likely points to a fundamental feature of his thought. If in the *Apology* he denies knowing anything that is both, the *Gorgias* suggests that that denial was provisional, evidently referring to a popular notion of the noble as something that is not thoroughly good but that entails a great loss. Here in the *Gorgias* Socrates appears at first to be affirming that whatever is conventionally judged noble, including the conventional rules of justice, must be noble and therefore good. But he has already shown by his remarks on Archelaus and the Great King that his view of justice is highly unconventional. His deeper thought would seem to be not that justice is good because it is noble but that true human excellence is noble because it is good, not only beneficial but admirable, as the flourishing condition of a well-ordered soul that is essential for happiness.

Whatever the correspondence or lack of correspondence finally is between ordinary notions of justice and Socrates' view of virtue, the consequences of his insistence on the unity of the noble and the good are clear: no one in his right mind would welcome vice into his soul. And facing this truth seems to be the key to the medicine Socrates is urging Polus to take. Immediately before and immediately after his exhortation to submit to the argument as to a doctor, Socrates forces Polus to concede that he "would not welcome the more bad and more shameful rather than the less" (475d4–5) and that "neither I nor you nor any other human being would welcome doing injustice more that suffering it, for it turns out to be worse" (475e4–6). Facing and thinking through this insight is what Polus most needs. To do so would lead him to see that those who fall into a condition that is truly and not just conventionally bad must do so involuntarily, like people who contract cancer. If they seem to choose it, they are acting only out of ignorance of the true worth of things and are to be pitied. To be indignant towards them is to fail to understand the terrible state they are already in. It is no more rational than wishing to "get even" with a patient for trying to "get away" with having cancer, or with having a heart attack on the highway and causing injuries to others. This understanding is what undergirds the calm, humane equanimity with which Socrates regards the tyrants and other criminals whom Polus reacts to with such storms of envy and indignation. For if Socrates is right, anger is foolish and the retribution it seeks is altogether irrational. The next argument proceeds on the premise that indeed this is so, and that the law, recognizing this, always seeks through punishment to restore the disordered criminal's soul to health.

Proof that Paying the Penalty Is Better than Not Paying It (476a3–79e9)

With this next argument Socrates addresses his second major disagreement with Polus, his assertion and Polus' denial that it is better for one who has done injustice to pay the penalty. Socrates begins by asking whether everything just is noble, and Polus quickly agrees that it is (476b1–3). Then ensues a strange discussion in which Socrates claims that every action has an object and that whatever qualities pertain to the action of the agent also pertain to the experience of or effect on the object. Socrates is silent on actions such as dancing or thinking, which we name with intransitive verbs, and on actions such as washing oneself or improving oneself, which we name with reflexive verbs. As always in reading Plato, to get clear on what is inadequate in an argument is to begin to see the issues that a full exposition of the problem would ultimately need to explore and that a more promising interlocutor (such as the young Plato himself) would insist on raising. True, as Socrates says, to beat forcefully or to cut deeply is to leave one's victim forcefully beaten or deeply cut. We may also say that to teach effectively is to leave one's student well instructed. But to work for someone who exploits one profitably is not to be profitably employed, and to be conquered by someone who conquers gloriously is not to be gloriously defeated. The question is, what is the case with justice? Certainly it is a fine thing to be a partner in a just community, but what about corrective justice? We are sure—and this is doubtless why Polus does not balk at an improperly generalized claim here—that to be punished by one who punishes justly is to be justly punished, so that the case is not the same as being exploited or defeated. We are sure that a just act must be just on both sides. But we are not sure what we mean by that. For while nobility seems somehow intrinsic to justice, and justice seems intrinsically reciprocal, the nobility of an act of corrective justice is not obviously present on both sides in the way that even the shamefulness of an unjust act is—for we do consider it shameful both to abuse another and to be abused. But then is undergoing corrective justice after all more like suffering defeat or exploitation, where everything fine and good is gained by one at another's expense? If this does not seem to live up to what we mean by justice, are we not forced to doubt whether simply harming, even in return for being harmed, is ever wholly just? Are we not pushed to affirm with Socrates that if justice is indeed thoroughly noble, it must be at least good if not also somehow noble all around?

The argument Socrates makes here for the beneficial character of punishment is on its face comically inadequate. He moves rapidly from the thought that if just punishment is a noble thing to give, it must be a noble thing to receive; if noble, it must be good; if good, it must be pleasant or beneficial; and since punishment is never pleasant to receive, it must be beneficial (476d5–77a4). Polus could easily protest that being justly punished is good and even pleasant for others though not for the criminal, just as he could earlier have protested that acting justly is only good for others, but he does not. Something in Socrates' strange argument rings strangely true to him. Justice cannot be mere exploitation; it must embody a fairness and a common good that makes it a far finer thing than the harming of one person to benefit another.

But what good does punishment do for the criminal? Socrates argues that it must benefit his soul since it does not benefit his body and that it must do so by releasing it from some evil. At first he spells out a range of forms that the bad condition of the soul may take: "injustice, lack of learning, cowardice, and the like" (477b7–8), but quickly he replaces this list with injustice alone, without protest from Polus (477c2). This slippage again involves a certain plausibility, since it does seem likely that the main good effect of punishment on its recipients would be to make them more just. But the result is an inadequately supported claim that injustice, as *the* bad state of the soul, being more base but not more painful than the bad conditions of body and possessions, must be the worst of all evils, without any account of how this injustice may be related to lack of learning, cowardice, or any other vice.

The argument is striking not only for its incompleteness but for its negative focus. Not only is there no positive claim that justice is the greatest of goods, but there is not even a claim that injustice is the worst of evils for the positive reason that it is the corruption of our most precious possessions, our souls. Socrates works entirely from the premise that injustice is surpassingly base, a premise that Callicles will attack as mere prejudice. The negative focus and the lack of clarity as to whether injustice is one among a number of vices or the sum total of vice go together. Only if Socrates and Polus were to give sustained attention to the question of what the good condition of the soul is, how its elements, the various virtues, fit together, and how they make us happy, could they arrive at an adequate understanding of why injustice is bad, how much of vice it covers, and whether it is truly the worst of evils.

Without clarifying what the good condition of the soul is—and hence what the goal would have to be of any art that cares for souls—Socrates proceeds to identify that art as the art of the judge who imposes just penalties, on no stronger grounds than that it is to judges that we take the unjust, just as it is to doctors that we take the sick. While alternating between treating justice as the whole of psychic disease and treating it as only a part, Socrates now suggests that punishment releases one from all of it (478d4–5). As Stauffer observes, the suggestion that punishment can cure ignorance is especially problematic.[23] Equally questionable is the unstated assumption that in taking others to court people are simply or chiefly seeking a cure for their souls. But Polus is again free to object and again he does not. Is there not something to this thought, something we get at when we speak, for example, of "correctional facilities" and of "teaching the offender a lesson"? Just as Polus somehow recognizes the unhealthiness of the unjust soul, he sees the power of the demand that corrective justice must aim at straightening out the offender and restoring a common good between him and his community. Socrates is silent on the concurrent and usually much more prominent demands societies make that justice should avenge wrongs and deter others from repeating them. This striking silence may signal a profound reservation as to the justice of both aims: vengeance accomplishes nothing good at all, and even deterrence, if accomplished by harming the offender, fails to meets the standard of reciprocity or the promotion of a truly common good that seem essentially to belong to justice.

While Socrates is silent on the darker motives behind the vengefulness that is at work in criminal prosecutions, he is not inattentive to them; a central purpose of this whole argument is to cure Polus of the envy that drives such vengefulness. Socrates administers the medicine for Polus' envy by teaching that, contrary to appearances, most miserable of all is "he who, doing the greatest unjust deeds and using the greatest injustice, brings it about that he is neither admonished nor punished and does not pay the just penalty" (478e4–79a1). Such a person is no better off than a patient who conceals his symptoms and never gets treatment, "fearing, as if he were a child, the burning and cutting, because it is painful" (479a8–b1). And with this thought Socrates returns to the same solid point, not affected by the flawed details of the argument he has made. It may not be true that from judges and juries we get the proper treatment for our psychic ills. This would be the case only if legal justice sought the individual's good as much as that of the community, if laws and judges were wise, and if legal penalties were well suited to reform delinquents. It might not be true that injustice as conventionally and legalistically understood is the worst of evils. But to whatever extent injustice is or expresses something unhealthy in the soul of one who has it—and even the tyrant-envying Polus can't help recognizing that in some deep sense it does—the conclusion is inescapable that such unhealthiness is a condition to be pitied, and all the more so if the one who has it fails to face the problem and avoids ever addressing it. Like children who run away from doctors, Socrates says,

> those who flee justice run the risk of doing something of the same sort, Polus: observing its painfulness, but being blind to its beneficial quality and ignorant of how much more wretched a thing than an unhealthy body it is to dwell with a soul that is not healthy but rotten, unjust, and impious, whence they also do everything to avoid paying the penalty and being released from the greatest of evils. (479b4–c2)

If escaping punishment only deepens the unhealthy soul's disorder, what would the treatment look like that would best address it, that would be in this account most perfectly "just"? If the process is to bestow the benefits that Socrates attributes to it, it must address the root causes of the soul's disorders, including the ignorance that Socrates here as so often elsewhere characterizes as the core of vice. True punishment, then, would seem to be very close to true education. Socrates has also stressed that it must be noble on both sides; it must be a process in which "punisher" and "punished" both participate in the same spirit, as teacher and student do in the process of successful education. In the best of cases, the remedy will include even more participation on the part of the "punished" than the "punisher," or indeed both will be the same person and the process will be one of self-reform or self-education. For only with self-reform is the nature and character of what the reformer does precisely the same as the nature and character of what the reformed experiences. Might the only perfectly just and noble "punishment" be the correction a thoughtful soul gives itself? But how is this any longer reasonably characterized as punishment at all? The term is still fitting because the goal is correction and because the process is often painful, a fact that Socrates emphasizes with his comparison of punishment to painful surgery and his observation that those who flee the treatment they need do so out of childish fear of pain (479a5–10). The willingness to accept one's needed medicine is as much a matter of bravery as it is of intelligence: the bravery to face hard truths and the bravery to acknowledge our own defective condition.

And here is where Socrates' chastening of Polus fails. Polus has a wise teacher but his teacher does not have a dogged student; even the wisest of teachers cannot give his pupil the courage he needs to press forward through his inner self-contradictions to resolve them. And so Polus remains divided, believing that justice is good and not good, envying the tyrant his boldness and freedom and yet disgusted by his baseness, incensed at what he gets away with and yet evidently wishing that he could do the same; showing daring only in speech and not in action. Polus, for all his bluster, is soft. Why is it so hard for him to work his way free of a confusion that embroils him in such angry and envious passions? Part of the problem surely is his strong attachment to external goods that Socrates' medicine would require him to give up. But part may also be a deep attachment to his own sense of what is noble and base, which restrains him from pursuing tyranny himself and which powerfully resists the thought that we are all somehow at bottom similar in pursuing the good, however it appears to us.

The Just Use of Rhetoric (480a1–81b5)

Facing this failure of his powers of persuasion (which Socrates must surely have expected from the beginning) what does he do, and how does his strategy here shed light on the broader purposes of his exchange with Polus? Let us return to the question of rhetoric, for as Socrates repeatedly reminds us, this dialogue is as much a display of the merits of his own mode of rhetoric as it is a critique of Gorgias'. Rhetoric at its best is not empty display or exploitative manipulation but rather wisdom's self-presentation to the unwise or the not yet wise, aimed at conveying as much of the truth as is mutually beneficial while protecting both sides from harm. Throughout the exchange with Polus, Socrates is addressing his rhetoric directly to Polus but indirectly to Gorgias, who is learning something important from the exchange, and addressing it even more indirectly but perhaps most seriously to the numerous potential students in the audience for whom he and Gorgias are competing. Especially with an eye to these, Socrates gives pointers to many serious features of his own understanding with his strange and incomplete arguments. Moreover, as Plato's creations, Socrates' speeches are addressed to potential students in future times as well as to less astute readers who may not become philosophic but to whom Plato may nonetheless wish to convey a politically beneficial teaching. Let us see, then, if we can disentangle some of these possible lessons.

For Polus himself, who remains mired in contradictions and ever prone to anger, Socrates can offer only a palliative treatment—one which takes a strange and comical shape, however. Socrates asks Polus what use rhetoric can have, since it now seems that a sensible person would never want to use it to commit injustice or escape the penalty for it. To the contrary,

> If he or anyone he cared for did do injustice, he would go voluntarily where he might pay the penalty as quickly as possible, to the judge just as if to a doctor, hurrying lest the disease of injustice, having become chronic, should make the soul fester and become incurable. (480a6–b2)

This sentence, odd as its claim is, provides two important supplements or correctives to what Socrates has said to Polus hitherto. First, Socrates now acknowledges, if only in passing, that wayward souls can become incurable and indeed may do so rapidly. He is not, as he earlier appeared, naively hopeful that for every disorder in the soul there is an appropriate punishment that can remedy it. And second, he now acknowledges what his discussion of tyranny seemed to deny—that a healthy and sensible person does indeed care for others besides himself. In that discussion, as in many of his appeals to interlocutors to take more care for the virtue of their souls, he begins by encouraging the listener to be not less selfish but more serious about seeking out his own good: the real fault of most of us is not too much but too little seriousness about our true long-term happiness. But here Socrates complements that argument with an acknowledgment that of course every normal person will care also for others.

When one or one's loved ones have committed injustice, Socrates continues, rhetoric can be of no use in defending against deserved punishment, then, and is useless altogether,

> unless someone takes it for the opposite purpose and supposes it necessary most of all to accuse oneself, and then whoever else of his relatives and friends happens to do injustice, and not to hide the unjust deed but to bring it to light, so that he may pay the penalty and become healthy, forcing both himself and the others not to play the coward but to grit his teeth and submit well and courageously, just as to a doctor for cutting and burning, pursuing what is good and noble and not taking into account what is painful. (480b9–c8)

Dodds notes the comic irony of this suggestion, as well as the absence of any acknowledgment that rhetoric may sometimes be needed to defend the innocent against unjust accusations.[24] Socrates is still proceeding on the assumption that the law courts are strictly benevolent in their intentions as well as curative in their effects. To the extent that Socrates can persuade Polus to see even a grain of truth in this assumption, the result will be to calm his indignation and introduce into his thoughts and actions—and those of present and future political men who may be influenced by Socratic rhetoric—a more humane and constructive attitude towards lawbreakers.

But now comes the strangest twist. If one must do evil to anyone, Socrates says—and admittedly he makes this hypothetical, and he warns of the danger of being wronged oneself—then one should do it by providing that one's enemies *avoid* punishment.

> If the enemy does injustice to someone else, one must provide in every way, by acting and by speaking, that he not pay the just penalty nor go to the judge. And if he does go, one must contrive that the enemy escape and not pay the just penalty, but if he has stolen much gold, that he not give it back but that he keep it and spend it on himself and his own, unjustly and impiously, and if he has done an injustice worthy of death, that he not die—in the best case never, and become immortal in his wickedness—but if not, that he may live for as long as possible being such. (480e7–81b1)

In encouraging Polus to use the criminal justice system in this way to help his friends and harm his enemies, Socrates creates a comic inversion of the way all law-abiding citizens normally use the police and courts to help their friends—if only their fellow lawful citizens—and to harm their enemies.

The irony is that if Polus *could* be as frankly and thoroughly calculating as this picture suggests (even on behalf of his friends as well as himself), he would no longer feel the tangled resentment that makes him crave a triumph over the unjust in the first place. Whatever habits and qualities he decided were healthy and essential to living happily he would judge good and not shameful, and those who displayed them he would admire without vitriol, even if his self-interest required him to compete with and try to defeat them. Whatever habits and qualities he decided were unhealthy and ill-suited to happiness he would consider more pitiable than a body wracked with disease. And whoever he found himself in irreconcilable enmity with, including both foreign and domestic enemies to his country and its decent laws, he would wish to render harmless but not more miserable. If he did not feel sufficient compassion for those who suffer from psychic disorders to make an active effort to cure them, he might make that effort simply in order to prevent them from harming him and those he cared for, but at the very least he would regard them with a sadness free of anger and resentment because free of all envy. This is Socrates' state, giving him an inner calm and an attitude of gentle humanity to others. But Socrates has watched Polus and has seen that he lacks the strength to work his way free of his anger. Even as half of Polus' soul grasps the truth that the unjust soul is diseased and pitiable, the other half reasserts its resentment and wants to see that soul suffer even more. And what is curious is that Socrates actively invites Polus to take pleasure in contemplating the rot of the unjust tyrant's soul. In this way he encourages a crazy mixture of the doctor's humanity and the executioner's punitiveness. What is gained by this bizarre halfway house?

Socrates' thought seems to be this: if it is impossible to cure Polus' envy and desire for vengeance, it is better to leave him with a confused mixture of punitiveness and humanity than with only the former, and that by giving his anger this strange new direction, it can be made less painful for him and less dangerous for others. The mixture of disparate elements extends through Socrates' whole account of what is wrong with the unjust man's soul and what is to be wished for him. Socrates calls such a soul unhealthy and rotten—suggesting a natural disorder that is bad because intrinsically destructive of happiness—but also impious, suggesting a selfish pride that is bad because likely to bring upon him divine wrath and punishment (479b8–c1). Significantly, this mention of impiety comes only at the end of Socrates' education of Polus, when it is clear that Polus is not going to embrace the arguments in a spirit that will allow a resolution of his confusion. When Socrates enumerated the elements of psychic disorder a little earlier (at 477b7–8), impiety was not among them. At the end of the dialogue Socrates will say much more about the gods and the afterlife in the myth he constructs for Callicles, whose education also fails. There he will cast the gods as themselves inspired by a curious amalgam of Socrates' own naturalist, medical outlook with the punitiveness traditionally ascribed to gods; nowhere are the gods presented as simply sharing his own gentle sadness at the sight of psychic disorder. Here in the discussion with Polus Socrates says nothing about the afterlife, but he does allude to death with the comment that in the best case the criminal on whom one wishes to avenge oneself will "become immortal in his wickedness" (481a7). Anger craves for the unjust a speedy death even as it judges such a death too good for them, while it yearns for the just to be spared death altogether. Even as Socrates acknowledges this anger he brings Polus a step closer to the far gentler view that it is not length of life but the quality of life that matters, a view that the Stoics would later adopt with enormous benefits in their freedom from the corrosive poison of anger and resentment. In Polus we have only the barest beginnings of either a philosophic outlook, a reformed piety, or a Stoic calm. The mixture of Socratic humanity with traditional piety remains an undigested hodgepodge for Polus, albeit one less destructive than the mixture of admiration and disgust towards tyrants that he began with. Polus will at times rest content with the thought that the evil are altogether pitiable; at other times he will want to see them suffer and will be able to remind himself about their inner rot; at other times, if he finds himself even half-inclined to believe in the gods, he will take further pleasure in the thought of the criminals' likely sufferings in Hades; at still other times, when his sophisticated doubts about any providential gods are clearly in the ascendancy, his thoughts about vice's natural sanctions will again give him comfort. There is no stability in such a brew, but to whatever extent Socrates' outlook takes hold, the less corrosive and less dangerous Polus' resentment and his doubts about the gods' providential care will be.

More clues as to the broader effect Plato's Socrates may have intended these arguments to have on others who never become philosophic but who come in some degree under the influence of philosophy will be seen in Plato's *Laws*. There the Athenian Stranger inculcates a Socratic, medical view of injustice as psychic ill-health right alongside a largely traditional but austere piety in which the gods continue to sanction justice but stand much more as models of sublime self-sufficiency than as rulers. An important difference with the *Gorgias*, however, is that the Athenian Stranger never encourages in the citizens the twisted punitiveness Socrates encourages in Polus. This would seem to be because the citizens of Magnesia are to be far simpler and healthier than the corrupt, cosmopolitan Polus. It is also because they are to remain citizens first and foremost, and hence their laws must foster their public-spiritedness and in particular the zeal in prosecuting crime that is needed to prevent its recurrence (see esp. *Laws* 730d, 731e). This zeal may be fueled either by moral indignation or by the humane thought that criminals must be stopped and taught to live better lives for their own good, and the Athenian Stranger encourages the latter without trying to eradicate the former. But civic zeal is not compatible with a propensity to gloat over the unhealthiness of uncured delinquents.

This final suggestion of Socrates to Polus, in which he encourages the perverse punitiveness of refraining from punishing delinquents in order to leave them in the worst possible state, may show how far gone he considers Polus to be in needing a sedative that does no other positive good. But this teaching is likely in the end less important as a treatment for Polus than as a dramatic portrayal for Gorgias and even more for observant onlookers of the incredible power and persistence of indignation and the extreme difficulty of purging its ugly venom from our souls. In encouraging in Polus a comic mixture of philanthropy and cruelty towards those who do wrong, he reminds us of our own confused response to wrongdoers both individually and collectively. For, after all, what is our own society's treatment of criminals but just such a strange mixture of philanthropy and cruelty? And what is every outburst of our anger but a confused mixture of envy and disgust, a desire to prevent the one who offends us from "getting away" with his wrong, with the implicit thought that he would have the last laugh if he did, revealing a painful envy of the freedom of action he has shown and the triumph he must not be allowed to keep; but a simultaneous intuition that there is something deeply base or contemptuous and hence profoundly unenviable about being the being that would do such a thing.

For his most promising listeners, Socrates' most serious suggestion here may be the one that pertains to their treatment of just this disorder in themselves. The highest use of rhetoric may be pointed to in the advice to "accuse oneself"—the application of forensic scrutiny to uncover one's own confusions, to state clearly and honestly what one does not know, and to submit oneself and one's confusions to the knife of rigorous logical analysis. Socrates provides here a spectacular display of our characteristic confusions about what the happy and admirable life is, what the relation is between wisdom and virtue, and what virtue and vice each deserve. But he offers only the most incomplete sketch of the arguments that would need to be considered to come to a stable and unconfused view of these matters. Because of Polus' limits as an interlocutor, Socrates has argued for the goodness of virtue without analyzing it and without more than a cursory argument for the power of knowledge or wisdom. But Callicles, who takes over the discussion from him, will prove just as limited. At first Callicles seems bolder in his departure from conventional moral opinion and his embrace of hedonism, but Socrates will soon show that he, too, cares about the noble and especially about justice (e.g. 511b–c). Callicles is thus unable to refute Socrates' thesis that doing injustice is worse than suffering it or to escape the same profound self-contradictions that Polus is entangled in. If Callicles could be consistent in his hedonism he could consistently oppose Socrates' claims for the goodness of virtue, but pure hedonism does not seem humanly possible. Thus the only way forward is to identify and embrace the core of virtue that is not merely conventional but is rather the health of the soul. The search for this core of virtue, however, awaits a better interlocutor than either Polus or Callicles. If the *Apology* is an example of Socrates' popular rhetoric, the *Gorgias* is rhetorical too, in approach as well as in theme. Meno and especially Protagoras will prove more interested in and thoughtful about the nature of true virtue, and in the *Protagoras* we see a deeper encounter with the hedonist premise, a better exploration of its most serious limitations, and clearer indications of where Socrates does and does not agree with it. Let us turn, then, to those two dialogues. In doing so, we shall begin to see some of the distinctions and qualifications that will make Socrates' own thesis clearer and more persuasive.

THREE

Virtue and Knowledge: *Meno*

More than any other dialogue, the *Meno* makes its theme the relation between virtue and knowledge, and in it appear many of the same characters and motifs that we have seen in the other dialogues that treat this subject. As in the *Apology* and the *Gorgias*, Socrates propounds his strongest and most counterintuitive claims both for virtue and for knowledge in contexts that highlight his dubious standing in and ultimate deadly conflict with the city of Athens, his associations with the equally disreputable sophists and rhetoricians, and his project of distancing himself from these men even as he shows great interest in their teachings.[1] As in the *Gorgias*, allusions to Socrates' impending trial and conviction are rife. As in the *Apology*, the question of education is linked to the issue of corruption, and now in a most dramatic way. We here see Socrates conversing with the young Meno, who has come to him eager to know how virtue is acquired and leaves persuaded that it can be neither taught nor learned. According to Xenophon, Meno would later become a notoriously impious and immoral leader in the Greek expedition into Persia under Cyrus the Younger.[2] At the end of the dialogue we also see Socrates antagonizing Anytus, who three years later would join Meletus and Lycon in bringing Socrates to trial for impiety and corrupting the youth. To be sure, the *Meno*'s ostensible conclusion is that virtue is not knowledge. For it seems that what is knowledge should be teachable, yet the *Meno* both expounds and dramatizes the myriad of reasons why virtue is so hard to teach to others. At the same time, the dialogue ends with the thought that if virtue is not at bottom knowledge or active wisdom, it has no coherence, and the opinions that guide noble human beings are as irrational as the murmurings of the intoxicated priestesses at Delphi. What are we to make of this conclusion? I will argue that the dialogue, by showing the limitations of the Socratic thesis, also shows us its solid core that is not subject to these limitations and thereby vindicates its essential truth.

Opening (70a1–71d8)

Meno begins the conversation with an abrupt but complicated question that seems to have special urgency for him:

> Can you tell me, Socrates, whether virtue is teachable? Or whether it isn't teachable but is rather acquired by practice? Or whether it isn't acquired by practice or learning, but is present in human beings by nature or in some other way? (70a1–4)

An admiring student of Gorgias, Meno reports that Gorgias always claimed that virtue cannot be taught and professed to teach only rhetoric (95c1–4).[3] Gorgias may well have shared the skepticism of many of the sophists as to whether what conventionally passes for virtue is ultimately anything coherent or good for its possessor, but if so, the gentlemanly rhetorician was far more circumspect than the bold sophists, and indeed we will see that as a young man Gorgias' student Meno shows great respect for traditional, public-spirited notions of virtue. But something in Gorgias' reticence has left Meno dissatisfied. If Gorgias taught him the technical skill needed by statesmen but averred that the manliness or magnificent public-spiritedness needed to put it to its greatest use was an unteachable gift of nature, might Meno have had some reason to hope that this was not so? If he did, would it have been the courage to seize what was best for himself or the splendidly generous dedication to the good of others that he especially feared he might lack?

The eagerness of Meno's opening question, whatever its motive, is not matched by analytical precision. Meno suggests four or five different possibilities—that virtue might arise through teaching, through practice, by nature, or in some other way—perhaps divine grace—but he substitutes learning for teaching at 70a3 while seeming to equate them. Is this legitimate, or might virtue be something that can be learned but that each one must learn for oneself? Socrates replies with a complicated piece of ironic praise for Meno and his teacher Gorgias in which he playfully addresses just this distinction that Meno should have drawn.[4] If it were as easy for wise men to impart their wisdom to others as to acquire it for themselves, then Gorgias would have made all the Thessalians wise, as Socrates claims

Gorgias has done, and Socrates himself would have made all Athenians aware of their ignorance about the true nature of virtue, as he playfully insinuates that he has done, and they would know with him that it is pointless to investigate how virtue is acquired before first determining what it is. As it is, the Thessalians remain uncultivated horsemen and the Athenians remain so far from acknowledging any doubts about virtue that they, led by Anytus, will soon condemn Socrates to death for undermining it. Perhaps Gorgias can at best inspire his students with his magnificent style, and Socrates can at best infect his compatriots with a perplexity that is still as likely to leave them irritated and hostile as to lead them to discover the truth (cf. 79e7–80b7).

But in the midst of this complicated irony Socrates makes an astonishing admission: he is so far from knowing whether virtue can be taught that he claims to know "nothing about virtue at all. And concerning what I do not know *what* it is, how could I know *what sort* of thing it is?" (71b2–4). We are back to the radically agnostic Socrates of the *Apology*. If Socrates seems to know what virtue is when confronted by brash immoralists like Polus and Callicles, he leads with his perplexities in speaking to one who seems eager for virtue, as Meno is. Of course Socrates raises questions about virtue as often as he sings its praises, but he usually seems to be seeking the essence of something that he, like everyone, recognizes when he sees it. If that were his state, however, we would expect him to be especially interested in identifying virtue's common features, including whether it is teachable. For just as it is essential to our concept of language that it is acquired and not possessed by nature, is it not essential to our commonsense understanding of virtue that it is both teachable and improved by practice? But Socrates speaks now as if he had no knowledge of which members constitute the class "virtue"; it is as if one were to ask him whether witches are given to irony and he were to answer that he does not know who, if anyone, counts as a witch in the first place. Meno is appropriately shocked: "Do you truly not know what virtue is, and are we to report these things about you back home as well?" he asks, to which Socrates answers, "Not only that, comrade, but also that I have not yet met anyone else who knows, as it seems to me" (71b9–c4). Perhaps this is as good a statement of Socratic ignorance as we get anywhere: it pertains somehow especially to virtue, and consists at bottom in a deep suspicion that the essential qualities people attribute to virtue do not in fact come together to characterize any real phenomena any more than the essential features of witches do.

But as soon as Plato lets us glimpse this radical doubt, the conversation moves on. Meno asks whether Socrates did not find Gorgias wise on the question of what virtue is; Socrates professes forgetfulness and asks Meno to "recollect" what Gorgias said, or simply to answer for himself, "for doubtless you share his opinions" (71d1–2). In this dialogue famous for its teaching on recollection, the first mention of recollection thus reminds us that when we look within for knowledge, we are likely to recover not truth but erroneous opinion picked up from others—which Socrates is especially "bad" at retaining.

First and Second Definitions: The Elusive Unity of Virtue (71e1–74a10)

Meno now offers in his own name his first and most spontaneous definition of virtue, giving us our best indication of what he had in mind when he pressed Socrates on whether it could be taught.

> First, if you want the virtue of a man, that's easy. This is the virtue of a man: to be capable of carrying out the affairs of the city, and in doing so to benefit one's friends and harm one's enemies, and to take care not to suffer any such thing oneself. If you want the virtue of a woman, it is not difficult to say: she should manage the household well, preserving its contents and being obedient to the man. (71e1–7)

Meno adds without elaboration that the virtues of children, old men, and slaves are different yet again, for "the virtue belonging to each of us is related to each task appropriate to each action and time of life" (72a2–4). Evidently we have here a descending hierarchy of virtue, with manly virtue as the fully realized form or the focal case. While the woman's job is to obey the man, Meno says nothing about the man's duty to obey the sovereign ruler or people; a man's virtue par excellence is the virtue of the ruler.

Meno's definition of virtue is flexible and, in its primary form, both traditional and highly political, like Polemarchus' definition of justice in the *Republic* (334b). He may not have succeeded in reducing virtue to a simple formula, but why is that a failing if virtue is not a simple phenomenon? Meno indeed has Aristotle on his side:

> Those who speak in general terms deceive themselves when they say that virtue is the good condition of the soul, or acting rightly, or something else of the sort. Those who, like Gorgias, count off the virtues speak much better than those who give such definitions. (*Politics* 1260a25–27)

Aristotle's point, like Meno's, is that the virtue of each individual is relative to his or her function. But Socrates insists that if virtue is one phenomenon, however many varieties it may exhibit, it must have a single essence or principle. The condition of being well adapted in any way for any purpose is not a thing or even a class of things but only a relation. On the other hand, if all human virtue can be understood as excellence in serving the greater community of which one is a part, that common purpose would indeed give it unity. Is that what Meno means, however, or does he think of manly virtue rather in terms of self-fulfillment, and ruling as the opportunity for that fulfillment? Or is he simply divided, and is his understanding of virtue not only manifold but incoherent? Socrates' next question—what it is that make all bees bees—is both open-ended and indirectly suggestive of the answer that virtue is serving the community well, but it makes Meno no more inclined to give it. Indeed, it even seems to discourage such a response, by calling to mind, instead of the splendor of ruling and performing great benefactions and crushing enemies, the lowly service of worker bees. When Meno thinks of manly virtue, does he at once both associate it with serving the interests of others and consider it to be not service at all but the best kind of personal fulfillment?[5]

Meno's attachment to the virtue of ruling becomes more manifest when Socrates gives fresh examples pointing to this second way we might find unity in all of the virtues. Perhaps, he says, virtue is something like health or strength, essentially the same wherever it is present in male or female, young or old, a quality indeed useful to each in doing one's job but above all good for oneself. Meno agrees that health and strength have this character but denies that it is the same with virtue. The source of his resistance seems to be not a reluctance to identify virtue with the conditions of one's own thriving, but rather his sense that virtue in its truest sense is accessible only to a few. Socrates then asks whether both male and female do not need moderation and justice to manage well what is assigned to them. Thus he points to a third possible unifying feature of all virtue besides its benefit to others or to oneself: virtue entails a moral constraint on one's inclinations and on the use of one's powers. Meno agrees that all need moderation and justice to manage their responsibilities well, but he resists Socrates' conclusion that "all human beings are good in the same way, for by attaining the same things, they become good" (73c1–3). True virtue, as he sees it, is not something that can be possessed by just anyone or exercised in just any station in life.

Indeed, so highly does Meno regard excellence at ruling that when Socrates presses him a second time to define virtue, Meno casts aside his own careful distinctions between types of virtue and simply defines it as "the ability to rule human beings" (73c9). Socrates assails this definition by asking whether ruling well could possibly characterize the virtue of a child or slave. Of course it could not, Meno concedes, and immediately abandons his second definition. Meno seems to lack the courage of his convictions. If he really thought the central, highest, most noble virtue was the capacity to rule well, why should he not say that this is human excellence wherever it appears, even in a child or a slave, who might thereby win influence over all the adults around him as Xenophon's young Cyrus does, or succeed in gaining his own freedom and rule over others as Polus' Archelaus does?[6] Why should he not even say that the human being capable of gaining rule and ruling well is more truly a human being than those who can only obey?

One reason Meno cannot stay with this simple answer becomes clear in the next exchange. When Socrates asks whether virtue must not include, in addition to being able to rule, being able or willing to rule justly, Meno is so certain that justice is essential to virtue that he replies, "I think so, for justice *is* virtue" (73d9–10). But still his opinion will not stay put. Socrates asks whether there are other virtues and he agrees that there are; when pressed, he lists the three other traditional cardinal virtues—courage, moderation, and wisdom—and adds magnificence, the distinguishing quality of Gorgias that he so admires. Evidently courage, which he puts first, and magnificence, which he adds, have special importance for him, whether he believes himself to be distinguished by them or whether he hopes but also doubts that he has them. Once again Socrates hones in on this multiplicity of virtues as a problem, pointing out that they have failed to identify "the one that is present through all of these" (74a9). The famous Socratic problem of the elusive unity of virtue, as it unfolds in the concrete case of Socrates' conversation with Meno, is not so much a problem of virtue taking many specific forms as it is the deeper problem of virtue having no clear common principle. Meno cannot say what makes a virtue a virtue because he simultaneously holds in his mind conflicting answers to the question. Indeed, his admiration for great political virtue is likely even rooted in this ambiguity: ruling seems to promise an activity at once splendidly devoted to bringing benefits to others, supremely fulfilling for oneself, and nobly self-restrained in its dedication to principle.[7] And what is true of Meno is true generally of young people with the highest political ambitions. They are likely to feel especially keenly all of these strands of attraction to virtue, strands that need sorting out in any effort to give a rational account of human excellence. Engaging them in dialectical inquiry, especially at this time of life when they are most open to questioning, may hence be especially fruitful for Socrates' efforts both to educate and to test his hypotheses about virtue and the human soul.

Perhaps a more deft and dogged Meno might insist that these elements of virtue *are* united in the paradigm case but only the paradigm case of the ruler. Virtue in its lesser reaches, he might say, is indeed a fragmented thing, in some instances serving the individual's good and in others the community's, in some instances manifesting itself as moderation and in others as justice, at some times promoting its possessor's own welfare but at others limiting it, because life in its proper unfolding is possible only for a few, and virtue in its wholeness is the excellence only of human life at its very best, the life of ruling. The activity of the great ruler is of all things best, on this view, because it is most intrinsically satisfying, inasmuch as it involves mustering and honing great capacities to surmount great challenges and shining before others in doing so. The activity of complete virtue thus resembles that of an Olympic athlete, the paragon of physical excellence or virtue (*aretē*), but in an arena far more significant and more fulfilling to the highest and most uniquely human aspects of human nature. Such virtue is generous but not servile—as generous as it is possible to be towards those human beings whose defective natures admit of incomplete thriving—self-fulfilling but not utilitarian, demanding of great sacrifices in the short term but by no means bad for the one who engages in it. If the active life of virtue, so understood, could answer Meno's hazy but glowing hopes, it would seem to leave nothing to be desired, and virtue's unifying principle might well be defined as "that which fulfills human nature." Perhaps it would not be fair to expect Meno or anyone to develop such an answer in the heat of Socratic cross-examination, but it will be important to try to see from what follows what there might be in Meno that stops him even in principle from developing such an answer—and that will soon leave him hostile to all Socrates' attempts to probe his fractured view.

Definition and Dialectic (74a11–77a5)

Socrates succeeds in finding common ground with Meno when he elicits Meno's intuition that he should be able to give an account of virtue that makes sense. There follows a complicated and curiously hypothetical discussion over the proper way to define the essence of anything, shape and color being taken as examples. Two prominent things that emerge from this exchange are Socrates' preference for clear definitions that cleave as close as possible to ordinary experience without relying on hypotheses about the underlying nature of things, and Meno's unwillingness to "try" and "practice" giving such clear definitions as a preparation for defining virtue (75a1, 8–9). When Meno asks Socrates to define shape for him, Socrates agrees to do so if Meno will at least promise to make another attempt afterwards to define virtue. After Meno agrees, Socrates says, "Then it's necessary [for me] to be eager to do so, for it's worthwhile" (75b6). Something in Socrates' soul follows most closely the logic of what it is necessary not only to do but also to desire in order to reach the ends he considers good. But Meno is more flighty, more petulant, and unwilling to keep his promises. He objects to Socrates' first definition of shape and demands another; when Socrates gives him a second, more to his liking, he demands as well a definition of color, whereupon Socrates calls him spoiled and tyrannical on account of his beauty. Meno wants definitive answers without having to work for them.

Third Definition: The Primacy of the Good (77a5–79e6)

Pressed yet a third time to define virtue, Meno finally borrows from an unnamed poet an account that appears to avoid the fragmentary character of his earlier definitions while preserving the grandeur of virtue defined in terms of rule:

> It seems indeed to me, Socrates, just as the poet says, that virtue is "to rejoice in noble things and to be capable." And I say this is virtue: for one desiring (*epithumounta*) noble things to be capable of providing them. (77b2–5)

On the basis of this definition Socrates will launch an intricate argument that seems designed to prove that virtue is knowledge of and vice ignorance of one's own good. Hence, without specifying the most fulfilling life as the life of rule, he seems to be moving in a direction similar to the possible resolution sketched just above. But the argument is left unfinished, and the disturbing conclusion is instead drawn that virtue is merely an outstanding capacity to get for oneself the mundane goods that everyone wants. What does the argument show and why does Socrates allow it to misfire?

The first thing we observe is that Meno makes two potentially far-reaching changes in rephrasing the poet's statement, and it will be Meno's definition and not the poet's that Socrates interrogates. Where the poet speaks of "rejoicing" in the noble, which might equally include the noble deeds of oneself, one's friends, strangers, and even enemies, Meno speaks of "desiring" the noble, which could mean desiring to do it but seems especially to mean desiring to have it for oneself. The noble, for Meno, thus comes to sight as something eminently desirable, rather than a sacrifice of what is good, and indeed there is already something curiously acquisitive or aggrandizing in Meno's stance towards it. Second, where the poet speaks cryptically of "being capable," which might include the capacity to perform noble deeds, to defend nobility wherever one finds it, or to instill it in others, Meno specifies that he means the capacity to provide what is noble, again evidently for oneself.[8] This phrasing strengthens the impression that Meno is thinking mainly of noble possessions, such as the gold and silver and honors and offices that he mentions at 78c6–7, not noble deeds. Might the doing of noble deeds not quite add up to all that Meno longs for?

We may also ask whether Meno is aware that he has changed the poet's definition, or whether he thinks he has simply restated and perhaps clarified it. If he is unaware that he has at least changed its emphasis, then Meno shares a noble-minded imprecision that seems characteristic of gentlemen everywhere: an imprecision as to whether the noblest deeds are ends or a means to something further, and likewise an imprecision as to whether one's love of nobility is fundamentally "disinterested," as George Washington liked to describe the best leaders' motives, or fundamentally a love of honor, as Washington also characterized the ruling passion of the noblest minds. The accounts that Xenophon's Ischomachus and Cicero's Laelius give of themselves illustrate both aspects of this imprecision, as does Aristotle's rich account of the gentleman's outlook in the *Nicomachean Ethics*.[9] Aristotle gently suggests, however, that there are serious limits on the extent to which the love of the noble can ever be simply disinterested (*NE* 9.8). Might the poet disagree, insisting that *truly* noble people do exist who love the noble in a disinterested way, even if they are very rare? Socrates does not pursue this possibility here, although he will return to it at the end of the dialogue.

In examining Meno's definition, Socrates begins by subsuming the noble under the good. "Do you say that the one who desires the noble is a desirer of good things?" (77b6–7). Socrates secures agreement here quite easily, perhaps too easily. Unlike Glaucon, Meno is confident that the noble is good for its possessor, evidently because the noble things at the center of Meno's attention are in his judgment the good things par excellence—magnificent honors and offices and fine possessions—and he ranks human beings according to their degree of desire for these highest goods. He does not, like Glaucon, focus on the doing of just deeds, despite the fact that when pressed he has just said that justice is virtue (73d9–10) and that virtue means abstaining from providing what is good when it is not just

(78e3–6). Thus he remains thoughtlessly confident that everything noble is good without examining either the nature and grounds of his confidence or the lingering doubt in his mind.

Socrates' next step is to challenge the premise of Meno's ranking of human beings. To Meno's implicit claim that only the virtuous desire noble things—which he has now agreed are good things—Socrates asks, "On the grounds that there are some who desire the bad things, and others the good things? Don't all people, you best of men, seem to you to desire the good things?" (77b7–c2). Here again is a clear statement of the fundamental Socratic premise as to the primacy of the good, now framed in terms of desire (*epithumia*) instead of wish (*boulēsis*). The ultimate motive of all human action is a desire or wish for what is good; there is no choice of what is bad as bad; there is no radical evil.[10] But in stating his thesis so categorically, Socrates leaves many questions unanswered. If people never desire what is bad because it is bad, but always for the sake of some real or apparent good, are there not still healthy and unhealthy, noble and base desires that distinguish better and worse human characters? And if no one desires what is in every way bad, do people not sometimes feel intense desires for objects that are and are even known to them to be on balance bad? Meno, thinking about either or both of these questions, understandably refuses to grant Socrates' point.

Socrates then probes the mental state of those who desire what is bad, and in particular the connection between passion and judgment. To Meno's insistence that some desire the bad things, he asks, "Supposing that the bad things are good, do you mean, or even knowing that they are bad do they nevertheless desire them?" (77c3–5). Socrates implicitly concedes now that people desire things that are in fact bad, but he is preparing the argument that all such desire involves ignorance. But Meno will have none of it. Some people err out of ignorance, to be sure, he thinks, but others desire bad things in full knowledge that they are bad. Socrates now presses further into what it means to desire, confirming now that by "desiring" Meno means "desiring to have something for one's own": can anyone really desire to have bad things for oneself?

Socrates then changes the terms from good and bad to beneficial and harmful. Does the one who wishes for the bad things, he asks, do so "believing the bad things will benefit him who comes to possess them, or knowing that the bad things harm the one who has them?" (77d1–3). Meno does not protest this change, as one might, with the moral objection that the wicked choose to do what is ignoble and to that extent bad, but beneficial for themselves. This objection was rendered less likely by the previous exchange in which Socrates focused attention on the good and bad things we possess, not those we do: it would be harder to say that people knowingly acquire what is bad than that they knowingly do it. But Meno is already quite disposed to look at the good and bad in the way Socrates suggests. Whatever wavering belief he has that what is noble and hence good may demand a sacrifice of one's own good (cf. 78e3–6) is allowed to slip unnoticed out of sight as Socrates elicits and reinforces the predominant strain in his thinking—perhaps the deepest strain in everyone's thinking—that identifies the noble as fundamentally and essentially good, and the good for each person to do as what is, at least for the most part and at least in the long run, beneficial for oneself. So thoroughly does Meno endorse this view that he even accepts Socrates' suggestion that to believe that a bad thing is beneficial is not to know at all that it is bad (77d4–7).[11] What Socrates is eliciting from Meno is of great and universal importance, then, but it is a problem for Meno that he fails to attend to the also important countercurrents of belief and attachment in his own soul.

Yet Meno still insists that while some desire the bad in the belief that it is beneficial, others do so knowing full well that it is harmful. And this reservation too accords with common sense: people do seem to feel all sorts of unhealthy desires in full knowledge of how unhealthy they are. Socrates' next step, then, is to secure agreement that at least the first group Meno has just spoken of, those who think the bad things are beneficial, really desire something good.

> So it's clear then that these are not the ones who desire the bad things—those who are ignorant of them—but they desire those things that they supposed to be good but that are in fact bad. So that those who are ignorant of them and suppose them to be good clearly desire the good things. (77d7–e3)

This passage has elicited much scholarly controversy, and justifiably so: it is devilishly difficult. As Gerasimos Santas points out, the acknowledgment here that some people desire things that are in fact bad seems to contradict Socrates' earlier claim that all people desire the good things (77c1–2). The only way to make sense of Socrates' argument is to see that his use of the term *desire* (*epithumeō*) is growing progressively more precise in response to Meno's objections. His first suggestion that everyone desires good things was imprecise in failing to specify whether the object of desire should be taken as the particular thing that one seeks (e.g., supreme power), the apparent good that one may mistakenly believe the objects contains or will bring (e.g., honor and wealth) or the ultimate goal of all striving (true happiness, whatever that turns out to be, even if it should have a very different character from what one imagines). The ensuing argument shows that Socrates uses *desire* in all of these ways but increasingly in the second sense. At the same time, he uses the term *want* or *wish* (*boulomai*) especially in the third sense.[12] Even before making the point that we have seen him make in the *Gorgias*, that whatever particular things people pursue, what they all really *want* is to be happy and not unhappy, Socrates draws here a subtle, important distinction as regards immediate desires. Pressed by Meno, he concedes that one can in a real sense desire an object that is not good. But even as one desires just this particular thing (the first and simplest meaning of desire), one desires it *as something good* (the second and fuller meaning). Desire is inextricably bound up with judgment, and an erroneous judgment makes the desire itself mistaken.

This connection between thought and desire is both important and subtle. To say that we desire the object as something good is not necessarily to say that we desire it only because we first judge it good; it may be more accurate to say that desire springs up and brings with it the belief that its object is, as desirable, necessarily good, if only because it conveys an expectation of pleasure. The key thought is that our judgments and emotions constitute inseparable aspects of one and the same response. When desires are confused or contradictory or volatile, so are their accompanying opinions. In its fluidity and tendency to lack adequate grounds, desire resembles opinion, whereas our deepest wants or wishes are more stable in the way that knowledge is, being rooted in the abiding needs of our nature.[13]

Next, Socrates turns to the people who, according to Meno, know the bad things are harmful but desire them anyway. Do they know that *they* will be harmed by them? he asks. Do they know that to the extent that they are harmed they will become unhappy? Meno says they do. But to Socrates' final question, "Is there anyone who wants to be miserable and unhappy?" (78a4–5), Meno can only say no. As Socrates introduces happiness and misery into the discussion, he underscores the fact that he is now speaking not of immediate desires and aversions but of their ultimate root by using the word for *wish* or *want* (*boulomai*). Whatever the status of those things we desire, the ultimate wish behind every desire is to be happy. Meno cannot help but agree. "Then no one wants what is bad, Meno, if he does not want to be such. For what else is it to be miserable than to desire what is bad and to obtain it?" (78a6–7) This part of the argument seemed at first to be aimed at showing that the alleged class of people who know that the bad things are harmful but desire them anyway has no members, or in other words that all desire perfectly follows judgment as to what is good.

This view that desires or indeed all passions are perfectly in accord with judgments we may call the "radical alignment theory." Thus a number of commentators have taken Socrates to mean that desires for anything that seems bad are wholly impossible, with the result that virtue requires nothing but insight and that neither self-control (*enkrateia*), understood as difficult self-overcoming, nor lack of control (*akrasia*), understood as acting contrary to one's own better judgment, is possible.[14] But by switching from *epithumia* to *boulēsis* at the culmination of the argument, Socrates leaves open and even implicitly concedes that human beings can and do desire bad things and even things that they somehow judge bad, or less than the best that is available to them.

If Socrates is making important concessions to Meno as Meno pushes back against him, making his use of *epithumia* more precise and in the end claiming that the possession of bad desires is only involuntary, not impossible, how far does this concession go? If he is granting here, as he affirms more directly elsewhere, that human beings are subject to bad and irrational desires that they must vigilantly resist, which sort of irrational desires would he agree are possible? For desire might be irrational in the sense that its object is in fact bad, or is consistently known by the agent to be bad, or is normally known by the agent to be bad but at present believed good, or is both generally and at present believed bad, or is generally believed bad but at present believed good. By bad, we may mean what is wholly bad, on balance bad, or on balance good and yet less good than some other available alternative.[15] Socrates' quietly precise use of *boulēsis* suggests that he thinks human beings fundamentally *wish* only for what is truly, thoroughly good (even if it is unavailable), and that in a derivative sense we wish at each time to do and to have what is best among available options. But by connecting desire especially with pleasure and with appearances and by pulling back from his implicit claim that we never desire anything bad, he leaves open the possibility that we may desire many things that we otherwise know or believe to be bad but do not at present judge bad, and even things that we concurrently judge to be on balance more bad than good or less good than some available alternative, as long as we in some way judge them good. For if prospective pleasure begets desire, there is no reason to think, or to think Socrates is saying, that general opinions or general knowledge or even present, clearly perceived knowledge of countervailing evils will make a desire for some intense pleasure simply evaporate, any more than a soldier's knowledge that fighting hard is his best chance for survival will make fear evaporate. All that Socrates clearly affirms here is that we desire nothing that we think simply bad, that we truly want only what is good, and that all desires for what is not the best available to us are in a deep sense involuntary, involving an inner division or confusion that we could never wish to have.[16] The *Meno* leaves for later the argument that those with knowledge of what is best will follow it, and it leaves for the *Protagoras* a full treatment of the problems of mixed motives and competing desires.[17]

Having concluded his analysis of desiring and wanting, Socrates returns to Meno's definition of virtue, rephrasing it now as "to want good things and be capable of providing them" (77b4–5). But since all want what is good, no one is better than another in this, so that "if in fact one is better than another, he would be better with respect to the 'being capable,'" and virtue would be simply "the capacity to provide what is good" (78b7–8, c1). In his restatement Socrates preserves his two substitutions of the good for the noble and wanting for desiring, and Meno silently accepts both. As for the first, Meno seems to have realized that the good for each individual is in fact what he meant by the noble all along, and as Jacob Klein observes, he never goes back on this substitution, a fact that may be important for the course he will choose in life.[18] Equally important is Meno's failure to protest the substitution of wanting for desiring. Socrates' logic up to this point has been sound, but he has left important questions unexplored. He has leapt lightly from the diversity of human desires—wise and unwise, healthy and unhealthy—to dwell on the unity of the ultimate wish for happiness behind those desires. He has not explored the question of how people come to have the wrong desires and what it takes to get free of them. He has brought Meno to a point where, if he is at all promising, he should begin to see for himself that a crucial difference between the virtuous and the vicious is in the degree to which they see clearly and steadily what is and is not worth pursuing. When Socrates reformulates the definition of virtue as wanting the good and being capable of providing it, then, a more promising interlocutor would object, "No, Socrates, I said that virtue is *desiring* the good or noble and being capable of providing it. You have pointed out that no one *wants* to desire what is bad, which raises the question of why some people do. What stops them from getting straight and keeping straight what is really good?" Then he might explore the key question of the relation of knowledge to passion and probe more deeply into the roots of human motivation and action. But in fact, rather than inquire into the problem, Meno embodies and illustrates it. And at the heart of the problem seems to be a reluctance to look closely into what is at work in his own soul. In particular, we see that as soon as Meno has made explicit his identification of the noble with the good, his concomitant attachment to the other sense of the noble—the difficult or heroic demands of duty—has again slipped out of view. Something about that aspect of the noble is important enough to keep Meno's view of virtue fragmented and yet is extremely hard for him to examine squarely.

Once Meno has identified the noble with the good, it no longer seems credible to him that people differ significantly in their ends. If everyone seeks what is good, what is good seems obvious to him: it is the health and wealth, the gold and silver and honor and political rule that he assumes everyone wants or envies (78c5–7). Even when Socrates asks whether he has nothing else to add, Meno includes in his list of goods neither wisdom nor any other qualities of soul. Socrates replies that virtue must, then, be the capacity to provide "gold and silver, as Meno the guest-friend of the Great King asserts" (78d1–3). The natural result of Socrates' insight into the primacy of the good, in the absence of deep thoughtfulness about the needs of the soul, is to unleash one's existing desires, which for Meno means above all his desire for wealth and political power. Even if Socrates is bringing Meno up against this result in hopes that he will recoil from it and become more thoughtful, the enterprise is most risky.

Socrates is indeed able to show that Meno's view of the human good is not as simple or as simply crude as he expresses it here. When he asks, "Do you add to this providing, Meno, doing it justly and piously, or does it make no difference?" (78d3–5), Meno replies that of course these provisos must be added, but somehow it did not occur to him to add them himself. Given the way he keeps forgetting about justice, it is apt that Socrates should now introduce piety for the first time: only piety can check the tyrannical inclinations of a Cyrus. But it is also interesting that Meno readily embraces Socrates' addition of "justice or moderation or piety" to their definition of virtue at 78d8–e1. Something in this politically ambitious young man deflects him away from focusing on and seeking clarity about the true good of his soul, drawing his attention to mundane goods that present temptations to tyranny or vice; yet something else in him is uneasy about this trajectory and welcomes the constraints piety and justice bring—and this despite the evident indifference to piety he showed just before (76e6–9). Meno wants the dignity of doing splendid or noble things; he wants these activities to be good for him; he does not want his pursuits to be simply, crudely selfish; but he does not want to think about how all these concerns fit together. Does he sense at least dimly that just as a life spent doing noble deeds would not answer all of his longings, neither would any such goods as he is likely to acquire in a straightforwardly aggrandizing way? Is he harboring hopes for something further that he does not want to examine too closely? If Meno is ever to resolve his self-contradictions, he needs to accept his ignorance and seek wisdom. But in fact, when Socrates again points out Meno's ignorance as it manifests itself in the fractured character of his view of virtue, Meno attacks him as a wicked trickster.

Perplexity, Knowledge, and Recollection (79e7–86c3)

Meno's complaint, beginning at 79e7, is a mixture of honest perplexity, petulant impatience, and dishonest evasion. Like the stingray that numbs all who touch it, he complains, Socrates infects others and has now infected Meno with his own bewilderment and has left his soul and tongue both numb, even though on many other occasions he has spoken well about virtue to large audiences. Meno acknowledges his perplexity only as something Socrates has inflicted on him, not as an underlying ignorance he has uncovered. In the same spirit, Meno speaks of the soul here for the only time in the dialogue only to reproach Socrates for bewitching it, not to acknowledge the importance and difficulty of cultivating it. He even makes a veiled threat: anywhere but in Athens, such behavior would get Socrates into serious trouble. Meno's irritation at having his confused opinions about the most important things exposed is, in incipient form, the same anger that will soon drive the city of Athens to execute Socrates for corrupting the youth.

At the same time, Meno asks how Socrates can expect anyway to learn what virtue is, given his professed total ignorance about it: "In what way, Socrates, will you seek that about which you don't know at all what it is?" (80d5–6). If Socrates really knows nothing about virtue—neither which phenomena it includes, so that he might seek their common elements, nor its general definition or characteristics—how can he ever come to know it? In fact Socrates seems to know well both what qualities virtue is thought to include and what principles are thought to govern it, but perhaps he also knows that these do not add up to a single coherent whole. Socrates in response points out that Meno's thinking is on a trajectory that will likely lead him to give up on learning altogether, since no one can learn either what he already knows or what he does not know at all, and Meno is implicitly placing all potential knowledge in these two categories. Socrates thus points to the realm in which all learning in fact must occur, the realm of things that we do somehow know, but not with sufficient clarity. And is this not indeed the realm of everything of serious concern to us as human beings?[19] Meno has shown an impatience with definitions that rely on terms not yet themselves perfectly defined; he wishes for a certainty free of hypotheses. By contrast, Socrates' first and likely preferred definition of shape as that which always accompanies color (75b) suggests that the best we may be able to do is to notice and gain clarity on our experience as it is given to us, observing how the phenomena as we experience them relate to one another and affect one another. There is no way for us to understand anything from the ground up without reference to other things that are themselves imperfectly known. But the disheartened Meno needs courage and determination if he is to make any progress. To remedy this deficiency, Socrates tells a story.

The story is Socrates' famous account of knowledge as recollection and the soul as immortal. Socrates begins by claiming to have heard "certain men and women wise in divine matters"—and before he can even say what they teach, Meno eagerly interrupts: "saying what speech?" (81a5–7). Especially now that his confidence in his understanding of virtue has been shaken—and now that he has been brought to see the self-aggrandizing trajectory of his concern with virtue—Meno shows himself to be more attracted to piety than he at first seemed (cf. 76e6–9). Socrates cites a poetic account of divine providence that holds out hope for glories in future lives to those who are pious now.[20] He then offers his own mystical account of knowledge as recollection, which, departing radically from the common-sense perspective of his model definition of shape as that which always accompanies color, alleges that knowledge comes not from careful attention to what is before us, but from recollecting what we once knew, completely and with certainty, in a previous life or lives of which common sense has no inkling. The connecting thread of these two "divine" teachings is a claim about the immortality of the soul. Why is this the right medicine for Meno's own soul, and in particular for the softness and laziness he has shown in the search for knowledge? Socrates' chosen medicine suggests that the root of Meno's failing may be an inability to come to terms with mortality. As much as Meno wants to possess virtue and exercise it on a grand scale, he does not want to inquire closely into the nature of the human soul, its true perfection, or its future fate. Might his attachment to virtue be tied to a subterranean hope for immortality that he does not want to examine out of fear that it may prove ill-founded? Philosophy requires courage to bring such hopes into the daylight and to try to determine whether the cosmos supports them. Might the lack of courage that becomes evident in Meno through the drama of this dialogue be the most important answer to the questions Meno failed to pursue, the question of what else besides intellectual aptitude distinguishes those who see the good clearly from those who do not, as well as the question of what so often prevents people from applying the knowledge they have?

Socrates opens his own account of knowledge and recollection with a tale—we are surely not far off in calling it a myth—about the soul and its previous lives, in the course of which it has seen and hence learned all things.[21] The result could not be more encouraging for philosophic inquiry:

> Inasmuch as the whole of nature is akin, and the soul has learned everything, nothing prevents someone, once he has recollected just one thing—what human beings call learning—from discovering everything else, so long as he is courageous and doesn't tire in the search. (81c9–d4)

Socrates focuses Meno's attention on the conclusions that all knowledge is somehow already present in him, that what we call "learning" is really nothing but recollection, and that nothing but application is needed to achieve it. The question that he thereby distracts Meno from considering and indeed never answers is how the original learning occurred that recollection purportedly recovers. It seems to have been a matter of mere sight, as if inquiring, reflecting, calculating, analyzing, hypothesizing, and testing played no part in learning—a problem already. But to whatever extent we do learn by simply seeing, can we not do it now as well as before? Why would it follow from the soul's immortality that *all* learning is recollection rather than, in most cases, a fresh, direct grasping of what we have perhaps grasped before and may someday grasp again? To be sure, there are some matters about which we have no possibility for direct apperception in this life—the things that happen in Hades, for example, and those that occurred before our births. Curiously, however, Socrates speaks of these things, and especially of his tale of recollection itself, not as things he has seen and recollected but as things he has "heard" and "trusts" (81a5, e1). If hearsay and trust fall short of adequate knowledge, does Socrates really give good reason to think that any knowledge comes from recollection rather than from direct observation and analysis? Might not the active exertion that Socrates calls on Meno to make here and now be the sole true cause of such knowledge as Meno stands to gain, and the myth a crutch to help him begin to exert himself, not in recollecting but in thinking?

Indeed, so defective is Socrates' whole account of recollection that he himself will openly admit at the end of it,

> As for the rest of it, I wouldn't affirm the argument very confidently. But that, by supposing it necessary to seek what one doesn't know, we would be better and more manly and less lazy than if we should suppose that what we don't know is neither possible to find nor necessary to seek—about this I certainly would do battle, if I could, both in speech and in deed. (86b6–c2)

The story's factual claims may not be worth defending, but its practical import, that knowledge is attainable and that we must strive for it—this Socrates affirms with conviction. In doing so, he incidentally acknowledges that he knows something quite solid about virtue: courage and diligence in the search for truth make men good and hence are virtues. The story's rhetorical function, then, is clearly to encourage the disheartened Meno to exercise these virtues and make an effort to learn (81d5–e1; 86b1–4; cf. 84b6–c9). But if the story is so defective in its literal teaching that it is not worth defending, why would Plato give it pride of place as his most memorable statement on human knowledge? Might an admittedly defective statement about human learning still teach something important, despite and perhaps even by means of its defects?[22]

Socrates' "demonstration" that learning is a matter of simply recovering knowledge that we once saw and grasped in complete form in some prior life is his famous geometry lesson with the slave boy. The truth that Socrates fishes out of Meno's unschooled slave is this: to find a square whose area is twice that of a given square, one must construct it on a diagonal drawn between opposite corners of the first square. As Socrates says, he does indeed only ask questions and provide no answers (82e4–5; 84c10–d1). But the slave shows such ignorance and needs Socrates to lead him so carefully, step by step, until he stumbles over the right answer, that the claim that this knowledge was ever present in his mind before Socrates planted it there seems absurd. Still, there is something impressive in what Socrates accomplishes. He shows that a completely uneducated person, so long as he has grown up among human beings and learned ordinary language (82b4–5), can be prompted to discover the solution to a challenging problem in mathematics. The answer is present in him only as the barest of potentialities, but it is still present in the sense that he need only attend carefully to the things he already is thoughtlessly aware of to solve the problem.[23]

What is seldom noted is that Socrates shows quietly that learning is as much a matter of discovering and rejecting our implicitly or explicitly held false opinions as it is a matter of replacing them with true ones. The slave must first free himself from two false opinions before he is able to see the correct answer. But curiously, the errors he must overcome seem as much a product of Socrates' leading questions as of the slave's own preexisting views (82d8–e3 and esp. 83d4–e2). Again, might it be that the most important false opinions that we need liberation from are ones that we acquire under the influence of others? If so, the process of "recovering" true knowledge would be identical to the process of liberation from the cave, appropriately called "recollection" in the sense that it constitutes a recovery of a natural or politically unmediated understanding that, ironically, is accessible only to human beings who grow up in society and then subject that society's authoritative opinions to rigorous scrutiny.

The first result of seeing the inadequacy of our thoughtlessly held false opinion is a new awareness of ignorance.[24] Socrates points out that whereas before the slave boy "supposed he knew" the length of the side of a square whose area is eight square feet, "now he does consider himself to be at a loss, and just as he does not know, neither does he believe he knows" (84a6–b1). Meno agrees that the slave's prior state of ignorant confidence was worse than his present state of conscious perplexity and that the slave has likely benefited from being refuted—even though Meno has just blamed Socrates for throwing him into a similar perplexity. For as he sees, now that he is watching with detachment and is untroubled by shame and pride, it is only with awareness of ignorance that we are motivated to seek the knowledge we lack.

To be sure, many things cannot be discovered by mere reflection but must be learned by going to see them or inquiring of those who have. Socrates cannot recollect but must ask Meno whether the slave knows Greek; the slave cannot recollect but must be told the Greek word for "diagonal"; and most importantly, Meno is expected to learn something important from watching the demonstration. Are these interactions not cases of teaching and learning too? True, Socrates implies at 82a1 that teaching does not exist and that all learning is only recollection, but in asking Meno to say whether he is teaching the slave or merely asking questions, and in asking Meno whether the slave has ever been taught geometry, Socrates implies that the activity we commonly call teaching does indeed go on all the time. His use of the terms *teaching, learning,* and *recollection* seems intentionally, provocatively inconsistent, but perhaps if Meno were attentive enough to demand consistency Socrates would say this: that teaching in the precise sense means telling or showing, and that whatever we acquire by being told is not genuine knowledge but is mere ungrounded opinion, at best the material out of which, through a process of testing and inquiry and reflection, learning can arise. This implied meaning of the word "teaching" may be important for interpreting the dialogue's final argument that virtue cannot be taught. Learning, by contrast, occurs through an active process of inquiry by which we reflect on what is already in our minds, test what is grounded, what is ungrounded, and what is altogether incorrect in what we assume, and recognize what is implicit in what we already know. To the learning process we bring natural powers of insight or "recognition" of what makes sense and what does not, powers that are evident even in an individual with the most impoverished education. The structure and capacity of our minds make certain truths "already" necessary and hence in a way already implicit in us even before we consider them, especially mathematical and logical truths. Yet to forge them into true knowledge takes sustained, active effort.

But what about the knowledge sought so far in vain by Socrates and Meno, the knowledge of what virtue is? Socrates suggests that the answer is already present in Meno in the sense that he need only put together what he somehow already knows to solve a puzzle that is as elusive and perplexing as the problem of finding the square root of 2. Thus Socrates suggests that in the world of human action, just as in the world of space and quantity, we work from certain little-examined premises that guide and structure everything we do, and that our truest, deepest judgments about what is good and noble are, like mathematical truths, things that we can access though our own experiences and actions and yet that we can only discover and clarify and cannot arbitrarily posit or freely choose. Like the objects of geometry, our notions of virtue have a purity and perfection greater than anything we encounter in the world of experience; yet still we trust or hope that they, like our mathematical notions, are capable of a perfectly unified and consistent articulation. The demonstration lends support to the hope that they are, if it also suggests that the solution we must come to in the end will not be the first or second that occurs to us but one that will come from an unexpected direction. Perhaps, like the geometrical example Socrates has chosen, the problem of virtue can be fully solved only by recognizing that it involves incommensurable elements: we may never be able to define virtue in a way that satisfies all the expectations of both goodness and nobility that we initially bring to it, just as we cannot express the relation of a square's side to its diagonal with any ratio, as early mathematicians at first assumed could be done. But we can show what things are incommensurable and how they are in fact related.

The demonstration indicates, moreover, the difficulty of attaining genuine knowledge of the solution to a difficult problem even after we seem to see it. Socrates observes at the end of his demonstration that the slave still does not have knowledge but only true opinion (85c6–7), and that his now correct opinions are no more solid than "a dream that has just been stirred up" (85c9–10). But, he adds, if someone should lead him through these and similar inquiries "many times and in many ways . . . he will in the end know them as precisely as anyone" (85c10–d1). The sober conclusion of all this is that genuine knowledge of serious matters can be acquired only through a process of inquiry that each must undertake for oneself. It cannot be taught in the sense in which we naively think of teaching—as the dispensing of knowledge from one mind to another—although it certainly can be set in motion and assisted by apt questioning or dialectics, so long as one has an able and willing student. This process is necessary in every field but perhaps not equally necessary. Especially in matters of politics and morality, where students begin with deep-seated beliefs that require searching self-examination, a dialectical ascent from the political community's received opinions may be the only ascent.

All of this is important and persuasive. But having shown this much, Socrates now rapidly catapults Meno to several astonishing conclusions. If the slave is somehow "recovering knowledge within himself," it must be knowledge that he "either got hold of at some time or possessed always" (85d6–10); if he got hold of it at some time, it was not in this lifetime, since he has never been taught geometry before; hence he either acquired it before he was a human being or he always had it.

> If, then, in whatever time he is and in whatever time he is not a human being, there are present in him true opinions, which when roused by questioning come to be knowledge, will his soul always be in a state of having learned? For it is clear that for all time he either is or is not a human being. . . . So if the truth about the beings is always present for us in the soul, would the soul be immortal? (86a6–b2)

What has happened here? Socrates has pointed to but now leaves aside the sensible thought that knowledge is always, throughout our lives, incipiently present in us by nature in the form of an ability to "recognize" what makes sense and what does not. He ignores the fact that he demonstrated and even emphasized just before—that truth can be present in different degrees, from a bare potentiality to a transient awareness that flickers into consciousness like the memory of a dream to the solid grasp that comes through repeated practice—making it possible not only to be born with the first but to gain the second with a teacher's help and the third through our own efforts. Having first distinguished these stages and called the first two "true opinion," he then conflates opinion with knowledge (85d9) in order to suggest that complete knowledge was always present in the slave, and thereafter he uses the terms *knowledge* and *opinion* interchangeably. Having said that the slave must have either acquired his true opinions in *some* previous time or always had them, he proceeds as if he has just proved that he had them in *every* previous time (86a6–7). Finally, he glides from the sensible assertion that, so long as we exist, we either are or are not human beings, to the assertion that we have always existed either as human beings or as something else.

So poor is this proof of the soul's immortality that it throws us back upon the question of what serious thought Socrates could possibly mean to convey with his claims at 81c5–d4 that all knowledge both begins with sight and is somehow already present in us from birth, that the human soul is coeval with all the things it comes to know, and that the whole of nature is somehow "akin," so that knowledge of one part of it can lead us directly to knowledge of the whole. The dialogue spells none of this out. It points us to the possibility, however, that built into the structure of the human mind is at least an implicit knowledge of the world around us; perhaps this is the sense in which all nature is akin, inasmuch as it is all "akin" to us or commensurate with our powers of perception and analysis. Might the orderly structure of the world and hence, in a sense, the being of the things in it and even the being of the world as a world depend in some decisive respect upon the contribution of the human mind, so that the human soul would be in that sense coeval with the world? If so, then perhaps, much more than we tend to think, coming to know the whole has the character of looking within, reflecting on what is already present, and thinking carefully about the nature of our own experience and the processes of our own thought, a character suggested at the most basic level by Socrates' definition of shape. To be sure, this account seems to suggest that the kinship of all things means that grasping any one of them brings them all into one's possession, as if all truths were fish and all the fish in the sea were interconnected, so that one need only catch one to have them all. But reading more carefully, we see that one particular truth is key—the truth of what it is to learn and what the relation is of learning to mortality, or of human knowing to truths that do or do not exist permanently outside of us. Thinking through these questions, Socrates suggests, and coming to understand the way our concern for mortality and our hopes for immortality shape our self-understanding and our understanding of virtue, is the key to unraveling the confusion that impeded Meno's efforts to define virtue and that entangles every beginner in the quest for knowledge.

So strong is Meno's longing to believe in immortality, however, that he fails to "recognize" the astonishing lapses in the proof of it for what they are. Socrates has succeeded in giving him a faith that allows him to press on in the inquiry, but what Socrates cannot give him is the courage to examine himself and his own hopes that would allow him to become a full partner in the search for the truth. Meno remains resistant to the inquiry into the nature of virtue that threatened to pull those hopes apart; he still prefers to focus only on the less troubling question of whether it can be taught; he has not grasped at all that virtue can be taught only by a process of questioning that would leave the chief work to him.[25] He even fails now, in restating his original question, to include the possibility that virtue is acquired by practice (86c7–d2). If the purpose of the recollection myth was to inspire Meno with courage and doggedness in the search for truth, the gulf between the spirit of his inquiry and that of Socrates now confirms again that those qualities cannot be taught.

Is Virtue Wisdom? (86c4–89a5)

Socrates chides Meno again for his careless impetuosity but throws up his hands and agrees to investigate whether virtue is teachable, even though they have not succeeded in defining it. He complains that while Meno tries to rule and indeed succeeds at ruling him, he fails to rule himself as Socrates rules himself; Meno fails even to try, out of an excessive love of freedom (86d3–e1). Between the contradictory claims that Meno rules Socrates and that Socrates rules Socrates, we might be well advised to regard the former as ironic—and hence to expect that, in the coming discussion, Meno's question about virtue's teachability will not after all displace Socrates' question about its essence. Might self-rule indeed be a central part of that essence, in contrast to the capacity to rule others that Meno so admires? If so, we must watch for further indications as to whether that self-rule requires mere insight, on the grounds that passions and actions will automatically pursue the good that the mind sees (as Socrates is generally taken to believe), whether it involves a forcible overcoming of passion, so that virtue would require dispositions that are not in any way knowledge, or whether it requires something in between, an unusually deep penetration of all the passions by knowledge to bring them more and more into alignment. But we may note for now that this and Socrates' other jesting comments about Meno's ruling him (76b4–c2; 80b8–c6) likely point to one reason such exertion is needed and thus to one component of self-rule that Socrates considers crucial: the resistance to the charms of the beautiful and to the erotic intoxication that it brings.

In agreeing to let Meno have his way, Socrates asks for one small concession. He proposes that they first examine a preliminary question that will help them determine whether virtue is teachable, just as a geometer, when asked whether a triangle of a given area may be inscribed within a given circle, might propose examining a preliminary question, on the hypothesis that it will be possible to inscribe it only if certain conditions are met. The geometrical example is obscure, to say the least.[26] The problem seems to be that only if the area in question has in fact first been successfully inscribed in the circle can we identify the lines referred to in the "preliminary" test. But if the test is not useful in the way Socrates claims, as a starting point, it still points to certain facts about a triangle that has been inscribed in a circle, and confirming the existence of the relations Socrates observes can also confirm that the figure has been correctly drawn.

Socrates' preliminary test in the case of virtue's teachability concerns its resemblance or identity to knowledge.

> Socrates: "What sort of thing, among the beings pertaining to the soul, would virtue have to be for it to be either something teachable or something not teachable? First, if it is different from the kind of thing knowledge is, is it something teachable or not—or as we were just now saying, something recollectable? Let it make no difference to us which of the two names we use: is it something teachable? Or is this at least clear to everyone: a human being is taught nothing other than knowledge?"
>
> Meno: "It seems so to me, at least."
>
> Socrates: "But if virtue is a certain knowledge, it's clear that it would be something teachable."
>
> Meno: "Of course."
>
> Socrates: "We disposed of this quickly, then—that being of the one sort it is something teachable, of the other sort, not." (87b5–c9)

Socrates has indeed moved quickly, more quickly than a careful interlocutor ought to allow. In particular, he moves from the cautious but cryptic formulation that a thing, to be teachable, must be "the kind of thing knowledge is" to the less qualified statement that it must be knowledge itself (87b7, c2–3). But surely not everything taught is knowledge—unless we wish to say that we are imparting knowledge when we teach a puppy not to chew the furniture. This shift calls attention to a fundamental problem in the argument to come: it will entail a pervasive imprecision on the relation between knowledge per se and other things that may resemble or involve knowledge. Nor, as we have seen, is all knowledge teachable in any ordinary sense. Might it be that there is one kind of autonomous virtue that is at its core a knowledge that each must ultimately acquire for oneself, and another kind that is good habituation, being at best "the same sort of thing as knowledge" in the sense that habitually following the rules of a wisdom that one does not oneself possess is "the same sort of thing" as wisdom? Might philosophic and ordinary civic virtue in fact have these divergent characters? Although the argument to come is one of the ones in the Platonic corpus in which Socrates considers the relation of virtue to knowledge most explicitly, it is set up and proceeds with such imprecision of language that we must expect it to leave Meno more confused than enlightened; it is likely to require especially careful attention to its ambiguities if it is to shed light on our basic question.

Proposing now that they examine whether "virtue is knowledge or is other than knowledge" (87c11–12), Socrates continues,

> Socrates: "Do we say virtue is anything other than good itself, and does this remain our hypothesis, that it is good itself?"
>
> Meno: "Absolutely."
>
> Socrates: "Then if there is something good that is other than and separate from knowledge, probably virtue would not be a certain knowledge. But if nothing is good that knowledge does not encompass, then in suspecting it to be a certain knowledge, we would suspect correctly." (87d2–8)

Having made much of the claim that one cannot know the qualities of a thing without knowing what the thing is, Socrates now hangs a whole argument on the unproven assertion that virtue is good. But perhaps in the case of virtue this procedure is not unreasonable: by virtue we know we mean something good, even if we do not know what else we mean. Might we not begin with this recognition and discover what virtue is by discovering what is good? This approach would take us on a long path if we were required to identify the many things that are good for human beings and the many qualities needed to secure them. It would require a shorter path, however, if virtue turned out to be the only good thing in the world, as Socrates almost suggests here that it might be, or if, as he suggests more seriously, there proves to be just one thing so fundamentally and consistently good that nothing else can be good in its absence, or alternatively, as Meno seems inclined to believe, so fundamentally and consistently good that everything else is assured of being good in its presence.

Before considering what else besides virtue might be good, Socrates raises the issue of what we mean by good. He immediately reasserts the identity of the good with the beneficial, underscoring now the thought that the good is relative and the human good is defined by human needs (87d8–e3; cf. 77b2–78b2). But he makes the point in a curious way. Since it is by means of virtue that we are good, he says, and since all that is good is beneficial, it follows that if we are virtuous, we are beneficial; only after establishing this does he make the simpler point that if virtue is a good thing, it must be beneficial. This manner of proceeding calls attention again to two very different ways of understanding virtue, as selfless service to others, and as shrewdness in benefiting oneself, thus simultaneously evoking both the most moral and the most utilitarian aspects of Meno's concern with virtue. Yet once again it is the latter that will come increasingly to the fore.

What, then, is the character of the good that virtue secures, and of the good that it is? Socrates begins simply by asking what is beneficial, and he and Meno seem at first to have a plethora of answers. They quickly agree on the identity of many beneficial things, including goods both of the body and of the soul, but they do not succeed in putting these into any order on the basis of the ultimate human good that virtue ought to serve, and the distinction between means and ends is never clearly drawn. Pointing to a path of inquiry that would answer the question of whether or to what extent virtue is knowledge by determining what human fulfillment consists in and then identifying the qualities it requires, the argument follows instead a lower path, considering in a general way what seems to be useful even if we do not know what it ought to be for. Yet even so, Socrates makes a plausible case that without knowledge human beings are unable to make good use or at least reliably good use of any of the other things we call good.

> Socrates: So let's take up each point in turn and examine what kind the things are that benefit us. Health, we assert, and strength and beauty and of course wealth: we say that these things, and those like them, are beneficial, no?
>
> Meno: Yes.
>
> Socrates: But we assert that these same things sometimes also do harm—or do you speak in a manner different from this?
>
> Meno: No, but in this way.

> Socrates: So examine this: when what guides each of these do they benefit us, and when what guides do they do harm? Isn't it when correct usage guides that they benefit us, and when not, they do harm?
>
> Meno: Certainly.
>
> Socrates: Let's examine in addition, then, the things pertaining to the soul. Do you call something moderation and justice and courage and ease of learning (*eumatheia*) and memory and magnificence, and all such things?
>
> Meno: I do indeed.
>
> Socrates: So examine whether some of these don't seem to you to be not knowledge but other than knowledge—if these don't seem at one time to harm but at another to benefit. For example, courage—if courage is not active wisdom (*phronēsis*) but a certain sort of boldness. Isn't it the case that when a human being is bold without intellect (*nous*), he is harmed, but when with intellect, he is benefited? (87e5–88b6)

Socrates suggests now not only that knowledge is necessary for making good use of anything else but that it is sufficient—so absolutely, invariably good that fortune has no power to defeat it. He gives no argument for this premise, but Meno readily accepts it, evidently out of an intuition or a yearning to believe that virtue has such sublime goodness and reach. Meno now proves quite ready to agree that many of the things he was certain were virtues, and therefore good, are not good in the absolute sense that he demands and hence must not be virtues. His certainty about what virtue is runs less deep than his desire for it to be proven supremely and invariably good.

What exactly is the intellectual quality that constitutes or lies at the core of virtue? Socrates uses a cascade of different terms to describe it, moving rapidly from knowledge to correct usage, back to knowledge, then to active wisdom and intellect, back to active wisdom, and finally to good sense, but increasingly the focus is on active wisdom rather than knowledge (87d1–89a4). This movement is prepared by Socrates' initial statement that if virtue is teachable it must be not precisely knowledge but "the kind of thing knowledge is" (87b7). Yet Socrates makes these replacements without discussion and, in particular, without pausing to investigate precisely how active wisdom resembles factual knowledge and whether this resemblance extends to the crucial quality of being teachable.

As Socrates enumerates the qualities of soul that are unreliably good at 88a7–8, he almost lists the cardinal virtues but replaces wisdom with three other things: ease of learning (*eumatheia*), memory, and magnificence. The first two of these seem to be preconditions for wisdom and the third a natural expression of it, but all three can also give the appearance of a wisdom that is in fact absent. The first, *eumatheia*, contains an important ambiguity: it can mean a facility for true learning but can also mean mere tractability or docility. Magnificence, in Meno and perhaps also in his teacher Gorgias, whom he imitates, conveys the promise of wisdom, but if that magnificence is prematurely acquired it may even impede wisdom's development. Memory, previously identified with learning or wisdom, now turns out to need the guidance of intelligence or active wisdom if it is to be good at all. Most interesting is Socrates' discussion of courage, the virtue he chooses to illustrate the defectiveness of all other attributes in the absence of active wisdom. He gives two ways of understanding it at 88b2–4, as a boldness that is as likely to be harmful as beneficial and that needs the addition of active wisdom to be good, or as active wisdom itself, which would seem to be at once understanding and a virtue of character.[27] Socrates does nothing to help Meno understand the second alternative, which expresses the thought, elaborated in the *Protagoras*, that courage is nothing but "wisdom about what is terrible and not terrible" (360d4–5), perhaps meaning the capacity not only to see but to hold onto the truth about what is best in the face of every kind of fear. Socrates does not here settle the question of which alternative best defines courage; perhaps boldness that needs wisdom's guidance applies best to civic courage and active wisdom itself to philosophic courage. At the same time, Socrates identifies the wise use of courage as that which benefits its possessor: "Isn't it the case that when a human being is bold without intelligence, he is harmed, but with intelligence, he is benefited?" (88b4–6). Even as he makes the claim that active wisdom is the only unconditionally good thing, then, Socrates suggests that its goodness lies in its unerring power to secure other, unnamed good things, and to secure them for oneself. Thus he shows that Meno is in a strange condition regarding virtue, expecting it be utterly pure and unconditionally good, yet at the same time thinking of it mainly as an instrument of one's personal advantage. And once again, it is the self-interested thought that comes to the fore.

Socrates now asks Meno,

> In sum, then, do all the undertakings and acts of endurance of the soul result in happiness when active wisdom guides, but when folly guides, in the contrary? . . . If, then, virtue is one of the things in the soul, and it is necessary for it to be beneficial, it must be active wisdom, since indeed all the things pertaining to the soul, themselves by themselves, are neither beneficial nor harmful, but when active wisdom or folly is present in addition, they be-

> come beneficial and harmful. So according to this argument, virtue, being beneficial, must be a certain active wisdom. (88c1–d3)

Or, as he encourages Meno to agree a little later, with rather more caution, "Do we say, then, that virtue is active wisdom, either in whole or in part?" (89a3–4). As Bartlett and Bluck both observe, the qualification "in whole or in part" is ambiguous; it could be taken to refer to virtue, reopening the possibility that active wisdom is only part of virtue after all, but it could also be taken to refer to active wisdom, suggesting that it may be partly a virtue and partly something else.[28]

There are many difficulties with the argument that in fact give ample reason for the qualification of Socrates' final conclusion. Terms shift; premises are not defined; what is good as a final end is not specified; the power of chance is altogether denied. The argument elicits Meno's fractured hope that virtue as he conceives it, an intelligent form of the political virtue that governs the practical and political life and secures the goods conventionally pursued by that life, might be at once surpassingly good and the unerring means to acquire other good things for oneself. Socrates thus brings to the surface the extreme hopes that animate Meno's interest in virtue and that must also fuel his political ambition, leaving him ultimately dissatisfied with the moderate achievements that are possible through peaceful, lawful means.

If Socrates does not share this fractured, unrealistic hope for virtue understood as ordinary prudence, could there be some other sense in which active wisdom does meet the strong claims that Socrates makes for it, being somehow at the heart or at the helm of everything good and somehow invariably good in a way that does not depend on luck? His shifting use of the terms *knowledge, correct usage, intellect, good sense,* and *active wisdom* certainly invites us to ask which virtue or quality or possession he is ultimately making these strong claims for. Might the claims that do not hold for active wisdom as even the highest form of prudence be true for it when understood to comprise theoretical wisdom? Might the strangely qualified conclusion at 89a3–4 that virtue is active wisdom, in whole or in part, point to the true conclusion when the ambiguity is taken both ways? That is to say, active wisdom may be virtue in part, or part of virtue—constituting the whole of the highest virtue but only a part of popular virtue—and in part virtue—being also in part that theoretical knowledge which is not a virtue but an understanding whose possession and exercise are unqualifiedly good as ends, and as immune to the vicissitudes of fortune as anything human can be? And might the presence of the wisdom that is both practical and theoretical be essential to every possession or experience that is truly good? This is a radical thought; it would mean that no good quality, no bravery or generosity, no gift of fortune, none of the simplest pleasures, not even life itself, is intrinsically worth having except as informed by the thoughtful reflections of a rational mind. But it does accord with Socrates' initial suggestion that nothing is good that is "other than and separate from knowledge" (87d5), his statement that "all the undertakings and acts of endurance of the soul" and "all the things pertaining to the soul are, themselves by themselves, neither advantageous nor harmful" except when used by active wisdom (88c1–d1), and his claim in the *Apology* that the unexamined life is not worth living. Without at least a rudimentary self-understanding, every experience is but a hazy dream or a cauldron of confusion that is as such not good. In its complete form the human good comprises the possession and exercise of active wisdom, which includes a deep knowledge of ourselves and our diverse concerns, the strength to hold fast to our insights about the proper ordering of those concerns, and a basic and growing understanding of the cosmos and our place within it. True, to be enjoyed fully the activity of wisdom must be unimpeded, and this means that the human good requires freedom from such evils as debilitating pain and many resources that are good only when guided by wisdom, but these are refinements rather than refutations of Socrates' basic point. Thus the key claim of the *Meno* about virtue and knowledge proves to have a wholly coherent if radical meaning when it evolves, without fanfare, into a claim about virtue and active wisdom. Virtue in its highest sense is nothing but active wisdom, and active wisdom in turn is alone unqualifiedly good and encompasses or guides everything else that is truly good, even if it can never bring the invulnerability that Meno hopes for.

Socrates of course offers no proof here that active wisdom constitutes the human good in this radical way. He seems to come to this discussion already quite confident that it does and merely makes claims for it that are mystifying until we read them as claims for a wisdom that is at heart theoretical. In the same way, in the geometrical example he began with, he does not show how to determine the location of the lines he is discussing, but the relations he points out make sense and reveal something interesting once we have found them. Comparing the ratios between them, we can now confirm that the area is indeed inscribable and the figure was indeed correctly drawn. Perhaps Socrates, too, in going through this defective proof for the supreme value of knowledge, is engaged more in confirming something he has already figured out than in finding anything new.

Is Virtue by Nature?

Meno understands none of these far-reaching Socratic hints. Just as he fails to grasp the difference between teaching and learning, so he fails to grasp the difference between inert factual knowledge that can be "taught" and the wisdom that rules a self-governing soul, and likewise between habit-bred conventional virtue and the dialectically attained wisdom that Socrates calls true virtue. With a comical argument that abstracts from all of these distinctions, Socrates suddenly contends that the good people must not be good by nature.

> For if they were, I suppose the following too would be the case: if those who are good did arise by nature, I suppose there would be men who recognized for us those among the young whose natures are good. These we would take aside, once they had pointed them out, and guard them in the Acropolis, having them sealed up much more than we do gold so that no one might corrupt them, but rather, once they came of age, they might be useful to the cities. (89b1–b7)

Let us consider the premises of this proof. If virtue exists by nature, it must be born complete, like Athena from the head of Zeus, in need of no cultivation; if left to itself in society, virtue is nonetheless as likely to be corrupted as unguarded gold is to be stolen; despite the city's tendency to corrupt virtue, virtue is in fact supremely valuable to every city and will be recognized by at least some citizens; their efforts to protect it will have the full support of the rest, among whom must nevertheless be many would-be corruptors. The first premise is logical but extreme; this is indeed what it means for any quality to exist strictly by nature—like green eyes—but it is not the way most "natural" gifts are given us—such as a gift for playing baseball, or for eloquence. The other premises are surprising, and add up to such a strange supporting argument for the claim that virtue is not by nature that it provokes us to consider the extent to which the opposite claim might be true. Might true virtue indeed depend above all on having a most rare nature? Such is the suggestion of a similar but more cogent account of the relation of the good by nature to the city that Socrates gives in book 6 of the *Republic*. There he says that virtue is in need of cultivation as well as protection from corruption, that if anyone in a city is wise enough to know what the most promising youth really require, these people are so few and so isolated that they are rarely able to provide it, and that the gifted are in such danger of corruption because the fulfillment of their potential, culminating in the philosophic life, is in tension with the qualities and habits that the city wishes to cultivate to produce law-abiding citizens and especially leaders eager to serve them. Comparing that account with the one here in the *Meno* helps us see what this one ignores or abstracts from—most significantly the crucial distinction between philosophic and civic virtue and the possibility that the highest virtue does require rare natural gifts.

The more adequate version of this story in the *Republic* points back again to the fact that if virtue is "the kind of thing that knowledge is," it still must include not only the knowledge possessed but also the qualities of doggedness and courage needed to acquire it in the face of strong societal pressure against questioning received opinion. Contrary to Socrates' claim that active wisdom is the whole of virtue, doggedness and courage might seem to be additional virtues that belong to the subrational soul, requisites for gaining active wisdom but in no way that wisdom itself. But the curious thing about the drama of Meno is that in his subsequent career he will show no lack of boldness in battle or of doggedness in pursuit of gain. Precisely what does he lack, then, that Socrates possesses and cannot give him? It would seem to be a certain uncanny gift for seeing clearly what he needs and an ability never to lose sight of it. This capacity to grasp and not lose hold of insights in the face of pleasures and pains cannot properly be called knowledge, though knowledge is its goal. But is such steadiness and strength of vision not an aspect of active wisdom, perhaps indeed its most important part? And if one were to object that a strong *desire* for knowledge is also essential, being no part of wisdom, might Socrates not reply that the strength of this desire is nothing other than the steadiness of one's insight that knowledge is the good one needs above all others?

Thus while the argument about nature helps make clear why virtue cannot be solely the gift of nature or solely knowledge, it leaves intact the hypotheses that virtue is largely dependent on natural endowments and that it is active wisdom. This exploration of the sense in which virtue might be knowledge and the reasons why it cannot be simply knowledge, culminating here at 89b, may indeed be the high-water mark of the dialogue. But Meno gains no more clarity from the discussion than he has earned. The argument on its surface assumes that Socrates and Meno have shown that virtue is in no way the gift of nature and therefore must be altogether attainable by learning, which the careless Meno takes to mean is altogether teachable. Socrates will so easily refute this conclusion that Meno will give up on the equation of virtue with knowledge, so that the last part of the dialogue seems to undercut everything established in the first. But nothing stops both of the main arguments of the dialogue from being true: that virtue is active wisdom and that it is *not* in any ordinary sense teachable.[29]

Anytus and the Education of Citizens

Abandoning the distinction between knowledge and active wisdom that Meno has failed to grasp or to reflect upon, Socrates now concedes Meno's premise that all that is knowledge is teachable, even as he raises the suspicion that they have made a mistake somewhere in their equation of virtue with knowledge. Meno is reluctant to reopen a question that seemed settled, but Socrates insists that "it is necessary for it to seem nobly stated not only a moment ago, but also now and in the future too, if there is to be anything healthy in it" (89c8–10). To have a healthy soul is to live by principles that are persuasive when you look at them in every light, rather than at one time seeming noble and at another foolish, or at one time wise and at another ignoble or incomplete; it is to be free of Meno's characteristic waffling. Socrates continues, "As for its being something teachable, if it is knowledge, I don't retract this as being ignobly stated. But consider whether I seem to you reasonable in distrusting its being knowledge" (89d3–6). Since Meno has grasped neither the rarified meaning that Socrates gives to virtue nor the very limited extent to which this virtue is teachable, the rest of the dialogue will work from a conventionally political understanding of virtue, and likewise from an ordinary citizen's assumption that whatever is sensible in virtue can be taught through ordinary means by anyone who has it. As Socrates describes Meno's aspiration for virtue to Anytus, who has just come in, he desires "that wisdom and virtue by means of which human beings nobly manage both households and cities and tend to their own parents and know how both to receive and to send off citizens and guest-friends in a manner worthy of a good man" (91a1–6). But the two premises that virtue is both teachable and civic in character will soon collide. Socrates will argue that virtue must not be knowledge after all, because he can find no teachers or students of it and especially because the great men who most display it have been spectacularly unsuccessful in imparting their own virtue to their sons. His final conclusion will be that virtue must be an irrational gift of the gods, like the gift of prophetic inspiration.

What can Socrates' purpose be here? Most commentators, interested chiefly in the dialogue's teaching on knowledge, neglect this last, most political section, despite its obvious relevance to Socrates' conflict with the city of Athens. We may provisionally hypothesize that Socrates, finding Meno insufficiently intelligent or dogged to win philosophic virtue for himself, wishes to give him a second-best form of virtue, in the form of opinion supported by pious hopes. It quickly becomes clear, however, that Socrates' intentions in this section are at the very least more complex. What is most strange is the way he baits Anytus. Anytus, the son of a leather tanner and a popular leader in Athens, shares and gives vehement expression to the Athenian demos' hostility towards philosophy and especially towards the foreign sophists who are befriending the elite and educating their sons, teaching them to question traditional morals and to use rhetoric to gain political power. Immediately after telling Meno that he suspects that virtue is not teachable because he can find no teachers of it, Socrates turns to Anytus and provocatively suggests that the sophists are such teachers and that Meno's friends should send him to one of them. Then Socrates details with devastating thoroughness the failures of Athens' leading statesmen, past and present, to produce virtuous sons—again to the visible ire of the patriotic Anytus. Anytus' closing word to Socrates is a threat of prosecution if he does not stop making such speeches, to which Socrates gives an insulting reply (94e3–95a6). This is the last Plato's readers see of Anytus until he appears in the *Apology* as one of Socrates' prosecutors. Is Socrates deliberately provoking this indictment? Is there something crucial that the already elderly Socrates still wants to learn and hopes to learn from the discussion with Meno and Anytus, something valuable enough to risk alienating this dangerous man? Or might both be true: that having necessarily alienated such men and having worn out philosophy's welcome in Athens through an ongoing attempt to confirm his answers to crucial questions, Socrates must provoke a dramatic confrontation with the city in order to make it subsequently regret its hostility and become more tolerant of philosophy?

Whether Socrates learns anything new here, he certainly succeeds in eliciting from Anytus a strikingly vehement and ungrounded set of judgments about the sophists, their students, and the parents who allow those young people to study with them. In this exchange Socrates uncovers not only the ignorance behind Anytus' judgments about who possesses virtue but his confusion about the mental state of those who lack it. When Socrates suggests sending Meno to one of the sophists to learn virtue, Anytus swears,

> By Heracles, Socrates, hush. May no such madness seize anyone among my family or relatives or friends, whether citizen or foreigner, so that he goes to them to be ruined, since these plainly are the ruin and corruption of those who associate with them. (91c1–5)

Socrates only grows more provocative, professing astonishment that Protagoras in particular could have earned so much money and lived so long and even continued to that very day in such high repute if he had been an impostor—ignoring the fact that Protagoras died in a shipwreck fleeing charges of impiety after his books were burned at Athens. If such people were impostors who ruined their students, Socrates asks (anticipating his questions to Meletus about himself in the *Apology*), did they ruin them knowingly . . . and knowing what kind of hatred and ignominy they were sure to incur? Or were they completely deceived about themselves? Either way, he suggests, should we not count them as mad? (92a2–6). Socrates simplifies the picture of human motivations even as he tidies up Protagoras' life, suggesting that people are as capable of judging what is good for their souls and as intent upon getting it as they are able and ready to demand good shoe repairs (and, he comically suggests, as ready to stone bad cobblers as they are moral corruptors). As he did in the exchange with Meno at 77b2–78b2, Socrates leaves out the whole intermediate realm in which people desire and choose things that are bad for them, as well as the possibility of teachers' conspiring with their students to gain unfair advantage over others.

Anytus, by now almost apoplectic, replies that far from being mad, the sophists know exactly what they are doing; it is rather their students and especially the students' parents and cities that are mad for tolerating them. Under questioning, Anytus admits that he himself has never been harmed by a sophist, has never known any of them, and never wants to know any, but he knows who they are and is sure that they are wicked. If Anytus' prejudice is comical, his inability to give an account of the motives of the sophists and their students is more interesting. It seems to him insane to go or to send one's child to a corrupter: to be corrupted seems to him clearly the ruin of one's happiness. But if what is good and bad is as obvious as Anytus thinks, why do parents and children ever make this mistake? He can only say with exasperation that the whole enterprise is mad. At the same time, he cannot help believing that the corrupters themselves know what they are doing and are somehow gaining at the expense of those they prey upon. But again, he cannot give an account of what motivates them. He does not want to admit that there is something powerfully appealing, even to decent people, in what the sophists offer. If he were to acknowledge that they have found a sure path to prosperity and honor in the city, he could not present the simple life of decent, law-abiding people as obviously the best route to happiness. He is left viewing those who disobey and subvert the laws as just perverse, and evil as inexplicable. But at the same time he is sure that these people are not insane but rather are diabolically calculating and benefit themselves at others' expense. His incoherent rage grows out of this storm of shifting opinions.

To all this Socrates replies that Anytus must be a prophet to know such things on the basis of so little experience (92c6).[30] Anytus somehow represents the ancestral education and its claim that ultimately good men get their wisdom from the gods. But as Klein says, Socrates' statement also looks in the context like unflattering irony: Anytus does not know what he is talking about even if he happens to be right.[31] Still, Socrates professes himself ready to listen. Who of the Athenians are good teachers of virtue to the youth? he asks, just as he will later ask Meletus in the *Apology*. As Meletus does there, Anytus answers that all the gentlemanly, decent citizens are virtue's teachers. "Or," he asks, "isn't it your opinion that many good men have arisen in this city?" (93a3–4). To this Socrates replies, "It seems to me, Anytus, that there are those good at politics here and that there were such in the past no less than there are now. But they haven't been good teachers of their own virtue, have they?" (93a5–7). Socrates silently shifts the subject from virtue as a whole to political virtue. He thus implies that virtue in the full sense of complete wisdom may indeed be nowhere in evidence in Athens and that the best the city can offer is the virtue of its outstanding leaders. At the same time, he leaves out of consideration the ordinary civic virtue that is inferior to both but that at least has the advantage that it very often is successfully cultivated by ordinary parents in their ordinary children. Socrates reminds Anytus of what undistinguished men the sons of Themistocles, Aristides, Pericles, and the aristocratic leader Thucydides became, despite their purportedly good natures, their fathers' success in teaching them such skills as horsemanship, and their fathers' presumably greater desire to make them good men than good horsemen.[32] In focusing on such cases and omitting to discuss all the cases in which ordinary decent men raise decent sons, Socrates makes the case for the teachability of political virtue look far more hopeless than it is.

Why should ordinary civic virtue be more easily taught than the virtue of great statesmen? The difference seems to lie both in the availability of the necessary talents and the goodness for the individual of the life required. On one hand, any ordinary nature may be habituated to an ordinary respect for the laws, whereas great leadership ability requires talents that nature does not reliably bestow on sons of eminent men. On the other hand, it is possible to instill common law-abidingness in most ordinary human beings because, under any decent regime, they really are on the whole happier as decent men than as scoundrels, and they can be brought to see this, whereas it is less clear that the most gifted will be happiest in lives of public service. Extraordinary political virtue thus requires both rare gifts and a rare dedication to the common good that may be unteachable because it is less demonstrably good for the individual.

Socrates' first claim in this section—that the sophists teach virtue—and his second claim—that no one teaches virtue—may seem to have little in common except their success in outraging Anytus. But together they begin to illuminate for Meno the fork in the road that he faces. His choice, Socrates will suggest, is either to pursue excellence understood as cleverness in attaining what is best for himself, and to do so in the sophists' spirit of skepticism about traditional moral virtue, or to seek excellence in promoting the good of the city, taking seriously the possibility that this may not ultimately be a rational science and may result from or at least depend on belief in divine inspiration. Nevertheless, perhaps the most important thing Socrates has drawn out of Anytus—whether for his own edification or Meno's or that of someone else to whom he will relate this conversation—is that Anytus, who represents that noble aspect of virtue that Socrates will increasingly characterize as a kind of divine madness, still adamantly insists that virtue is thoroughly rational and as teachable as any craft.

Theognis on the Teachability of Virtue

Meno is by now completely bewildered. He says he admires Gorgias for never claiming to teach virtue and even laughing at the sophists who do, yet he himself still voices uncertainty as to whether there might not be teachers of it among the sophists. Socrates replies that all of the political men share Meno's ambivalence as to whether virtue can be taught, ignoring what would seem to be the strong contrary evidence just given by Anytus. Thus he implies that, somewhere beneath Anytus' loud confidence that virtue is teachable, he too must harbor a countervailing belief that virtue is at its core uncalculating and so not reducible to rational analysis or demonstration. Socrates also adduces the poet Theognis as an example of this ambivalence, quoting almost in full a cryptic but intricate poem in which Theognis seems to say that virtue both can and cannot be taught. Again, evident contradictions come to make sense once we distinguish the civic from philosophic virtue and their different modes of acquisition. Socrates begins with these lines:

> With them drink and eat, and with them
> Be seated, and be pleasing to them whose power is great.

> For from the noble you will have yourself taught noble things. But if with the bad you mingle, you will lose even the intellect you have. (95d4–e1)

Socrates gets Meno's ready concurrence that Theognis is implying here that virtue is teachable. But is Theognis' message quite so simple? What he says, more precisely, is that if one takes the initiative to seek out great men with a view to becoming like them, one will learn many noble things. Theognis does speak of learning but does not quite specify what is learned beyond saying that it is something noble; he does not say that one will learn the truth or gain intelligence or good sense. Surely one who associates with the great is likely to pick up their noble spirit and refined manners, as Meno has picked up the proud bearing of Gorgias, but how much else can one simply pick up, and can it ever include true understanding?[33]

On the other hand, Theognis says, associating by choice with the bad will bring one to resemble them and also make one lose what good sense one has. Theognis associates virtue with good sense, then, and vice with foolishness, but these connections are not quite symmetrical. Both natural good sense and a desire for improvement are needed to benefit from the company of even the wisest. And even if understanding does not rub off from good company, it can be ruined by bad company. Virtue and good sense have a certain vulnerability, then, especially when they rest mainly on habituation, imitation, and a desire for honor, but perhaps in every case in which virtue is not grounded in comprehensive, stable self-knowledge. Vice is more impervious than virtue to outside influence, in part because it involves an indulgence of natural pleasures and a coarsening and hardening of the soul against the influence of opinion.

After getting Meno's assent to a simple reading of these lines as implying that virtue is teachable without qualification, Socrates quotes the following from later in the poem:

> But if understanding could be produced and instilled in a man
> . . . [those who could do this] would earn much great pay . . .
> Never from a good father would there have arisen a bad man,
> If he is obedient to sober words. But by teaching
> You will never make the bad man good. (95e4–96a2)

The words "obedient to sober words" might equally well be translated as "persuaded by moderate myths." If every young person were willing to listen to reason, or at least to the stories that instill moderation, then indeed there would never be a bad son of a good man. Like Socrates, Theognis denies not that virtue can be learned but only that it can be imparted at will, pointing to the need for both natural ability and correct inclination as preconditions for its attainment. But once again Socrates does more to hinder than to help Meno in putting together the puzzling and seemingly contradictory opinions about virtue that he finds in himself and others, and in this case to see how Theognis' poem might indeed be thoughtfully coherent. Socrates' reserve, if not malicious, suggests a high threshold indeed for the independent contribution he judges it necessary for students to make in order to gain wisdom.

Knowledge vs. Opinion: The Statues of Daedalus

At this juncture Socrates begins pushing Meno towards the conclusion that there must not be a teachable science of virtue after all, since all the self-professed teachers of virtue are agreed to be worthless at cultivating it and all those agreed to be noble and good cannot make up their minds whether it is teachable or not—and no one can be an effective teacher of something about which he is so confused. A better student than Meno might object that the general negative opinion of the sophists is neither so unanimous nor so decisive as Socrates says, or that not all gentlemen would admit to any such ambivalence as Socrates attributes to them. He might also object that even if none of the famous sophists or statesmen teaches virtue, it still does not follow that no one anywhere has discovered or might discover the true nature of virtue and a means to teach it. Socrates twice gets Meno to agree that if there are no teachers of a thing there can be no students of it (96c1–2 and 8–9) but this would only hold if nothing were ever discovered by anyone for the first time—which a better student might also point out. Any of these objections would bring the conversation sharply back to the fundamental question of what virtue is. In the absence of such a response, Socrates quietly continues to narrow their working definition of virtue to its higher civic meaning: the virtuous man is above all a good leader. In doing so he moves (at 96e7–97a4) from the "correctly" made agreement that the virtuous man is beneficial, to the "nobly" made agreement that he is beneficial to others. Then, contradicting his earlier argument, he says that knowledge or active wisdom is not the essential precondition for human prospering and hence the essential core of virtue after all; correct opinion will do just as well (97a6–c5; contrast 87d2–89c4). And whereas before he denied any role to fortune in determining human happiness, now he begins preparing a dizzying elevation of something very much like fortune as *the* source of human prospering.

Meno does raise the sensible objection that opinion is less good because less reliable than knowledge; Socrates replies that so long as opinion is correct opinion, it will guide correctly (97c4–5). Thus he implicitly claims what he will explicitly affirm in the *Protagoras*, that not only knowledge but also opinion, at least when "correct," is efficacious in action. Meno cannot deny that correct opinion will guide correctly and immediately wonders why knowledge is so much more highly regarded. Socrates answers with essentially the same point Meno has just made about opinion's unreliability. Besides putting on display the ridiculous flightiness of Meno's opinions, what is Socrates up to?

Socrates' introduction to this important section of the dialogue sharpens for us the question of just what it is that makes opinion such an unreliable guide. Is it only its incompleteness? But is not all human knowledge incomplete? In fact, as Socrates now suggests, opinion is worse than incomplete: not only is it easily dislodged from its grounds but it has a positive proclivity to run away, like a human slave who longs for liberty, or like the lifelike statues of the mythical sculptor Daedalus. These statues, he says,

> if they haven't been tied down, escape and run away, but if tied down they stay put. . . . To possess one of his creations that's been untied isn't worth a very high price, just like a fugitive slave—for it doesn't stay put—but one that's been tied down is worth much. For the works are very beautiful (*kala*).
>
> In reference to what, then, do I say these things? In reference to the true opinions. For the true opinions, too, for so long as they stay put, are a noble (*kalon*) thing and accomplish all good things. Yet they aren't willing to stay put for a long time but run away from the soul of a human being so that they aren't worth much until someone ties them down by means of a calculation of cause. This, Meno, my comrade, is recollection, as was agreed to by us before. And once tied down, they first become knowledge, and then lasting. (97d4–98a6)

In describing the opinions that can become knowledge Socrates uses the term "true opinion," but in the surrounding discussion he alternates this expression with the not quite equivalent "correct opinion." Correct opinion may be correct because it is true, or merely because it instills good habits. Much of traditional civic education inculcates opinion of the latter sort. To some extent the statue analogy applies to both types of opinion, but Socrates makes it clear that the main function of the image is to explain a defect in true opinion.

In comparing human opinions to statues, Socrates highlights the imitative character of opinion and its potential to deceive in seeming to represent perfectly and even to be the things it in fact presents in embellished or distorted or simplified form. In calling the statues noble or beautiful and valuable, he suggests that a degree of nobility fairly obtains both in conventional moral opinions and in true ones. In comparing opinions to statues that run about, Socrates further suggests a comical resemblance between the fluidity of opinions and the spontaneous motion of living beings. The problem with opinions is not quite that they are easily pushed aside by the passions, like sentries made of stone; the problem is that they themselves contain or are bound up with desires in such a way that they are their own source of often ridiculous instability. In comparing opinions to slaves that yearn to flee, Socrates points to something in us that actively resists and chafes at the rule both of authoritative opinion and of truth. Correct opinion teaches citizens to obey their superiors, to stand their ground in battle, to remain faithful to their spouses, and always to tell the truth; in moments of temptation each of these opinions wavers and what seemed good before does not seem best now. When Socrates assures Meno that correct opinion guides as well as knowledge does, for as long as it is correct, he is abstracting from the crucial fact that mere opinion has a preternatural tendency to desert us, especially at the moments when we need it most.

What is the source of opinion's uncanny mobility? If true and correct opinions are like restless slaves who chafe at constraints upon both their desires and their dignity, then opinions' reasons for taking flight likely include both desire and spiritedness—desires for the pleasures and material gain that slave owners, authoritative civic opinion, and philosophy all seek to curb, and perhaps even more powerfully, the spirited yearning to feel one's freedom unobstructed by any external authority. Socrates' image of the loosened statue fleeing suggests that something tends to untie opinions and something else implicit in those opinions themselves sets them in motion. Perhaps it is in general countervailing desires that first loosen both our most noble correct opinions and our most thoughtful true ones, after which it is spirited pride that especially gives them feet and makes them rebels.

But while authoritative opinions do often run about and fail to govern those they should govern with a steady hand, they seldom run far. Socrates' image in the *Republic* of the cave and the fierceness with which its denizens attack those who seek to liberate them is a reminder of their enormous tenacity. Soldiers flee in battle but soon are ashamed; Meno himself displays flighty opinions in shifting from utilitarian to very noble views of virtue, but each of these views has a deep hold even on him, in spite of his unusually liberated education at the hands of Gorgias. Socrates makes clear that his real purpose with the statue analogy is to illuminate a problem in the progression from true opinion to knowledge (79e). Something in the experience even or especially of those who escape the cave causes their new insights to want to take flight. Socrates says that true opinion becomes knowledge "by means of a calculation of cause" (98a3–4). What sort of thinking about causes can tie down true opinions? We can best hold onto any truth if we know why it is so, and most of all if we know why it is necessarily so. In the case of truths about virtue, the tie would be provided by a deep understanding of human nature, the nature of human choice, and the causes of virtue and vice—just such things as Socrates has discussed in his two proofs that all wish for the good and that virtue is active wisdom. In moral knowledge the tie is especially necessary because here the opinions in us that ought to follow reason obediently are most inclined to rebel.[34] If the driving force behind the rebelliousness of both the slave and conventional opinion is a simple love of freedom and self-assertion, the tendency of true opinions to flee our grasp may be rooted in something related but even deeper in human nature, our desires to attribute to ourselves more cosmic importance than is justified, or to believe ourselves the uncaused causes of our characters and actions in a way that is not justified, with all the accompanying tendencies to place extreme demands on the world for recognition or recompense for our noble self-overcoming.

In the next line Socrates again obscures the meaning of this investigation that is needed by calling it "recollection" (98a4). But if we apply what we have seen about the full meaning of the recollection passage, we can say that the needed "tying down" is a version of the same process that we saw Socrates take the first steps through with the slave boy. The movement from true opinion to knowledge involves a process of clarifying an understanding that is somehow already present in us, drawing out the implications of what we already know, pruning away false opinions that we have picked up along the way, bringing our opinions into harmony, and then anchoring our insights by considering them "many times and in many ways," as Socrates says the slave must do to turn his opinion about the square root of two into knowledge (85c9–d1). Meno's slave probably lacked the intelligence to do this for himself, but as a servant evidently well-trained to listen to his master's commands and humble enough to admit his ignorance (unlike his master), he exemplifies the compliant qualities that our thoughts need if they are to serve us well.

But of course a servant needs practice in his work as well as docility, as does our incipient knowledge. Socrates underscores the importance of practice in his striking comment about the order of progress towards stable knowledge: once tied down, he says, true opinions "first become knowledge, and then lasting" (98a5–6). Not only correct opinion and even true opinion but knowledge itself is prone to slip away unless we habituate our souls to accept and live by it. And this is again true especially of the knowledge that is the chief subject of the *Meno*, knowledge of virtue. Is not "recollection" an apt characterization of the lasting, efficacious knowledge or active wisdom that is virtue, inasmuch as to be wise means repeatedly "recollecting" what one has come to know about the good, especially in the heat of provocation or temptation when we are most inclined to forget it?

Xenophon expresses the same thought with the same sober realism in *Memorabilia* 1.2.12–16, where he describes Socrates' failure in educating Alcibiades and Critias. It was not that these young students failed to learn what Socrates had to teach; in a sense they grasped his insights clearly and could even entrap others in the contradictions that he had shown them in themselves. But their knowledge had no staying power. Behind and even perhaps somewhere within their opinion that Socrates was admirable was a contrary thought that made this one take flight when Socrates was not there to remind and chastise them, a thought that said that not Socrates but the popular and powerful leaders of democratic Athens had a dignified life worth emulating. Xenophon even takes the occasion to rebut a popular interpretation of the Socratic thesis, in a way that accords perfectly with Socrates' emphasis here on the practice needed to tie insights down:

> Now perhaps many of those who claim to philosophize would say that one who is just would never become unjust, nor would the moderate one ever become insolent, nor would anyone who had learned anything else that can be learned ever lose that knowledge. But I, for my part, do not reach the same judgment about these matters. For I see that, just as those who do not train the body are unable to do bodily work, so also those who do not train the soul are unable to do the work of the soul. For they are able neither to do what they should nor to refrain from what they should not. . . .
>
> I, too, am a witness to these things. For I see that, just as those who do not practice forget verses composed in meter, so also forgetfulness occurs in those neglecting the speeches that teach. And when someone forgets the speeches that admonish, he has forgotten also the things that the soul experienced when it desired moderation. As he has forgotten these, it is no wonder that he forgets moderation as well. (*Memorabilia* 1.2.17–21.)

Xenophon does not deny that virtue is some kind of knowledge, but it is a knowledge that requires practice if it is not to desert us. Both the account of the statues of Daedalus in the *Meno* and this passage from the *Memorabilia* suggest the same thing: that knowledge when present is efficacious, but not effortlessly so, nor does its mere presence guarantee its own stability. On a small scale and the short term, we can see this phenomenon in struggles with moderation. Even in extreme cases, when the penalty for immoderation is most immediately vivid and the knowledge of what is good is most easily available, knowledge can fail us. A person who suffers from lactose intolerance may possess all the information he can possibly need to tell him that he really has this deficiency and that the pleasure of the ice cream he desires is not worth the price he will pay subsequently in sleepless indigestion. If he keeps his knowledge clearly in view, it will be efficacious. But since knowledge of what is the best among our imperfect options does not necessarily dispel the desire for everything else that would be pleasant, he may still need to make an active effort to remember the unpleasant consequences that his desire makes him want to forget. His knowledge, Socrates would say, is intermittent and not yet lasting. More generally, the soul that desires moderation in Xenophon's account may have sufficient information about why a moderate life will bring him more happiness than an immoderate life, but he still must practice attending to that knowledge so that it becomes not just a passing notion but a stable and lasting part of the knowledge that governs his life. Then in times of temptation he will prevail, not effortlessly but reliably, which is why Xenophon presents Socrates as a master of self-control or *enkrateia* rather than effortlessly virtuous.

But if Socrates grants the need for self-control, is this not to admit that the failure of self-control (*akrasia*) is possible, and does Socrates not famously deny this? No, not wholly: he denies that we may act against knowledge that we possess, but he does not deny that we may act against knowledge that we usually possess and have temporarily lost and may again have when we see and regret what we have done. A wise person's knowledge will be more steadily available because he has schooled himself to keep it in view, but at moments of temptation he will still need vigilance to do so, rather as a good hiker needs vigilance not to slip on a steep path, but being a good hiker, he will exercise that vigilance and will not slip.[35]

Socrates, however, is in fact very cautious in his claim that knowledge is attainable at all. He says to Meno,

> I say this not as one who knows but as one who conjectures. But that correct opinion is something different from knowledge, it doesn't seem to me that I'm conjecturing this, but if indeed I would say I know anything else—and I

> would say this of few things—I would put down this too among those things that I know. (98b1–5)

That the knowledge that we need is attainable, that it emerges out of true opinion through a dialectical process of questioning and examination and repeated consideration, and that it requires some such process of "tying down" as a slave needs to become a useful servant, all remains in Socrates' mind only an excellent conjecture. The strongest alternative in his mind is presumably the pious view that the knowledge we need comes not through any such human efforts but through divine inspiration. Indeed, this whole dialogue may be at bottom one more attempt of the already old Socrates to tie down his thesis about the accessibility and character of human knowledge a little more firmly. But that knowledge is not the same thing as correct opinion, this Socrates already knows with full confidence. Even if he were certain of nothing else, he is still sure that the opinions that guide communities well are not knowledge, for they contain confusions and self-contradictions, and we know that by knowledge we mean something intelligible and clear. But even to be certain of this much is to know we know that some knowledge is possible, if only knowledge about thought itself; hence perfect skepticism is untenable. Significantly, however, Socrates claims certainty only about the difference between correct opinion and knowledge, not about that between true opinion and knowledge. We know that an opinion that is confused and self-contradictory cannot be knowledge. We hope that we have access not only to true opinions in the form of intelligible and clear thoughts that express well what we experience, but to knowledge that goes beyond this in accurately representing permanent truths about the world, but Socrates claims no certainty that we do. Perhaps the difference between true opinion and our necessarily incomplete knowledge is at most one of degree. But that our original, defective opinions are not knowledge, that we need knowledge, and hence that we need with courage and perseverance to pursue it, by all means possible, this we know, and this is all we need to know in order to know what we most need to do (cf. 86b6–c2).

Philosophy's Collision with the City

For a moment, in response to Meno's objection at 97c, Socrates has offered a fascinating glimpse of his own thought about what wisdom is and how it is acquired, a glimpse that Meno would require careful questioning and reflection to understand. But in the absence of further active engagement from Meno, Socrates returns at the end of the dialogue to praising correct opinion, which he now identifies as the source of all the great Athenian leaders' wisdom and which he attributes in turn to divine inspiration. Thus the pregnant discussion of the statues of Daedalus is left behind as a forgotten digression.[36] So completely is the argument of the Daedalus passage neglected now that right after acknowledging the existence of practical knowledge (beginning with the most mundane and undeniably attainable knowledge of which road leads to Larissa), explaining how it differs from mere opinion, and indicating what work one must do to secure it for oneself, Socrates concludes that if virtue is not given by teachers then it must not be knowledge, that knowledge must be unattainable, and that true or correct opinion (which he no longer bothers to distinguish) must be the only source of guidance in human affairs. The argument mirrors perfectly the human drama of the dialogue: what is hopeless for Meno because of his character is presented as hopeless altogether.

The result is extreme indeed. Denying that any of the great Athenian statesmen had knowledge, Socrates says they did what they did only by divine inspiration (99c3–5 and 7–9). In the absence of true knowledge of the good, virtue can arise only through divine inspiration—or perhaps through belief in divine inspiration or support, whether explicit or deeply submerged. But Socrates is harsh in this denial: he claims that Themistocles at the helm of Athens no more knew what he was doing or saying than the priestesses mumbling oracles in a trance at Delphi. He points out five times in short succession the mindlessness of those who have only opinion and not knowledge, saying that these statesmen "were not wise" (99b5), that like soothsayers and prophets, such men say many things in an inspired state and yet "know nothing of what they say" (99c3–5; cf. Plato *Apology* 22b8–c2); that they "don't possess intellect" (99c8), that again they "succeed by speaking about many great matters, though they know nothing of what they say" (99d4–5), and that they are "without intellect" (99e6). Almost his last word in the dialogue is a comparison of such statesmen to gibbering shades flitting about mindlessly in Hades (100a2–7). What Socrates says guides these statesmen is indeed not even quite true or correct opinion but *eudoxia* (99b11). Since this word most often has the meaning "good repute," or conformity to generally reputable opinions, Socrates may be suggesting that the statesmen guide affairs in a way that seems divinely inspired mainly by attending closely to common opinion.[37] This Socrates implies ironically when he likens Anytus to a diviner after it becomes clear that Anytus' judgment of the sophists rests only on a popular prejudice.

Anytus, a statesman who believes himself rational and sensible, is predictably furious at the suggestion that statesmen do what they do only by divine inspiration. But Meno is surprisingly open to this idea. Though Meno is a student of Gorgias drawn to the view that virtue is the capacity to secure what is good for oneself and an evident rationalist who had no time to stay in Athens for the most solemn of its religious festivals, Socrates has uncovered in him a deep attraction to the divine and an admiration for the splendor of uncalculating self-forgetting. No doubt it is easier for Meno than for the politically active Anytus to attribute irrationality to outstanding political virtue, but that does not stop him from admiring that virtue from afar, perhaps in the way that Shakespeare's Cassius admires but cannot quite join or judge as sensible the intense moral purity of Brutus, or the way ordinary religious believers tend to regard ascetic saints as noble and inspired but perhaps not completely sober. This is the admiring view that Socrates leaves Meno with. Will it stick? To Anytus' obvious anger Socrates gives a rude and dismissive reply; in response to Meno's admiration he reminds him that they still do not know what virtue is, and with a lame excuse he takes his leave.

What has Socrates done with Meno? To put the most benevolent interpretation on his actions, we might say that he is testing Meno to see if he is philosophically promising, finds that he is not, and so gives him a pious story in hopes of at least partially replacing for him the unattainable wisdom that would have given a solid grounding for virtue. To assess this hypothesis we would have to determine when Meno's lack of promise becomes evident and consider what Socrates says and does not say after that point; if his lack of promise is clear at least by the stingray comment at 79e7 ff., we would have to explain why Socrates returns after that point to suggesting that virtue is active wisdom about one's own advantage (88a2–b6). An alternative interpretation is that Socrates is studying and even experimenting on Meno. Having found him poor material for philosophy, he may still wish to lay before Meno two memorable but incompatible ways of thinking about virtue—as shrewd, selfish knowledge of one's own good, and as divinely inspired selflessness—and then step back and see what happens. His first interest may be simply in confirming for himself that everyone who is honest must acknowledge a powerful attraction to *both* of these ways of viewing virtue. Second, knowing that Meno is thoughtful enough to keep reflecting on what he has said, Socrates deliberately leaves him with an unsatisfactory conclusion as the best way to keep him thinking.[38] Socrates may want to see how Meno will change if he comes to side more fully with one or the other of these inclinations, now that they have both been brought to the surface and into explicit competition. Perhaps Meno will become a pious civic-minded leader, or perhaps (as turns out) a hard-boiled self-aggrandizer who thinks active wisdom is achievable after all and that the only difference between superior and inferior people is the former's ability to get for themselves the vulgar goods most people envy. Either way, Meno's development may confirm a Socratic hypothesis about the connection between morality and piety. But if Socrates is experimenting in this way, is it not dangerous and perhaps inexcusably reckless? Could the *Meno* be Plato's own indictment of Socrates, on the grounds that he gave too little thought to the character of those upon whom he tried out his arguments—a charge that Xenophon too suggests might at least be reasonably raised?[39]

And what is Socrates' purpose with Anytus? If in Meno Socrates has taken a politically ambitious youth who seemed enlightened and irreligious, who showed no indignation and little evident concern with justice or desert, and brought him to a state of perplexity and frustration that cracked open his yearning for the divine and uncovered in him a deep admiration for the noble as something irreducible to or even incompatible with one's own good, with Anytus he has done just the opposite. He has taken a political man with an intense spirit of moral indignation even on behalf of people he does not know, a man who hates the rationalist sophists even without any experience of them, and has shown that nonetheless he is profoundly committed to the view that virtue is rational, is good for the virtuous man, and is teachable. If Anytus could be persuaded that virtue is just a matter of divine grace, a selfless form of service that is not and need not be rational, Socrates would trouble him less and he in turn would pose less danger to Socrates. Whatever Socrates might say, Anytus could shrug and say to himself, "The gods have not spoken to Socrates." For this very reason, however, Anytus' sublime self-confidence would pose a serious challenge to Socrates' rationalist philosophy, for how can Socrates *know* that Anytus is wrong? As it is, Anytus' anger shows that Socrates, like the sophists, has gotten under his skin, revealing a deep, uneasy recognition that their rationalist enterprise is by no means just craziness or foolishness and that it poses a serious challenge to the beliefs he is committed to. Socrates cannot be surprised by Anytus' anger; at best it only confirms hypotheses he has long held. Yet the way he provokes and departs from Anytus also suggests that he is deliberately courting the hostility that will result in his execution.

What, lastly, is Plato doing here with us? This dialogue has shown us the limitations of, and at the same time the deep element of truth in, the claim that virtue is knowledge. This claim would be unqualifiedly true only if virtue were a body of knowledge that one person could bestow on another and that needed nothing but mental acuity to grasp and to put to use. This in turn would hold only if the truths that nature or the teacher offered to our attention were opposed by no important passions in us that need to be overcome. As it is, powerful passions in us resist the truth when we begin to glimpse it, resist our following it when we think we have accepted it, and resist our sorting out the confusions and contradictions that keep us ambivalent and that our lapses ought to spur us to think through. A key reason for all of these difficulties that has emerged in the dialogue is that virtue in fact has two separate meanings, as philosophic and as civic, which are not wholly compatible but which are both powerfully attractive.

What qualities does true virtue need, then, besides intelligence? This dialogue illustrates them both by their presence and by their absence. Clearly needed first of all is the desire for knowledge, which both the slave boy and Anytus lack but which Meno seems to possess in common with Socrates. But also required are several qualities that Meno lacks but that his slave possesses in common with Socrates: a willingness to admit ignorance and error, a docility in following the lead of reason wherever it may take us, and a willingness to apply oneself diligently to the task at hand, however little it may please or flatter one's pride. By their absence in the slave we note the passions and the habits that most oppose knowledge: spirited pride and a false love of freedom understood as indulging one's whims, one's pride, and one's laziness. In Meno we see the stew of pride, conflicting hopes, and softness that keep his opinions unmoored. In Protagoras we will see a far superior interlocutor, one who claims both to know and to teach virtue, and in the dialogue that carries his name a richer exploration of the nature of human excellence and of the inner unity that virtue in its full flowering possesses. For as Socrates says at the end of this work, he and Meno have explored the question of how virtue is acquired but have not yet adequately answered the question of what virtue is: that exploration is pursued nowhere more deeply than in the *Protagoras*.

FOUR

The Unity of Virtue: *Protagoras*

Introduction and Framing Scenes (309a1–16a5)

The central theme of the *Protagoras* is the unity or disunity of the virtues. This issue is intimately connected to our question of whether virtue is knowledge or wisdom. For if virtue is either, it is clearly a unity, and if the particular virtues are ultimately unified, they must be different expressions of a single principle of action, a comprehensive understanding of what is good being one of the best candidates for such a principle. Again we find in the *Protagoras*, as in the *Apology*, the *Gorgias*, and the *Meno*, explorations of the power of knowledge or wisdom linked thematically with discussions of the rationality of retribution; of education and corruption; of the relationship between rhetoric, sophistry, and philosophy; and of the tension between the intellectuals who practice these arts and the ancient polis. Here again, as in the *Gorgias*, we have a dialogue named for one of the famous but somewhat disreputable intellectuals of Socrates' day, in this case the sophist Protagoras, who turns out to have much in common with the younger and at this point much less well-known Socrates. Both Protagoras and Socrates are engaged in luring promising young men away from their fathers and guardians; both have unconventional views on justice and the gods; and both have an interest not only in politics but in investigating the things in the heavens and under the earth. Ultimately both would die as a result of the hostility of the city of Athens, Socrates by execution and Protagoras in a shipwreck, fleeing the city after his books were burned there in the year 420.[1] In this dialogue we have some of Socrates' most impressive interlocutors, not only an assembly of sophists gathered in the house of Callias and led by the wily Protagoras but, by proxy, the wise poet

Simonides. In it, we will thus see more of what Socrates shares and does not share with his most enlightened fellow Greeks, more of how he understands the wisdom that he identifies with true virtue, and an especially rich investigation of the relation between wisdom and the one virtue that seems hardest to subsume under it, courage.

In the opening scenes of the dialogue, however, Socrates is at pains to emphasize the differences between himself and Protagoras. The dialogue's framing story of Socrates' early morning encounter with Hippocrates has the function of emphasizing this distance. Socrates presents himself as a simple, sturdy citizen of democratic Athens, in contrast to the sophisticated foreign sophists who lurk almost shade-like in a kind of underworld in Callias' house. When the young Hippocrates shows his "courage and impetuosity" (310d3) by rushing to Socrates before dawn and demanding that he take him to Protagoras and persuade the famous teacher to accept him as a student, Socrates engages him in a discussion "to test his resolve" (311b1). Impetuosity is not yet resolution or strength, without which learning would seem to be futile and perhaps even harmful. But Socrates also warns of the dangers of ingesting into the soul the "learnings" of the sophists without knowing in advance whether they are beneficial or harmful (313c4–14b4), implying not only that virtue is not knowledge but that some knowledge may be fatal to virtue. In the same way, he will voice to Protagoras the democratic view that the ability to grasp moral and political questions is not a matter of expertise but something possessed equally by all (319a8–20b5). Therefore, he suggests, Protagoras' professed art of teaching the political art to the young is almost certainly a sham.

But clearly there is also much that is ironic in this anti-sophistic stance of Socrates, as Plato reveals from the very beginning of the dialogue. For the framing story of Socrates and Hippocrates has itself a framing story in which Socrates relates his whole conversation with the sophists to some nameless companions, and if Socrates is eager to tell them all about the warnings he has given Hippocrates, he also confides to them that he himself is totally smitten with Protagoras. While Hippocrates and the other companions learn of Protagoras' unpublicized arrival in Athens only on the third day, Socrates has known of it from the start and has evidently been spending time with him, even if he has waited until today to take him on in a public contest.[2] Socrates, for all his protestations that he is not a sophist, is taken for one by the lowly doorman who hears him conversing on some theoretical topic with Hippocrates in the courtyard. Finally, although Socrates will adopt here the democratic position that there are no expert teachers of virtue (319a8 ff.), it is at least strange, as he himself points out (361a3–c2), that he should be the one to do so, when he is also the one who argues that virtue is knowledge or something akin to it—and when elsewhere he argues that only a few teach virtue and the many are corrupters (*Apology* 24d1 ff., *Republic* 492a–c and 494b–e).

Now if Socrates does much and perhaps Plato still more to distance Socrates from the sophists in popular opinion, these ironic elements of the *Protagoras* raise the question of whether the difference may not have been considerably smaller than is usually supposed—and whether Plato does not wish this truth too to be somehow preserved. Plato encourages us to view Socrates as the radically original inventor of political philosophy and the only genuine heir of the pre-Socratics, who defended philosophy against the distortions and abuses of the mercenary sophists. But Stauffer, in a thoughtful essay on Socrates' relation to the sophists, makes the intriguing suggestion that it may be more accurate to view Socrates as "a new kind of sophist, practicing a modified version of the sophistic art."[3] If it is part of Socrates' and especially Plato's rhetorical project to present Socrates as the moral opponent of the immoral sophists, and if at the same time it is a requisite of Plato's philosophical project that he provide access to the full truth of who Socrates was, may we not find important clues to Socrates' own thought in the statements of Protagoras, who boasts of saying openly what all of the ancient wise men, beginning with Homer and Hesiod, have secretly thought in common (316d3–17c5)? In particular, might the idea that virtue is knowledge or wisdom be an important part of the common ground between Socrates and all of the sophists?

But if Socrates was a different kind of sophist, we would also expect to find significant differences in the way he and the others understood the equation of virtue with knowledge or wisdom. The impression Socrates gives at the beginning of the *Protagoras* is that he rejects the thesis entirely on the basis of moral and political beliefs he shares with democratic Athens; the impression he gives at the end is that he accepts it even more thoroughly than Protagoras does. But if there is, then, much irony in the first suggestion, might there not also be a serious thought there—that Socrates, living as a citizen and taking more seriously than does the itinerant cosmopolitan Protagoras the civic and moral outlook of the citizen, or the moral aspirations of the city to be a worthy object of reverence and love, understands objections to the virtue-is-knowledge thesis that Protagoras, in his overly hasty dismissal of conventional opinion, has missed? Hence, having thought through these objections, Socrates may have articulated more clearly the sense in which the thesis is still true, and may have digested this truth more deeply than Protagoras. Thus, in making the extreme claims for knowledge that he makes in this dialogue, Socrates would be both using a piece of defensive rhetoric adapted from the sophists and also giving indications as to the core of his most serious thought.

Intriguing further clues as to the way in which Socrates may have been a different kind of sophist may be found in the rich references to Homer throughout the first part of the dialogue. In retelling the dialogues to his companions in the first framing scene, Socrates compares the charm of Alcibiades to that of Hermes. He alludes to the passage in book 24 of the *Iliad* where Hermes protects Priam against the hostile Greeks, and, in the only reference to nature in all of Homer, the passage in the *Odyssey* where Hermes shows Odysseus the plant whose "nature" is to make one immune to the spell or enchantment of the gods (10.280–306). In the third framing scene, after Socrates arrives with Hippocrates at the house of Callias, Socrates compares the sophists Hippias and Prodicus to the shades of the Greek heroes that Odysseus encounters in Hades in book 11 of the *Odyssey*. By implication, then, he compares himself to the wily Odysseus, very much the old companion of these shades. But unlike the shades, Odysseus has his wits fully about him and will succeed in winning his homecoming against the opposition of a hostile god, by using the root whose nature is to make one resist the charms of the divinities, by coming to Hades to investigate the thing under the earth, and by questioning the prophet Teiresias. May Socrates have found a way to contend with the challenge posed, by the gods or revelation, to philosophy in a way that the other sophists did not? Protagoras, on the other hand, Socrates compares not to the shade of a hero in Hades but to Orpheus, who like Odysseus went down alive into the underworld but failed to accomplish his mission of rescuing Euridice because, in a moment of fear, he looked back; the myth has it that he later died at the hands of women. This comparison would suggest that Protagoras of all the sophists is the shrewdest and most perceptive, but less courageous or steadfast than Socrates and hence unable in the end to win a satisfactory homecoming.

The Wisdom of the Ancients and the Art of the Sophists (316a6–320c1)

When Socrates tells Protagoras that he and Hippocrates have come especially to see him, Protagoras, who needs no introduction to Socrates and shows no curiosity about Hippocrates, asks merely whether they wish for a private interview or a public one. The fact that Protagoras is prepared to break off a lecture he is giving before many admiring followers to talk privately with Socrates testifies to the esteem he already has for him. Socrates suggests that Protagoras should choose between a public and private interview after hearing why they have come; he then proceeds to introduce Hippocrates as a potential student in terms that are at once carefully respectful and carefully guarded. While explicitly raising the subject of Hippocrates' nature, Socrates vouches only for his good family and good reputation (316b8–c2). We are not told whether Socrates considers it wisest for a teacher to interview a potential student in private; if so, it might be either to encourage frankness on the student's part or to provide greater safety for the teacher.

Protagoras, however, shows no interest either in hearing about Hippocrates' nature or in testing if for himself: he addresses only the potential concern with his own safety. Thanking Socrates for his solicitude or forethought,[4] Protagoras acknowledges the dangers of envy and hostility that he faces as a foreigner who comes to great cities and who encourages the noblest of the youth to prefer his company to that of their kinfolk. What he does not mention is the hostility much worse than personal envy that citizens often displayed towards these men who taught students to take their bearings from nature and to despise as mere conventions the laws and moral teachings of their fathers. Protagoras asserts, nonetheless, that he seeks his safety in frankness rather than in secrecy. In this he claims to have found a new approach to the old art of sophistry, which he says very many of the poets and famous wise men and others have covertly practiced, beginning with Homer and Hesiod.[5] Protagoras, the greatest of the sophists, thus claims a far closer resemblance than was normally suspected between his activity and that of the revered educators of Greece.[6] Even if Homer and the other great poets never taught students for pay, still Protagoras suggests that they, no less than the fifth-century sophists, had revolutionary teachings that they wished to shield from public gaze. But Protagoras, whose name means "first to speak out" or "first to address the public assembly," argues that the sophists of old did not escape detection and that their secrecy only brought them into ill repute. "So for the one who tries to run away and is not able to escape but is clearly seen, the attempt is very foolish, and it necessarily makes human beings much more ill disposed to him. For in addition to everything else, they consider such a person a scoundrel" (317a6–b3). By acknowledging openly that he practices the art of sophistry and by taking other precautions that he declines to specify, Protagoras boasts that he has lived safely to a great age.

All of this is most intriguing, but does Protagoras' account of his and the great poets' contrasting strategies make sense? In what way were they found out? Even if sophisticated Greeks agreed in attributing to their poems great subtlety and wisdom beyond what is at first apparent, none of the poets was ever prosecuted as Protagoras would be. In the passage just quoted, Protagoras presents his predecessors as foolish and his own approach as purely prudential. But if the brilliant Protagoras' policy was in fact less prudent, might it not also have been motivated by something other than a concern for safety? Given the pride he expresses in his speech, it seems likely that a distaste for disowning a profession he was proud of contributed to his departure from his predecessors' more cautious esotericism. And yet, if Protagoras is distinguished from his predecessors especially by a manly love of frank speech, is he even wholly courageous in his practice of it? After all, he is speaking out not in the agora but virtually underground, in the midst of a friendly gathering in Callias' well-guarded house, which he seldom if ever leaves during his stay in Athens. Moreover, even in praising bold frankness he proves himself a flatterer of his aristocratic audience, with his claim that the "many" perceive so to speak nothing at all and merely repeat whatever the great men in their society say, while the great are impossible to deceive (317a2–b3). But lest we attribute to Socrates a prudence that Protagoras lacked, we must remember that Socrates in the end met the same fate as he. If there is any difference between the two in point of prudence, perhaps it is only that Socrates was not driven by pride to take risks without reason.

Of course the possibility remains that Protagoras is only pretending to be hiding in plain view and only pretending to think that the elite parents of his students have seen through the guise of Homer and others, as a way of flattering and disarming them. If so, his Promethean courage may be only an act. Or the truth may be even more complex. Protagoras may think that in his pretended openness he is fooling most of the people most of the time—and yet he may harbor a secret admiration for Promethean courage that undercuts his cautious prudence and his willingness to say that cautious prudence is the sum of virtue. And this possibility will in fact be borne out by the rest of the dialogue.

When Protagoras has expressed the desire to display his educational wares before the whole gathering and his host has obligingly assembled all the guests, Protagoras asks Socrates to repeat his reason for coming so that those who were not present before might hear it. Socrates repeats his statement (cf. 316b8–c4 with 318a1–5), but, since no repetition in Plato is ever simply a repetition and every revision is potentially significant, we note that Socrates now omits his prior comments on Hippocrates' nature. Evidently he realizes that Protagoras is not interested in his potential student's natural endowments, an inference immediately confirmed by Protagoras' first words to Hippocrates:

> Young man, it will be possible for you, if you associate with me, on the day you do get together with me, to go home in a better state, and the same holds for the next day as well. In fact, every day you will continually progress in improvement. (318a6–9)

Protagoras thus expresses confidence that his art may be profitably taught to anyone with any ordinary degree of alertness and will reliably produce virtue of some kind. On the question of whether and to what extent virtue is knowledge or wisdom, Socrates appears to differ significantly from the sophists in giving much more weight to the natural soil in which learning must take root if it is to bear good fruit. But again, we may ask, does Protagoras really believe his own advertising, or is he exaggerating for the sake of money and fame? Either way, Plato indicates here that he may not be thinking enough about natural differences and the dangers that learning may pose to the wrong natures; this carelessness may be connected to a limitation in his understanding of the origin and essence of virtue itself.

And what Socrates immediately presses is the question of what virtue is. One way of understanding virtue is that it is an art. Exactly what kind of art do you profess, he asks Protagoras, and what kind of virtue or improvement are you promising? To make his question perfectly clear, he gives as examples a painter and an aulos player, who are both skilled practitioners of relatively high arts and able to teach their skill to students. Protagoras, however, replies that he, alone among the sophists, does not subject his students to the study of any art at all.

> "For the others abuse the young. For although the young have fled the arts, they lead them against their will and plunge them back into the arts, teaching them calculation and astronomy and geometry and music"—and as he said this he glanced at Hippias—"but coming to me he will not learn about anything except what he came for. And this study is good counsel about his own affairs, that he may best manage his own household, and concerning the city's affairs, how with respect to the city's affairs he might be most capable of acting and speaking." (318d9–19a2)

The arts, as he presents them, are full of drudgery and petty in their exacting demands for precision; what he teaches is in every way more noble, more magnificent, and more satisfying.

Socrates, however, wonders whether Protagoras has an adequate account to give of this ability that he claims to teach, and he probes him by continuing to insist that it must be some art, and even coining a name for it: "Do I follow your argument? . . . For you seem to speak of the political art and to promise to make men good citizens" (319a3–5). By adding what Protagoras did not say, that he makes men good citizens, Socrates offers him a respectable presentation for his enterprise; Protagoras' own statement is compatible with his teaching students to manage both private and public affairs in whatever way is most profitable to themselves. Protagoras, taken with Socrates' definition, replies, "That is indeed, Socrates . . . the very profession that I profess" (319a6–7). He turns out to be ambivalent on the question of whether what he teaches is an art, just as he is evasive and perhaps ambivalent on the question of who the chief beneficiary of his activity is—whether it is the public, his students, or himself.[7] But if one is not even perfectly clear about whose good one's activity is intended to secure, can what one practices be a true art?

And indeed, no sooner has Socrates introduced the art of politics than he questions whether anyone is in fact a master or at least a teacher of it: "'It is, to be sure, a noble craft you possess,' I said, 'if in fact you do possess it. . . . For I didn't suppose this to be something teachable'" (319a8–b1).[8] Socrates' argument that the art of politics cannot be taught has two parts. First, he observes that the Athenians summon experts to consult on everything they consider to be a matter of teaching and learning, but they treat everyone as competent to deliberate about the management of the city's affairs. Hence they must consider this competency to be one in which there is no school of experts, and being wise, they must be right. Surely there is no small irony in this proof. The fact that the Athenians allow just anyone to enter into the discussion of the greatest affairs may be taken to illustrate the folly of democracy as much as it does the unteachable character of political prudence. But Socrates is also pointing to a curious fact: though almost any layman would immediately show his incompetence in a craft for which he had no training, democracies are not obviously less competent in managing their common concerns than are other regimes.

The second part of Socrates' argument takes its sights not from the ordinary practices of democratic Athens but from the experience of its greatest leaders: "Not only is this the case with the city's common affairs, but in private, too, the wisest and best of the political men are not able to bestow on others the virtue that they have" (319d7–e3). Now Socrates makes a subtle shift from the ability to give sound advice, which many may have, at least sporadically, to the virtue of a great statesman as a rare possession that presumably includes both excellent judgment and great public-spiritedness. Not the nonexistence but the unteachability of political excellence in this sense is what makes democracy a plausible regime, even in a world in which only the wealthy have money and leisure for education. But as Socrates brings virtue to the fore, he also equates it with wisdom, taking as his chief example the failure of Pericles to educate his own sons and other dependents in "those thing in regard to which he is wise (*sophos*)" (320a1). In doing so Socrates raises the important possibility explored in the *Meno* that virtue is not quite knowledge but wisdom. At the same time, he offers in passing a surprisingly frank acknowledgment of the questionable character of his own protégé Alcibiades, whom, he says, Pericles sought to keep from corrupting his sons. Or could it be that what Socrates found promising in Alcibiades was the very thing that made him look corrupt to Pericles?

None of this proves that either political excellence or any other virtue is simply unteachable. But it does bring out how important a good nature and a willing mind are in those who are to acquire virtue, as well as how difficult it is to identify any experts in teaching it. Socrates professes himself unimpressed by the sophists' claim to have mastered that art, but he does grant one of their main premises. While his explicit contention is that virtue is unteachable and there is no such art as Protagoras professes, he makes his argument most perplexing by quietly assuming in the course of it that virtue is in fact some kind of knowledge or wisdom.

Protagoras' Myth: Epimetheus and Prometheus (320c2–22a2)

Protagoras promises to enlighten Socrates on his reasons for believing virtue is teachable. To this end he offers both a myth and an argument, answering in turn Socrates' two arguments against virtue's teachability based on the practice of the *dēmos* and the experience of the great. Myths are a device commonly used by the wise men of old and by Socrates too; Protagoras is more frank than they, however, in calling his myth a myth and in attributing it to no one but himself, thus signaling that we should not believe in its literal truth.[9] This myth is a subtle and graceful account of how it has come to be that justice, unlike the arts, is not the province of specialists but is known by all. It is a charming story of the imperfect providence of the gods, which seems to affirm the gods' benevolence but which under closer examination suggests that human beings have in fact been left on their own to work out their own happiness in an inhospitable world, without natural defenses, natural sociability, or a naturally fulfilling end.[10] While the myth teaches that the gods made humans and all the mortal races, it also states that the gods formed them beneath the earth through a blind mingling of the elements without any plan for their welfare. The task of ensuring their survival was assigned afterwards to the improvident Epimetheus and the desperately improvising Prometheus. Even Prometheus' foresight seems to develop only as a kind of afterthought, a lesson learned from hard experience of the results of being too careless and too trusting. So far are the gods from teaching men forethought that they lack it themselves.[11]

Epimetheus is not a complete bungler. Though "not very wise" (321b7), he is in fact, like nature itself, fertile in invention and generous if not profligate with his gifts, through which he provides well for all of the animals except human beings. Yet this benevolence seems to come as an imperfect response to nature's own deeper harshness. The first thing Epimetheus gives each animal, even before a source of food, is defense against the others, suggesting that the world is brutally competitive in ways not simply explained by scarcity. The second thing (and the occasion of Protagoras' first mention of any Olympian god by name) is defense against "the seasons that come from Zeus" with fur and thick skins and hooves that give them warmth, bedding, and protection against the hard ground (321a3–4). Each description of a provision Epimetheus makes for the animals only highlights a deprivation suffered by humans, who are by nature left "naked and unshod and without bedding and weapons" (321c5–6). Man is not even endowed by nature with reason but only with the potential for reason, which desperation and daring will call into play: while the other animals are called irrational or without speech (*alogon*), man is not yet called rational. Only later will he acquire both practical reasoning and speech.

So helpless are humans left by Epimetheus or nature that only Prometheus' gift of the arts allows them to survive.

> So Prometheus, being at a loss as to what means of preservation he might find for the human being, steals from Hephaistos and Athena the wisdom of the arts together with fire—for there was no way for anyone to possess it or make use of it without fire—and so gives them to the human being. So in this way the human being obtained the wisdom that pertains to life, but the political wisdom he did not have, for it resided with Zeus. (321c7–d5)

Protagoras uses the present tense in speaking of the theft: a crime and even an ongoing crime is the essential precondition of all human thriving—and not any crime but a crime of impiety, which only for want of opportunity is not directed against the highest god.[12] Originating as the arts do in an act of hubris, they are a sphere of human activity distinct from and in tension with the realm of law and morality.[13] Although not provided by nature, the arts are a direct and rational response to the needs of nature. Within this realm, excellence or virtue is a matter of knowledge or wisdom, and yet, we may note, it rests on a foundation of courageous daring. This daring is needed because the gods are careless and unreasonable, for the arts the gods begrudge man would cost them nothing to give and would win them lasting gratitude. In his story Protagoras presents the divine realm as neither wholly wise nor unified; it comes to sight as somehow both intelligently benevolent and as inexplicably harsh.

Since the story of Prometheus is explicitly called a myth, what is meant to be true and untrue in it, and what is Prometheus meant to represent? Prometheus seems to embody the spirit of rare, independent-minded inventors and discoverers among primitive humans, wresting control of their own destiny from a hostile environment. If on Protagoras' reading the poets and sophists all teach the same wisdom, Prometheus' spirit would be their spirit as well. But then in what sense is Prometheus divine? A clue comes in Protagoras' next observation on primitive humanity.

> Since man had a share of the divine allotment, first, through the kinship with the gods, he alone among the animals believed in gods; and he took it in hand to build altars and statues of the gods. He then articulated speech and names through art, and provided housing and clothing and shoes and bedding and food from the earth. (322a3–8)

Language develops only after other arts: Protagoras is radical in his denial that humanity is naturally political or even social. But curiously, piety seems to come even before language, suggesting the thought that human beings could not have become makers had they not first recognized in themselves a divine spark of reason and foresight and the ability to control fate. Whether it makes sense for Protagoras to speak of men's awareness of their kinship with the gods when they seem as yet to have no speech and no communities of kinship with one another is doubtful. His strained chronology suggests that he is trying too hard to deny that man is by nature a political being. At any rate, primitive man populates the world in his imagination with other kindred beings who, he senses, should care for him and yet who seem not to; thus he is inclined by turns to tremble before them, to place the highest hope in them, and, more rarely, to defy them.

Yet even in defying them he imagines himself emulating some divine being who must in similar spirit defy blind, stupid fate and make himself free. Thus the great benefactor of early times perhaps became in the popular memory a benevolent god, yet a god who was now strangely at odds with the other gods and whose motives had become obscure. Despite or possibly because of this obscurity, Prometheus with his unselfish courage is the hero of Protagoras' myth. Whether Protagoras in his own mind admires him simply as a human being or as in some way still divine, Plato does not disclose.

Protagoras' Myth: Zeus and Hermes (322a3–d5)

In the second part of the myth, which explains the origin of justice, Zeus and Hermes replace Epimetheus and Prometheus as the leading characters. Now Protagoras makes it explicit that the arts came before any communities. Politics is even further removed from nature or more wholly shaped by convention than the other arts are. Men form alliances and found cities for protection from the beasts, Protagoras says, against which they are individually too weak for defense, since "they did not yet have the political art, of which the art of war is a part" (322b5). Yet for the same reason, they can no more live together than apart, and thus they are perishing miserably. Finally Zeus steps in and orders Hermes to bring humans shame (*aidōs*) and justice or punishment (*dikē*) so that the race might not be utterly destroyed. Hermes finds Zeus's instructions insufficiently precise, however. He asks whether he should distribute shame and justice in the same way the arts are distributed (which, he helpfully explains, means giving each to only a few individuals) or whether he should distribute them to everyone. Hermes, the god of thieves and to that extent akin to Prometheus, has been more attentive to the fate of human beings than Zeus has been. Prompted by Hermes, Zeus replies, "To everyone" (322d1–2). Yet somehow foreseeing that his order will not in fact suffice to endow everyone with shame and justice, Zeus adds that anyone found incapable of sharing in them should be put to death as an illness to the city.

Protagorean man, in sum, is apolitical and solitary, so solitary that he is not a family or even an erotic being. While explicitly describing nature's provisions for the survival of each kind of living being, Protagoras' myth is silent on the sexual coupling so essential to every animal species' survival as well as to the foundations of human society. Socratic man, by contrast, is by nature both political and erotic, and erotic by virtue of the most basic neediness that Protagoras agrees nature has left him in: Protagoras' formula for the miserable condition of natural man is precisely Socrates' formula for the condition of eros in the *Symposium*.[14] The erotic and political aspects of human nature are connected in Socratic thought not only because the family serves as the building block of the political community but because nature, in making us mortal, gives us a yearning for a transcendence of our mortality, and one of the chief ways human beings seek this transcendence is through great political deeds. If Socrates is right in claiming eros to be a universal human impulse, then Protagoras has underestimated its power not only in others but also in himself, and we should see some signs of that lack of understanding in the rest of the dialogue.

Protagoras ends his myth without explaining how the gods give human beings justice. Nor is he quite explicit as to whether the two dispositions that Zeus orders Hermes to distribute, shame and justice, constitute the whole of the political art that humans lack. The myth invites the assumption that they do, but this assumption does not withstand scrutiny, most obviously because the art of war belongs to the political art and yet is no part of shame or justice (though justice may direct and limit its exercise). "Zeus" has provided the willingness to submit to law that political authority must build upon, but he has taught neither the art of commanding, which war especially requires, nor the art of legislation. Nor has Zeus assumed the part of the effective leader himself. He has not implemented an education in justice that would make individuals understand its reasonableness or love its beauty, as humans later do in Protagoras's account (325c5–26e5); he has not given any laws except the one instituting capital punishment for injustice; even this law he has only proclaimed without establishing any means of enforcement; and finally, he evidently does nothing to discover and punish those who feign justice unjustly. Heaven gives only the most rudimentary materials that daring leaders need to employ if they are to win wars and keep order at home, without endowing anyone with the shrewdness or courage to become such a leader. If Prometheus' original gift of the arts gave humans the technical wisdom needed for survival without the political wisdom that still "resided with Zeus" (321d3–5), then a second Prometheus and a second theft would seem to be needed to bring humanity the political art. Might "Hermes" represent this second Prometheus, akin to the first in his bold thievery but more of a political being and less of a free spirit, more outwardly deferential to authority and more crafty, who teaches "Zeus" to think prudently about human needs and presents himself to his fellow men as the agent of Zeus's will? The parallel with Machiavelli's teaching on the wise use of prophecy is striking.

If Hermes is the original founder who subjects his fellows forcibly to the political yoke and teaches them pious awe and justice, however, he is not simply the inventor of these things. For in the myth piety predates even language, and although Protagoras does not say the same of the sense of justice, his account of the chaotic character of the early societies suggests that humans were likely not only robbing one another but taking vengeance on one another, and it was this vengeance that made life especially unbearable. Yet vengeance presupposes a sense of justice. Hence Hermes or the original human ruler, in teaching justice and pious awe, would only be using and shaping inclinations whose source is deeper and older than himself. But if this is so, is man quite so naturally apolitical, and are law and justice quite so conventional, as Protagoras seems to think?

Protagoras' Argument for the Teachability of Virtue (322d5–24d1)

Although the myth is silent on the origin of political authority and law, Protagoras adds supporting arguments for his claim that political virtue is shared by virtually all human beings, arguments that at least begin to show the source of civic virtue in ordinary citizens. Yet these arguments go much further than the myth in suggesting that civic virtue and justice are entirely conventional—that despite their almost universal prevalence among men, they are the result not of a natural or divine gift but of human teaching and practice. Adroitly responding to Socrates' reminder that he is in democratic Athens, however, Protagoras presents these claims not as his own ideas but as the common opinions of everyone, which he will merely defend as sensible. But his arguments in fact turn out to be playfully ironic, and one of them surprisingly reminiscent of Socrates' own claims about moral responsibility. Protagoras continues both to close and to obscure the gap between civic virtue and the political art by affirming the good sense of citizens' refusing to allow nonexperts to testify on technical matters while welcoming everyone's advice on matters of "political virtue," which, he says now in his own name, "must as a whole follow justice (*dikaiosunē*) and moderation (*sōphrosunē*)" and which ought to belong to all if there are to be cities (322e2–23a3). Political virtue, like the endowment Zeus ordered Hermes to distribute, includes some form of justice and some form of reverence or self-control. But Protagoras now replaces *dikē*, a word for justice that can also mean prosecution or punishment (as Protagoras uses it in reporting that Prometheus was said to have suffered for his philanthropic theft at 322a1–2), with *dikaiosunē*, the word for complete justice or fairness. Protagoras is beginning to minimize vengefulness and emphasize a practical pursuit of the common good in his account of the virtue that citizens need, as opposed to that which Zeus ordered. Likewise, he now replaces *aidōs*, pious awe or shame, with *sōphrosunē*, moderation or sensible sobriety. While moderation is compatible with piety, it can also serve to replace piety and even justice. For in general, Protagoras goes on to explain, moderation means truthfulness, yet where justice is in question it means having the sense to at least claim that one is just even when one is not and even when at least some others know one is not. Protagoras says that everyone must "somehow" have a share in justice if there are to be cities (323b7–c2), but the previous statement suggests that this "somehow" may include possessing it only in appearance. Thus the political virtue that "follows moderation and justice" seems to have more than one form. In the good citizen it means the possession of justice as lawfulness and the moderation that accords with this, while in the shrewd leader or the free spirit it may mean feigning justice in ways that are compatible with one's sensible pursuit of one's own interest. But Protagoras indicates that such feigning is as essential for the community as for those who engage in it: the city can survive citizens' injustice but not their openly scoffing at justice and being treated as anything but mad (232b5–7). Protagoras concludes that everyone believes that everyone does have a share in justice. Even when we know certain individuals to be unjust, we must also think that they, too, believe in justice at some deep level if they are not insane, so much does anyone's respect for justice require the belief that everyone recognizes its claims. While pretending simply to endorse the common belief that everyone shares in justice, Protagoras in fact indicates his ironic distance on this belief.

Protagoras turns next to the issue of virtue's teachability. "But that people don't believe it to be by nature or automatic, but rather something teachable and present in those in whom it is present as a result of diligence, this I'll try to demonstrate to you next" (323c5–8). He is moving further and further from the claim that Zeus gives virtue to human beings in anything more than a most fragmentary and problematic form, and towards the view that justice exists by convention, while still taking cover under the claim that he is merely explicating everyone's view. He bases his claim that justice is teachable on the indisputable fact that people exhort one another to virtue and blame and punish vice all the time, obviously assuming that doing so will make a difference. He begins with the sensible observation that one is not angry with but rather pities others for such defects as shortness or ugliness that one regards as the result of nature or chance. He then adds that "the noble things and their contraries" all come from nature and chance (323d5–6), with the implication that what is of human origin, such as law, is not noble. Just and unjust action, depending not on nature or on chance but on us, are responsive to the application of incentives and disincentives—and this he now insists is *all* that is at work in punishment.

> For no one corrects those who are unjust with this in mind and for the sake of this, that he did injustice—anyone who isn't imposing retribution irrationally like a beast. But the one who undertakes to correct rationally does not impose retribution with a view to the wrong that has been done—for that would not make undone what has been done—but for the sake of the future, so that this person himself may not do injustice again nor may another who sees him being corrected. (324a6–b5)

Thus Protagoras attributes to virtually everyone—everyone who is not utterly senseless—the unconventional Socratic view that the anger that seeks retribution as an end is irrational and that the only rational end of punishment is correction. This attribution can only be ironic. Of course it is true that blaming and reproaching always presume on the part of their object a capacity to do better and usually involve some attempt to engage that capacity, but passionate anger also demands that wrongdoers suffer, whether that suffering is constructive or not. Protagoras shows that he recognizes this fact when after using the word for punishment that means to check or correct (*koladzō*), he reverts to describing what the Athenians do when they punish as "imposing retribution" (*timōreō*). Socrates earlier used the Athenians' alleged wisdom to argue for the unteachability of virtue; now Protagoras, in ironically attributing to the Athenian people a coolheaded rationalism that he knows they do not have, is besting Socrates at his own game. At the same time he shows that he shares Socrates' striking detachment from the ordinary experience of indignation and the ordinary view of moral responsibility.

But interestingly, in keeping with what we have seen about Protagoras' and Socrates' opposite assessments of the importance of eros in human psychology, they seem to come at the problem of moral responsibility from opposite directions. Socrates in his discussion with Polus in the *Gorgias* treats virtue as the natural perfection of the soul and the essential core of any real happiness. Hence he teaches that the right response to injustice is to pity the one afflicted by it and seek to cure him. In keeping with this claim, he argues often that virtue is knowledge or wisdom and that only ignorance makes men vicious; hence again the right response to vice is pity or education, not vindictiveness. Protagoras, as we would expect of one who views justice as merely a conventional device for keeping order in the artificial construct that is political society, makes no such argument from the premise that justice constitutes the health of the soul. His gentleness starts from the opposite premise. If justice is conventional, then a sensible person will not be indignant towards those who seek to profit at society's expense, even if he recognizes that society must punish them in self-defense. And in keeping with this thought, Protagoras treats justice as the product not of rational enlightenment but of habituation. Both the wholehearted lover of justice and the wholehearted conventionalist are free of vindictiveness; anger lives only in the shadowy realm of confusion in which we both believe virtue to be good for us, truly better for our happiness than vice, and also believe the vicious to be getting away with an unfair advantage.

Given the flaws we have seen in Socrates' argument in the *Gorgias*, however, we may well ask whether Socrates and Protagoras do view the matter from quite such opposite perspectives as first appears. Even if Socrates considers true virtue to be essential for happiness and true vice most pitiable, his way of understanding virtue may be almost as unconventional as Protagoras', as his professed ignorance as to whether the great king is happy or unhappy in the *Gorgias* suggests. Neither Socrates nor Protagoras is shocked by skeptical questioning of traditional authority or by the refusal to obey unwise laws, for example, and so both will be free of anger towards these "vices" for the same reason. While Plato explicitly ties Socrates' freedom from anger only to his hypermoral stance, this dialogue with Protagoras allows us to see another major reason for gentleness that must also be at work in Socrates at the same time.

But if Protagoras' freedom from anger arises from his rare degree of detachment from ordinary moralism, how does he understand that moralism? Is his awareness that not everyone shares his coolly pragmatic approach to punishment—that real moral indignation is much more prevalent than he pretends—not in tension with his implicit teaching that justice is merely conventional? Has he thought deeply enough about the roots of the pious and indignant inclinations that preceded rational lawgiving in his own account?

Protagoras' Account of Education and Its Failures (324d2–28d2)

The last part of Protagoras' great speech is a response to Socrates' second argument, in which Socrates reasoned from the failure of great men to give their sons virtue to its unteachability. Protagoras says that to answer this he will give "no longer a myth but an argument" (324d6–7), implying that only now is he turning from myth to reason, whereas in fact the myth ended at 322d5. We can understand this discrepancy in two possible ways. First, and especially if we are reading quickly and casually, this comment may highlight and fix in our memories the charming myth about the gods and the divine origin of justice—and likewise the memorable argument to come of how diligently the whole polis inculcates virtue—and cast into the shade the more radical suggestions Protagoras has just made about the importance of feigning justice and the irrationality of retribution. But it may also be a signal that everything he has said so far is a story—a pious story about the gods and an ironic story to the effect that everyone shares in justice and everyone is a diligent, rational teacher of justice—and that only now is he going to reveal his deepest thought. For even if the middle of his speech is the most open in a sense, it is not the most radical when read carefully. The next argument goes even further in shedding doubt on the premise of the myth that the gods have given human beings justice. Its teaching is that humans are by nature more savage than the worst criminals (327c4–e1) and that only the continual exercise of compulsion, from infancy to old age, imposed by human beings and human institutions, makes anyone fit for society. Here we have conventionalism in its purest form.[15]

Protagoras' reply to Socrates' second point is that great men do teach their sons virtue to the best of their ability, for indeed everyone teaches everyone virtue to the best of his ability, since everyone's well-being depends upon it. Hence the individual differences that remain reflect differences not in education but in natural receptivity to society's instruction. Like language, a degree of virtue is thus universal but not innate. In this argument Protagoras again shows his cultivation and his deft rhetorical skills by managing to flatter by turns both the demos and the elite, attributing to everyone a share in giving and receiving a serious education in virtue while ultimately acknowledging that the higher reaches of this education are pursued above all by the rich and powerful. He manages this, however, at the cost of obscuring the difference between the common decency that most people do indeed more or less convey to most of the young and the high-level art of statesmanship that men like Pericles exhibit and that Protagoras prides himself on teaching. This conflation becomes evident as Protagoras identifies the "one" virtue that all must have as, by turns, "justice and moderation and piety," "the virtue of a man (*anēr*)," and the thing that everyone, "child and man and woman" must learn if he is not to be forcibly expelled from the city (324d7–25b1).

Yet even in its most elementary form the civic education Protagoras proceeds to describe is more thoughtful than the harsh injunctions of Zeus in the myth. It employs exhortation, praise, appeals to honor, and the spirit of emulation, using punishment only as a last resort. Its higher reaches are high indeed, involving intensive study of music and of the great poets. Protagoras acknowledges cultivated Greeks' seriousness about instilling a love of nobility through these studies, even while emphasizing the compulsion that underlies this process (325e5; 326b2). Finally he mentions the ancient lawgivers, attributing to them the wisdom of having framed laws that teach virtue (326d6). Through all of this, citizens educate one another so assiduously that they all become experts, as it were, in virtue. In the same way, they all would become tolerable aulos players

> if everyone taught this to everyone else in both private and public and rebuked one who didn't play nobly and didn't begrudge this, just as now no one is begrudging or secretive when it comes to the just and lawful things, as they do in the case of the other arts—for I think reciprocal justice and virtue are profitable for you. (327a4–b2)

Protagoras now presents virtue as an art, but one that differs from other arts in this small way: that it profits everyone for everyone *else* to practice it.

What Protagoras professes to teach is the same virtue that everyone teaches, but perhaps a bit more skillfully, sailing in like a world-class aulos player and holding master classes in all the major cities of Greece, and unlike everyone else charging a fee since he, as a foreigner, does not suppose himself the beneficiary of the virtue he thus advances. His message, at least on the surface, could not be more respectable. He has even managed to exculpate the notorious Alcibiades and to hold out hope for the disappointing sons of Pericles, since they are still young. So skillfully has he woven a story to flatter both demos and aristocrats of Athens, in response to Socrates' warning that he is only a foreigner among proud democrats, that he has all but caused his own unique art to disappear from view. This is the one failing of an otherwise masterful performance, a comic failing if the whole purpose of the speech was to advertise his wares to a prospective new student, but perhaps not a serious one if Protagoras' interest has all been captivated by the contest he has found himself in with the intriguingly wily Socrates.

To Socrates' challenge, Protagoras seems to have given a good answer. Is civic virtue not teachable and taught in just the way that he says? Socrates might reply that civic education, even at its best, proceeds more through habituation than through rational persuasion and hence falls short of true teaching, while the result, including as much irrational prejudice as clear understanding, falls short of true virtue. But surely Protagoras would agree.

The education he prides himself on teaching is really quite different, an education free from compulsion, proceeding by enlightenment and not blind habituation, and giving his students freedom and an Olympian perspective on their city's political life, if also the wherewithal to shine within it. He has not explicitly distinguished this education from the civic education the laws provide, but everything in his speech has pointed to its presence and has encouraged us to reflect on how the two must differ. And thus his speech is helpful in adumbrating the important sense in which virtue cannot be knowledge: ordinary civic virtue cannot be, resting as it does on force and habituation and perhaps, as Protagoras indicates, conducing as much or more to the good of others than to one's own. But by these very limitations, civic virtue indicates the need for a higher virtue that may indeed be a kind of knowledge, knowledge of where we each stand in a world shaped by harsh natural necessity and knowledge of what we must do to thrive. Has Protagoras not quietly indicated how this virtue can be taught, building on the civic education that the city provides and proceeding by provoking questioning on one hand and by developing rhetorical skills on the other? Would this virtue not, like ordinary civic virtue, depend in considerable degree on the student's nature and yet be capable of adding much to whatever nature provides?

The Unity of Virtue: Justice and Piety (328d3–32a1)

Socrates reports that he was filled with wonder at Protagoras' performance and persuaded that Protagoras is right that it is after all "through diligence that the good become good" (328e1–3), thus summing up succinctly the quietly atheistic thrust of the whole speech. Indeed, Socrates tells Protagoras, he has only one small question to ask before he will be entirely satisfied. At the same time, he adds, the splendid Protagoras is worth little if he can only give a speech that any of the popular speakers could have given without being able to answer a simple question with something new that the audience has not already heard. Thus Socrates' and Protagoras' deliciously urbane wrestling match continues in high style.

Socrates' sole question—the one that he thereby indicates we should especially be puzzling over at the conclusion of Protagoras' speech—is whether virtue is one or many. Most obviously, this question refers to the gap Protagoras has both pointed to and obscured between the polis' civic and his own sophistic education. But in some form Protagoras and Socrates clearly agree on the divide between ordinary civic virtue and philosophic virtue. Socrates also seems to be curious about one or two other potentially important gaps that are further in the background of Protagoras' speech but potentially more important for understanding him: the difference between the virtue of the statesmen he trains on the one hand and his own virtue as a thinker and teacher on the other, and (if it is ultimately different) that between the shrewd selfishness that his account would seem to present as the rational response to our natural condition (akin to Socrates' transmoral-utilitarian account of virtue) and the bravery of his myth's hero, Prometheus. Does the essential core of virtue in Protagoras' mind really reduce to enlightened self-interest, or does a critically important part of it oppose self-interest? If the virtue that Protagoras in fact most deeply admires is that of Prometheus and the virtue that Socrates most admires is that of the detached philosopher, then their true positions will be the opposite of the ones they take in their first dispute. Protagoras will turn out to think that a key part of true virtue is not knowledge or wisdom (and hence that virtue is not a single whole), and Socrates will turn out to think that that the whole of it is knowledge or wisdom (and hence that it is one). And this they will indeed prove to do.

The way Socrates puts his question is this:

> You were saying that Zeus sent justice and shame to human beings, and in many places in your speeches justice and moderation and piety and all such things were spoken of by you as being some one thing taken together, virtue. So go through these very things precisely for me by means of argument—that is, whether virtue is some one thing, and justice and moderation and piety are parts of it, or whether these things that I was just now speaking of are all names of what is in itself one and the same being. This is what I still desire. (329c2–d2)

When Protagoras tries to go right up the middle, replying that these virtues are all parts of virtue, which is one, Socrates presses further: are they like the parts of a face or like the parts of gold, which do not differ at all "except in respect to bigness or smallness?" (329d8). Protagoras naturally chooses the more obvious answer that the different virtues are like parts of the face. This answer will be explored but never endorsed by Socrates, however, who explicitly distances himself from it at 330e7–31a1. Does Socrates think, then, that all acts of virtue really are rather like pieces of gold, just more or less important expressions of one and the same quality or principle? Or does he in some way still recognize differences of kind as well as of degree between the virtues?[16]

Socrates proceeds now by asking whether each of the virtues is always found together with the others, as eyes are found together with noses. It would seem both easy and prudent for Protagoras to say that each virtue, at least in its full realization, does require the others, but he emphatically denies this. "Some are courageous but unjust, and others just but not wise." Socrates responds with innocent surprise, "Are these parts of virtue too, then . . . wisdom (*sophia*) and courage?" (329e5–30a1). In Protagoras' long myth and argument about civic virtue, wisdom and courage were almost nowhere in evidence, but now Socrates' suggestion that virtue is a single organic whole causes Protagoras to disclose his true belief that virtue has very different kinds that by no means come naturally and automatically together. Protagoras replies that wisdom and courage are indeed parts of virtue and that wisdom is the greatest of them. Perhaps Socrates' apparent failure to see that virtue goes far beyond lawfulness strikes Protagoras as irritatingly naïve, as his hypermoral claims about virtue strike both Polus and Callicles. At any rate, we have now an evident divide between the lesser, civic virtues of justice, piety, and moderation, and the greater virtues of courage and wisdom that according to Protagoras neither imply nor are implied by the former. Protagoras does not say whether one may be moderate without justice or wise without courage. Nor, more seriously, does he say that one could be wise without justice, but neither does he rule it out.

What Protagoras does say in response to Socrates' further questioning is that the power and scope of each virtue are distinct, just as the powers and objects of the different parts of the face are. Thus, as Socrates puts it and Protagoras agrees, each part is "not such as another," and in particular "none of the other parts of virtue is such as knowledge, or such as justice, or such as courage, or such as moderation, or such as piety" (330a7–b1, b3–6). Divining the importance of courage to Protagoras, Socrates puts it in the middle, simultaneously replacing wisdom with knowledge, a substitution Protagoras neither protests nor seems to notice. May Protagoras at once overestimate the importance of courage and give too little thought to the difference between the knowledge he possesses and can transmit to others and the wisdom that requires profound reflection on oneself, one's limitations, and the limits of what one knows?

Socrates next, with no small amount of legerdemain, draws the conclusion that if justice is just and piety is pious and no virtue is "such as another," then justice must be impious and piety unjust.[17] In the process he makes clear that Protagoras' premises are not his, and that he himself considers justice and piety either identical or nearly so. It would apparently be honest as well as prudent for Protagoras to agree about justice and piety, yet something makes him resist. His first response is a dismissive one:

> "It really doesn't seem to me so simple, Socrates," he said, "as to concede that justice is pious and piety just, but there seems to me to be a distinction there. But what difference does this make?" he said. "If you like, let justice be for us pious and piety just." (331b8–c4)

Protagoras denies the unity of the virtues even though he cares so little about the particular distinction between justice and piety that it does not seem worthwhile to him to object to Socrates' bad logic. For him, evidently, these two virtues are both products of social conditioning, both grounded in fear and shame and both cultivated for the sake of social cohesion and peace. Only when Socrates insists that he not let things that he disagrees with pass unopposed does he critique Socrates' reasoning. Appealing to a meaning of justice that Socrates takes seriously—perhaps most seriously of all the meanings of this fraught term—Protagoras says, "it isn't *just* to call things having some similarity 'similar' nor to call things having some dissimilarity 'dissimilar,' especially if the similarity they have is very small" (331e2–4, emphasis added). Justice means assessing everything at its true worth.

But is Socrates not being unjust here, in insinuating that everything that is not justice or piety must be positively unjust or impious? What could be behind his bad logic, if not a shameless desire to win at all costs? His argument would seem justified by what he wishes to uncover as an especially deep though by no means uncommon fissure in Protagoras' view of virtue. The divide that Protagoras exemplifies is potentially present in any account of virtue that assigns to the different virtues different powers and domains of action without any clear ordering principle of unity to govern them. Without this, there is nothing to prevent their working at cross-purposes to one another, as in fact they often seem to do. Courage, for example, often seems to demand a militant response to insolence, even where prudence may call for forbearance.[18] Piety seems to some to require acts that oppose lawfulness or even reason altogether. Worse still, if the real principle of justice is the good of the city and that of wisdom is one's individual good, as Protagoras suggests, there is no reason they would not be frequently opposed. Only Socrates defines virtue in a way that makes it immune to such divisions.

The Unity of Virtue: Wisdom and Moderation (332a2–33b6)

Since Protagoras refuses to give Socrates any traction in his effort to expose a divide between his views of justice and of piety, Socrates turns to an example of the opposite problem in Protagoras' account of the virtues as separate and distinct wholes. He points out that moderation or sobriety (*sōphrosunē*) and wisdom (*sophia*) seem to overlap or converge in both being the opposite of folly (*aphrosunē*). To the extent that the virtues are separate they seem to be in potential conflict, but to the extent that they are in harmony they seem to overlap or converge, so little do they each govern a distinct sphere of life with a clearly independent principle of action.

Again Socrates' reasoning is slippery. He exploits the fact that the word *sōphrosunē* has a broad range of meaning, extending from the most basic self-control in food and drink to modesty to good sense, while its opposite, *aphrosunē*, means especially foolishness. Protagoras generally equates *sōphrosunē* with a low-level moderation born of shame and habit and reasonably expected of men, women, and children alike (325a6), while viewing wisdom as a distinct and much higher virtue. But Socrates, beginning with the obvious opposition between folly and wisdom, and getting Protagoras to agree that "for each of the contraries, there is only one contrary" (332c8–9), pulls out of his hat the conclusion that *sōphrosunē* and *sophia* must be identical. Socrates is tricky, but Protagoras is brilliant and clever. Why does he not reply that each concept that is simple has a single contrary, while words that have multiple meanings can have a different contrary for each meaning, and the sense in which *sōphrosunē* opposes *aphrosunē* has almost nothing in common with the sense in which *sophia* does? Is he afraid to acknowledge how wide a gap he really sees between the simple civic virtues he professes to teach and the shrewdly amoral wisdom he really admires and teaches? But then why does he not frame the difference as that between the simple moderation and sobriety needed by citizens and the greater practical wisdom needed by good statesmen—or between citizen virtue and a theoretical excellence that has nothing to do with politics?

The fact that Protagoras lets himself be trapped suggests that Socrates has caught him off balance. Protagoras seems to have held simultaneously in his mind two different thoughts about moderation—that it is a merely conventional virtue of self-control that benefits society, and that it is true good sense in the conduct of one's own life—without considering the relation between them. When Socrates presses him, it really does seem to him that there is something sensible about even low-level moderation and something foolish about being out of control: moderation is good not only by convention. But his conventionalism has evidently kept him from thinking carefully about what may be the natural and rational root of the virtues that social conventions demand.

Having ostensibly established the unity of wisdom and moderation,

Socrates says he next established or reestablished that justice and piety are "pretty much the same thing" (333b5–6). His brief reference to their agreement about justice and piety leaves it unclear whether there is any renewed discussion about their relation at this point, but clearly Protagoras makes no more difficulties about Socrates' identification of the two, confirming that he sees little of importance to distinguish them.

The Unity of Virtue: Moderation and Justice (333b7–34c6)

Finally, Socrates tries to get Protagoras to affirm the identity of moderation and justice. Protagoras has repeatedly spoken of moderation, justice, and piety as together making up a low-level civic virtue. If Socrates can get his agreement that they are essentially the same, he can use Protagoras' prior agreement that moderation is wisdom to prove the identity of piety, justice, moderation, and wisdom. He can thereby refute Protagoras' original claim that there are many who are just but unwise (329e5–6).[19] When Socrates asks Protagoras whether it is possible to act moderately (or sensibly) in doing injustice, Protagoras says he would be ashamed to say for his own part that it is, but he asks Socrates to proceed on this basis, for the first but not the only time taking refuge behind popular opinion. Unlike at 331c, Socrates allows the evasion, suggesting that he recognizes that it is indeed Protagoras' own opinion that is on the table and that he has no wish to embarrass him needlessly. But this maneuver wins Protagoras little breathing room. For though he has avoided conceding outright that moderation is justice, he must either stand by and watch Socrates refute the contrary, "popular" view, or actively come to its defense.

Caught in this dilemma, Protagoras first drags his feet and then digs in his heels, opposing Socrates with an oath on what seems to be an extraneous matter, resorting to speech making, and finally refusing outright to continue the discussion on Socrates' terms as an exchange of question and answer. We never see the proof Socrates would have offered for the unity of justice and moderation. It is replaced first by a debate over the meaning of the word "good" and afterwards by a general discussion among those present about the fair way to conduct a philosophic conversation. If, as is often or always the case in Platonic dialogues, the interruption or substitution of one subject for another is in fact the continuation of the first by other means, what can we make of the discussion about the good that takes the place of Socrates' proof regarding justice and moderation? Let us look closely at the way it arises and unfolds.

"Come then," I said. "Answer me from the beginning. Do some seem to you to act moderately in doing injustice?"

"Let it be so," he said.

"And by 'being moderate' (*sōphronein*) do you mean 'thinking correctly' (*eu phronein*)?" He said so.

"And thinking correctly is deliberating well, because they are doing injustice?"

"Let it be so," he said.

"If they fare well doing injustice, or if they fare badly?"

"If they fare well."

"Do you say, then, that some things are good?"

"I do."

"Then," I said, "are those things good that are beneficial for human beings?"

"Yes, by Zeus," he said, "and even if they are not beneficial for human beings, I at least call them good!" (333d3–e2)

This outburst, the first swearing we have seen in Callias' house, is as ambiguous as it is unexpected. Is Protagoras objecting to the ignobility of what he sees as an attempt to reduce moderation to whatever is beneficial for human beings, and calling in divine support to oppose it? Or is he objecting to the naïve moralism of an argument he anticipates Socrates is preparing to make in support of the prudence of always acting justly? The oath itself might suggest the former, but his subsequent responses to Socrates' gentle probing all suggest the latter. Is is it possible that both are at work in a strange tangle in Protagoras' soul—that lurking within his very vehemence in opposing naïve moralism is a streak of fugitive piety?

When Socrates asks the crucial question, "Do you mean . . . things that are beneficial for no human being, or things that are not beneficial at all? Do you call even such things good?" (333e5–34a2), Protagoras makes it clear that he does not call things that benefit no one or nothing good. He rejects any thought that it is good to do what is commanded by divine or human laws when no one benefits. His point, rather, is that the good is far from being a monolithic whole; it differs endlessly depending on whose good we consider; it is relative not only to the beneficiary but often to the specific part or specific condition of the entity affected. For example, he says, manure is good for the roots but bad for the young shoots of plants, and ingesting olive oil is fine for healthy human beings but bad for weakened ones. If Protagoras is not simply choosing examples at random without reference to the real question at issue, he seems to be indicating indirectly that what is good for one part of a community may not be good for others, and that what is good for the most healthy and vigorous human beings would harm others—and thus that there are no universal rules of justice that apply to everyone and secure their good in common, as he imagines Socrates is going to argue. Perhaps he has in mind the daring acts of founders or tyrants as examples of the strongest individuals securing their own good.

But the oath suggests another thought, one that is admittedly speculative but that is reinforced by the striking place of Prometheus as hero of Protagoras' myth. Even or precisely at the point of affirming what he takes to be a bold, courageous insight, an insight that shows his toughness in facing up to the hard truth that man has been left alone to work out his fate in an indifferent universe and that the soothing pieties of the multitude are foolish, Protagoras opposes Socrates with an appeal to Zeus. Might he think or hope in some way that what is truly divine is on the side not of the piously moral but of those who are breathtakingly daring in their clear-sightedness? Or, if indeed nothing in the cosmos supports such men from outside, might they be, like Prometheus, somehow divine themselves? Thus, while Protagoras sees a divide between what is good for the common citizens and what is good for the leaders, he may see an even more important divide between what is good for ordinary, conventional citizens and leaders alike and what is good for the wisest, most daring individuals. At any rate, he refuses to be corralled by Socrates' questioning, and Socrates, unable to force him to keep answering against his will, fails to pull tight the noose he has prepared for him. Instead of a Socratic argument for the unity of moderation and justice leading to the conclusion that justice is indeed inseparable from wisdom, then, this dialogue gives us a Protagorean argument that the good is neither absolute nor common but radically relative. And this claim Socrates fails to refute.

Dramatic Interlude (334c7–38e5)

Socrates' unsuccessful attempt to prove through speech the identity of justice and wisdom is now replaced by a dramatic struggle between Socrates and Protagoras over whether and how their discussion should proceed. This struggle soon involves the whole audience in debating and adjudicating a dispute over the just means of conducting a philosophical discussion. If the prior discussion of the good shed some light on Protagoras' submerged views on the question ostensibly left behind, that of relation between justice and wisdom, this practical dispute about justice between men who consider themselves wise will shed further light on both the problematic character of that relation and Socrates' own views on it.

As often happens in quarrels, part of the argument is about what the argument is really about. Is the assembly of intellectuals debating the rules for a contest over the zero-sum good that is the honor of supremacy, or the rules for a collective search for the common good that is knowledge?[20] Somehow they are at one and the same time doing both. Socrates begins by asking for special consideration as a man with a handicap. Pleading for brief answers, Socrates—the same man who is narrating this entire dialogue verbatim to his friends—now claims with breathtaking audacity to have such a poor memory that any such long speech as Protagoras has just given (181 words, to be precise) makes him forget what the discussion was all about. Protagoras immediately makes the question one of what is adequate to the subject, not the listener, and of who is to be the judge of how much elaboration each question requires. The point is to give questions the answers they deserve, and no one has the right to judge that for another—or at least not for the wise Protagoras. Socrates immediately makes the question more personal and contentious: Protagoras, he claims (whether truthfully or not we will never know) has boasted of his ability to speak at will either more fully or more briefly than anyone and to teach others to do the same; let him show off his ability. Protagoras will have none of it: I would not be the world-famous Protagoras, he says in effect, if I let my opponents decide whether I am allowed to come to the net and what sort of spin I am allowed to put on the ball. Socrates at once picks up his ball and prepares to go home, alleging that he has no desire to force Protagoras to talk in a way that he does not wish—and besides that it is improper for Protagoras, who can use either brevity or length of speeches, not to accommodate one who is capable only of the former—and anyway that he has a pressing engagement elsewhere. Lest we ourselves become forgetful, we must recollect that the framing dialogue gives the lie not only to Socrates' poor memory but also to his pressing engagement, just as the rest of the dialogue will give the lie to Socrates' reluctance to push Protagoras where he does not wish to go. Can there be any excuse for such lies?

If we were to be so squeamish as to seek refuge in casuistry, we might say that what Socrates really means by his forgetfulness is that long speeches cause not him but his interlocutor and the audience to lose sight of the question at issue, loosening Socrates' tight grip on the uncomfortable problem he wishes to press and allowing everyone to slip away into comfortable evasions: Socrates is in fact being modestly ironic in calling the fault his own (cf. 336c4–d4). And is not modesty a form of moderation? Likewise, perhaps by his claim that he does not want to force Protagoras to continue against his will, Socrates really means that he wants to do nothing against Protagoras' true interest, and Protagoras stands to benefit by learning from Socrates. And perhaps by the claim that he has pressing business elsewhere, he really means that his quest for the truth is so pressing at all times that he cannot waste time watching idle displays, enjoyable though they might be. These excuses are even helpful. If to tell a lie is to do an injustice, Socrates is most unjust, but if to act justly is to pursue only the highest purposes in the most effective way possible, without allowing either incompetence or squeamishness to cause harm to no purpose, then Socrates is just.

Socrates of course also has somewhere else to go because he is a citizen and has no need for the protection of Callias' house, in contrast to the wealthy, effete foreign intellectuals who shelter there. As a simple citizen he is beholden to no one, he needs to impress no prospective students, and neither can he be detained by force, try though Callias might to hold him by his threadbare cloak (335d1). To Callias' plea that he not deprive the company of a delightful spectacle, Socrates praises him for his philosophic spirit but pleads inability: since I am slow and cannot go at Protagoras' pace, he ought to go at mine, for otherwise the conversation is impossible. Again, this outrageous pretense of feeble-mindedness has perhaps a sensible kernel at its core. Socrates can proceed in his thinking only methodically, taking and examining one step at a time; he cannot do otherwise because it is so clear to him that to do otherwise is unprofitable. This would make sense if Socrates were to insist that the conversation is a friendly, mutual search for the truth, but he confuses the issue by comparing it to an Olympic race, while still demanding that his opponent adjust his pace to him. Allowing a superb golfer with a bad leg to use a golf cart is one thing, but demanding that an Olympic runner "race slowly" against the hobbling Socrates in absurd. What is his point?

Ultimately Socrates is forcing us, his listeners, to ponder the complicated ways in which at one and the same time he is and is not engaged in a contest for supremacy. He is seeking the truth about whether and how virtue might be one, not victory for victory's sake, yet his activity is still inescapably a contest because it is essentially refutative, and refutation is invariably resisted. For this reason Socrates needs a certain courage or toughness in addition to his intelligence and love of wisdom in order to carry out his investigations. More immediately, setting up a situation in which the whole gathering wishes to see the discussion continue and laying down his terms in such a ways as to entangle the needs of productive discussion with the requirements for fair contest, Socrates forces the onlookers to propose an accommodation between the parties that must at once address the requisites of justice as the common good and of justice as fair competition. Then he is able to step back and await the collective proposal, which when it comes he will need to revise only slightly in order to have exactly what he wants. The dispute about justice turns into the founding of a small city in speech—not in imagination as in the *Republic* but in actuality, if only for a limited purpose and for an hour—and Socrates comes out as king. What does this drama reveal about the participants' views of justice and about the possibility of securing justice, at least in the most favorable case—among such friendly, reasonable men as are gathered here? Is there ever a true common good to be found, or is all human society inevitably a wolves' fight for supremacy, more or less muted and disguised?

Callias is the first to respond, and on cue he immediately makes an argument about justice. He approvingly attributes to Protagoras the claim that it is just for each to speak in the way that he thinks best: justice is equal liberty for all. Callias never quite admits that what is at issue is a contest, though clearly it is this that he is enjoying. Alcibiades in turn takes up Socrates' cause, in a spirit at once frankly agonistic, playfully debunking of Socrates' purported bad memory, and noble-minded. He treats the exchange as unquestionably a contest for supremacy, showing that he understands half but only half of what is at work in Socratic dialectics. But he says that Socrates already grants Protagoras' supremacy in speech making. Let Protagoras, then, either grant Socrates' supremacy at dialectic (which of course he cannot afford to do) or resume the contest on Socrates' terms. Therefore what Socrates demands is "more equitable" (336d4): justice is fair play in a frank contest for glory. Ironically, it is the future tyrant Critias who now attempts to be peacemaker by splitting the difference.[21] He points out that both Callias and Alcibiades are partisans whose fair speeches are calculated to favor their own champions. But even as he shows his readiness to dismiss appeals to justice as hypocritical, he makes his own appeal to the justice of impartiality. It is proper for us to side with neither and simply ask both parties to continue: justice is treating everyone the same.

Prodicus now replies with a pedantically hairsplitting speech, distinguishing such near-synonyms as "disputing" and "quarreling," "praising" and "esteeming," and "delighting" and "pleasing." He agrees with Critias that the onlookers should listen to both speakers but insists that more regard should be given to the most deserving and in particular to the wisest: justice is proportional, not numerical equality. He calls on Protagoras and Socrates to compete in a spirit of goodwill, not enmity. For even if human society is fundamentally competitive, he argues, there is a common interest in ensuring that the competition be fair, and this for two independent reasons. All stand to benefit by learning from those who are wise, and all want merit to be recognized. Thus, despite its pedantic style, this speech by the man Socrates calls his teacher (341a4) is in fact eminently sensible, and there is little here with which Socrates would disagree. The chief difference is that Prodicus identifies the common benefit to be derived from conversation as pleasure—albeit the high pleasure of learning something new—whereas Socrates is rather too rude, too dogged, too competitive, too practical, altogether too much the shrewd, thrifty plebeian, to share Prodicus' spirit. This difference in manner reflects the deeper difference that for Socrates, philosophy is an urgent need and not a delightful luxury. Socrates' sense of urgency fills him with a robust energy, even an erotic energy, that contrasts sharply with Prodicus' effete feebleness (cf. 317d10–e2). Prodicus' is the first speech that Socrates reports wins the approbation of "very many" though not all of those present (337c5–6).

Hippias, the last of the audience to speak, draws everything together with a stirring proposal that everyone applauds. Appealing to the assembly's shared love of knowledge and the sophists' shared respect for nature (*phusis*) as opposed to law or convention (*nomos*), he includes everyone in his exhortation and his praise. Calling them "kindred and relatives and fellow citizens by nature, not by law" (337c8–d1) and "the wisest of the Greeks" (337d4), he urges the assembled luminaries to find agreement on the basis of their natural kinship, using reason and not force; he urges both contestants to accommodate one another with speeches of measured length; and he suggests that the onlookers elect overseers to supervise the proceedings. Here is the original proposal for a republic of letters, founded by rational men for the common purpose of hearing good speeches. And this audience of sophisticated sophists, all of whom evidently agreed with the covert teaching of Protagoras' myth that man is by nature not a political being, that justice is mere convention, that appeals to justice are inevitably foolish or self-interested, and that the wise man lives his life only by the light of nature as discerned by reason, all applaud his proposal for a little republic based on natural justice. The social and political nature of man is after all unanimously accepted, and Prodicus' claim that there is a common good to be found in fair competition is confirmed.

Why, then, does everyone applaud Hippias' speech, while only "many" approved Prodicus'? Nobly stirring speeches are never quibbling, as Hippias himself says in urging Socrates to unfurl his sails a bit, and neither are flattering ones. May there be a connection? The drawer of fine distinctions seems inevitably to be wasting time with trivialities or seeking petty victories or reproaching us with imprecision; the painter of great inspiring images sweeps us along in a sense that we already understand with adequate clarity everything that really matters. Moreover, and comporting with his more flattering style, Hippias silently opposes the inegalitarian thrust of Prodicus' speech. As much as we recognize the value of learning from those who are wiser and as much as we want to honor true merit, our pride resists acknowledging any deficiency in ourselves and any superior among our fellows. As pleasing as it is to learn, it is even more pleasing to be called wise; as satisfying as it is to see the most deserving win, it is even more gratifying to be judged worthy of presiding over them as judges. Pride deflects the goal of any community away from what is truly most beneficial towards what is pleasing. Even in the best of republics, wisdom must be diluted by the consent of the less wise majority.

But by the same token, consent may be redirected by wisdom. At once Callias, the host, uses his own judgment to amend the resolution of the assembly. Aware that Socrates needs more accommodation to be willing to continue, he asks him to elect the overseer. Still Socrates demurs. The very things that made Hippias' speech so pleasing to the assembly makes it unacceptable to him. First, Hippias has blurred the essential differences between ranks, whereas in truth only the wisest are worthy to judge wise speeches. Doubtless Socrates thinks no one is a better judge than himself of the kind of answers his questions deserve, but what he says is that no one present is worthy to sit in judgment on Protagoras. Socrates, unlike Prodicus, understands the uses of strategic flattery. With equal deftness Socrates addresses the second problem with Hippias' proposal, its call for compromise in the length of speeches without regard for the serious purpose of the discussion and what that purpose requires. Hence Socrates substitutes for one reasonable-sounding compromise another more to his liking. He will let Protagoras choose whether to ask or answer the questions, and when it is Socrates' turn to answer he will teach Protagoras how it is properly done.[22] If Protagoras subsequently fails to stick to the questions, everyone will join Socrates in pressuring him to do so, without any need for an overseer. Everyone assents, and Protagoras is compelled to agree to ask and answer briefly in turn.

Socrates has won a complete victory. He is to be the supervisor of the wise Protagoras, with everyone as his enforcers, like a philosopher king supported by his trusty auxiliaries. He proves his ability both to manage his own affairs and to do what he pleases with this little republic of letters, showing that he and not Protagoras is the master of the art that Protagoras professes to teach. Protagoras, by contrast, has had nothing to say in this litigation scene after his initial insistence on playing his own way. He is unobliging, uncompromising, and either unwilling or unable to make an effective appeal to justice on his own behalf—perhaps because he regards justice with too much disdain to think seriously about it, but perhaps, by contrast, because he is too high-minded to resort to the deceitful flattery and trickery that Socrates employs with breathtaking ease. Either way, he lacks political skill, even or especially among men most like himself whom he ought most completely to understand.

True, Socrates carries out this successful coup in the house of Callias and not in the city of Athens, and while Callias cannot force him to remain, Athens will in the end force him to drink hemlock. But the strategy he employs here prefigures the strategy that he and more successfully Plato and Aristotle will use to win at least a sturdy foothold for philosophy, an alliance with the elite in every cultivated polis and nation who pride themselves on their love of wisdom, even if wisdom is not wholly welcome among them; an alliance therefore built partly on flattery, but in a way that always includes an open and occasionally accepted invitation to join Socrates in his rewarding quest.

What understanding of justice does the devious Socrates demonstrate through his little coup? Clearly justice for Socrates is rule of the wise, softened but as little as possible compromised by an accommodating exterior. Procedural justice counts for little with him; the only thing that matters is the good end towards which one intelligently employs one's skill. But what is that end? If it is not the common good of the whole assembly, it is at least the highest good of Socrates and of anyone else who will listen and profit. Yet it is telling that even Alcibiades, who knows Socrates well, regards the whole thing as a contest for supremacy and not a shared quest for the truth: Socrates' justice consists in a willingness to teach wisdom, the virtue he most cherishes, but the drama of the dialogue demonstrates the limits of this virtue's teachability.

To return, then, to the question that Socrates was forced by Protagoras' intransigence to stop pursuing, the question of the unity or disunity of wisdom and justice, we see that Socrates has in fact succeeded in pursuing it through this dramatic interlude. The answer he suggests is that, according to any conventional understanding of justice, wisdom and justice are not one. To be sure, wisdom will in most cases dictate an extensive compliance with society's expectations, for it teaches the unimportance of most of the contested goods and the value of acceding to the demands of law, although under the right circumstances wisdom might lead one to stage a successful coup against the prevailing laws and rulers. But wisdom and justice are indeed one if, with Socrates, we understand justice as wisdom exercised in pursuit of a common good, and especially wisdom exercised in pursuit of the unconventional and uncommon but still irreplaceable and shareable good that is an ever firmer possession of wisdom itself.

The Poem of Simonides: Is it Contradictory? (338e6–42a5)

Forced to take the lead, Protagoras proposes that they pursue the same question of virtue in a different medium, that of poetry. He now makes an important addition to his earlier account of education: the critical interpretation of poetry, he says, is in fact "the greatest part of the education of a man" (338e7). If a reverential reading of poetry is essential to ordinary civic education, evidently it is especially through teaching students to read closely and critically the works of the greatest poets that Protagoras undertakes to give them an Olympian perspective on the conventional wisdom of their cities. The poet he chooses is the celebrated Simonides, a contemporary and friend of both Pausanius and Themistocles, who wrote odes to the Greek heroes in the Persian Wars, but who was also a friend of tyrants and who earned great sums from his writing. Simonides was, according to the ancients, a religious skeptic, but evidently less open in his freethinking and less boastful of his wisdom than the sophists would later be.[23] Protagoras earlier listed Simonides together with Homer and Hesiod as examples of the wise men of old who used poetry to conceal their teaching (316d). Thus Simonides' way of life stands as a middle way between those of the itinerant self-proclaimed sophist Protagoras and the citizen-philosopher Socrates.

The poem Protagoras chooses is an ode to the tyrant Scopas, which is cited by other ancient sources as well, although the largest number of lines come from this dialogue. It is, as Protagoras says, most germane to the subject of the dialogue, being all about the relation of wisdom to virtue and whether and how virtue is attainable for human beings. Here is what we have of the poem:

> Now a good man in truth it is hard to become,
> In hands and feet and mind foursquare, wrought without blame . . .
> Nor do I deem well-tuned the word of Pittacus,
> Albeit spoken by a wise mortal: "Hard," he said, "it is to be noble."
> God alone could have this prize,
> but for a man it is not possible not to be bad
> whom unmanageable misfortune brings down.

So long as he does well, every man is good,
but bad if he does badly.
And such for the longest time [or for the most part] and best are those
whom the gods love.
Therefore never shall I cast away my mortal lot,
seeking that which cannot possibly come into being,
an empty and unachievable hope: a wholly blameless human being
among us who consume the fruit of the broad earth.
If I find him I will give you the news.
But everyone I praise and love
willingly who does
nothing shameful; but against necessity not even the gods fight.
. . . for me he suffices who is not bad,
nor excessively wild, a healthy man, who knows justice as the benefactor of
the city.
Him I will not blame, for of fools the number is infinite.
All things are noble, with which the shameful is not mixed.

When Socrates acknowledges that he has studied this poem and claims to find it well-written and consistent, Protagoras quotes the beginnings of the first and second stanzas, asking whether they are not contradictory. As Socrates tells the story to his companions afterwards (and we must remember that the whole account is a fiction within a fiction, Plato's account of Socrates' retelling of a dialogue that is largely or entirely Plato's own creation), Socrates is flummoxed and alarmed by Protagoras' suggestion that the poem is inconsistent. Protagoras proceeds pedantically to point out a tension that is right on the surface—that Simonides seems to blame Pittacus for saying something virtually identical to what he himself has just said—and for this Protagoras receives thunderous applause from his illustrious audience and Socrates staggers dizzily from the blow. Stalling for time, Socrates says, he calls Prodicus to his assistance against Protagoras, whom he compares to the raging Achilles attacking the river god Scamander. Can there be some serious sense in which Socrates considers Protagoras to be, in his treatment of the poets, excessively impious, or rash, or irrational in his demand to be honored for a courage that he carries too far? In his infatuation with courage or his excessive ambition to shine, does Protagoras threaten to do violence to the essence of Simonides' thought?

It never becomes quite clear, however, where Protagoras has in mind to go with his critique of Simonides. Possibly he intends only to argue that Simonides is being unreasonably contentious out of love of honor, but his earlier classification of Simonides among the secretive sophists of old, together with his comment that examining this poem will give them a different way of pursuing the same question of virtue (339a3–6), suggests that he may intend to unpack some hidden teaching of the poem that will reconcile the two statements he quotes. Thus he might plan to argue that the *goodness* of a dutiful citizen is hard to attain and hence rare, but that it is attainable through human effort and indeed is necessarily present where circumstances and teachers cooperate to give it sufficient support, whereas *nobility* is a rare, divine gift, which allows the best souls to rise above all adversity. If these two aspects of virtue are different and spring from different sources, then virtue is not one. Such an interpretation is likely to elicit serious admiration from the assembled company and to give Socrates little hold against Protagoras. But Socrates, recruiting Prodicus as an ally, foils Protagoras by exasperating him with such a series of crazy interpretive suggestions that Protagoras finally throws in the towel. Protagoras is not skilled at developing a thesis by means of dialectic at the best of times, and he is helpless against Socrates' barrage of wild volleys.

First Socrates clowns by pretending to think that the great Protagoras has never considered the difference between becoming and being. Protagoras is of course famous for his provocative teaching that all being is becoming, but perhaps Socrates is signaling that central to Simonides' poem and its teaching on virtue is its adumbration of the underlying, permanent necessities that constrain all beings and even the gods, and that Protagoras has not thought enough about the evidence for such necessities. Building on the distinction between being and becoming, Socrates throws Protagoras further off balance with the surprising proposal that Simonides really means to say that becoming virtuous is hard, but remaining so is easy. He quotes Hesiod's famous lines, "Before virtue the gods placed sweat," but whenever someone "reaches the apex of it, then it is easy to possess, difficult though it was" (340d2–5; cf. Hesiod *Works and Days* 289–92). This interpretation makes Protagoras so annoyed that he forgets Simonides' poem entirely. "It would be great ignorance on the part of the poet if he said virtue were such a paltry thing to possess, which is of all things most difficult, as all human beings hold it to be" (340e5–7). Protagoras does not even bother to cite the next line of the poem, which contradicts Socrates' interpretation directly: "God alone could have this prize" (341e3). But perhaps that line goes too far for him; Protagoras' outburst and the fact that he ignores the next line both bespeak a passionate belief that true virtue does exist among human beings as a thing of great rarity, difficulty, and nobility. Can Socrates have a serious thought behind the apparently clumsy error of assimilating Simonides' thought to Hesiod's? Perhaps it is that, despite his disclaimer in the next line of his poem, Simonides is pointing to a deeper sense in which true virtue, based on wisdom, is not only achievable but once acquired is lasting and even pleasant, rather than heroically difficult. This thought would accord with the words of Hesiod that Socrates quotes and their immediate context, which concerns the distinction between wisdom and folly, and would suggest an important disagreement between Protagoras' view of virtue on one hand and the view held by Simonides, Hesiod, Socrates, and Prodicus on the other. This suggestion, however, Socrates does not yet develop.

Instead, Socrates launches a second interpretation of the line, even more far-fetched than the first. Using the slow and pedantic Prodicus as his straight man, he proposes that Simonides did not understand what contemporary Athenians do by the word "difficult" (*chalepos*), but instead understood it to mean "bad," and is reproaching Pittacus for saying, in effect, "It is bad to be virtuous." Protagoras responds that this is nonsense: Simonides meant what anyone means by "difficult." Socrates immediately concedes this, pointing out that Simonides in the next line attributes nobility to the gods and surely their nobility is not bad; he and Prodicus were only joking. With all his illogical twists and turns, Socrates has left everyone in the room dizzy and has reduced Protagoras to silence. Aside from putting an end to Protagoras' attempted cross-examination, what is Socrates' point? Could he mean seriously to suggest that in Simonides' eyes nobility really is bad—because it involves pain, or a sacrifice of one's true good, or a fanatical raging, like Achilles', that betrays a lack of self-knowledge? But how could Simonides attribute any such thing to the divine beings? Might he mean by nobility a capacity and disposition to dispense favors with magnificent freedom, unconstrained by calculations of utility and indeed unconstrained by the good and bad as one finds them, and thus simply gracious or simply inexplicable in one's benefactions? Might Simonides, and Socrates with him, see something ultimately bad in humans' attribution of such radical freedom to the gods and, by extension, to themselves at their best?

The Meaning of Simonides' Poem

When Socrates secures a free hand to offer his own interpretation of the poem, he now does what he has given everyone to understand he can neither do himself nor abide from anyone else: he spins out a long speech, by turns quoting and interpreting almost all of the poem. Evidently he agrees with Protagoras about the value of studying the great poets, and certainly he demonstrates his long reflection on this one; perhaps such meditations have constituted a significant part of his own education. But the interpretation he now offers is a fantastic mixture of helpful insights with a fresh succession of outlandish claims.[24] Socrates does Protagoras one better by claiming that not just the ancient poets but the whole citizen body of Sparta engages in secret philosophizing. He continues to put strange constructions on words and to offer strained readings of Greek syntax. He claims on each point to be in perfect agreement with Simonides, even attributing to him his own unconventional claims that virtue is wisdom, that virtue is one, that the only thing truly worth having is understanding, that no one does wrong involuntarily, and, by implication, that virtue is not a sacrifice of happiness but the core of happiness. If Socrates is, after all, capable of speaking in a lengthy monologue, he is perhaps not capable of finding safety in boring inanities; he takes refuge instead in statements so unqualified that they are absurd and to that extent obscure. Given the wild character of Socrates' interpretation of Simonides' poem, then, it may be useful first to read what we have of the poem carefully on its own terms, guided by those suggestions of Socrates that seem most sensible, before considering what Socrates is trying to accomplish with his stranger interpretive suggestions.

At first reading, the poem seems to embody the traditional, tragic spirit of pagan piety. According to Socrates' third and most obviously sensible interpretation of the opening lines of the first two stanzas (344b6–c3), Simonides is saying that hard as it is to become good, it is impossible for humans to remain permanently so. When overtaken by misfortunes, we cannot avoid falling into sin. Nobility of spirit belongs by nature only to the gods, and human beings whom the gods favor possess it only for a time, as a merely borrowed grace. Therefore the best that we can do is to acknowledge humbly our dependence on the gods and to avoid hubris at all costs. Since all of us must bow to necessity, we ought not to blame others when they do so, but we may reasonably praise those who are no worse than fortune forces them to be—those who are not willfully bad. It is good to recognize our need for law, to eschew unreasonable demands on one another, and to welcome those who are not gratuitously evil or shameful.

But the reflections expressed in the poem invite questions that may point to a deeper current of meaning, flowing in a different direction. That such a current may exist is suggested also by Protagoras' attribution of a secret teaching to Simonides as well as by the statement in the penultimate line of the poem that the vast majority of human beings are fools, implying that Simonides may be addressing only the very few. If the gods do not love men because they are good, but men are good only because favored by fortune or the gods, how are the gods, at least in their actions towards human beings, noble at all and not simply arbitrary? If all human beings are as good as fortune permits, if human beings and even the gods must bow to necessity, how is the divine law that embodies the spirit of retribution just and not irrational?

These thoughts lead, then, in the third stanza, to a new spirit of humane realism. Accepting that human nobility and baseness are subject to fortune and that perfection is not to be sought among human beings, Simonides says he praises and loves those who at least do wrong only under compulsion. But this thought, too, proves incoherent on close inspection and in need of revision. For how could anyone do wrong willingly, if "so long as he does well *every* man is good"? Shameful acts would only be driven by necessity, but "against necessity not even the gods can fight." Must Simonides not ultimately agree with Socrates, then—as Socrates claims he does at 345d6–e4—that all evil is the necessary consequence of either compulsion or ignorance? This is why, as we shall see, Socrates reads Simonides to be saying here not that he praises those who do nothing shameful willingly, but that he willingly praises those who do nothing shameful.

Thus, in the final stanza, Simonides moves to an even more gentle spirit of realism. He embraces the "healthy" human being who is not excessively wild—perhaps meaning he who avoids on one hand the madness of excessive hopes for human perfection, which can lead to destructive anger or to debilitating self-hatred, and on the other the wildness of those who would openly scorn as unnatural the human law that we all need. Without expecting any human being to leave behind the concern for his own good, the wise person seeks such common good as is available and respects the beliefs that give necessary support to the laws. But if nobility is to be found neither in the gracious gods nor in self-sacrificing heroes, is a different kind of nobility not coming to sight here, in Simonides' own spirit of sublime humanity? This noble spirit seems to depend only on human wisdom and not at all on divine dispensation. It comes through seeing that the world is governed by necessities deeper and more immutable than the will of any god and through living rationally in light of those necessities. In exemplifying this outlook Simonides is silent on the justice of the gods, but he does attribute justice to humans who secure the good of their cities. Thus Simonides teaches that in the end we are not after all simply at the mercy of an arbitrary fate or of inscrutable divine beings, but that the wiser we can become, the more we can be pilots of our own ships. In its modest realism and frank, generous candor, the humanity he exhibits may indeed be the best of all human goods, if also very rare.[25] For Simonides as for Socrates, what is healthy and soberly sensible comes to the fore at the end as the ultimate standard of human merit.

Socrates' Interpretation of the Poem of Simonides (342a6–47a5)

The interpretation just given is of course only one reading and is based on an incomplete text. But it accords with Protagoras' comment that Simonides wrote esoterically, which Socrates does not contest, and with Cicero's comment on Simonides' free thinking. It is informed both by Socrates' pointers as to how to begin to understand the poem and by this interpreter's long meditations on Socratic philosophy, on the basis of which Simonides' thought does appear strikingly Socratic. Hence it accords as well with Socrates' indications here that he and Simonides are in agreement, as well as with Xenophon's choice of Simonides as a dramatic substitute for Socrates in the *Hiero*. Assuming provisionally, then, that Socrates understood the poem in some such way, let us now examine the interpretation he offers to the gathering and especially to Protagoras, considering what purpose he may have in launching his more outlandish suggestions and what sober kernel of meaning each might contain.

Socrates begins with the startling claim that "philosophy is most ancient and most abundant among the Greeks in both Crete and Lacedaemon, and the greatest abundance of sophists on earth are there" (342a7–b1). In our astonishment at hearing the xenophobic, militaristic, and anti-intellectual Sparta called the home of philosophy, we scarcely notice that Socrates is virtually equating philosophy with sophistry, confirming that the sharp distinction between them drawn by Plato is in some degree a fiction. But the Spartans philosophize or pursue wisdom surreptitiously, Socrates continues, lest other cities learn the secret to their preeminence among the Greeks, which lies not in "fighting and courage" but in wisdom (342b4–6). For evidence of the Spartans' esoteric philosophizing, Socrates cites their habit of remaining for the most part boorishly silent, while occasionally letting loose pithy volleys of devastating incisiveness. He cites as well the respect Sparta enjoyed among the famous wise men of old, whose proverbs are inscribed in the great temple to Apollo at Delphi: "Know thyself," and "nothing in excess." The ancient sages, among whom was the Pittacus whom Simonides takes on in this poem, not only admired the Spartans for their wisdom but imitated them in practicing Laconic brevity in speech.

What can Socrates' serious thought be with these strange claims about Sparta? For all the absurdity of calling the Spartans philosophic, Socrates' account in fact points to a number of curious resemblances between himself and the Spartans. Both practice brevity of speech and oppose showy intellectual displays; both are suspicious of projects of popular enlightenment; both prefer staying at home to traveling; both honor citizen virtue; and both are given to concealment. In all these ways they are aligned against the cosmopolitan Protagoras. More importantly, both Socrates and the Spartans prize moderation and self-knowledge—again perhaps more seriously than Protagoras does. Might this comical account of Sparta provide a clue to the reason why Socrates was himself a citizen-philosopher and even a Laconizer in comparison with Protagoras, inasmuch as he considered Sparta's political arrangements to provide good soil for human excellence? But if this account reveals a surprising kinship between Socrates and Sparta, it also illuminates an unbridgeable gap—precisely by pretending that the gap is not there. For the account adumbrates what would have to be true if the boldest claim of Socrates and the deepest thought of Simonides' poem were true without qualification—that is to say, if genuine virtue were knowledge or wisdom—and if at the same time, as all the Greeks agreed, the Spartans were outstandingly virtuous. The Spartans and wise men such as Socrates would have to understand moderation and self-knowledge in the same way; they would have to share the other traits Socrates has sketched for the same reasons; and courage would have to be either no part of virtue (and hence, as Socrates says at 342b6, not the reason for the Spartans' superiority) or a necessary part of wisdom.

In fact, the Spartans understand the Delphic command "know thyself" to call for simple piety and acceptance of one's place in the polis, under the rule of the elders and the law, whereas Socrates seeks a deeper self-knowledge through the critical questioning of ancestral and lawful opinions with a view to understanding the more fundamental and permanent truths of nature. Spartan moderation is a self-restraint born of lawful habituation and shame, whereas Socratic moderation is an inner harmony resulting from deep independent confrontations with the sources of irrational anger, pride, and hope in the human psyche—all of which are embodied in the raging Achilles to whom Socrates compares Protagoras. Thus the differences between the Spartan and Socratic understandings of self-knowledge and moderation come down to the difference between the kind of virtue that is grounded in shame and habituation, which cannot possibly be reduced to knowledge or wisdom, and the kind of virtue that is grounded in independent thought, which can.

The other differences follow on these. The Spartans' pithiness of speech is born of a confidence that the important questions are settled and a preference for action over words; Socrates' penchant for the short exchanges of dialectics is born precisely of his awareness of human uncertainty about the most important questions and his consequent persuasion that words and what lies behind them should be examined closely, one at a time, so that he and his interlocutors may each make what progress he is capable of towards understanding the truths that the authorities of his society have *not* adequately settled. The Spartans' hatred of showy speech reflects their view that honor should attach only to deeds and in the best case to the city, not the individual; Socrates shares neither of these preferences but is moved instead by a dislike for the boastful pretense of knowledge one does not have. The Spartans, confident that the truth is simple to see and hard to live by, hold that openness to other customs and ideas can only be corrupting; Socrates, omnivorously curious for his own part, is kept at home by his judgment that the best route to wisdom is careful examination of oneself and the opinions that one finds all around one. Yet in a way the civic Spartans and the philosophic Socrates are nonetheless aligned against the cosmopolitan Protagoras.

Only when it comes to secrecy does the agreement between the Spartans and Socrates appear to run much deeper than the surface, even if this agreement, too, is imperfect. Socrates gives two reasons why the Spartans practice secrecy: they want to protect from prying eyes that which gives them superiority over the other Greeks, and they want to protect from corrupting influences the virtue of their young. Might not Socrates, too, have a dual motive for concealing his wisdom? Holding a higher estimate of what may be learned from ordinary moral opinion than the sophists did, Socrates seems to have believed that even true, philosophic virtue depends more on a healthy polity than Protagoras thinks. Yet seeing so clearly the ways in which the political community's foundations are questionable, he knows even better than the Spartans the dangers of corruption that the sophists pose to traditional civic virtue. Hence the esotericism that Socrates shares with the ancient wise men and that Protagoras claims is unnecessary has as much to do with protecting the city from philosophy as it does with the direct self-protection of the philosopher. But once again, if Socrates considers philosophic wisdom to be true virtue, he must either defend his rejection of the Spartan view that courage lies at the heart of virtue, or show how courage in fact reduces to wisdom.

With this strange Spartan preface, Socrates now proceeds to go through Simonides' poem in detail. He begins by hanging on the thin thread of the Greek particle "*men*" the doubtful claim that the whole poem was intended as a polemic against Pittacus, made simply out of envy, in hopes of advancing Simonides' fame. Since this particle is Socrates' only evidence for his harsh claim, and since he in fact clearly regards the poem to be a beautiful work that rewards the closest scrutiny (cf. 339b5–8, 344a7–b3), what can his point be? At the least, Socrates seems to be indicating that he regards the republic of letters to be less perfectly harmonious than Hippias imagines. This exaggerated attribution to Simonides of envy against the Spartophile Pittacus might be a signal that Socrates considers even the relatively careful and patriotic Simonides to have been already too open in his skepticism out of an eagerness for fame, and insufficiently respectful of the rich soil of moral and political seriousness that both citizens and philosophers need in order to be optimally nurtured. But this will not be his last word on Simonides' reasons for challenging Pittacus.

Next, Socrates makes the tenuous claim that the first line, which is most naturally rendered "Now a truly good man it is hard to become," must instead be read to mean "Now a good man it is truly hard to become," on the grounds that no one could sensibly claim a distinction between a good man and a truly good man. In our own examination of the poem, Simonides did seem to be pointing to just such a distinction between true human goodness and what is commonly understood as nobility. If Socrates' explicit and Simonides' implicit claim that virtue is knowledge or wisdom holds, if it holds for all virtue without qualification, then as Socrates says here, all virtue will be true virtue. But if the civic virtue exemplified by the Spartans and the true virtue born of wisdom are in fact fundamentally different, then the Socratic thesis may well apply only to the philosophic and not to the civic form. Socrates is signaling that he will read Simonides' poem as if Simonides failed to distinguish the true philosophic form of virtue from the less true, popular form. If this is a strange step for Socrates to take in interpreting a poem that evidently is reflecting on just such a distinction, perhaps Socrates would justify it with this thought: that Simonides has not yet fully earned the right to his distinction, having not yet adequately proven that true virtue as he quietly depicts it is grounded in solid understanding of the human condition. Consequently, Socrates may think that Simonides' own virtue is in some sense more subject to the vicissitudes of fortune than he thinks.

Reiterating that the intention of Simonides' whole poem is to refute Pittacus' saying that it is difficult to be noble (344b3–5), Socrates now offers the reading of the first five lines of the poem that we adopted above as the most plausible surface meaning, interpreting them as teaching that virtue is hard to attain but impossible to keep, so that they fit smoothly with the next line,

> but god alone could have this prize. (344c2–3)

But when he takes up the following two,

> but for a man it is not possible not to be bad
> whom unmanageable misfortune brings down, (344c4–5)

he again gives a strange interpretation. Asking what it means to be brought down, Socrates gives three examples: "A great storm that strikes may make a pilot unable to manage, and a harsh season that comes may leave a farmer unable to manage, and these same things may happen to a doctor" (344d2–5). The examples all involve misfortune of a particular kind, ones that overwhelm the capacity of the human arts, and moreover ones that either come literally from the heavens (storms and seasons) or were traditionally thought to come from the gods (illness). Socrates curiously considers only these misfortunes' effect on the practitioners of the arts. He says nothing of the pilots' passengers or the farmers' families or the doctors' patients being brought down by misfortune, even though patients' misfortunes, in particular, would seem far graver than their physicians' when the medical art fails—as if the entire point of life were to pilot well a ship of a sort that can have no passengers. He says furthermore that men's good and bad character follows the vicissitudes of fortune only in the case of good men, as if bad men were invariably bad, and that all of the wise are eventually brought down by unmanageable misfortunes—as if no captain were able to keep his wits and his dignity about him when his ship is going down, and no doctor were immune to despair when his treatments fail. All this comes as a surprise, given that we thought Simonides' claims about the vulnerability of virtue applied only to vulgar, habit-based virtue and not to wisdom.

Equally strange is the way misfortune is replaced by ignorance in Socrates' interpretation of the next two lines:

> So long as he does well, every man is good,
> But bad if he does badly. (344e7–8)

The phrase translated here as "does well" is the infamously ambiguous *eu prattein*, which can mean equally to fare well or to act well. In our interpretation above we rendered it as faring well, since these lines seem most obviously to be expanding on the thought of the previous two about the power of good and bad fortune to make men virtuous or vicious. Socrates, however, takes the phrase to mean acting well, and that only in one very specific sense. "What, then, is good action when it comes to letters, and what makes a man good at letters? It's clear that it is the learning of these things" (345a1–2). Socrates might seem to be affirming his own thesis that thinking correctly is the cause of virtue and thinking badly is the cause of vice. But in fact, thinking correctly, as he puts it here, is identified not as the cause of acting well but as the whole substance of it.

Two clues as to Socrates' thought lie in his strange claim that only one who was once a good physician can ever become a bad one, and this equally strange remark about knowledge: "So also the good man could at one time become bad either as a result of time or suffering or illness or some other calamity—for this alone is doing badly, to be deprived of knowledge—but the bad man could not become bad, for he is always so" (345b2–6). Socrates' claim about physicians seems partially but only partially true. Those who practice medicine without any knowledge of the art are indeed not bad physicians but only quacks; yet it is not the case that bad physicians were necessarily ever good ones. But his claim is perhaps quite true of philosophers: only one who is very wise is ever a philosopher at all. And the other claims he has made fit philosophy better than they fit the arts he uses as examples. In the search for the truth for its own sake, only autonomous seekers and not passive passengers can ever benefit, and for one who is single-minded in pursuit of the truth, doing well and faring well are indeed the same. Now we are at the opposite pole from the Spartan perspective according to which victory, political freedom, and rule are the goods that matter and that constitute the aim and test of virtue. Socrates is showing now what would have to be true if virtue understood as knowledge or wisdom were the only human excellence, and if that virtue were the only good worth having.

But why, then, would great calamities ever unstring the human mind, as Socrates claims Simonides is arguing they necessarily do, when he insists that "becoming noble is difficult yet possible, but to be it impossible" (344e5–6)? If Simonides is identifying theoretical wisdom as the sole good in life, why does Socrates confuse matters by taking all of his examples from the practical arts, and why does he grant such power to storms, droughts, and plagues? Or is there something else that comes from the heavens that does have the power to destroy human virtue, to which these examples are merely pointers? No doubt terrible calamities, like serious illnesses, do sometimes derange the mind, but perhaps it is other unsettling challenges that come from "heaven" that pose a more serious threat to the autonomous goodness of Simonides' humane wisdom—perhaps above all the unsettling phenomenon of prophecy, which Socrates may not think Simonides ever adequately addressed. The lack of autonomy and permanence that Simonides attributes to ordinary virtue, then, Socrates attributes to Simonides' wisdom itself—and likely by extension to Protagoras'.

So far in his interpretation of the poem, Socrates has seemed to endorse first the Spartan view that wisdom is valuable chiefly or exclusively as a means to victory and freedom and then the most extreme philosophic view that wisdom understood as an end in itself is all that matters. Both positions are incomplete, the first in reducing philosophy to a tool, the second in denying our need for such goods as health and security, and consequently our dependence on both luck and the prudence and goodwill of other human beings. The last part of Socrates' interpretation of the poem indirectly addresses this disjunction, by indicating the sensible way that a wise person will recognize his lack of self-sufficiency and accommodate himself to those that he finds himself attached to as a matter of necessity. Reiterating once again that the poem is directed against Pittacus, he explains now that Simonides and indeed all the ancient sages shared his own view that vice is involuntary, in his gloss on the lines,

> But everyone I praise and love
> willingly who does
> nothing shameful; but against necessity not even the gods fight. (345d3–5)

This time without doing violence to Greek syntax, but still with slender direct textual evidence for his supporting argument, Socrates insists that the adverb "willingly" must be understood to refer to Simonides and not those he is judging. "For I pretty much think this, that none of the wise men believes that any human being willingly errs or willingly carries out any shameful or bad deed, but they know well that all those who do shameful and bad things do them unwillingly" (345d9–e4). This thought agrees with the deepest currents of thought that we found in the poem as well. The breadth of Socrates' claim is still surprising, but it is worth considering seriously; perhaps in reading all the ancient poets it would be fruitful to begin with the hypothesis that they shared this understanding of moral responsibility and see what new understanding of the text that hypothesis may open up. Protagoras has already expressed such a view, and it seems likely that many of the pre-Socratic philosophers, at any rate, agreed with Simonides that "against necessity not even the gods fight" (345d5), or that, driving not only inanimate nature, but also all living and human and even divine beings, are knowable necessities. Consequently, they shared the calm spirit of Protagoras' and Simonides' realism, judging anger and retributive punishment to be irrational. Still, one may hold all this and still not be quite Socratic. For implicit in Socrates' claim about virtue and knowledge and the ignorance at the root of vice is the thought that understanding is really key, that not blind passion but a certain failure of understanding and indeed a confused mixture of contradictory judgments is at work in all moral failings. It was above all to test and explore the implications of this hypothesis that Socrates undertook the dialectical investigations into moral opinion that set him apart from all his intellectual predecessors and contemporaries.

But Socrates immediately confuses matters again. He interprets Simonides to be saying with his verse on willing praise that he gladly praises those who do nothing base, in contrast to the reluctant way he or any sensible man compels himself to praise certain others who are less worthy, for example, parents or a fatherland that have been unjust to him, or the tyrants who were Simonides' patrons. So far, so good. The problem comes when Socrates contrasts the decent man who unwillingly praises his estranged parents or fatherland and who patiently endures their injustice with the "wicked" who eagerly seize upon their faults and blame them so as to exculpate themselves for their neglect: "As a result, they . . . heap willful enmities on top of those that arise from compulsion" (346a7–b1). Is this not a case of uncompelled wickedness, just the thing that Socrates said Simonides did not believe was possible? The whole picture is painted in moral terms quite incompatible with the thought that everyone does what he does because it is the best that he can do; here we have a moral man angered by injustice that he views as willfully, unnecessarily harmful, restraining himself and denying himself the honor to which he is justly entitled, in what he understands to be a free choice to follow his duty. In attributing to Simonides this series of reflections, is Socrates not taking back his implied classification of Simonides among the wise, "none of [whom] holds that any human being willingly errs" (345d9–e2)?

Perhaps so; perhaps Socrates means to indicate that Simonides took the first important step towards understanding moral responsibility but failed to carry his insights out consistently, so that even as he taught that human choices are all necessitated, he took credit for the uncompelled (or freely chosen, self-compelled) generosity of his own judgments. Thus he left it to Socrates to build on his initial insights a more consistent account of the phenomena. It is also possible, however, that Socrates sees no daylight between his and Simonides' understanding of the necessities that underlie both virtuous and wicked actions, and that he is deliberately giving a misleadingly moral, civic account of those cases in which wise men speak well of those who do not deserve it. These cases would include both Simonides' flattery of tyrants and Socrates' own loyalty to the city of Athens. Perhaps indeed, in first saying that neither Simonides nor any wise man believes that people ever willfully do evil and then attributing to Simonides the view that he has just rejected, Socrates is precisely imitating the movement of Simonides' own rhetoric, in which the boldness of his comment on necessity is softened by a suggestion at the end that there is still willful evil and unnecessitated nobility after all. That would imply that Simonides and Socrates both saw a need for "short speech" where moral responsibility is concerned: they both voiced their true views only with great caution, precisely out of the humane realism that sees how rare true wisdom and hence truly autonomous virtue is, and how much support is needed to keep the less wise on a good path.

But if Simonides' and Socrates' real reasons for gentle speech are not as dutiful as this story implies, what precisely are their reasons for going beyond caution and actively praising the unwise? In Socrates' case, at least, might it not have been a simple, human affection for the community that bore him? This thought might seem to be underscored in the present passage with its references to love for parents and fatherland, until we reflect on the fact that he says the wise man "compels" himself to love them and compares this compulsion to Simonides' less savory self-compelled flattery of tyrants. Somehow a hard necessity is at work, and if in Socrates' case it is partly the desire to make Athens a better home for future philosophers, it is clearly also in both cases partly individual self-protection. The fact that anyone wise would find necessary such flattery as Simonides engaged in casts a shadow over Socrates' bold claim that thinking well is the whole of faring well, with its implied claim that the wise are sublimely self-sufficient. So perhaps we have here an implicit correction of Socrates' moral and hypermoral-eudaimonist claims, an acknowledgment that even the philosopher's wisdom must be practical and political as well as theoretical out of self-preservation, and an acknowledgment that even if his wisdom is immune to being unstrung by challenges that come from heaven, his happiness is not. Still, we might ask Simonides, why should it ever be necessary to flatter tyrants? Does this choice not betray too great a willingness to debase his wisdom for the sake of money and fame? Perhaps. But Simonides might ask in turn why, if Socrates was equally wise, he remained in a city that would execute him rather than live more freely and safely abroad. And why did he increase this danger by choosing to state more openly what Simonides had stated so quietly? Both of these differences bring us back to

Socrates' project of dialectics: perhaps only if this was essential are the risks he took fully rational.

Socrates' last word on Simonides is that he was not, after all, so contentiously honor-loving in his criticism of Pittacus as Socrates previously charged, but that (as a good citizen, if on a pan-Hellenic scale), he reproached Pittacus only reluctantly and only for "stating utter falsehoods about the greatest things" (347a2). This, too, is strange, because Pittacus' statement that "it is hard to be noble" does not seem egregiously wrong according to Socrates' more sober-sounding third account of the disagreement, according to which Simonides taught that virtue is not "hard" to sustain but rather hard to attain and impossible to keep. With his repeated insistence that Simonides' whole purpose in writing the poem was to explicate his disagreement with Pittacus on this point, Socrates confirms our suspicion that his Hesiodic interpretation of the disagreement was his most serious after all: Simonides would thus be aligned with Hesiod's, Prodicus', and Socrates' view of virtue against Pittacus' and the Spartans' agonistic view, and the central point of the poem would be that virtue, when fully developed, is not a great ongoing struggle of self-overcoming but is instead the core of the greatest happiness. But if this is so, the famous, reputedly wise men of old do not all belong to the class of wise men whom Socrates says all agree about moral responsibility, and the republic of letters is not simply an island of idyllic harmony.

Second Dramatic Interlude (347a6–49a6)

As Socrates ends his interpretation of the poem, Hippias himself displays the competitive character of his little republic. He praises Socrates' account (whether altogether willingly is not clear) but he also wishes to display his own. Alcibiades comes again to Socrates' aid to keep the joust between Socrates and Protagoras on track. Socrates challenges Protagoras' dignity by suggesting that, after all, the interpretation of poetry is a party game for unlearned boors who have no ideas of their own to discuss and who in effect need hired flute girls to have a good time. As he reduces Simonides to the level of a flute girl, he flatters the assembled company. More seriously, he addresses the great limitation of the written word. Only gatherings of educated men who are noble and good, such as the assembled guests claim to be, "require neither a foreign sound nor poets, who cannot be asked what it is they are saying" (347d2–e4). Socrates has just shown his ability to engage the thought of a poet and to draw out of a poem many thoughts both openly and implicitly stated. He is obviously equally good at observing much that writers and speakers betray unintentionally, an essential skill without which he could not ask the probing questions that he asks in conversation. The one thing he cannot do with an author is "to put him to the test" (347e7), by forcing him to answer questions he does not want to answer and to choose between cherished opinions that are in conflict. This is what he is eager to do with Protagoras and what makes him such an unwelcome fellow-citizen to Protagoras in their little republic.[26] But as becomes increasingly clear, such uncomfortable contests are Socrates' chief reason for wanting to be there at all. Protagoras has no clear route of graceful escape and yet continues to delay and demur, no doubt hoping that some fresh distraction will arise to relieve him, but once again Alcibiades prevents that from happening. Appealing to the host Callias, Alcibiades asks whether Protagoras is not behaving ignobly in refusing either to converse or to state openly that he is unwilling to converse—in refusing either to reenter the lists, that is, or to declare defeat. Socrates tells his companions that Protagoras was ashamed and only with the greatest reluctance bade Socrates to ask whatever he wished. Whether Protagoras' shame was the deep shame of recognizing an important failing in himself or only the annoyance of being trapped by a more clever speaker may be questioned, as may his wisdom in resuming the contest with such an opponent. Does his prudent self-interest as a teacher demand it, or is Socrates' victory by now so likely that only a rash, shame-bred bravery urges him on, like a Hector returning for the final fight against Achilles?

Socrates now immediately changes his imagery, welcoming Protagoras not as an opponent but as a fellow warrior on a hunt for the same quarry or a raid against the same enemy in search of "what I myself am continually perplexed by," quoting Homer's line, "when two go together, one observes before the other" (348c6 and d1; *Iliad* 10.224). He thus reminds Protagoras what sort of contest they should be engaged in, a common quest for the truth. Yet we cannot help noting that Socrates still compares himself and Protagoras to Homeric heroes, who never ceased to be rivals even when allies in a desperate fight. Curiously, he also casts himself now not as Odysseus but Diomedes, putting Protagoras into the role of the wily Odysseus. And now Socrates makes even clearer what his own project is: it is not so much an attempt to enlist an ally who he hopes may see something crucial before he does as it is a search for confirmation: "When one alone sees, he immediately goes about looking for one to whom he may point it out and with whom he may confirm it, until he finds him" (348d3–5). The refutation of the reluctant Protagoras will corroborate an insight Socrates has had but which he cannot rely upon without further testing. And essential to that insight is the question of the unity of virtue.

The Status of Courage (349a6–51b2)

Asked again to state whether he views the virtues of wisdom (*sophia*), moderation, courage, justice, and piety as fundamentally similar or distinct from one another, Protagoras replies,

> "But I tell you, Socrates," he said, "that these are all parts of virtue, and that four of them are reasonably close to one another, but that courage is quite different from all these. And here is how you will know that I speak the truth: you will find many human beings who are most unjust, impious, immoderate, and unlearned, and yet who are exceedingly courageous." (349d2–8)

Protagoras no longer insists on any gap between wisdom and justice and no longer even suggests that civic virtue may be unwise. Evidently Socrates has taught him to be more cautious. At a deeper level, he would likely agree with Socrates that there is a version and perhaps the best version of each of the other virtues that is nothing but the application of wise judgment. But courage seems different; it is much less clearly reducible to any sort of wisdom.

Focusing on the relationship of courage to wisdom, Socrates asks whether the courageous are bold. The word he uses, *tharraleos*, means both daring and confident; its cognate, *tharsos*, denotes especially the confidence one needs to stand one's ground or to press forward doggedly. Protagoras replies, "They're even impetuous . . . in the face of things the many fear to advance towards" (349e3). Socrates himself may think of the virtue of courage chiefly or solely in terms of steadfast endurance, rooted in the confident knowledge that one is strong enough to bear whatever may arise; Protagoras seizes upon the eagerness to face dangers that is the rare and impressive mark of a hero. What is the source of this eagerness, and can it possibly be reduced to or even fully compatible with wisdom? Rather than take up that question directly, Socrates approaches the problem from the other side. In all cases in which impetuosity in the face of danger is not wise, is it noble or virtuous at all? He begins by asking whether virtue, which Protagoras teaches, is noble, and when Protagoras replies that he is as certain of its nobility as of his own sanity, Socrates asks again, "So is it partly shameful and partly noble . . . or is the whole of it noble?"

(349e6–7). The first alternative could be taken in several ways. Virtue might be judged to have some roots that are shameful—for example, anger or excessive pride or false opinion—and some that are noble—for example, love of country. Or it might be judged to have certain expressions that are shameful, such as fighting bravely against one's country, and others that are noble, such as fighting bravely for it. Or again, individual acts of virtue, even when done for the best of motives, might be thought to be partly shameful and partly noble, for example, the execution of a criminal by a wise judge, which might be considered shameful for the criminal and shameful also in a sense for the city that failed to prevent crime, but still noble as an affirmation of the city's principles. Socrates' formulation is open-ended enough to elicit any of these reservations about virtue's nobility if Protagoras has them, but Protagoras, like Meno, proves passionately committed to the view that true virtue must be thoroughly noble in every way: "The whole, surely, is as noble as anything can be" (349e7–8). Will Protagoras, then, call any act of physical daring noble courage, however mercenary or criminal or irrational its motive? Or will he refuse to call courageous some acts that normally are considered to be? If he does, what criteria will he apply? To count as courageous, will an act have to be perfectly rational—or to the contrary will it have to be free of rational calculation?

Socrates now probes this question with a series of examples. Avoiding the most interesting but also delicate case of citizens who die for their country, he begins instead with cases that are especially governed by calculation, the boldness of divers who risk drowning for profits. Establishing that divers are bold "because they have knowledge" (350a2–3), Socrates then asks about skilled cavalry and light-armed troops in comparison to their unskilled counterparts. Here he does not attribute the men's boldness simply to knowledge: perhaps no soldier's eagerness to fight is ever simply calculating, but some element of anger, pride, devotion, shame, greed, or ambition for glory is always at work in the eagerness to fight that Protagoras calls courage. Thus we have on the table one case in which knowledge is the source of a boldness that is not especially noble and one in which knowledge—at least the technical know-how that Socrates is calling attention to—seems at most to add to a boldness that has other roots. If Socrates is preparing to ask Protagoras whether knowledge is *the* cause of that boldness which is noble and hence true courage, his examples in fact seem chosen to elicit the answer that it is not.

Protagoras readily agrees that skilled fighters' knowledge makes them bolder than they otherwise would be. Sophist that he is, he even overgeneralizes the conclusion to affirm that knowledge in all cases makes people bolder, forgetting that knowledge often brings new reasons for fear. When Socrates reminds him that it is sometimes ignorance that makes people bold, Protagoras agrees, but on further questioning he denies that those who are bold for this reason are courageous and even calls them madmen. Thus guided by Socrates, Protagoras has excluded the irrational from the ranks of the courageous but has not explicitly excluded the overly calculating. On this basis Socrates tries out a possible conclusion:

> "Then are these," I said, "who are bold in this way not courageous but manifestly mad? And then again those wisest ones are also boldest, and being boldest, most courageous? And according to this account, wisdom (*sophia*) would be courage?" (350c1–5)

As many commentators have observed, this conclusion is not logically justified. From what has been agreed, it follows only that courage requires knowledge, perhaps only as one essential ingredient. Nothing that has been said would rule out the conclusion that each act of courage is an exercise of a subrational passion or habit such as anger, love, or pride, guided in part by a knowledge that may be only technical. Protagoras has not made clear what kind of knowledge he thinks courage requires, but he has never said that it depends upon, let alone is, complete wisdom. Clearly he would not count as courageous a man who is bold only because he does not understand the dangers he is facing. But would he refuse to call courageous a brave patriot who does his best with unfamiliar weapons, knowing that he is facing a serious risk, or the brave patriot who does not realize how grave a predicament he is in but would not have been deterred from fighting if he had known? Might Protagoras at one and the same time believe that true courage must be well informed and sensible and that it is a splendidly noble virtue whose goodness has nothing to do with calculation? But if so, is this confusion in any way unique to Protagoras?

To see this ambivalence is to see better what is at stake in Socrates' abrupt substitution of wisdom for knowledge. In presenting a view that the argument has not prepared Protagoras for, Socrates is actively provoking Protagoras' resistance so that he may probe it, but in moving the discussion to the level of wisdom, he is at the same time giving a glimpse of his own deepest thoughts about virtue. As we saw in the *Meno*, knowledge may be technical or strategic but is always partial and does not seem to amount to a virtue; wisdom includes a comprehensive, unified understanding of oneself and of the ends that are worth pursuing that may much more plausibly be held to define one's whole character. If courage as ordinarily understood involves an often fiery collision between what one desires or considers sensible and what one views as noble, a courage that was simply the expression of wisdom would be very different. In the former case, the experience of inner division and self-overcoming is central, and an aspect but only one aspect of judgment seems to be guiding something very much devoid of calculation—some anger or pride, for example—to overcome contrary desires and fears. Reason is at best a small rider upon a great stallion, whose acts can by no means be called knowledge, and though reason may be the judge of time and place and manner of acting, it is not at all clear that it is ultimately the rider's and not the stallion's ends it is pursuing. In the case of the wisest courage, however, the role of reason is vastly expanded to inform all the passions. Here we have a kind of centaur (an admittedly scarce but perhaps not quite chimerical being where the soul is concerned) whose actions all are the expressions of the wise soul's grasp of what everything is worth and what is good to pursue, fully desired because so clearly seen. In this case courage would be nothing other than a strength in one's ability to grasp and to hold onto and to act upon one's knowledge of what is genuinely fearful, which would depend, finally, on knowledge of what is best. Yet even if a few souls should have access to complete knowledge of everything important about themselves and the human condition, we may still ask whether adequate knowledge of what is best to do is generally available at those times when courage is required. Is courage not needed especially where incalculable risks must be taken and the best course is by no means clear?

As Socrates has failed to prepare the ground for his radical claim about true courage or to address any of these questions, it is no surprise that Protagoras emphatically rejects that claim—and he does so despite his proclivity to overestimate the importance of knowledge. What, then, does this provocative maneuver elicit from him? He reacts sharply, asserting accurately that Socrates has misrepresented what has been established, but his correction is itself inaccurate. He charges Socrates with having failed to ask a question (whether all the bold are courageous) that Socrates not only asked but used Protagoras' answer to (namely, that the foolish are not) to draw his conclusion that courage must be wisdom. Protagoras is rewriting the last steps of the argument to erase his concession that courage must be sensible. And what he goes on to do is to give an elaborate account of courage as he understands it that is in some ways revealing but that is most evasive on the key question of courage's relation to knowledge. Socrates has not closed the noose on him this time, and Protagoras does not want to allow him the rope to try again to show that courage must be perfectly prudent.

In giving his new account of courage, Protagoras compares the difference between boldness and courage to that between strength and power. On the basis of his previous insistence that foolish boldness is not courage, we might have expected Protagoras to say that the mere animal energy of boldness needs to be guided by intelligence to become true courage, in just the same way that mere brute strength needs to be guided by intelligence to produce real power—as Socrates argues in the *Gorgias*. Instead, Protagoras denies the importance of knowledge almost entirely while radically elevating that of strength. Thus he says that power can come from knowledge or craziness or spiritedness, while strength, evidently a finer thing, comes from "nature and the good nurturing of bodies" (351a3–4). Likewise, boldness can come from technical knowledge or spiritedness or craziness, whereas courage comes from "nature and the good nurturing of souls" (351b1–2). Courage in this revised account is neither rational nor simply a product of teaching or training, but a natural gift like the strength and coordination that an athlete needs, the sublimely steady hand that a surgeon needs, or the unflappable coolness under fire that a general needs, which human art cannot instill but can only bring to perfection. And in the case of both body and soul, the perfection entails a beauty that is by no means reducible to rational utility. Once again Protagoras has slipped the leash and has given a long and stirring account that succeeds in obscuring Socrates' central question, the relation of virtue to knowledge. Socrates has elicited important responses, but he must again take a new approach in order to pin Protagoras down.

Pleasure as the Good (351b3–52b2)

Having made Protagoras feel strongly that virtue cannot be knowledge of any ordinary sort, Socrates now prepares to explore the deeper and more serious possibility that virtue nonetheless is wisdom in the sense of a complete and architectonic knowledge of what is good and how to live well. But what is curious now is that he immediately tries to elicit from Protagoras, and seems to endorse himself, the view that the good is the same as the pleasant. True, he calls hedonism the view of the "many," but he nonetheless uses it as the premise of his most explicit defense of his thesis that virtue is wisdom. This is puzzling because hedonism does not in fact seem to be Socrates' view; in his exchange with Callicles in the *Gorgias*, for example, he makes a long and powerful argument against it. Nor will Protagoras ever concede that it is his. Why should Plato in this way associate Socrates' signature thesis with hedonism? Perhaps this passage is meant to show that Socrates' view is less simply opposed to hedonism than it usually seems, so that under the guise of expounding the popular view, Socrates is also revealing important things about his own. Yet a divide must still remain, for the desire for the truth does not seem reducible to a desire for pleasure. Why he makes hedonism his premise, then, remains for now a puzzle.[27]

Socrates begins his new line of questioning with the following exchange:

> "Do you say, Protagoras," I said, "that some human beings live well, and others badly?" He said so. "Does it seem to you that a human being would live well, if he should live with pain and suffering?" He said not. "And what if he should die having lived his life pleasantly? Would he not seem to you to have lived well?" "To me at least he would," he said. (351b3–7)

This is also a curious way to introduce the hedonist position, with a direct reference to death, raising the question of the relation of pleasure to our knowledge of our mortality. Does the certainty of death not cast a grave shadow over the life of pleasure? More seriously, does there not lie behind death's certainty an uncertainty about its finality and the possibility of further pleasure or pains that might utterly dwarf those we experience here? At the same time, precisely these problems and the difficulty of solving them can make hedonism attractive as an escape. One attempt to pursue hedonism more wakefully and wisely is the Epicurean one, which argues that we can know that death is nothing terrible. This claim originates of course in the *Apology*, where Socrates makes it at least with regard to the good man, although with comically inadequate arguments. For those who consider such certainty unavailable, the alternative way to pursue a life of pleasure wakefully in the face of mortality would be as a deliberate gamble, in full recognition that heaven might be against one as it was in the myth of Prometheus, and still following one's own autonomous judgment as to what is best. To the extent that Protagoras considers himself a hedonist, it is likely in this spirit. For the Promethean soul in contrast to the Epicurean, such knowledge as is humanly available would then seem to be insufficient and in need of heroic courage as a supplement. But for Socrates, the conclusion to be drawn from our insufficient knowledge of the divine is that neither pleasure nor courage is what we most need but rather a dogged pursuit of the knowledge we lack and that we precisely do not know to be unavailable.

Protagoras, then, evinces both a hedonist stance and a secret admiration for outstanding courage so intense that he seems to regard courage as the noblest and perhaps the best of all things. Socrates' next question is designed to elicit his reservations about the simple identification of pleasure with happiness, precisely by stating it baldly: "Living pleasantly, then, is good, unpleasantly bad." Protagoras now responds, "If, that is, one should live his life taking pleasure in the noble things" (351b7–c2). Continuing to probe, Socrates pushes and even tries to shame Protagoras into avowing a hedonistic standard of the good:

> "What is this, Protagoras? Surely you don't, like the many, call some pleasant things bad and some painful ones good? I mean, inasmuch as things are pleasant, aren't they good, unless something else results from them? And again, in the same way, aren't the painful things, inasmuch as they are painful, bad?" (351c2–6)

It is surprising to see Socrates now identify the moral position, normally associated with gentlemen, as that of the vulgar "many." Clearly, however, he is appealing to Protagoras' pride as a member of an elite that takes its standard from nature and looks down upon all moralism as mere convention: from the pre-Socratics' and sophists' standpoint, the gentlemen themselves belong to the "many"—and so they do, in a sense, from Socrates' standpoint as well. The position from which Socrates himself denigrates vulgar moralism, however, is distinct both from the position Protagoras takes here and from simple hedonism. He is arguing that pleasure is as such good, though not the only good, and while he suggests that the beneficial and harmful may constitute an independent standard from which pleasures may be evaluated, he implicitly rejects the idea that the noble does.

Protagoras, overlooking these nuances, takes Socrates to be saying that all pleasures are simply good and all pains simply bad, and this he refuses to grant, saying that it is "safer" to divide both pleasures and pains into the good, the bad, and the intermediate (351d3). He refuses to side with Socrates against the many and even refuses to grant that pleasure as such is good, recommending instead that they investigate the question. When Socrates agrees to do so and invites Protagoras to guide the inquiry, Protagoras says that it is just for Socrates to take the lead on the grounds that this hedonist line of argument is Socrates' and not his own. What he does not do is actively come to the defense of the noble against Socrates. If odds-defying courage is his cardinal virtue, it is at present not in evidence. With this cagy response Protagoras has become Socrates' imitator, the cautious Odysseus to Socrates' Diomedes.

Socrates responds with what looks like the beginning of a deeper inquiry into hedonism but that rapidly changes direction. He suggests that "it"—presumably the question of whether pleasure is the good—will become clearer if Protagoras uncovers for him more of his thought. Somehow the question about hedonism is one that must be pursued dialectically with just such a man as Protagoras. But then Socrates suggests that Protagoras has already shown his thinking about pleasure and it is something else that needs investigating. Comparing himself to a doctor and Protagoras to a patient, Socrates continues,

> "Having observed that you stand in regard to the good and the pleasant as you say, I must say something like this: 'Come, now, Protagoras, uncover for me this aspect of your thought as well: how do you stand in regard to knowledge?'" (352a6–b2)

What Socrates is saying, in effect, is that Protagoras has already made it sufficiently clear that behind his gentlemanly demeanor he identifies pleasure as the true good, so that courage and the other virtues would be good only as means, and that he is prevented only by prudential caution from declaring his true beliefs. And yet at the same time something about this very question remains hidden and will come to light only through probing Protagoras' understanding of the power of knowledge. Beneath his strategic pretense of openness, beneath even the hedonism that he quietly embraces with what he may still regard as intellectual daring, lies a deeper stratum of belief and attachment that cannot be separated from hedonism by focusing on the merits of pleasure but can be unearthed only by eliciting first Protagoras' agreement and then his resistance to the thesis that virtue is knowledge—the coldly calculating thesis that virtue is the knowledge needed to maximize pleasure rather than the more powerful but by the same token less provocative thesis that virtue is the wisdom that perfects the soul. In so doing, Socrates will be the physician who will bring to light the hidden fractures in Protagoras' own soul.

Once this deepest aspect of Protagoras' soul is uncovered, it becomes clear that the hedonist premise of the whole argument is profoundly unpersuasive even to this man who looks like one of the best candidates for a life of clear-sighted hedonism. From this result, Plato invites two possible conclusions. First, the reader might infer that virtue *would be* knowledge if the good were pleasure, but it is not. On this view, Protagoras thinks that he thinks that virtue is knowledge of an instrumental sort, but Socrates shows him a deeper concern for virtue as an end in itself—a concern that is universal, in one form or another, and that when properly grasped invalidates the hedonistic premise of Socrates' argument for his thesis, showing why virtue is in fact not knowledge. Thus we might say that Socrates deliberately seeks out the considerations that will defeat his never seriously intended thesis and thus leave the dialogue in *aporia*. And this *aporia* seems inevitable, given Socrates' procedure in this last part of the dialogue, for all he will really show is that sophists are eager to agree that knowledge is all-powerful in the human soul and that the common people are inarticulate in accounting for any other ends they have except pleasure. Ending as he does, Socrates leaves it to us to put together a richer understanding of virtue as much more than a merely intellectual quality.

But against this reading is the fact that Socrates says more than once that the arguments he is making hold true for any conception of the good, not merely for the good understood as pleasure. He also asks repeatedly whether the "many," in whose name they are ostensibly exploring the interrelations of virtue, knowledge, and pleasure, would have anything else to say than the answers they are giving to Socrates' questions, thus inviting us to consider whether a more nuanced and qualified version of his thesis might not be true. The second possible conclusion, then, is that Plato is giving us in simplified form the argument that must be elaborated to see why virtue in fact is something like knowledge, deliberately leaving it to us to do the work. If so, then the concerns that Socrates is drawing out of the depths of Protagoras' soul, however universal they may be, do not falsify Socrates' thesis but only keep Protagoras from seeing and accepting it. Socrates may be interested in confirming that it is a confusion on Protagoras' part, rather than an insight that Socrates has failed to take into account, that stops Protagoras from agreeing with him. He may wish further to confirm that in Protagoras as in everyone the deepest attachment is to what is intelligibly good and not what is irrationally noble. Finally, he may be looking for evidence that it is an unresolved and even unacknowledged tension between these two attachments that keeps Protagoras unsettled on the theological question. With these two possible conclusions in mind, then, let us carefully trace the remainder of the argument.

Is Knowledge Sovereign? (352b3–58c6)

Socrates now asks about the power of knowledge, in a passage famous for its bold claim and its memorable imagery.

> "Come, now, Protagoras, uncover for me this aspect of your thought as well: how do you stand in regard to knowledge? Is your opinion about this too like that of the many human beings, or different? The opinion of the many concerning knowledge is something like this, that it isn't a strong thing characterized by either leadership or rule. They don't think about it as though it were any such thing at all, but often when knowledge is present in a human being, they think that it is not the knowledge that rules him but something else—at one time spiritedness, then pleasure, then pain, sometimes eros, often fear. They simply think about knowledge as they do about a slave, that it is dragged around by everything else. So is your opinion about it something like this as well, or is it that knowledge is both noble and capable of ruling a human being, and that if in fact someone discerns the good things and the bad ones, he won't be overpowered by anything so as to do anything other than what knowledge commands, but rather active wisdom is competent to come to the person's aid?" (352a8–c7)

Whereas before Socrates emphasized the moralism of the common people, he now emphasizes their low estimation of the power of knowledge to govern the passions and especially pleasure and pain. Their moral outlook and their denigration of reason go together. Common moralism perceives a gulf between what is noble or right and what is good for oneself.[28] Reason may command what is good for oneself and perhaps compel it in cases that are overwhelmingly clear and immediate, but even the ability to govern passion in the interest of one's own long-term advantage strikes most people as mysteriously elusive. And they judge reason to have even less power to command noble acts of self-denial. Nor, according to ordinary opinion, would moral acts retain their glow of nobility if the mere recognition of their goodness were sufficient to determine their performance: what is noble seems to be necessarily uncompelled, even by internal causes. The conventional moral outlook thus entails, from Socrates' perspective, a serious demotion of reason. It will be part of his project to recommend, as an alternate way of understanding virtue, the tranquil, clear-sighted rule of reason as the highest thing in us, which, when it fully and firmly perceives what is best, necessarily loves and chooses it. But this is a major shift in perspective that the *Protagoras* only begins to undertake.

So provocative an account has Socrates given of the common people's contempt for reason that Protagoras feels himself honor-bound to come to reason's defense and affirm its sovereignty over the human soul. Socrates has insisted that both particular knowledge and active wisdom (*phronēsis*) rule in the human soul, or perhaps more precisely that knowledge when present will rule with the support of active wisdom when present, leaving it open whether it is opinion or something else such as passion that rules where either knowledge or wisdom is not available. To this Protagoras affirms that both wisdom (*sophia*) and knowledge have such power and are indeed "the strongest [or most excellent] (*kratiston*) of all human things" (352c8–d3). To this position Socrates contrasts the popular opinion that "though many know what the best things are, they are unwilling to do them—despite their being able to do them—but do other things instead. And indeed all those I've asked what in the world the cause of this is contend that those who do these things are overcome by pleasure or pain, or are overpowered by one of those things I was just now speaking of" (352d–e). The many believe in *akrasia* against Socrates' and Protagoras' claims about the power of knowledge. Protagoras' agreement with Socrates should not obscure the fact that Protagoras shares something of the popular view, to the extent that he has denied that wisdom is either necessary or sufficient to guarantee the possession of every other virtue. Yet when Socrates invites him to join in explaining what is really going on when knowledge seems to be overcome by passion, he resists, asking why it is worth even paying attention to the opinion of the many human beings, "who say whatever happens to occur to them" (a7–8). Socrates' reply is that it has a bearing on the issue of courage and how it is related to the other parts of virtue. What might the investigation show? The most extreme alternative to the Socratic thesis would be that courage is only loosely related to the rest of virtue in having not only a different source but a different end, in not being governed by the good as the other virtues are. The other alternative would be that courage, inasmuch as it is a true virtue and is not just a kind of subrational fierceness or rashness, is directed to the same end that the other virtues are, human happiness, and is an indispensable asset for attaining it, but that in drawing upon independent strengths in the soul that have nothing to do with knowledge or wisdom, it provides an essential supplement to wisdom. But if Socrates can show that human beings *always* choose the good as they see it, then each act of courage will be just one example of such choosing, one manifestation of wisdom, and courage will not be a separate requirement of human flourishing.

Socrates focuses on cases in which the many would say that they do what they know is base because they are overcome by pleasure, simplifying the picture by leaving aside the other passions that the many allege as causes for reason's failures. He asks them, through Protagoras, which of three possible ways they understand what might make pleasant things base.

> "Is it because they supply this immediate pleasure and because each of them is pleasant? Or because they subsequently cause illnesses and poverty and supply many other such things? Or even if they supply none of these things later on but just cause delight, would they nonetheless be bad, simply because they make them learn to take delight in one way or another? Do we suppose, Protagoras, that they would give any other answer than that they are bad, not as regards the production of the immediate pleasure itself, but on account of what subsequently arises, illness and the rest?" (353d1–e1)

When Protagoras concedes that the many would not say anything else, he and Socrates agree further that they would call illness and poverty bad for the sole reason "that they result in pain and deprive one of other pleasures" (353e6–54a1). Now he is characterizing the people as simple hedonists, which is surprising since he earlier cast them as moralists who fail to see that pleasures as such are good "unless something else arises from them" (351c5), and since he will presently list, among the good things that the majority prize, "health . . . the preservation of cities, empire over others, and wealth" (354b3–5)—vulgar goods, perhaps, but not themselves pleasures. But Socrates will go on to establish to the assembled group's satisfaction that these goods' value in the popular view lies in the fact that "they ultimately issue in pleasures and the release from and averting of pains" (354b5–7). And in one of a long succession rhetorical questions he hypothetically poses to the many, he asks "Or can you state any other end with a view to which you call them good, other than pleasures and pains?" (354b7–c2; cf. 353d6–e1; 354b5–c2; 354d1–3; 354d7–e2; 354e8–55a5; 356c2–3). Bad pleasures, he assures us they will answer, are simply those that conduce to greater pains in the end; good pains are simply those that result in greater pleasure or prevent greater pains. By the end of the passage quoted above, the word "base" itself disappears to be replaced simply by "bad." If Socrates is not merely humoring Protagoras, he is suggesting that the popular pretense of having an independent standard of nobility is hollow or at least very inadequately thought out.

But to say that the many would have nothing else to say is not to say that there is nothing else to be said, or even that the many themselves really hold the position they could easily be reduced to defending. Of the three possible reasons Socrates has given for considering certain pleasant things as base—that pleasure as such is base, that these things have bad consequences, or that they give delight in a certain way—Socrates has dismissed the first as perhaps impossible for anyone to maintain seriously, and he has shown that the second still collapses into hedonism in the absence of an independent standard of the good, but he has said nothing about the third. Is there not a strong case to be made that even if the chief thing we all want is pleasure, it is better to put at the center of our lives pleasures that fulfill our natures as rational beings rather than ones that can be enjoyed only in a state of mindless intoxication? And does this ranking not suggest further that beneath the general desire for pleasure may be a deeper desire for goods that are not simply reducible to it—goods such as life itself, knowledge, meaningful challenges, meaningful engagement with others, and dignity, at the heart of which is again a solid self-knowledge, a full awareness of our true condition, and an ability to make autonomous choices in accord with that knowledge? If the many would have nothing else to say than the hedonist arguments Socrates gives them, might it be because only a recognition of the worth and dignity of possessing and living according to wisdom can keep one's viewpoint from ultimately collapsing into hedonism?[29] If the majority of people sense the independent importance of wisdom without being able to articulate it, then their souls contain the same three levels of belief as Protagoras'. Protagoras in his fractured condition at times looks down on the many as confused moralists and views himself as clear-sighted; at other times he looks down on the many as vulgar hedonists and views himself as noble-minded. But perhaps in both Protagoras and the common people there is the same surface commitment to morality, covering a more hidden hedonism, which in turn conceals a deeper intimation that undifferentiated pleasure is not in fact the stuff of the best life. In exploring the thought of the many, then, Socrates is diagnosing the divisions within Protagoras' own soul.

The account of the good as pleasure simplifies the issues and makes them clearer. If, as the many are said to believe, the good is pleasure, and if, as they are also said to believe, it is by pleasure that they are overcome or defeated when they fail to follow the knowledge they allegedly have, then the absurdity of their position is easily shown as soon as the word "pleasant" is replaced by the word "good." Socrates, trying to help the many articulate their position, allows this absurdity to be pointed out by a hypothetical interlocutor. "You speak of a laughable thing," Socrates says he might say, "if someone does bad things, though he knows them to be bad and doesn't have to do them, because he's overcome (*hēttōmenos*) by the good things" (355d). The absurdity lies partially in the idea of being overcome or defeated by what is good, since we think of being defeated as involving a struggle against something bad that ought not to win, and partially in the contradictory assumptions that the alleged defeat seems necessarily to involve. For the many imagine the error to consist in choosing bad things, else it would not be an error, but also to consist in choosing good things, else they would never have been chosen, and (the interlocutor implies) it is ridiculous to think that anyone can at one and the same time judge an act to be on balance bad and also on balance good, or judge it on balance bad because it has less of what is truly good than the alternatives and yet choose it because it has so much.[30] This would seem to amount to both knowing and being deceived about one and the same thing (what is good) at one and the same time. What Socrates' interlocutor is giving here is ridicule and not a proof: he does not prove that we are overcome by pleasure only when we are deceived by it. But it is ridicule that brings out something important in human experience and our universal intuitions about the meaning of that experience. We seek what is good and, when asked, are able to give no account of why we or anyone would ever act except in pursuit of something that seems good. The interlocutor's ridicule and our response thus constitute a kind of dialectical confirmation of the primacy of the good. But if the good is what we always seek, then what, other than confusion about the good, would prevent us from choosing it? Thus we seem forced to acknowledge that knowledge can never be controverted in action.

To be sure, by considering only desire for pleasure among the passions that allegedly defeat knowledge and by considering only pleasure to be good, Socrates speaks as if human beings never had to contend with competing passions or choices between competing kinds of goods. But he focuses on the key question that must be answered whether the good is simple or manifold: "In what respect . . . are the good things undeserving vis-à-vis the bad, or the bad vis-à-vis the good? Is it in any other respect than when some are larger, others smaller?" (355d). What does not deserve to win in our calculations can be nothing other than the lesser good or the greater evil. In other words, all errors in action must involve errors in evaluating the respective quantity of goodness in each option. As Michael Morris observes, this argument requires not hedonism per se but only a claim about the commensurability of our wants and ends, a claim that good action means choosing the single best, if it is evident, and one of several equally plausible options if it is not, and likewise that bad action means failing to do this.[31] To be overcome by a bad or "undeserving" pleasure thus can only mean being kept by a smaller good from pursuing a greater one or avoiding a greater evil, or, as Socrates now puts it, "taking greater bad things as the price of obtaining fewer goods" (355e).[32] But (Socrates asks innocently) how could the smaller ever have such a power? The obvious answer that occurs to the many is that we are distracted by immediate pleasures into forgetting about their cost. And some such version of this problem seems to be involved not only in addictions and compulsions but in almost every failure to do what we allegedly know is best, so great is the power of immediate pleasures and pains to overwhelm the judgment when that judgment is not solidly grounded.

Socrates' response, however, is to argue that the experience of being overcome by immediate pleasure is still nothing other than being overcome by distorted perception.

> "For if someone should say, 'But, Socrates, immediate pleasure differs a great deal from subsequent pleasure as well as pain, I would say, 'Surely not in any way other than in pleasure and pain?' For no other way is possible. But like a human being good at weighing, adding up the pleasures and adding up the pains, putting the nearness and farness in the balance as well, say which of the two is greater. For if you weigh pleasures against pleasures, you must always choose those that are greater and more numerous; if pains against pains, the fewer and smaller; and if you weigh pleasures against pains and the distressing things are outstripped by pleasures, whether those near are less than those at a distance or those at a distance are less than those near, you must carry out that action in which these [greater pleasures] are to be found.'" (356a5–b)[33]

Granting that the same magnitudes always look bigger when they are near than when they are far away, Socrates continues,

> "If, then, for us doing well consisted in this, in doing and taking the greater lengths and avoiding and not doing the lesser, what salvation for our lives would come to sight? Would it be the art of measurement or the power of appearances? Or does the latter not make us wander up and down, often changing our minds about the same thing and having regrets both in our actions and in our choices of the greater and the lesser? And wouldn't the art of measuring render this appearance powerless? And by showing the truth wouldn't it set the soul at peace, remaining in the truth, and so save its life?" (356c8–e2)

In the same way, if the task of choosing well is one only of determining what will bring greater pleasure instead of less, is it not merely a problem of seeing straight and weighing correctly, and will it not be the knowledge-producing art of measurement that provides "salvation" (57a5–b3)? If so, it would be impossible to choose badly in full knowledge of what is best. One would take less of a good thing instead of more only when one misperceived or miscalculated or simply failed to think, as people so often do. Socrates then makes a pitch for the art of Protagoras and his fellow sophists:

> "And you yourselves know, surely, that an erring action without knowledge is done through ignorance, with the result that this is what being overcome by pleasure is: the greatest ignorance, for which Protagoras here claims he is a physician, as do Prodicus and Hippias." (357d7–e4)

In sum, there is an art of virtue, a wholly teachable art, but the many, being penny-wise and pound-foolish, refuse to go to its teachers and so remain mired in ignorance and error.

When all the sophists present agree that what Socrates has said about the power of knowledge is "true to an extraordinary degree" (358a4–5), Socrates elicits their agreement as well to what has hitherto been presented as the premises of the vulgar, that the pleasant is good and the painful bad, without any qualification being offered or demanded. Socrates has stripped away the topmost cloak obscuring the true thought not only of Protagoras but of all those in the room: their gentlemanly respect for the noble as something other than the pleasant or what conduces to it is now implicitly acknowledged to be mere lip service. The company goes on to agree to Socrates' characterization of the noble as well as of the meaning of self-control and its absence:

> "What, then, men," I said, "about the following sort of thing: all the actions that conduce to this, to living without pain and pleasantly, are they not noble? And is the noble deed both good and beneficial?" They agreed. "If, then," I said, "the pleasant is good, no one who either knows or supposes that other things are better than what he does, things that are possible, then does these things when it is possible to do better ones. And this 'being overcome by oneself' is nothing other than ignorance, nor is mastering oneself anything other than wisdom (*sophia*)." And everyone agreed. (358b3–c3)

This conclusion is most pleasing to all the sophists who are present. But is it true?

The Sovereignty of Knowledge Considered

The most obvious objection to Socrates' argument is that its hedonist premises are incorrect. Yet Socrates has made a point of insisting that the same argument holds whether we use the words "pleasure" and "pain" or "good" and "bad." This substitution was, to be sure, premised on his equation of the good with pleasure, but he has also asked repeatedly whether any other answers could be given to each of his questions, thereby inviting us to consider whether his equations are not true regardless of what meaning of the good we apply. Do they not hold for every understanding of the good, so long as we regard all of the goods that we care about to be measurable and weighable on a single scale, even if they are of different kinds? So long as we can say that knowledge and bodily pleasure and friendship are all components of happiness and so long as we can articulate their relative importance—indeed, so long as we can say that all concerns we have, whether for ourselves or for others, can be weighed correctly in terms of our deepest, most abiding wishes, or so long as we say there is always a best thing to do, as every moralist would say—does the argument not hold that the failure to choose the one of the available options that we judge most truly choiceworthy can happen only when we are at least momentarily confused?

Our objector might reply, however, that pleasure and the desire to avoid pain are still significantly different from other possible kinds of goods, in having an immediate power to grip us that others lack. Thus Robert Bartlett, in his thoughtful analysis of the dialogue, suggests that virtue is knowledge if and only if the good is pleasure or at least is consistently pleasant. Knowledge may indeed be the greatest good, as Socrates suggests Simonides and all the wise agree. But "if knowledge about the most important things comes at the price of our initial and perhaps dearest expectations about the world, it would to that extent be profoundly unpleasant or painful and hence would require some capacity in addition to a great intellect not only to grasp it but also to live in accord with it." If the truth is hard, in other words, virtue will require a subrational toughness or courage in addition to knowledge. This is a powerful argument. Indeed, so long as there is not a perfect correspondence between what is good, however the good is understood, and what is not only ultimately but immediately most pleasant for us, is such courage to endure pain or strength to resist immediate gratification not necessary in addition to understanding, if one is to choose well?[34]

The question Socrates keeps pressing us to ponder, however, is how pleasure and pain and fear and anger and eros all work when they defeat our better resolutions. Do they leave insight intact and simply bypass it? Or do they not invariably cloud the judgment?[35] When a political man "knows" that fidelity to his wife is the better choice but still propositions an aide, does his mind retain a crystal-clear knowledge that a life of integrity will bring more happiness than illicit sex will, and still ignore the knowledge? Or is that knowledge clear only in the abstract to the self that is not tempted, and obscured by the sight of lipstick and heels, which suggest the thought that the life of abstinence is the life of a foolish moralist? And if this is so, do similar reassessments not take place when terrible and vividly imminent pains or dangers overwhelm a soldier's resolutions to endure steadfastly, or when anger drives one into injustice? The question can be answered only by careful introspection. Socrates' suggestion that errors always involve a breakdown in the capacity to see straight or to weigh correctly offers an invitation to such introspection, and in particular, careful attention to the relationship between passion and opinion. For his claims in both the *Protagoras* and the *Meno* that bad choices involve cognitive error suggest that passion in a rational being cannot exist in isolation from opinion; that passion moves us with and through opinion, carrying with it assessments about what matters and how things stand for us, and that when knowledge of good and bad is present, it likewise awakens or produces corresponding inclinations and aversions. To be sure, knowledge alone does not produce desire, but in the presence of an underlying wish it can bring new desires into being: the knowledge that one needs more votes to pass a bill, for example, may produce the desire to find them. In sum, Socrates seems to say, knowledge cannot be dragged around by desires and fears because our desires and fears precisely *are* our present, vividly felt opinions about future goods and evils. And to be even momentarily under the sway of an erroneous opinion is to be at least momentarily confused about what is best: it is to be ignorant.

But then if, as Socrates has been suggesting, passions and opinions are two sides of the same coin, should passion not align itself effortlessly with whatever judgment determines to be best? Here in the *Protagoras*, where Socrates has given his fullest exposition of the claim that virtue is knowledge, he has also given his strongest endorsement to what we have called the radical alignment theory, the theory that passion and opinion are always in perfect accord. Moreover, in stating at 358b–c that not only wisdom, not only knowledge of a particular case, but mere opinion is sovereign in the human soul, he suggests that thought not only agrees with but controls passion, and he affirms explicitly that it controls action.[36]

Experience, however, does not seem to confirm that thought has such power. In the cases Socrates himself mentions, where present pleasures and pains loom large out of proportion to their true worth, thought seems rather to follow passion than the reverse, passion that in the form of immediate desires and fears often diverges substantially from our long-term wishes for ourselves. And thought seems moreover to follow passion imperfectly. Even if every desire contains an implicit opinion about the goodness of the object of the desire and every opinion about what is good implies some desire or wish, desires and fears and angers are more bodily, more elemental than opinions are, often burning with a fierceness unjustified by any reason and often persisting, if in an attenuated form, even when the weakness of their justification is seen. Is the problem immediate desires and fears pose really only a perceptual problem, cured by the art of measurement and perspective? Would having this art really guarantee its use, or does Socrates himself not often say that one who knows an art may also misuse it? But if the strength of our desires does not simply depend on the strength of the arguments that support their accompanying opinions and if knowledge of a pleasure's bad consequences does not necessarily make the desire for that pleasure evaporate, then as Santas asks, might the misalignment of passion and reason not provide another explanation for weakness of will than the ignorance Socrates alleges as its sole cause?[37]

Socrates spells out his answers to none of these questions, but I believe he would grant the force of many of these observations. Indeed, the very statement that seems to take his claims for the power of thought and his denial of *akrasia* the furthest, the assertion at 358b–c that not only knowledge but opinion rules where it is present, in fact undercuts the special status he seemed to give to knowledge at 352a–c. For in saying that "no one who either knows or supposes that other things are better than what he does, things that are possible, then does these things when it is possible to do better ones" (358b–c), he implies that even passing opinion has the same authority he has claimed for knowledge. But now his statement that knowledge is never dragged around like a slave begins to seem most paradoxical. For while he at first appeared to be asserting knowledge's great power to resist all temptations and distractions, his argument now seems to serve equally as a comment on knowledge's vulnerability—if not to being dragged around in its fully articulate and persuasive condition, then still to being muffled and silenced by passion, which brings with it its own pseudo-knowledge that seizes the citadel knowledge ought to hold. Even if we cannot succumb to passion without somehow changing our opinions, Michael Morris argues that the *Protagoras* is a poor expression of the view that virtue is just a kind of knowledge. All that the argument shows, he says, is that one cannot do wrong while thinking it wrong, but it does not prevent one from changing one's mind, and is not changing one's mind having one's knowledge dragged around?[38]

In the end, Socrates' most serious claim is not a claim about the power of all knowledge to prevail over passion: recall that in the *Meno* he says that true opinion when tied down first becomes knowledge and only afterwards lasting (98a6). It is not even a claim about the impossibility of giving way to inclinations that in our better moments or in some sense even at present we know are bad: recall also in the *Meno* his observations on the way desires can keep us from pursuing what we truly wish (78a). It is, rather, two things, more limited but still fundamental: that confused or erroneous judgment is still always implicated in erroneous choices, and that, when a person has knowledge of what is best, "active wisdom is competent" to make his choice right (352c6–7). Thus, at the most serious level, Socrates' claim about the power of knowledge resolves into a claim about the sovereignty of judgment in the human soul and a claim about the power not of any kind of knowledge but of active wisdom. How, then, is judgment both sovereign and prone to being corrupted, and how does active wisdom come to its aid?

Socrates' portrait of the human soul grants the possibility of competing, often incompatible, and sometimes impossible desires, each with its accompanying implicit opinions about what is good. But deeper than all these passing desires is our fundamental wish for happiness, and standing above our shifting opinions is the capacity to judge them and determine what is true and what is best. As single beings who live one moment at a time, we *must* at each moment take one course from among available options. In doing so, Socrates suggests, judgment comes into play, however well or carelessly, to survey the scene and settle upon the one thing that seems best to do. When judgment functions well it holds our deepest wishes clearly in view, evaluating passing desires and fears in light of ultimate goals, seeking out and scrutinizing relevant information, and choosing appropriately. When it functions poorly, which is to say routinely, it is a lazy gatekeeper that uncritically waves through whatever visitors appear familiar or perhaps respectably dressed or unusually importunate. Thus it can approve intense, even obsessive desires for objects that in moments of close attention it judges not worth pursuing. But what Santas calls a misalignment between the strength of desire and the judgment as to the value of the object, Socrates brings chiefly under the heading of unstable judgment, in which desire at one moment inflates its assessment of the object's importance and more careful attention subsequently cuts it back down to size.[39] This is why Socrates stresses the instability of shifting opinions and regrets that characterize those who lack the measuring art (356d–e). In sum, his view is that we may *feel* several passions at once, sometimes with degrees of intensity or apathy that we ourselves are capable of at least intermittently seeing as unreasonable, but we may at any moment *judge* only one thing best to do, and if we can do it we must do it, so that to *act* on an irrational passion one must have one's judgment at least momentarily obscured.

If we do somehow know better, these errors can happen only when we do not attend to and hold clearly in view the knowledge that we have and the deepest wishes that should guide us. Likewise, if we have the art of measuring and do not follow it, this can only be because we have lost sight of its importance or do not know how to follow and apply it consistently. It is not, then, particular knowledge of particular facts that always has the stability and strength to resist unreasonable passions, but knowledge of the value of the measuring art, knowledge of human nature, and knowledge of oneself, such that one is able to see and pursue what one needs, making use of one's strengths and avoiding the pitfalls posed by one's weaknesses. In short, knowledge is reliably sovereign with and only with the support of active wisdom.

This argument of Socrates has great power. It is also probably the case that virtually everyone is inclined to resist it and at least initially to find it troubling, unlike the sophists who are so flattered by Socrates' praise of their art that they immediately embrace his reasoning. But if the argument is compatible with even a very comprehensive and even benevolent conception of the good, why should it be so troubling? A clue as to the source of our resistance may be provided by Socrates' curious repeated use here of the term "deserving" (*axios*) as well as of references to the art that brings "salvation." Like the reminder of death at 351b6, both of these words point to another set of concerns that calculation about pleasure and indeed calculation altogether seems unable to address, the concern with mortality.

Socrates uses the word "deserving" at 355d3–56a5 in a restrictive sense: what is most deserving is simply what is most eligible to be chosen because it carries greater value for us. But he is also pointing out that if this analysis is right, this is all that "deserving" can ever mean. Good things deserve to be taken and bad ones avoided, good actions admired and sought and bad ones deplored, but good men do not deserve to be happy or bad ones to suffer, if good choices are the inevitable result of correct measurement and bad ones of confusion. This will be true whatever content the good turns out to have, even if the highest good is a noble selflessness. If choosing what is best depends on seeing it clearly, then it is not a free act of the will, and the radical freedom that we suppose people have when we impose and demand rewards and retributive punishments does not exist. Those who choose what is worse over what is better must invariably do so in a state of confusion or ignorance about what matters most, and no one chooses to be ignorant of the most important things. Thus neither demands for rewards nor retribution nor even forgiveness would make sense, but only admiration for the good, understanding for all choices, good and bad, sympathy for those whose ignorance blights their happiness, and resolute, humane, nonvindictive determination to stop people from needlessly blighting one another's happiness. In accord with Socrates' restrictive use of the word "deserving" is his equally restrictive use of "salvation" as the preservation of life and life's essential goods, rather than as something that transcends mortal life.

This, in sum, is the Socratic thesis in its full form and its most explicit presentation. By having Socrates prove the thesis only on the basis of questionable hedonist premises, and by having him disavow all his arguments at the end, the dialogue allows readers who may be profoundly troubled or angered by the thesis to conclude that virtue would be knowledge if the good were pleasure, but that it is not, so that the belief that everyone freely chooses both good and bad appears unrefuted.[40] Whether this reasoning is valid, or whether Socrates' arguments apply in fact to the human good in its fullest articulation, Plato leaves to us to ponder.

Courage Revisited (358c6–60e5)

One line of objection we have been considering to the Socratic thesis that virtue is knowledge is that a correct understanding of the good is essential for virtue and yet that that understanding is continually subject to being lost in the absence of a separate, subrational strength of soul. It is conceivable that this vulnerability might beset even the most comprehensive, architectonic understanding of the human condition and the human good, an understanding that in its intellectual reach could not fairly be denied the name wisdom. Then we would have to say that there are two independent cardinal virtues essential for living well, wisdom and strength of soul or courage. This is what Protagoras in fact holds. Therefore Socrates returns yet again at the end of the dialogue to the question of the nature and status of courage. In the prior discussion of courage at 349a6–51b2, Protagoras conceded that all the other virtues resemble one another and tend to appear together—so that each may reasonably be equated with a certain wisdom—but he defined courage as a separate quality of soul with a different root. We have suggested that he tends to view courage as having independent ends as well, so that it is free to disregard reason and its calculations about what is beneficial. Under the guise of establishing the power of knowledge, Socrates has in the interim secured Protagoras' agreement that nothing in the human soul is directed at anything other than the good as we perceive it. Socrates now reiterates that principle with a strong claim about human nature.

> "Isn't it the case," I said, "that no one voluntarily approaches the bad or what he supposes to be bad, nor does this, it seems, belong to human nature, to go voluntarily towards what one supposes to be bad instead of the good things; but when one is compelled to choose one of two bad things, no one chooses the greater one if it is possible to choose the lesser?" All of us agreed to all of these things. (358c6–d4)

Applying this reasoning to the domain of courage, Socrates asks now whether fear is anything other than the expectation of evil, and Protagoras agrees that it is not. Protagoras and the other sophists now agree with Socrates that all human emotions and practical judgments are at bottom a striving towards what seems good and away from what seems bad, and that the good as we see it is such a powerful magnet that our choices are not only guided by it but follow it of necessity. Socrates then asks whether every courageous choice is not likewise dictated by the good and bad as we perceive them.

> "If the former things are true, then will any human being be willing to go towards the things that he fears, if it is possible to go towards what he does not? Or is it impossible on the basis of what has been agreed? For it was agreed that that which he is afraid of he believes to be bad, and that which he believes to be bad, no one either goes toward or takes willingly." And these things seemed so to everyone. (358e2–59a1)

Even as he speaks of necessities, Socrates' language is precise: we may be compelled to choose between two evils (358d2), but we are not *compelled* to choose the apparent good, even though it is impossible not to choose it. For compulsion works only from without; inner necessities govern but do not constrain us, because there is nothing in us that seeks what is worse in the first place.

Socrates then forces Protagoras to revisit his earlier claim that courage differs in kind from all the other virtues, appearing often in isolation from the rest and consisting in an eagerness to advance towards what is bad. Of course courage seems to be such on the surface, but Socrates insists and Protagoras reluctantly agrees that in every brave deed one must in some way be pursuing the lesser of two evils or risking or accepting harm for the sake of some greater good one hopes to achieve. Courageous men seem eager for what is terrible and cowards for what is good, but this difference is misleading. It is really an evident good that moves the former as well. Protagoras' agreement on this point is a key concession. It seems to be one of Socrates' central purposes here and in all of his cross-examinations to ascertain whether anyone who is paying close attention and answering honestly can deny that all human choice is dictated by what somehow seems to one in the moment of choosing to be best. Protagoras, however, does not make this concession with a good grace. He even abandons his former view without conceding that it was ever his: when Socrates asks him whether cowards advance towards what they feel confidence about and courageous men towards what is terrible (as Protagoras previously claimed) Protagoras says, "So people say, Socrates" (359c6–7). Protagoras lacks the very courage he praises.

Socrates now draws his conclusion:

> "If this was correctly demonstrated, then no one advances towards what he considers terrible, since being overcome by oneself was discovered to be ignorance." He agreed.
>
> "But then all advance towards what they feel confident about, cowards and brave alike, and at least in this respect the cowards and the brave advance towards the same thing." (359d4–e1)

To do what is bad out of temptation or fear (to be "overcome by oneself") is possible, but only when one is at least temporarily ignorant of its badness; for all the difference in their appearance and specific deeds, cowards and heroes are doing precisely the same thing in pursuing whatever seems best to them at the moment of acting.

Protagoras cannot deny the force of this claim, yet he is not more than superficially convinced. He insists that courageous men and cowards advance towards quite contrary things, since the former go eagerly into battle and the latter run away. Socrates rightly guesses that behind this observation is the thought that what the two groups seek is radically different in kind, the former being moved by love of the noble and the latter by pleasure or personal advantage. And now finally Socrates is able to lay this thought about the difference between noble and base human beings immediately alongside the contrary thought that Protagoras holds but has forever avoided bringing into dialogue with it, that what is noble is nothing more than what is or conduces to the good, and the good nothing other than the pleasant. Establishing these equivalences, Socrates then asks, "Although they know this, are the cowards unwilling to go to what is noble and better and more pleasant?" (360a4–5). Protagoras sees that he cannot insist that cowards know what they are doing without destroying his previous agreement that no one chooses what he knows or believes to be worse among the available options. And that insight into the power of the good prevails over his intuition about the difference between brave men and cowards. Protagoras agrees that, after all, both the cowardly and the courageous are doing the same thing, pursuing what seems good. They differ only in that the courageous judge correctly how it is best to be found, while cowards, like rash men and madmen, have both "shameful fears and shameful confidence" as a result of ignorance (360b4–6). Socrates introduces without elaboration the thought that cowards, too, feel boldness or confidence as well as fear, but clearly they do: they are confident, for example that safety is good, even if they have less confidence in themselves than the courageous. In the same way, the brave have fears as well as confidence, for they are afraid of whatever they view as shameful. Here again the two types are more similar than they seem.

Next Socrates proves with a pair of precise syllogisms that cowardice not only is produced by but *is* ignorance, and courage is wisdom. Establishing that "that on account of which the cowards are cowards" is cowardice, and that the cowards "were manifestly such on account of the ignorance of what is terrible," he concludes that "the ignorance of what is terrible and what is not terrible would be cowardice" (360c1–7). To this Protagoras at least nods his agreement. Likewise, since courage is the opposite of cowardice, and cowardice is ignorance of what is and is not terrible, and the opposite of this ignorance is "wisdom about what is terrible and what is not terrible" (360d4–5), courage must be just this wisdom. Once again we note that wisdom takes the place of knowledge in Socrates' conclusion. Just as truly admirable self-overcoming must be guided by something deeper than the knowledge one can quickly grasp and quickly forget, so it stands to reason that it takes something deeper than mere intellectual comprehension to produce true courage. But even so, the conclusion is so strange that we are compelled to question again the premises. Are cowards really such solely only on account of ignorance? Do weak, sickly bodies and naturally fearful constitutions not also contribute to their being cowards, and by the same token, is not a strong constitution, both bodily and psychological, a critically important foundation for courage? Is Protagoras not right when he presents the main root of courage as a strength that can be nurtured but that must come from a good nature, in just the way that bodily strength is?

Socrates does not deny that wisdom requires an elemental strength of soul in addition to intelligence. This strength would not matter much for virtue if virtue were nothing but the ability to see clearly and calculate well the best way to maximize pleasure and if no great risks or fears or temptations needed to be endured to do so, but in fact every life must confront risks and fears as well as the pull of immediate pleasures, and even the sublime pleasures of philosophy are accompanied by investigations so difficult that Protagoras himself is unwilling to complete them. But what Socrates is insisting on is that the steadfastness needed for living well is precisely a steadiness of judgment, and that the softness that causes people to flinch and panic in the face of pain is an inability to keep one's grip on what one knows to be best. Much of what we call courage is in fact a foolhardy disregard for danger, but true courage according to Socrates is just this capacity to see clearly and to hold onto one's clarity under fire, without any of the distorted judgments that fear tends to bring.[41] If he is right, he is reasonable in calling courage one part or aspect of wisdom, even if its foundation lies deep in the less rational elements of the soul.

What might the subrational roots of courage be, then? Some possibilities are a natural doggedness or implacability or simple toughness, which some individuals certainly seem to have more of than others, independently of intelligence; *thumos*, or a proclivity to fierceness or anger in the face of opposition, joined with a keen sense of dignity and deserving and a hunger for victory and glory; an intense desire for some other good that eclipses everything else, such as love, gain, or knowledge; and confidence, or a high assessment of one's own strength, either physical or psychological or both. Implacability and *thumos* certainly play a role in battlefield courage as normally understood, but the former taken by itself is rather a kind of mulishness than a virtue for human beings, and the latter contributes nothing to clarity of judgment but at best merely counteracts the irrationality of panic with an irrationality of its own. Intense desires can also overcome many obstacles but are often unstable. The most passionate desires, after all, are desperate desires, if not in the sense that one despairs of satisfying them then in the sense that one imagines one would die if one could not, and desperation is more often the source of erratic judgments than steady ones; such steadiness as it brings is often bought at a terrible cost in clarity. Might desire not work differently, however, when a great hunger for happiness is joined with great confidence and steadiness of spirit, when the chief good one seeks is not in anyone else's power to grant or to withhold, and especially when one desires above all to know the truth about oneself and where one stands, whatever that truth might turn out to be? This desire in its very nature would counteract both impatience and the tendency to cling stubbornly to errors, with the violent shifts in judgment that can result when cherished beliefs are finally abandoned. Thus, this desire would seem to be both essential for wisdom and capable of making a good ally out of the elemental steadiness and toughness that courage and especially philosophic courage evidently require. Probably essential to the desire for the truth are, in turn, two other aspects of strength of soul: a confidence that whatever the truth may turn out to be, one can stand it, and the self-respect that makes one active in rooting out one's comforting self-deceptions. With such confidence and self-respect, one would not seize hastily upon poorly grounded opinions or lurch from one conviction to another; one would make one's best judgments in doubtful cases and hold to them calmly until better evidence presented itself.

The paradigm for such toughness is of course Socrates himself, whose contemporaries portray him as extraordinarily immune to ordinary pleasures, pains, and temptations. Aristophanes in the *Clouds* expresses this quality comically as Socrates' inability to understand how anyone could be distracted from thinking by the bites of bedbugs (a trait no doubt connected to the extreme pride he also attributes to Socrates); Plato in the *Symposium* by Socrates' scorn for shoes and his immunity to the effects of alcohol; and Xenophon in the *Memorabilia* through what he describes as almost inhuman continence, with the significant additional information that Socrates assiduously schooled himself in such continence. All of this is far from *thumos* in its usual, fiery form, epitomized by Homer's raging Achilles and conspicuous rather by its absence in Socrates. Yet the strength we are now describing may constitute the deepest substrate of *thumos*, consisting in confidence and self-respect, a dogged determination to overcome obstacles, and even, as we see in Socrates in this dialogue, a pleasure in victory and in shining before others, which nevertheless remains free of anger or intoxicated hopes for glory.

Are any of these elements truly subrational, however, except perhaps the doggedness that without intelligence is no virtue at all? For what is a strong desire for the truth but an unwavering opinion that the truth is of all things the most important to have? What is confidence but a judgment about one's abilities, and what is self-respect but an opinion about what is worthy of oneself? And finally, what is strength of soul itself but the ability to keep one's head and give way neither to panic nor to temptation nor to despair? Thus the elements that come to sight as the subrational foundation of courage turn out to be themselves much more infused with reason than they at first seem.[42] What courage amounts to—what it essentially is—is the ability to pursue the truth boldly and to hold to one's best judgments with consistency—and this ability Socrates not unreasonably calls an aspect of wisdom.

This also means, however, that wisdom itself is not merely a cognitive quality. While it certainly requires the ability to grasp logical propositions and draw correct inferences from them, it equally requires the strength of heart and mind to focus on what matters and to keep what one sees steadily in view and clearly in perspective. It is a virtue of the human being as a thoroughly embodied being, whose passions and judgments are all intimately connected and whose confidence is a judgment rooted in visceral strength. Aristotle will show his agreement with this understanding of wisdom when he calls *phronēsis* both an intellectual virtue and a virtue of character that infuses all the passions and that is necessarily efficacious in action (*NE* 7.10). As such, wisdom is a product of nurture as well as nature, requiring both a training in rigorous thought and a habituation in withstanding pain and overcoming difficulties. Thus we see Socrates' own answer to the question of how the different parts of virtue are related to one another and to the whole of virtue. They are related not as undifferentiated parts of gold nor as the altogether separate parts of the face, but as the same power, wisdom, which when applied to pleasures is moderation, when used to secure a common good with others is justice, and when applied to things that are terrible is courage. In this way, Socrates indicates, the different virtues are each distinct and yet all parts of a single and indeed indivisible unity, since each virtue depends on a correct assessment of what everything is worth. Thus wisdom as a whole and each virtue in its particular perfection requires comprehensiveness, clarity, and steadiness of understanding, and each of these three elements requires the other two. To our question of whether virtue does not need courage in addition to wisdom, then, Socrates' answer would be that it does not because courage and the strength of soul it rests on are integral components of wisdom, without which it could neither develop nor persist.

To this conclusion about courage, however, Protagoras refuses even to nod. He tells Socrates to finish the discussion for himself, accuses him of seeking only to gratify his love of victory, and falls silent. Protagoras' response is striking both in what he is willing to concede and what he is not.

He finds the claim that all vice is ignorance troubling, but he finds the corresponding claim that all virtue is wisdom even more troubling. It is easier for Protagoras and perhaps for every student of political philosophy to see how the vicious are in the end misguided and pitiable than to agree that virtue reduces to an admirable wisdom, even though the two cases are parallel. Similarly, many students of Plato can rather easily be brought to see the folly of the claim that the vicious deserve to suffer retributive punishment, but to give up the claim that the virtuous deserve a reward is harder. Somehow virtue wants to be and does not want to be a clear-sighted embrace of what is good.

Socrates' questioning has revealed that the hedonism Protagoras pretends to attribute to the people and in fact endorses is not the only principle in him, that beneath his gentlemanly surface and deeper even than his covert hedonism is a belief in a nobility that by no means reduces to pleasure. If the bold and liberated Protagoras cannot stay with his hedonist premises, we must wonder whether anyone can. To go at Protagoras' failing from another side, what Socrates has shown about the primacy of the good for all human judgment and choice is something that Protagoras cannot deny and yet also cannot wholly accept. He must agree that the apparent good is compelling when he looks at the arguments closely, one at a time, and yet something in him flies away from the conclusion when applied to the virtue he most prizes. Here we have enacted before our eyes the problem of opinion's instability. The problem for Protagoras is at least in part due to his overly crude understanding of the good as pleasure, but even if Socrates had framed the argument in terms of a more comprehensive account of the good, something deep within Protagoras would likely still resist it. What he needs but refuses to do is to examine closely this fugitive attachment to a nobility that he cannot quite articulate, and essential to that examination would be a careful investigation of what he thinks virtue really is.

Paradoxes within Paradoxes (360e6–62a4)

When Protagoras lambastes Socrates' love of victory and falls silent, Socrates insists that he is motivated precisely and solely by this question, "how in the world things stand in regard to virtue and whatever this thing virtue is" (360e7–8). If they could answer this question, he says, they could answer the question that they have long been debating of whether it is teachable, but they have somehow gotten the cart before the horse. Socrates imagines their argument reproaching and mocking them, inasmuch as Socrates first asserted that virtue isn't teachable and "now urges things that contradict this, trying to show that all things are knowledge—justice and moderation and courage—in which way virtue would most appear to be teachable" (361a7–b3), whereas Protagoras maintains that virtue is not knowledge and yet that it is teachable. We note that Socrates is again using the word "knowledge" instead of "wisdom." The "argument" in its mocking reproach obscures the difference between communicable knowledge, which may indeed be efficacious as long as it lasts but which is not virtue, with wisdom, which he has argued is virtue. With this bit of irony Socrates is able to present his position and Protagoras' as paradoxical in equal and opposite ways, but we have now seen that behind Socrates' paradox is a deep unity of thought and behind Protagoras' is a deep conflict.

To express this paradoxical difference between Socrates and Protagoras in another way, we might say that Protagoras, who argues that virtue is teachable and who promises his students liberation from the drudgery of the arts, falls into the same error as Gorgias and Proxenus, the error of overrating the power of mere thought and argument. To be sure, Protagoras shows in his myth that he grasps well the importance of force in political life and of habituation for political virtue. But he subtly denigrates that virtue, and with it, the long, hard habituation that it rests on. What he does not seem to recognize is the way compulsion and habituation can be good for the citizen himself and the way they are needed in the highest education as well as in the simplest training of workers and citizens. He does not see how much doggedness and training and self-compulsion wisdom requires in order to overcome the temptation of distorting thoughts. And because he does not put himself through such difficult training, he fails to grasp fully the deep inner unity of courage and wisdom. Socrates, who gives greater weight to the importance of force in politics than Gorgias does, likewise gives greater weight to the importance of self-habituation and self-discipline for the philosophic life than Protagoras does. His deepest insight is then to come full circle and see that, after all, something like knowledge is all that we need to be perfectly virtuous: the comprehensive understanding of the human good that includes knowledge of when and to what extent a common good may be found, knowledge of what each pleasure is worth, knowledge of what is and is not terrible, and knowledge of how to keep a grip on the particular things one knows and how to put it into effect—all of which is preserved through the moderate habits the Greeks called *sōphrosunē* (preserver of wisdom). This insight he presents now in cryptic and misleading form, however, with his statement that justice and moderation and courage are all knowledge (361b1–2), so that his position appears as disjointed as Protagoras'.

Socrates invites Protagoras to take up the thread of the puzzle again, likening himself to Prometheus in his determination not to be bested by the deceiver Epimetheus, but Protagoras declines. Something that can almost be called nature prevents all but the most intrepid of human beings from seeing clearly and steadily the good that we all want. The lack of courage or determination that stops Protagoras from resolving the conflict within himself is what makes it impossible to impart by ordinary educational means the wisdom that Socrates possesses. Socrates can offer arguments and indicate problems, but he cannot give another soul his own thirst for the truth above all other goods and his intolerance for self-deception, his confidence that he can bear the truth, whatever it turns out to be, or his strong hope that his own life, at least, will be better for having seen it. Protagoras' reply is on the surface both evasive and condescending: he praises Socrates as a promising young man and declares blandly that it is time to turn to something else. But quietly and almost graciously he concedes that Socrates has what it takes and he does not. Accepting Socrates' assimilation of himself to Prometheus, Protagoras praises himself as a human being (*anthrōpos*) without envy and Socrates as one who is likely to become a man (*anēr*) held in renown for wisdom (361e1, 5). It is Socrates, then, who not only understands the significance of the virtue of Prometheus, but possesses it. And doubtless he could not understand it had he not schooled himself so assiduously in thinking clearly and holding himself to what he has seen, so rare and elusive a thing is wisdom.

FIVE

The Socratic Thesis Applied: *Laws*

Turning to the *Laws*, we enter a different world. Here Socrates is absent, his place taken by a wise old Athenian Stranger, who gives his attention for a day to laying out the framework for the best practicable regime and the best practicable code of laws. The Stranger's interlocutors are two elderly gentlemen from Crete and Sparta, Kleinias and Megillus, the former of whom has been asked to serve as a legislator for a new Cretan colony, Magnesia. Thus the *Laws*, like the *Republic*, consists in the construction of a city in speech, but this one unambiguously intended not only to provide food for reflection on the problem of justice but to serve as a model for actual legislation under favorable but not utopian conditions. Now the Socratic view of moral and criminal responsibility is in its pure form so radical that it is surprising to find it appearing in the soberly practical *Laws* at all. For as Socrates suggested in the *Apology*, if virtue is at bottom knowledge of what is good, knowledge so powerful as to guarantee its own efficacy in action, and vice is rooted in ignorance, it becomes hard to see how any political community can justify the criminal sanctions that the rule of law requires. Indeed, not only does the *Laws* explore deep problems with retributive justice, but it portrays punishment aimed at deterrence as almost equally problematic: only reform and education aimed at crime prevention meet Socrates' and the Athenian's high standard of justice. To grasp this standard is to see why a rule that satisfied it could never be implemented in practice in anything like its pure form. Nevertheless, the *Laws* shows how a wise lawgiver might go quite far in instilling a citizenry with at least a serious recognition of the power of the Socratic thesis, and how a city's political and moral life might become more rational and humane as a result. Plato has the Athenian Stranger introduce a number of devices—the preludes to the laws; legal reforms that encourage calm deliberation;

a new understanding of responsibility; the concepts of pollution, nature, and luck; the equation of justice with psychic health; as well as subtle but far-reaching reforms of both piety and *thumos* or spiritedness—to bring the citizen's outlook as close as possible to the gentle humanity of the philosopher. In so doing, he also shows where this project invariably breaks down in the face of the irreducible irrationality of human moral passions. The *Laws* thus offers a fresh analysis of the relation of virtue to knowledge and an unrivaled exploration of the extent to which it is possible to apply that insight in ordinary political life.

Virtue and Knowledge

From the outset, the Athenian argues that good laws should be aimed at the whole of virtue because virtue is what makes the citizens happy. Here we have on a civic level the familiar Socratic claims about the goodness of virtue. The Athenian first adumbrates a version of the hypermoral-utilitarian claim on the level of the city as a whole, in telling Kleinias how he should have praised his own laws—if indeed they are divinely inspired, as the Cretans claim.

> "O stranger," it should have been said, "not in vain are the laws of Crete in especially high repute among all the Greeks. They are correct laws, laws that make those who use them happy. For they provide all the good things. Now the good things are twofold, some human, some divine. The former depend on the divine goods, and if a city receives the greater it will also acquire the lesser. If not, it will lack both." (631b–d)[1]

The Athenian goes on to class among the "human" goods health, beauty, strength, and wealth, and among the "divine" ones all the virtues of soul, including justice. The divine goods are somehow both highest and the means to the other goods, a problem of priority that the Athenian does not here resolve. Equally troubling, however, is the extreme claim he makes for the power of the divine goods. Although good laws certainly conduce to peace and prosperity and national independence, can they possibly guarantee them, let alone the rest of the "human" goods?[2]

Silently withdrawing this extreme claim, the Athenian subsequently puts a new form of it into the mouth of the good Dorian poet, as part of a broader project of reforming traditional poetry. Now speaking on the level of the individual, he makes the good poet say that "the good man, being moderate and just, *is* happy and blessed, whether he be great and strong or small and weak, whether he be rich or not" (660e, emphasis added). The lesser goods do not inevitably accompany virtue, but one can be happy without them, whereas happiness requires and is even guaranteed by a good soul: here we have again the hypermoral-eudaimonist claim. There is much truth in this, but again, is it simply so? As Aristotle dryly remarks, "nobody" would call a virtuous man happy whose life was full of suffering and misfortune, "except for the sake of maintaining an argument" (*NE* 1096a1–3).

As if acknowledging the force of this objection, the Athenian goes on to give a more subtle and compelling version of his thesis at 661b–d, now speaking unambiguously in his own name. He argues now that the lesser things commonly "said to be goods," such as health, beauty, wealth, and even tyranny, "are all very good when possessed by just and pious men, but all very bad when possessed by unjust men" (661b). Excellence of soul is neither the only thing that matters nor a guarantee of the other good things that do, but it is the essential foundation for using any of them well and deriving solid happiness from them. Just as most of us would not exchange our condition for that of a lunatic, even the richest lunatic in the world, so the Socratic philosopher would never exchange the clarity and inner harmony of his soul for anything else at all. Indeed, he says, "To see, to hear, to perceive, and, in general, to live as an immortal for the whole of time, while possessing all the things said to be good except for justice and the whole of virtue, is the greatest of evil. The evil gets less as the time such a man continues to live gets shorter" (661c). Unless or until such a soul can be cured, its life is, like the unexamined life, not worth living. The Athenian concludes, "The things said to be bad are good for unjust men and bad for just men, while the good things are really good for good men but bad for bad men" (661d). The suggestion here is that the more wealth and power a wicked person possesses, the worse off he is, perhaps because more resources allow him to commit worse crimes, and because success in crime encourages arrogance, while failure sometimes brings a criminal to reform. Virtue, then, is the necessary but not sufficient condition for happiness. This is a powerful claim. Yet neither the precise relation of virtue to happiness nor the precise character of the virtue in question has yet been specified. Clearly we do not have here the standard moral-utilitarian claim: The Athenian is conceding that all of the possessions people call good can be had without virtue. But if these goods do not constitute happiness, what precisely is essential for happiness that they do not guarantee? Is it the simple possession of virtue, or its active exercise, or some other activity that virtue makes possible and that makes life worth having? Even if there can be no happiness without virtue, is every demand of virtue, and in particular, every demand of justice, perfectly aligned with the requisites of happiness?[3]

By leaving these questions unaddressed, the Athenian is able to give the impression that his strong claim is wholly true of all virtue, both philosophic and civic, and in particular that it is true of justice as normally understood—obeying the law and not taking more than one's share of the good things that everyone wants. In fact, as the Athenian makes clear in book 9, he defines justice as Socrates does in the *Republic*, as the proper order of the soul, in which passions and habits form a harmonious whole under the guidance of self-knowledge and a thorough understanding of the human good (*Laws* 863e–64a; cf. *Republic* 435b–444e). The unjust soul from this point of view is so foolish, chaotic, and unhealthy as to be the most undesirable thing of all. It is true that one can have a well-ordered soul and still be crushed by adversity. But a good soul is still the one possession most worth having and the essential precondition for making the best of whatever fortune brings. The consequence is clear: criminals have a terrible disorder in their most precious possessions, their souls; they are incapable of a truly happy life; they are pitiable.

Yet as we have seen, the strongest claim for the unity of virtue and happiness may in fact be perfectly true only of philosophic virtue, or wisdom.[4] Such virtue, entailing as it does a wholehearted pursuit of knowledge and hence a radical detachment from most of the contested goods, a generous benevolence towards friends, and a gentle spirit of humanity towards others, will dovetail almost perfectly with the demands of justice as usually understood. But for the ordinary citizen, justice as ordinary laws define it demands a more difficult form of self-denial. Even if the good order in the soul is essential for happiness, even if it holds for everyone and not just the philosopher that true happiness is best found in the active exercise of virtue, the ordinary person invariably counts as essential to happiness many goods and advantages that virtue does not guarantee and may often oppose. Kleinias voices this perspective as he responds with skepticism: he is not persuaded that a strong, healthy, rich, unjust tyrant lives unhappily, even though he does consider such a man's injustice shameful (661e–62a). In reply, the Athenian returns to a more public or popular level of the discussion, and on this plane he again makes his claim bolder. If he were a legislator, he says, he would try to compel the poets and everyone in the city to say that there is no divergence between virtue and pleasure, or between what is just and what is profitable (662b–c). This is a hard thing to show. Perhaps it is impossible to show. But the citizens will consistently put virtue ahead of worldly advantage—and therefore live the very best lives of which they are capable—only if they agree with the unconventional Socratic assessment of what makes life worth living, or are at least persuaded by a popular image of this perspective. This is why they need a civic religion to support their wobbly love of virtue.

It is fitting, then, that at this point the Athenian brings the gods into the discussion. Yet as he does so, he goes on the offensive. Unless the fathers and legislators of the city and the gods themselves can say that the most just life is most pleasant, he argues, they will be forever unable to speak in consonance with themselves. For if they say that the happy life is the most pleasant but not the most just, this is at odds with their praise of justice. And it is not only gods and lawgivers but above all parents, who love their children most of all and most want them to be happy, who urge them to be just. On the other hand, if gods, lawgivers, and parents should say that the happy life is the most just but not the most pleasant, they will not be able to say clearly what the other, greater good is that justice brings that outweighs the good of pleasure. It will not do to pretend that pleasure is a trifle that virtue can fairly demand we disregard; it is of the essence of happiness. Indeed, the Athenian insists that "no one would voluntarily be willing to be persuaded to do that which does not bring more joy than pain" (663b). Elsewhere he elaborates:

> By nature, the human consists above all in pleasures and pains and desires. To these every mortal animal is, as it were, inextricably attached and bound in the most serious ways. The noblest life should be praised not only because it is superior as regards the splendor of its reputation, but also because, if someone is willing to taste it and not become a fugitive from it because of his youth, it will prove superior in respect to that which we all seek—namely, having more delight and less pain throughout the whole of one's life. (732e–33a)

This claim is important for the Athenian's argument, because if he granted even an occasional divergence between the nobly virtuous life and the happy life, he would have to concede that the person who had his own best interest clearly in view would not invariably choose to act virtuously. He would sometimes face a choice between justice and happiness, and then something else other than knowledge, something like the good will of Kant's philosophy, which chooses what is right for its own sake without regard for its beneficial or deleterious consequences, would be needed to keep him just.

Certainly it seems and will always seem to many human beings that there are such divergences between the demands of justice and those of happiness; the Athenian hopes at best only that "the argument which does not split the pleasant from the just, and the good from the noble, [will be], if nothing else, persuasive in making *some* willing to live the pious and the just life" (663b, emphasis added). What he can say more confidently is that all who fail to close this gap in their own understanding will live lives of profound confusion or ignorance about what matters most. They will think at times, or with parts of themselves, that wealth, power, and pleasure are what matter and that virtue is at best a means to these, and a most unreliable one unless the gods intervene to right the scales; they will think at other times that virtue is what is noblest and best, and when they do they will vacillate again as to whether virtue is noble as a terrific sacrifice that needs a reward or whether it is in itself the good most worth having. All such divisions the Athenian calls ignorance. Indeed, he calls it "the greatest ignorance of all" when a man

> doesn't like, but rather hates, what in his opinion is noble or good, and likes and welcomes what in his opinion is wicked and unjust. This dissonance between pleasure and pain on the one hand, and the opinion that is according to reason on the other, I assert to be the ultimate and greatest ignorance, because it belongs to the major part of the soul. In the soul, you see, the part that feels pain and pleasure is like the populace and the majority in the city. So when the soul opposes knowledge, or opinions, or reason—the natural rulers—this I call lack of intelligence. (689a–b)

The Athenian here acknowledges that people often find the noble course painful and the base one more pleasant, but he insists that the root cause of such dissonance is still ignorance. Not only when the mind holds an inadequate opinion about the good but even when it apprehends the truth, the Athenian insists, there is some kind of ignorance at work whenever reason fails to prevail, and we are not perfectly free from ignorance until reason has permeated all the passions. Thus he asks how, without consonance, there can ever be active wisdom (*phronēsis*), and concludes that "the finest and greatest of consonances would most justly be called the greatest wisdom (*sophia*)" (689d).[5] In the same vein the Athenian says later,

> With regard to the things the lawgiver enumerates and sets down as shameful and bad, and the opposite, good and noble, whoever is unwilling to use every means to avoid the former and employ all his capacities in the practice

> of the latter—every such human being—is ignorant of the fact that in all these matters he is treating his soul, a most divine thing, in a most dishonorable and unseemly way. (728a–b)

In sum, Plato acknowledges throughout the *Laws* that no code of legislation, however wise, can instill in the majority of citizens the virtue that in Socrates' soul sprang from philosophic independence—the self-sufficiency, the strength to face necessity calmly, the humane spirit of moderation, and the freedom from tumultuous desires and ambitions and resentments that bend most of us out of shape and make us put the higher things in the service of the lower ones. Even the best laws can foster only a simulacra of true virtue in the form of shame-bred self-control. This is one reason the Athenian says that while the individual should try to acquire true reasoning and live according to it, the city must take its reasoning secondhand and, he implies, in diluted or distorted form (645b). The city must rely on pious fears and on other sanctions for virtue and not upon a simply autonomous love of virtue in its citizens, and it must to some extent bow to people's irrational demands for vengeance against those with unhealthy souls. What well-framed laws can do, however, is to remind citizens at every opportunity of the higher and truer perspective on virtue and criminal responsibility, so as to move them at least some distance from harsh vindictiveness towards a more healthy autonomy and a more humane way of regarding human failing. This, I would argue, is the reasoning at work behind Plato's complicated and seemingly self-contradictory pronouncements on criminal law throughout the *Laws*.[6]

Preludes and the Appeal to Reason

So what practical and workable solutions does Plato offer to pull citizens towards a more rational perspective? His starting point is the thought that society can do much better than it usually does in providing lifelong moral education and guidance, to make crime the rare and shocking exception that it should be rather than the dismal commonplace that it is among us. The law code that he offers is therefore one tailored to a small polis, the society that most nearly approaches the intimacy and educative potential of the family at its best. Its tiny size, in a world of warlike rivals for power, ensures that every citizen will be valued and that all will have a reason to help educate the young and push delinquents to reform.[7] Thus the polis, as Plato envisions it, enlists the entire law code and way of life to teach and persuade and charm the citizens into being good: it is as morally serious and at the same time as gentle and rational as Plato thinks a society comprising real human beings under optimal circumstances could be. The aim of everything in the laws is education, of a twofold character. First, through the education in poetry and music that shapes both taste and morals from childhood, and through the judicious use of honor and dishonor, the laws seek to instill in the souls of citizens a habitual love of lawfulness, rooted in pious awe and reverence for ancestral ways, and a horror at injustice. Even when this habitual disposition is not informed by a complete understanding of what justice is and why it is good, and when it therefore coexists uneasily with contrary desires, it still comes much closer to true virtue than the self-control that rests merely on fear of punishment. Punishment is of course a necessary part of criminal law, but Plato presents it as a last resort; to the extent that it is needed, it is a sign of the failure of civic education. Second, the laws encourage the thoughtful reflection that allows any citizen who carefully ponders them to progress towards a deeper understanding of ethics. Thus the code has at every point a curiously double and tension-freighted character. For much of what impressionable young people need to acquire moral seriousness is the sight of vice meeting with shame and punishment which all too often are inflicted in anger and do the criminal no good. But while the Athenian makes concessions to popular anger, he seizes every opportunity to write into the law signposts that point us towards his own truer and more humane perspective.

This better, more rational perspective is present nowhere more clearly and strikingly than in the Athenian's use of "preludes" to introduce the major laws, an innovation Glenn Morrow calls "almost unique in political philosophy."[8] Modern laws are sometimes introduced by brief preambles stating their purpose, but the aim of Platonic preludes is far more ambitious. Preludes, sometimes much longer than the laws themselves, use extended discussions to enlist the citizens as willing participants and at best active partners in the laws' educational project. Their aim is, if not to engage the citizens in philosophy, at least to make them "as persuadable as possible with regard to virtue," disposed to listen "in a more tame and agreeable mood" to the laws' injunctions (718c–d). The Athenian explains the need for this reform by citing Hesiod's famous observation that "the immortal gods have put sweat before virtue, and a path to it that is rough and steep," though the road becomes "easy to endure" when one reaches the top (718e–19a, citing *Works and Days*, 287–88). By assigning responsibility for this state of affairs to the gods, Hesiod seems to hint that popular religion has made virtue less appealing than it ought to be, given its inherent goodness. But are poets like Hesiod not themselves largely to blame for this error? And indeed, the Athenian parts ways with the ancient poets in giving a much bolder critique of popular conceptions of morality and popular piety. Shortly before this passage he even pronounces it "the noblest and truest of all principles" that the good man should commune continually with the gods but that the devotions of the wicked are a positive evil (716d–17a). Piety in defective human beings only reinforces the view that virtue is something painful that needs a reward and that vice is bad only because it provokes divine wrath, which may be appeased with gifts: it is better for these people to stand at an awe-stricken distance from the gods than to worship them in such a spirit. The inadequate divine support for human virtue according to Hesiod's portrayal would seem to be an example of the irresponsibility of the poets that made the Athenian insist in book 2 that they must be closely supervised by the legislator.

Yet here, unlike in book 2, the Athenian allows the poets to reply in their own defense. Or more precisely, he himself addresses the lawgiver on the poets' behalf, in what turns out to be a cascade of rapidly shifting and unfolding claims. Beginning with the plea that the poets merely repeat the words of the muse without understanding them, like intoxicated priestesses, or rather that they merely imitate life as they see it, in all its multiplicity, this defense from ignorance merges imperceptibly into an account of the poet's ability to praise "what is fitting" more adequately than the blunt law ever can. For while the lawgiver must "always exhibit one speech about one subject," the poet can take different individuals' circumstances into account and give guidance tailored to each. The ancient poets' apology or defense against the Athenian's implicit charge that they are not good educators of the young is that they are in fact masters of conveying different messages to different audiences. However much Plato may wish to reform their popular message, he here recognizes the subtlety of their work and adopts their methods.

The vehicle for incorporating poetic subtlety into the laws is the preludes. These work to soften the harsh, peremptory commands of ordinary laws—which threaten as tyrants do, or merely give their commands and rush away as "slave doctors" do (720c)—with the persuasive reasoning of the "free doctor" who treats free citizens by investigating the condition of each patient's soul "according to nature," reasoning with him about it and even learning from him (720d). The Athenian's use of preludes thus comes to sight as a radical and rational departure from the poetic presentation of virtue and its justification. The first example of a prelude illustrates the new aim of instilling a more autonomous dedication to virtue by showing the citizen how the law, in this case, the law requiring everyone to marry and procreate, is in fact good for his individual happiness, fulfilling his soul's profound longing for a share in "immortality" (721c). Whereas the poets rely too much on stories of angry gods, the preludes, like thoughtful doctors, make their appeal to nature, to reason, and to the individual's own truest good.

But when we look more closely, the picture is less simple. Since no prelude stands alone, the choice is not in fact between laws that compel and laws that persuade, but between simple laws that merely compel and "double" laws that also persuade through their accompanying preludes. The art of legislation may mix persuasion with force, but it cannot dispense with force (722b–c).[9] Moreover, although the Athenian's first example of a persuasive prelude appeals explicitly to nature—echoing the assertion that the free doctor investigates and teaches according to nature—the natural yearning that the prelude appeals to, the yearning for immortality, is, curiously, the one human longing that can never be satisfied on the plane of natural human existence. The individual's obedience to the marriage law does perhaps allow the species to partake of immortality, as the Athenian says (721c), but the individual's hope that this will bring him personal fulfillment entails something either more or less than perfect reason.[10] Hence it comes as no surprise that the Athenian in his summary says not quite that the preludes teach reason, but rather that they make the citizen "receive the command—that is, the law—in a frame of mind more favorably disposed and therefore apt to learn. That is why, according to my argument at least, this would correctly be called a 'prelude' rather than an 'argument' of the law" (723a–b). Preludes cannot serve as "free doctors" but can at best dispose some citizens to obedience and some to thoughtfulness. By moving the law in a more rational direction without making it wholly a matter either of persuasion or of reason, preludes turn out to be in every way an adaptation of the ways of the poet.

The Requirements of a Just Criminal Code

Book 5 goes deeper in expounding a prelude to all of the laws, and thereby showing more of Plato's radical thoughts on the impossibility of conforming law more than very incompletely to true reason. This theme is developed in a series of revealing but tension-laden comments about justice at the beginning of the book. After exhorting the citizens to take the good of their souls with utmost seriousness, the Athenian observes,

> No one, so to speak, takes into account the gravest of the so-called just penalties for wrongdoing: what is gravest is to become similar to men who are wicked, and, in becoming similar, to avoid good men and be cut off from good conversation, and instead to attach oneself to the bad by seeking intercourse with them. He who grows similar in nature to such people must necessarily do and suffer (*paschein*) what such men by their natures do and say to one another. (728b–c)

This much certainly can become part of a coherent and constructive public teaching, for everyone should be encouraged to see that the worst consequences of vice are the natural ones. But the next thought is more radical.

> Such suffering (*pathos*) is not, indeed, a just penalty (*dikē*), since the just—and the just penalty—is noble. It is retribution (*timōria*), a suffering that is a consequence of injustice. Both he who undergoes this and he who escapes it are miserable: one because he does not get cured, the other because he is destroyed in order that many others may be saved. (728c)[11]

Here the Athenian slides imperceptibly from natural consequences into purposeful deterrence or retribution, which are pursued by human beings who are precisely not willing to let nature take its course. But the clear message is that neither retribution nor the estrangement from good men that vice naturally brings is really just. As Socrates argues in his confrontation with Polus in the *Gorgias*, what is just must be something noble and hence good; there is nothing noble about an action or event that is wholly destructive (*Gorgias* 474d–75a). That is why Socrates always treats pure retribution as ignoble and irrational: it piles harm upon harm without accomplishing anything good. Even when punishment accomplishes some good for others by deterring them from the same error, that still does not make it noble according to this reasoning. For even the natural destruction that vice brings in its wake may do good in providing an object lesson to others, just as an obese person who dies of heart disease may serve as a warning to gluttons, yet we do not treat his demise as anything noble. The most troubling suggestion of the present passage is that even punishment calculated to work as a deterrent is no more noble, and in the final analysis no more truly just, than the bodily ills of the immoderate. Both are, in different ways, just grim necessities.

In book 9 of the *Laws* Plato sheds further light on the standard a perfectly just criminal code would have to meet. Here he continues not only his gingerly critique of retribution but also his insistence on the injustice of deterrence whenever it is severed from rehabilitation or other benefits to the criminal.

> Perhaps by paying the penalty [the temple robber] would become better, by becoming moderate. For no judicial punishment that takes place according to law aims at what is bad, but for the most part accomplishes one of two other aims: it makes the one who receives the judicial punishment either better or less wicked. (854d–e)

The Athenian insists that whatever is nobly done must be nobly undergone, and that it makes no sense to say (as we all tend to think) that a punishment that is noble and just to inflict may be base and harmful to suffer—for then society is simply using the criminal to benefit itself. Nor, if it is truly noble, can it be base but beneficial to suffer (859e). The Athenian censures "the many" for saying, "without consonance, that the noble things and the just things are separate" (860c), with the result that they vacillate endlessly between what they judge as good and what they judge as just. Unless we are to deny the nobility of justice, the only exit from this morass is to grasp that what is just is necessarily both noble and good and what is unjust is necessarily both base and bad, so thoroughly undesirable that no one in his right mind would willingly choose it, and hence that, as the Athenian says, "the bad are all bad involuntarily in every respect" (860d). They may at times be beyond our help, but they should never be beyond our pity, and if our treatment of them is to be truly just, it must be noble and good on both sides.

But how could any punishment be noble to undergo as well as noble to impose? The only punishment that could fully meet this standard would be the kind of punishment Socrates says crime deserves in the *Apology*: education. This line of thought has several counterintuitive consequences. First, any punishment is in fact noble to undergo if it results in true reformation, however much the criminal may resist it and however shameful it may seem to ignorant eyes. The benefit is of course likely to be deepest, and hence the punishment most truly noble, when the criminal himself accepts it as needed medicine, as an occasion to learn to do better and, if necessary, to restore what he has destroyed, so that he may return to a state of friendship with his fellow citizens (862b–c). At the same time, the best and hence most just punishment need not hurt at all. It need only improve the offender and repair the harm.

> To accomplish these things by deeds or words—with pleasures or pains, by honors or dishonors, even by monetary penalties or gifts, and in general by whatever procedure someone may use to bring about hatred of injustice and desire, or lack of hatred, for the nature of the just—it is this that is the task of the noblest laws. (862d)[12]

Finally, the most just punishment for a criminal who cannot be reformed—the one that in fact best expresses the nonpunitive spirit of compassion that a wise judge would feel—is death, not imprisonment. For death ends the evil of an irredeemable life as imprisonment cannot. With this judgment Plato shows both his humanity and his adamant toughness. If even the unexamined life is not worth living, how much less is the life in which ignorance and rage wreak havoc on oneself and others? Yet his logic demands that we first make every effort to teach and reform—unstinting efforts that do not begrudge the sick soul what it needs to heal—and that we reserve capital punishment for crimes that show an absolutely hardened disregard for law and human life. Punishment that simply restrains the criminal because the citizenry is unwilling to make a serious effort at curing him is no more just than a Victorian insane asylum. Plato would be dismayed by the prospect of a nation with over two million men behind bars, many of them languishing for years on death row.

In sum, the Athenian takes the common insight that justice must secure a common good and must not harm one person to benefit another, and he shows what drastic changes would be needed in our penal codes to attain this standard of justice. Not only retribution, not only deterrent punishment that fails to help the convict, but all attempts to make the punishment fit the crime by matching the seriousness of the crime with the painfulness of the punishment are unjust. They seem just only because we still harbor the thought that the criminal has gotten away with something and deserves to suffer even more harm on top of the terrible havoc he already suffers in his soul.

Obstacles to Implementing the Rule of Wisdom

Simply to articulate Plato's high standard of strict justice is to see why no actual penal code could even approach it in practice. No society is able to deter unhealthy souls from crime without imposing harsh punishments on its most unhealthy citizens, punishments that usually make their souls even worse. No society is willing to devote the time and resources to rehabilitating criminals that Plato's standard requires; nor, even if it were, could it help more than a few to attain complete health of the soul. Every system of justice must satisfy the outraged anger of crime victims and their families if they are to forgo private vengeance and accept the rule of law. Thus, in accepting the rule of law, society must give up not only personal vendettas but the truly forward-looking and constructive stance of Platonic justice, which would bring each unhealthy soul as far as practicable towards a complete cure. For to attain this standard, commands and prohibitions, even if applied to all citizens alike, would have to be enforced in ways that would differ endlessly depending on the character of the offender. One thief might need only a stern rebuke in order never to repeat his crime, another might need to be publicly shamed, a third would need to study Plato, and a fourth might be so incurable that death would be the only just penalty. But why, indeed, should the justice system wait for citizens to commit crimes before applying a remedy, if the remedy is meant to help them? Why should it not spring into action, admonishing and if necessary restraining the citizens, whenever they show any inclination to commit a crime, since surely prevention is the best cure? We now have an image of a justice system that, if wisely administered, would resemble the rule of a good parent over a young child more than the rule of law. If a government of fallible men and women ever tried to implement such a system, the result would be intolerable totalitarianism.

Plato accepts the need for the protection that comes from a rule of known laws and fixed penalties, but he forces us to see how seriously this compromises the highest standard of justice. He also prompts us to wonder whether divine justice might not succeed where human governments fail, and whether the only solution to our predicament would not be the rule of a wise god who needs no laws and who teaches and heals each unhealthy soul. But he also gently contrasts his standard with his own society's idea of divine rule. At 859a, he asks, "How do we conceive writing about laws in the cities should be: should the writings appear in the shapes of a father and mother, caring dearly and possessing intelligence, or, like a tyrant and despot, should they command and threaten, post writings on the walls and go away?" But a few pages later, returning to the problem of the confused notions of justice that result from our lack of clarity about the involuntary nature of all injustice, he asks, "Is the argument now being uttered by us going to say only this much and depart, as if it were being spoken by a god, giving no argument as to why it has spoken correctly, and just legislating in defiance of the difficulty in some way?" (861b–c). The divergence between his view of crime and the view embodied in the law codes of Sparta and Crete, which claimed divine inspiration, lies at the heart of the Socratic critique of all the claims to divine inspiration known to Greek antiquity.

Concessions to Irrationality: Nemesis and Shame

Implicit in the rule of law is the need for frightening deterrents. At the beginning of the discussion of criminal law in book 9, the Athenian calls it a disgraceful thing that, after legislating such a rigorous moral education, the founders of the new city should still be required to deliver threats in order to deter crime, but he accepts this necessity. Later he acknowledges that earthly sanctions alone are not enough, and that both punishments in Hades and further punishments when the soul returns to earth must be invoked (870d–e). Still later he acknowledges the limits even of these threats, and casts about for "some ultimate deterrent" (881a), but he never comes up with anything worse. Good laws can make crime rare but can never extinguish it. Otherworldly sanctions seem especially needed at both ends of the spectrum of social bonds. On one hand, they are required to ensure just treatment of those for whom ordinary social connections are too weak to provide adequate protection. Immediately after denying the justice of retribution, the Athenian finds himself forced to invoke the avenging gods to come to the aid of strangers from abroad, who have no champions to protect them (729e). On the other hand, extreme sanctions are also needed to reinforce what should be among the strongest bonds of all, children's sense of duty towards their parents. For parents in traditional societies demand an extraordinary degree of gratitude and deference, claims which no reasoned appeal to the grown child's own advantage can ever fully support. Thus the Athenian speaks of Nemesis for the first and only time in a speech warning about the rage of dishonored parents.

This rage is a vivid expression of the all but ineradicable human desire for vengeance against those who harm us. This desire, if it had its way, would punish every wrong, deliberate or inadvertent; it would punish citizens when they "refuse to believe" (887d) and "dare to misunderstand" (892a) the sacred stories about the gods; it would punish dumb beasts that kill people and rocks that fall and injure them. And popular anger demands not merely that crimes be judged and punished, but that the people at large have a direct say in the process. As the Athenian puts it,

> In regard to crimes against the public, it is necessary, first, that the majority have a share in the decision. For when someone does an injustice to the city

> everyone suffers the injustice, and they would justly be vexed if they had no share in such trials. . . . Even in private suits it is necessary that everyone take part as much as possible. For anyone who does not share in the right of judging considers himself not at all a sharer in the city itself." (768b; cf. Aristotle *NE* 1132b33–33a1)

This means that the people, in insisting on serving on juries, insist on being judge in their own cause, a thought troubling enough in itself. But why do people feel themselves so personally affronted when crimes are committed? Somehow the law-abiding citizen finds his own sense of dignity assaulted by a crime that goes unpunished, suggesting that if criminals routinely got away with their crimes, the value of law-abidingness itself would become questionable in his eyes. Thus the law-abiding citizen is vulnerable to being persuaded of the validity of the criminal's way of looking at the world; both need to see crimes punished if they are to have respect for justice and for just citizens.[13]

So powerful is the demand that injuries must be avenged that it is even assumed to persist after death, and even against those who were never really at fault. Thus, when a citizen has killed another by accident, the killer is required to go into exile for a time, on the assumption that

> he who dies a violent death after having lived with the outlook of a free man feels, when freshly dead, spirited rage against the perpetrator. Filled with fear and horror on account of his violent experience, and seeing his own murderer going about in his own accustomed haunts, he feels horror; being himself disturbed, he does all he can, having Memory as an ally, to disturb the perpetrator and his doings. (885d–e)[14]

Anger reaches its crescendo when it is parents who have been wronged and especially when they have been killed by their own children. Aeschylus in the *Oresteia* gives a gripping portrayal of the rage such parents are thought to carry with them beyond the grave, embodied as the Furies that hound Orestes out of Argos for killing his mother, despite the fact that her death was punishment for murdering her husband Agamemnon and was ordered by none less than Apollo himself. The furies are utterly savage, vengeful, and unwilling to listen to argument. They press their claim so unrelentingly that, in the third play of the trilogy, the *Eumenides*, they successfully threaten to ruin the young city of Athens if they are not given a place there. The achievement of the story is that the Areopagus is established as the final judge in all cases of homicide: law does replace raw fury. But Athena promises the Furies that those who kill their parents will be acquitted only when they have an exceptionally strong justification, as Orestes has, and even then purification and expiation will be required. Athena and the Athenian chorus recognize that it is in fact a positive good for Athens that the Furies be allowed to remain in the background. For they stand behind the law as the oldest and strongest source of awe, evidently embodying for Aeschylus the thought that there are some things to which we must bow simply without qualification or question (*Eumenides* 475, 690–98). The positive, written law of the city and its lawfully instituted courts never have quite this power, wise and good as they are. For like Apollo in Aeschylus's trilogy, the laws have arisen within memory in the clear light of day and they use the language of reasoned argument, which as such is always open to questioning and to counterargument. The *Oresteia* hence stands as a warning against placing excessive hopes in enlightened politics. To secure a rule of laws based on reason and public consent is an excellent accomplishment, but in the gloom behind the positive law must lie something more terrible that inspires us with shuddering awe and unquestioning obedience.[15] The official teaching of Plato's city Magnesia, by contrast, is that reason provides an adequate basis for all legislation and that unquestioning obedience is never demanded. Yet Plato's references to the power of Nemesis and the importance that he gives to civic piety in the *Laws* show a quiet, qualified agreement with Aeschylus' judgment on the need for some such supplement to reasoned arguments about justice.

Less irrational than the concessions to Nemesis, but still a compromise with human irrationality, is the Athenian's reliance on passions of reverence and shame. He puts great emphasis on cultivating a sense of reverence for the law—reverence that necessarily combines respect for its underlying moral principles with reflexive respect for what is simply old. Likewise, he encourages and makes extensive use of shame. Uniting these two closely related passions under the heading of *aidōs* or awe, the Athenian says that the lawgiver should "consider lack of awe to be the greatest evil for everyone both in private and in public life" (647a–b). To ensure its hold upon the citizens, the Athenian says it is not enough to do as most cities do and enjoin the young "to be ashamed before everyone"; the lawgiver must also "urge the elderly to be ashamed before the young, and to take care above all lest any young person ever see or hear them doing or saying anything shameful" (729b–c). Shame is a potent tool that the Athenian relies on especially to curb dishonesty among the magistrates. But, perhaps surprisingly, he also connects shame with battlefield courage (647b). For shame is in fact the obverse of the sense of honor that pervades every good army, including our own.[16] The shame or awe that Plato finds most valuable is not the debilitating shame at actual bad behavior that may or may not impel the offender to reform, but what we might call "preventative shame," the sense that one *would* be ashamed to behave in certain ways, which in the best case keeps one from ever doing so. While shame and honor normally involve the attribution of moral responsibility for one's faults and ignoble inclinations on one hand and for one's good qualities and deeds on the other, it is possible to emphasize the more rational aspect of these passions, focusing attention simply on what makes virtue admirable and what makes vice a proper object of dismay and disapproval. In this way, these passions are probably indispensable supports to human excellence, ones that classical republics all appreciated and utilized and that we pay a cost for neglecting.

Voluntary and Involuntary Crimes

More troubling even than his practical concessions to irrational anger is the way the Athenian finds himself forced to compromise in his very formulations of the basic principles of moral responsibility. After his careful argument that all injustice is involuntary, the Athenian is compelled by a stubborn Kleinias to write into the law some version of the common distinction between voluntary and involuntary injustices; this is the only time Kleinias simply digs in his heels against the Athenian's reasoning (861e). Thus Plato portrays wisdom bowing to the inescapable political power of the view that people deliberately do wrong and for that deserve retributive punishment. Immediately after emphatically refusing to retract his claim that all injustices are involuntary (861c), the Athenian capitulates and begins to delineate a class of "voluntary" injustices that should be punished.[17] But in an interesting shift, he now refuses to call *any* harm an injustice if it is *not* "voluntary" (862a). In this way he at least preserves the thought that nothing anyone does involuntarily deserves retributive punishment.

In order to satisfy Kleinias, the Athenian makes use of a sensible distinction between harms done on purpose, such as killing a man in anger, and those done by accident. He follows common opinion in calling the former voluntary and unjust, while refusing to call unjust any harm done inadvertently. The crucial difference is that actions of the first type show the character of the agent in a way that the latter do not (862b), and hence, the Athenian and ordinary opinion both agree, the former calls for a more serious response. But while most people see such acts as deserving more harm, the Athenian sees them as calling for more help. And while most people view them as in every respect voluntary, the Athenian's argument, taken as a whole, suggests that crimes committed "voluntarily" are at the deepest level even more *involuntary* than harm inflicted accidentally, for in corrupting one's own soul, one acts more against one's true wishes than in making a simple mistake.[18] In a similar spirit, the Athenian accepts the common thought that those who break the law while insane should not be punished (864d); but while others think it is because insanity provides an excuse, Socratic reasoning would say it is because reforming such a person is probably hopeless. Thus the distinction that others make for the sake of imposing retribution on some and excusing others is made by the Athenian only in order to identify some who can and should be cured and others who either need no cure or are incapable of it.[19]

A similar dynamic is at work in the discussion of ignorance and its role in crime. In the theoretical discussion of crime in book 5, the Athenian makes it clear that all wrongdoing is rooted in ignorance (see esp. 728b and 731c). Yet in the actual criminal code, the Athenian follows common practice in attributing only some crimes to ignorance and others to anger or desire (863c). He further distinguishes between "simple" and "double" ignorance. Simple ignorance is ignorance of a fact—for example, that it is against the law to divulge certain information. Such ignorance, he says, is responsible for "light faults" that deserve gentle punishments or forgiveness. By contrast,

> the double version occurs when someone lacks understanding because he partakes not only of ignorance but also of the opinion that he is wise, and believes he knows completely things about which he knows nothing; if this is accompanied by strength and force, the lawgiver sets such things down as the causes of great and unmusical faults. (863c)

The Athenian makes plausible the blameworthiness of "double ignorance" by reminding us of the arrogance of "unmusical" souls, those whose natural forcefulness and courage, perhaps strengthened by an education in the gymnastic and martial arts, has not been rendered thoughtful and gentle by a corresponding education in music and poetry, which would instill it with a reverence for the beautiful and an openness to reasoned persuasion. Such unmusical souls take no care to inform themselves about relevant facts and laws, believing that they are wiser than the law.

Yet even here the Athenian stresses the peculiar character of ignorance. The other faults that contribute to crime all present temptations, temptations to indulge anger or to pursue pleasure, against what we believe or think we believe is good. Because desire and anger come to sight as temptations that moral opinion tells us we have a duty to resist, we praise those who "master" or "control" these passions and blame those who "yield" to them. But no one blames in the same way one who "yields" to ignorance. For ignorance, especially ignorance of what is truly good and bad, offers no temptation (863d–e). We are ruled by it when and only when we are unaware, or insufficiently aware, of its presence: it is a trap most difficult to escape.

Immediately after making this observation, the Athenian returns to the thought that what is done in ignorance, even the deep ignorance of right and wrong, should *not* be blamed:

> The tyranny in the soul of spiritedness, fear, pleasure, pain, feelings of envy, and desires, whether it do some injury or not, I proclaim to be in every way injustice. When, on the other hand, the opinion about what is best (however a city or certain private individuals may believe this will be) holds sway in souls and brings order to every man, then, even if it is in some way mistaken, what is done through this, and the part of each man that becomes obedient to such a ruler, must be declared to be entirely just and best for the whole of human life—even though many are of the opinion that such injury constitutes involuntary injustice. (863e–64a)

Here we have a case very similar to the case of the "double fault" above, which the lawgiver was encouraged to blame harshly, yet now the soul in the grip of an error it does not even perceive is called "entirely just." Why so? The difference seems to be that we are speaking now of erroneous opinions that result in orderly self-control rather than lawbreaking, even though they still fall far short of the true rule of reason.[20] Thus we have three different views of moral responsibility on the table: the conventional one that measures injustice mainly by the harm done, while excepting legally justified harm and pardoning harm based on ignorance; the public teaching the Athenian is laying out for the city that measures injustice mainly by the condition of the doer's soul, treating the tyranny of passion as injustice and the spirited self-mastery that bows to prevailing moral opinion (as exemplified by the guardians in the *Republic*) as just, even when the opinion is erroneous; and the Socratic view of which this civic view is a reflection, namely that the truly just soul is ruled not by spiritedness obedient to opinion but by truth allied with healthy desires.[21]

The unsettling upshot of the two passages quoted above is to underscore the close resemblance between "justice" in this civic-minded definition and the "great and unmusical faults" of the doubly ignorant who are both ignorant and ignorant of their ignorance, and whose ignorance is "accompanied by strength and force" (863c). For what is the rule of law in any actual polity but a mixture of wisdom and ignorant folly, backed up by force? At 722e–23a it becomes clear that actual laws in real political communities have invariably been like the commands of the slave doctors, and that only the Athenian's innovation of preludes can make laws even partially acts of reasoned persuasion.[22] The practical result of the passage just quoted will be to give protection to citizens who in good faith obey even erroneous laws and mistaken notions of what their duty is, and protection likewise to doubters of the official religion, including philosophers, while unleashing punishment on those who knowingly break the law out of anger and especially out of greed and incontinence.[23] At a practical level this makes a certain sense. If the task of the law is to "teach and compel" wrongdoers to do better (862d), then those who with perfect self-control follow the wrong end need only be taught why their end is inadequate, while those who act against their own better judgment often need compulsion as well, to shore up their inadequate self-control. But the Athenian knows that no community will take seriously the task of enlightening citizens whose behavior is already orderly, nor, when compulsion is needed, can any community be relied on to exercise this compulsion in the compassionate knowledge that the ultimate cause even of arrogant violence is ignorance of what is truly best (728a–b), and that the worse the fault, the deeper and more pitiable the ignorance is that drives it.

The Criminal Code: Footholds for Reason

Even while the Athenian finds himself forced to dilute his own insight about the involuntariness of crime in offering legislation, however, he reminds us of his higher and more comprehensive perspective in many small ways throughout the exposition of the criminal law. This characteristic mixture of reason and unreason appears in the prelude to the first criminal law the Athenian takes up in book 9, that on temple robbery. In good Socratic fashion, the Athenian emphasizes the inner affliction of the souls of those who are drawn to crime and the misfortune of finding oneself in this condition. But the laws also teach people tempted by this most impious crime to look upon their own inclinations as a curse as well as a natural affliction (854b). These two descriptions are not compatible, but both support the thought that crime is never wholly voluntary. Likewise, throughout the exposition of the criminal code, Plato makes maximal use of the ancient and morally ambiguous concept of "pollution."[24] The thought that pollution accompanies great crimes deepens the seriousness with which society regards them but also softens society's vindictiveness, for a pollution is a thing so horrible that no one would choose to have it. In the concept of pollution the difference between voluntary and involuntary offences is minimized and the possibility for redemption is emphasized. Anger is given its due; the polluted one must make some expiation, but once he has done so, he is to be forgiven.

The notion of pollution carries with it a recognition of the interconnectedness of the community and a sense that one cannot simply dismiss crimes as someone else's business, but in a very different way from the angry tendency to see crimes against anyone as a personal affront to oneself. The thought that the community is polluted suggests that the evil tendency at the root of a crime is infecting the whole community and must be purged from it for everyone's sake. Such a notion of pollution is in general quite alien to our liberal, individualistic ethos, but it is felt in cases where crimes have become so atrocious that blame seems to extend from the direct perpetrators to everyone who failed to stop them, and even subsequent generations feel tainted by belonging to a community that could do such things.[25]

With his advice on how to view and handle one's own evil impulses, Plato gives a new meaning to the old idea of taking responsibility for one's actions. The individual or the society that takes responsibility in this way need not view crimes as the result of a radically free will; one may even, like Sophocles' Oedipus, believe that one's crimes were fated, but nonetheless one acknowledges them as one's own; one acknowledges the presence of the disorders that exist in one's soul or one's community and strives in every way to overcome them, taking an active part in the administration of justice and in one's own education and making no excuses. "The greatest of all evils for the mass of human beings is something which grows naturally in the soul, and everyone, by excusing it in himself, fails to devise any way to escape it" (731d–e; cf. 727b–c). To the would-be temple robber, the Athenian offers exhortations to pray for divine help, to seek out virtuous company, to "hear, and try yourself to say, that every man must honor the noble and the just things," and to "flee, without turning back, the company of bad men. If by your doing these things the disease abates somewhat, well and good; but if not, look to death as something nobler, and depart from life" (854b–c).

Further ways the Athenian builds footholds for reason in the criminal law include his frequent use of medical language that treats crime as a disease and the proper remedy for crime as a "cure," as well as his frequent language of luck and misfortune. Thus the slave or foreigner convicted of robbing a temple is to have the "misfortune" written on his hands and face before being executed and cast out of the city unburied (854d); the family that takes the allotment of a family of inveterate criminals is to be set up "with better luck" (856e); the Athenian, having defined injustice as the tyranny of passion over the soul, "whether it does some injury or not" to others (863e–64a), adds that if indeed it does harm others, if one succeeds in one's evil purposes, that is "bad luck" (877a). A further use of language that points to the Socratic perspective is seen in the Athenian's frequent references to nature and what occurs or grows naturally. Even the longing to rob temples is called a natural affliction (854b), and the divine punishment the Athenian says the city must hold up as a threat against the most stiff-necked criminals is presented as a natural consequence of crime (870e). Especially revealing is the glimpse the Athenian gives us of his own view of retributive punishment when he says that, were it not for the love of wealth, "there wouldn't occur in cities murders that require murders to purge them" (870c).

Finally, the law works in many ways to bring calm and reason both to judicial processes and, wherever possible, to criminal penalties. As Morrow has shown, the legal procedure Plato outlines in the *Laws* contains many innovative improvements on contemporary Greek practice, all aimed at introducing into trials more questioning of witnesses, sifting of evidence, and leisurely collective deliberation, as well as opportunities for defendants to appeal their verdicts before sentences are carried out; one notable reform is the rule that prevents trials for capital offences from being concluded in less than three days, addressing Socrates' criticism of Athenian procedure in the *Apology*.[26] This new spirit of calm deliberation reaches its peak in the laws on impiety in book 10 and the establishment of the nocturnal council, which must reform the impious by proving to them the error of their opinions—or allow the impious to persuade the council of the merits of their unconventional views.

With such civic education and such training in self-control, the Athenian considers it practicable to impose surprisingly light penalties for most crimes, especially first offences and especially when motivated by the sudden anger or the excessive vigilance in self-defense to which spirited men are naturally prone. In most cases even of murder the penalty is only two or three years in exile, although it is death for premeditated murder prompted by greed. Plato attempts to give reformable criminals every opportunity to regain their places as full members of the community. Likewise, the emphasis in cases of theft is upon restitution and restoring the severed connections between the offending member and the rest of society (862c). Like modern advocates of restorative justice, the Athenian argues that informal conferences of families and friends should be the court of first recourse when trouble breaks out between individuals—conferences whose first aim is likely to be mediation with a view to reconciliation, rather than punishment (766a ff.). And if criminals are, as often as possible, to be given a fresh start after they have paid the penalty or made right what they have destroyed, so much more does the Athenian insist that punishment not be visited upon their children. Indeed, the child of a criminal who overcomes his parent's shame and bad example and goes on to live an upstanding life is to be given special honor for this achievement. In all of these ways, the Athenian weaves a spirit of philosophic gentleness into the morally impressive but often unforgiving ethos of his Cretan and Spartan models.

The Rule of Law in Perspective

Again, however, the spirit of retribution is never left behind. We are now in a position to appreciate the full import of perhaps the most revealing statement on this spirit, which comes early in book 5. Here the Athenian contrasts the life that is truly blessed with the life and preoccupations of the political man as such. "Truth is the leader of all good things for gods, and of all things for human beings. Whoever is to become blessed and happy should partake of it from the very beginning, so that he may live as a truthful man for as long a time as possible," he says (730c). Life according to truth is one peak of virtue, and here, the Athenian indicates, the fullest happiness is to be found, as well as trustworthiness among friends. Yet such a man is distinguished more by a freedom from injustice than by a devotion to justice. Hence the Athenian adumbrates a second peak of virtue, which he associates with the greatest honor if not the greatest happiness. "Yet the great man in the city, the man who is to be proclaimed perfect and the bearer of victory in virtue, is the one who does what he can to assist the magistrates in inflicting punishment" (730d). Every political community needs spirited citizens who believe in punishing their enemies, abroad and at home.[27] The limits to the Athenian's efforts to overcome moral indignation reflect not only a bow to necessity but a recognition that indignation is an indispensable force supporting the rule of law.

> Every real man should be of the spirited type, but yet also as gentle as possible. For there is no way to avoid those injustices done by others that are

> both dangerous and difficult, or even impossible to cure, except to fight and defend oneself victoriously, in no way easing up on punishment. This every soul is unable to do, if it lacks a high-born spiritedness. On the other hand, in regard to the curable injustices men commit, one must first understand that no man is ever voluntarily unjust. For no one anywhere would ever voluntarily acquire any of the greatest evils—least of all when the evil afflicts his most honored possessions. Now the soul, as we asserted, is truly the most honorable thing for everyone; therefore no one would ever voluntarily take the greatest evil into his most honorable possession and keep it for the rest of his life. So the unjust man, like the man who possesses bad things, is pitiable in every way, and it is permissible to pity such a man when his illness is curable; in this case one can become gentle, by restraining one's spiritedness and not keeping up that bitter, woman's raging. But against the purely evil, perverted man who cannot be corrected, one must let one's anger have free rein. (731b–d)

As citizens we should be as gentle as possible towards first offenders and youthful offenders who give reason to hope that they may be cured; we should willingly expend time and resources to help them and should not let irrational indignation get in our way. Yet the political community still needs anger. In cases in which hopes for reform are slim and examples must be made to deter others (for no society can in fact avoid practicing deterrent punishment), anger is necessary if society is to have the stomach to hurt those who have broken the law.[28] In reality, of course, those with incurably sick souls are much more pitiable than the curable, for they are the ones in whom the cancer of moral decay has metastasized throughout the whole soul. The real condition of the political community is now illuminated for us in a nightmarish way: the fabric of society keeps being attacked by humans who have gone mad, who keep smashing into our houses and our windows and our children and doing grotesque harm to themselves, but harming us too. To get up the energy and determination necessary to stop them, we have to go a little berserk ourselves and blame them for being in such a bad condition and want them to be even worse off. Yet this passion to punish the mentally deranged is part of what characterizes "the great man in the city," the man with the great love of justice (730d). If moral indignation is a failing, it is a failing deeply intertwined with the best impulses and noblest deeds of many of the very best souls among us.[29]

Plato was as sensitive to the dangers of cynicism and political apathy as anyone in our time has ever been, and he acted thoughtfully and consistently to counteract these dangers. He was determined to support both "the great man in the city" and the philosophic observer of his own and all times. But his own assessment of these two lives shines quietly forth, and that assessment turns in the end on his estimation of the highest embodiment of the love of justice, the rule of law. The rule of law stands as a compromise between reason and unreasoned force, seeking to bring dispassionate uniformity to a process that at bottom rests on the irrational demand that wrongs must be punished and that punishment must fit the crime. Plato invites us to consider what a government would look like that did not bow to these spirited demands but sought to improve each citizen by ruling him with continual scrutiny and personally tailored supervision. Such a rule would be gentle in its freedom from vindictiveness but endlessly oppressive when entrusted to fallible human beings. Against this alternative Plato sides unambiguously with the rule of law. Yet he supplements the law with music and poetry and early habituation to deepen the citizens' appreciation for what is admirable in the best citizens' souls, and he tempers all of this with arguments that hint at the ways that human perfection surpasses good citizenship altogether. We are in the habit of thinking of Plato as an almost fanatical proponent of unrealistic ideals in politics, one who naively thought the political community could instill true virtue in everyone if only it tried hard enough. But this is propaganda invented by Plato's modern rivals, beginning with Machiavelli. In fact he was the original realist, who fully grasped the need to lower the sights of politics so as not to do more harm than good. The difference between him and his modern critics consists above all in this: that he saw more clearly how much higher true virtue and true justice are than what passes and must pass for these in every actual political community.

Reforming the Passions: Spiritedness and Strength of Soul

Yet even here, in the midst of his gravest concessions to irrational anger, the Athenian carves out one more foothold for reason. For if the *Laws* is a work of sublimely sober realism, it is equally an exercise in articulating the highest possible aspirations within the bounds of what is realistically attainable: a major leitmotif of the work is the graceful dance between repeated concessions to political reality and equally frequent, sinuous, subtle new steps to advance the humane perspective of the philosopher. Perhaps the deepest level of this project is the Athenian's sustained effort to reform spiritedness (*thumos*), the aspect of the human soul that in Platonic psychology is rooted in our vulnerability to death, that is called into play in the passionate defense of oneself and one's own, and that expresses itself in anger, fierce courage, the concern with dignity, and the love of justice.[30] Spiritedness is an indispensable support to moral seriousness, and in particular a crucial ally of reason both in controlling unruly desires and in defending the city's freedom, but at an even deeper level it tends to be hostile to the calm reasoning that philosophy requires and that simply rational preludes and laws would rely on. Spiritedness chafes at the limited happiness that nature and fortune offer; it demands divine support for our hopes, our dignity, and our outrage at injustice. Without cutting the root of spiritedness' vigilance, the Athenian works to make it less closed to reason and less of an obstacle to individual happiness and social harmony. He does this by encouraging it to assimilate itself to a related quality that is in fact subtly different—the calm strength and habitual self-reliance in the face of fortune's vicissitudes that the Athenian calls *eupsuchia*, a word that can mean simply courage but that denotes more generally the good condition or strength of soul and is captured well by the old-fashioned expression "stoutness of soul." If the Socratic philosopher is remarkably free of moral indignation, possessiveness, irrational pride, and the other manifestations of spiritedness, including heroic battlefield daring, he displays strength of soul in the highest degree.[31]

In characterizing anger in the passage quoted above as a "bitter, woman's raging" (731d), the Athenian directly challenges the traditional association of spiritedness with manliness and strength, an association epitomized in the popular imagination in the figure of Achilles. Although anger looks manly, Homer hints and Plato much more openly states that it is really an expression of the bitterness of one who is impotent to stop a harm and unable to feel whole again until one has lashed out in return.[32] Francis Bacon echoes this judgment, arguing that, though men with the keenest sense of honor may be especially prone to anger, real strength demands that they cultivate "an honor of a stouter web."[33] According to Plato, the greatest strength would be the quiet strength to hold on to what one knows about the sickness of all criminals' souls and to rise above anger entirely. Most citizens will never be able to adhere consistently to such gentle equanimity—Bacon indeed considers it impossible[34]—but the Athenian suggests that citizens can be taught to admire and emulate this equanimity in a way that will make their individual lives happier and civic life more humane.

Plato alludes metaphorically to this strength of soul when he asks early in the *Laws*, "Do we suppose someone is a worthy ruler in ships if he possesses only the knowledge of navigation, regardless of whether he is subject to seasickness or not? . . . And what of a ruler over an army? Is it sufficient qualification that he possess the knowledge of war even if he's cowardly in the midst of dangers, even if he's seasick with the drunkenness of terror?" (649b). A good ruler of any kind, including one who rules over himself, needs not only knowledge but level-headedness in times of turmoil. This passage could be taken to imply that virtue requires two quite disparate elements, knowledge and a simple, visceral strength that is quite independent of thought, opinion, or truth. For in seasickness, if anywhere, there would seem to be a human failing that is simply bodily, involving as it does no temptation to change one's mind and to succumb to distorted thoughts. And yet seasickness is perhaps the limit case that proves the rule that in human experience there is nothing that is merely physical. For seasickness is still a kind of confusion, and the immunity to it is an ability to keep a grip on one's knowledge of which way is up in the face of intense distractions that threaten to confuse the judgment. This passage is consistent, then, with the conclusion that the toughness or steadfastness that virtue needs in addition to reasoning power is at bottom just a steadiness of judgment.

Further light is shed on this problem in book 7, where Plato takes up education from early childhood. The Athenian seems here to be turning to the long-delayed treatment of gymnastics as the cultivation of the body and the counterpart to music, the cultivation of the soul. Yet once again it becomes clear that body and soul, and hence music and gymnastics, cannot be separated for human beings. We are somehow both rational and subrational to the depths of our being. The Athenian begins by advocating that pregnant women take long walks and that infants be swaddled and rocked and carried about in order to develop strong bodies, alluding to a then-common practice of carrying young birds to strengthen them for cock-fighting. But soon the Athenian acknowledges that in humans it is above all the soul that needs such treatment. Returning now in a very different way to his ship image, he calls for the infant to be continually rocked, adding that "it is beneficial for all, and not least for the very youngest, to dwell—if it were possible—as if they were always on a ship at sea" (790c). He does not explain why this is beneficial for most people after infancy, but he does compare this treatment of infants to the Corybantic rites that were used to cure madness with music, dancing, and sacrificing to the gods. Somehow the women who care for infants and the women who perform the mystery rite cures of the Corybantes divine that infants share with the mentally ill and to some extent with "everyone" a specific disorder in the soul that needs music and rhythmic motion and sacred incantations to cure it. In both cases, he explains,

> the passion being experienced is presumably terror, and the terror is due to some poor habit of the soul. When someone brings a rocking motion from the outside to such passions, the motion brought from without overpowers the fear and the mad motion within, and, having overpowered it, makes a calm stillness appear in the soul that replaces the harsh leaping of the heart in each case. This has wholly desirable effects. In the one case it makes them go to sleep; in the other case, with the help of the gods to whom each sacrifices and from whom each receives good omens, the process awakens them to dancing and influences the dancers through the aulos music. It thereby replaces our mad dispositions with prudent habits. (790e–91b)

How can newborns already possess bad habits? A certain madness, it seems, possesses us by nature in the form of a primal terror. In book 1 the Athenian defined fear as an expectation of pain (644c–d), but he reminds us now that infants experience this fundamental terror before they have any clear expectations of anything. If this is a bad habit, it is in our nature to have it. The Athenian alluded most obliquely to this same disorder on three occasions in book 2, while discussing also its musical and sacred "cure." The first reference is the most positive, or as we see now, euphemistic. At 653c–d he says that the gods have taken pity on the human race, whose education tends to run down under the debilitating effects of constant toil, and hence "have given as fellow celebrants the Muses, with their leader Apollo, and Dionysus—in order that these divinities might set humans right again" (653d). He goes on to explain that "every young thing" by nature "seeks to move and cry," as if "dancing with pleasure," implying that the sacred choruses work to restore this naturally happy and lively state. A little later he reiterates, in a less sunny manner, that "the nature of all young things is fiery, and unable to remain calm either in body or in voice, but is always crying and leaping in a disorderly way." But humans are capable of attaining order in their motions with the rhythm and harmony that the sacred choruses bring, for "the gods, we asserted, have taken pity on us and given us as fellow members or leaders of our choruses Apollo and the Muses . . . [and] Dionysus" (664e–65a). So now the divine gifts are educative and not merely restorative of our original natures. Then, in another restatement, he says that "every living being, to the degree to which it is appropriate for it to possess intelligence when fully developed, to this same degree it lacks intelligence by nature [or from birth]. During the time in which it lacks the active wisdom that is proper to it, every being is completely mad and cries out in a disorderly way; as soon as it can stand by itself, it jumps in a disorderly way" (672c). These motions and cries are the original source of music and gymnastics, he continues, which are developed through the use of rhythm and harmony, the gifts of Apollo, the Muses, and Dionysus. Now again the divine gifts educate humans, in accordance with their proper natures, but the Athenian is becoming more frank about the mad state in which we all begin life. Only in book 7 does he identify this madness as fear of death.

How do music and the gods cure this terror? The infant comes into the world out of a womb that was safely enclosed, bathed in the rhythmic sound of the mother's heartbeat, and frequently in motion. If the helpless infant is left alone in stillness for very long it will die, and it somehow instinctively knows this, or at least it responds instinctively to silence and stillness as if it knew it. When the mother rocks and sings to it, an assurance returns that it is safe and all is well. But is everything ever quite so completely well? The infant perhaps already senses dimly that with life comes a vulnerability that cannot be overcome, and this sense is never wholly overcome: the Athenian finally says in book 11 that almost all human beings are as much afflicted with terror as children are (933c). Like the rocking of the mother, the Dionysian gifts of music, dance, and wine sooth us by subsuming our restless motions into their cosmic embrace, assuring us that we are not alone and that something far greater than we are takes cognizance of our sufferings and ennobles our struggles. In book 2 the Athenian speaks of the gifts of the gods as putting awe into the soul, turning the primal terror that is mere fear into a pious awe that is still terrible but also beautiful and meaningful and to that extent comforting (672d). Now in book 7 he adds that the gods give "good omens" to "each" as part of the "cure" they effect, and that this is the source of "wise (*emphronas*) habits" (791a–b). More specifically, this cure is the source of subsequent courage, for "every soul that dwells with terror from the time of childhood would be especially likely to become accustomed to feeling fear; presumably everyone would assert that this is practice in cowardice rather than courage" (791b). While Kleinias agrees, the agreement is surprising. Does his city not train youths in courage by exposing and accustoming them to endure what is fearful?[35] The Athenian immediately adds this more conventional thought: "the practice in courage from earliest youth onward consists in triumphing over the terrors and fears that come upon us" (791c). But what he has indicated is that such courage to face what is frightening rests on a deeper assurance, whether wholly justified or not, that all is well and that one will never be utterly bereft of aid. Consisting as it does in a kind of opinion, this deep confidence is neither simply rational nor simply devoid of reason. It is equally distinct from the fiery daring that comprises battlefield courage at its most heroic and from the knowledge of what is and is not terrible that Socrates calls true courage in the *Protagoras*. Yet in different ways it conduces to both, one form of it inspiring acts of bravery and endurance through a hope that transcends reason, and another form providing the necessary strength precisely to seek the truth and to hold the knowledge one has steadily in view. Instilling in each citizen some version of stoutness of soul is the fundamental purpose of the gymnastic education in the *Laws*, which lays the foundation for a very few to become philosophic and for the many to live with a calm strength that mirrors that of the philosopher.

Seeming to leave fear, cowardice, and courage behind, the Athenian now turns to what we would expect him to characterize as a training in moderation. Yet he continues to frame his goal in terms of courage broadly defined, or *eupsuchia*: "Moreover, the absence or presence of ill humor in the soul is no small factor in determining whether strength of soul or weakness of soul would result" (791c).[36] Just as strength of soul is fostered by protecting the very young from excessive fears, so it is fostered by protecting them from excessive and hard-to-satisfy desires. Here again the correct handling of infants turns on countering their tendency to cry, not by trying to appease them but by stopping their tears at their source. From the outset infants can be gently schooled in accepting necessity and gently dissuaded from making clamorous appeals to others to get them what they think they cannot bear to be deprived of. The more one's happiness depends on what others have in their power to give or withhold, the less happy one will be. Thus the Athenian even calls the middle course between extreme pleasure and pain godlike: "And I assert that this is the habit that should be pursued by any one of us who is to be divine: one should not allow oneself to pursue pleasures headlong, thinking one can in this way avoid the experience of pain, nor should one simply flee pain" (792d). If human beings cannot attain the sublime, calm, painless self-sufficiency of a divine being, they can most closely approximate it through self-reliance and a calm acceptance of necessity, free from the tears that betray an inability to accept what cannot be averted or undone. *Eupsuchia* turns out to provide, then, a unifying principle of all the virtues for the citizens as well as a foundation for the clarity of the philosopher. It is this that will allow citizens to take full responsibility for their faults when their own actions prove destructive (727b); it is this that will make them view adversity not as a reason for rage or despair but as a "high, steep slope" that chance has given their spirits to climb (732c); it is this that will make them willing and able to submit calmly to the stiffest demands of the law; it is this that will allow the potential philosophers to regard necessities of another sort with similar equanimity. Despite the Athenian's criticism of his Dorian interlocutors for overemphasizing the virtue of courage, at the deepest level they failed to appreciate its full importance.

This schooling in *eupsuchia* is the keynote of the rest of the discussion of education in book 7 and especially the reform of popular piety that Plato adumbrates there. Just as the citizens are expected to defend themselves when assaulted rather than go running to the authorities, and even women, or at least their close relatives, are expected to fend off or punish sexual assaults (879c–e, 874c), so citizens both male and female are to defend their homeland when it is threatened and not rush to the temples to beg divine protection, "bringing down on the race of humans the reputation of being by nature the most cowardly of all the beasts" (814b; cf. 909e–10a). In keeping with this training in self-sufficiency and the calm acceptance of necessity, the citizens are to study mathematics and astronomy and thereby learn about the fundamental necessities governing all things. For "it's likely that whoever first formulated the proverb about god was looking to these when he said that 'even a god is never seen to fight against necessity'—meaning, I believe, whatever necessities are divine" (818a–b).[37] The penal law in book 9 encourages the same spirit. Even when the lawgiver appeals to sanctions beyond this life, he presents those sanctions as natural necessities rather than as the personal vendettas of angry deities (870d), although he also paints the gods as willing to help those who strive their utmost to be virtuous. In teaching the citizens to revere gods who are not vengeful, to rely as much as possible on themselves, to regard their own virtue as the basis of their happiness, and to regard criminals' disorderly souls with more pity than anger, the Athenian teaches a calm spirit of self-sufficiency that imitates if it does not grow entirely from the same root as the philosopher's own. For the citizens' toughness necessarily draws some of its strength from *thumos* or spiritedness. Yet they are so little encouraged to be angry, irascible, and glory seeking, and so deeply schooled to be calm and self-reliant, that their toughness comes as close as possible to the unthumotic strength of the philosopher.

For the citizens, there is a limit to this reform of piety in support of *eupsuchia*. The deepest questioning is something the citizens should be protected from, while the philosopher alone fords the swift-flowing river of skeptical doubt (829d ff.). The trust in the gods that supports the citizens' stoutness of soul is never to be more than trust. But what about the philosopher? If the opinion instilled in all the citizens by the swaddling and rocking and music of infancy is not quite true opinion, does this beginning not cast a shadow over the rationality of the courage of everyone brought up in this city, including the future philosophers? But perhaps it is better to say that those who are ultimately to awaken fully from the dreamy security of the rocking ship and gain full control of their own vessels must undergo a difficult transition: this city's childhood education does not point them by a straight path to their greatest fulfillment. Yet what it provides may well be essential. For out of the trust that all is well with the world may grow most easily the crucial trust that all is well with ourselves, that whatever we encounter, whatever the truth turns out to be, we can handle it. This confidence may at first not be well grounded. If it comes to be so, it will not be a trust that we can overcome any obstacle: the worst evils may be impossible to overcome. But it is a trust that whatever we meet, we can face it calmly without panic, without falling into the helpless despair from which we believe we need some outside force to rescue us, and without losing our grip on what we know about the things that matter most. Because this strength involves judgment, because its essence is a kind of level-headedness, and because at its best it involves self-knowledge and understanding of the necessities that define the human condition, it is better understood as an integral aspect of wisdom than as its merely nonrational foundation.

The Unity of Virtue

The Athenian returns again to the question of the unifying core of virtue at the very end of the *Laws*. Having established the shadowy nocturnal council as the guiding intelligence within the city, he presses the thought that this council will be the city's salvation, in the same way that, "when intelligence is mixed with the noblest senses and has become one," it is justly called the "salvation" of each animal (961d). Likewise, the piloting art brings about the salvation of ships at sea and the arts of medicine and generalship bring the salvation that consists in victory and health. As in each of these cases, so in the city whoever possesses the guiding and saving intelligence must know clearly the goal at which it should aim. Kleinias sees that this knowledge must belong to the nocturnal council if to anyone. The Athenian agrees: "it is necessary . . . for this council to possess every virtue, the ruling principle of which is not to wander and have many aims, but to look to one aim, and always shoot all things, like shafts, at this" (962d). Kleinias is confident that they have already identified the city's unifying goal as virtue, led by intelligence (963a; cf. 631b–d). But when the Athenian presses him further, asking "whatever is that one thing" to which this intelligence itself looks in guiding everything else, Kleinias cannot answer (963b–c). The possession of moral virtue seems to be and not be the end of everything else; it cannot be just a means to the bundle of lesser things that cities tend to pursue, and yet how could it guide us—how indeed could it have any standard to guide it—if its own simple existence were our whole end? Without giving Kleinias the answer, the Athenian defines precisely what the guardian council must understand in order to provide the guiding intelligence the city needs. It must understand how the four cardinal virtues, and in particular courage and active wisdom, are distinct and yet one. The Athenian explains why or in what sense courage and active wisdom are considered distinct: "it's because the one—courage—is concerned with fear, and even the beasts share in it, as do the dispositions, at least, of the very young children. For soul becomes courageous without reason and by nature, but, on the other hand, without reason soul never has, does not, and never will become wise (*phronimos*) and possessed of intelligence" (963e). Here he echoes a comment in book 4 about two kinds of moderation, in which he distinguishes "the sort one would speak of in a solemn way, compelling prudence to be moderation," from "the popular sort" that "blooms naturally, from the beginning, in children and beasts, and by which some lack self-restraint with regard to pleasures while others possess self-restraint" (701a–b). There may be little unity in the popular versions of the virtues, even while the highest forms of them do form a unity. When the Athenian now asks Kleinias to say in what way this is so, however, he is altogether unable to do so. But this earlier passage from book 4 points to the answer that virtue in the highest or most precise sense is all one because it is all wisdom.

What the Athenian does provide here in book 12 is an elaboration of what the council members require in order to be the city's saving intelligence. They must know not only why and how virtue is one, but what power virtue and vice have (964c), what the one idea is behind virtue's many manifestations (965c), whatever the one goal is to which virtue ought to look (965d), and in what sense the beautiful and the good are one and not one (966a); they must in addition grasp fully the proofs regarding the existence of the gods (966c–d). All of this knowledge remains beyond the scope of the city's leading founder, Kleinias, because it goes beyond the scope of civic virtue altogether. Central to the five questions is the question of virtue's goal. Civic virtue, consisting in law-bred habits, necessarily has many goals because the law invariably does. To the extent that civic virtue has a unifying principle, it is the sturdy strength to "stay the course" in obeying the law, anchored at one end by a deep trust in the cosmos and in oneself, cultivated from infancy, and at the other end by the assurance that the law is the embodiment of divine reason. For the philosopher, virtue will be unified by its overarching end, theoretical wisdom, which is good because it satisfies his deepest need and noble because it brings to perfection his highest capacity. Virtue will be unified likewise in the harmony of insight and strength that governs everything he does, giving him the capacity to grasp clearly, rank correctly, and hold steady his knowledge of what is good and to follow the divine reason that he himself possesses. Virtue is a single whole in him because it is the single, unbroken grasp of the good that is of concern to him in its entirety and its full context. Virtue is more than knowledge, but it is nothing more or less than complete wisdom.

NOTES

INTRODUCTION

1. Plato *Laws* 650b.
2. Irwin, *Plato's Ethics*. In chapter 1 of this work Irwin gives a good account of such evidence as there is for dividing the dialogues into early, middle, and late periods.
3. Brickhouse and Smith, *Plato's Socrates*, esp. 119.
4. For a good discussion of the political considerations governing Plato's complex rhetorical strategy, see Peter Ahrensdorf, "The Question of Historical Context and the Study of Plato."
5. These divisions are all my own. One of the few to try to give a schematic account of the different positions Socrates and his followers and interpreters have taken on the relation of virtue to happiness is Gregory Vlastos, in *Socrates*, chapter 8. Vlastos distinguishes what he calls three forms of eudaimonism: the utilitarian eudaimonist (under which he includes both what I have called the moral and the hypermoral-utilitarian positions), the eudaimonist view that virtue is partially constitutive of happiness, and the eudaimonist view that virtue is wholly constitutive of happiness. I think it better to call the claim that virtue is an instrumental means to happiness simply *utilitarian*, reserving the term *eudaimonism* for the claim that virtue is constitutive of happiness. My categories of moral and hypermoral eudaimonism are essentially the same as Vlastos' second and third variants of eudaimonism. He neglects what I call the heroic and transmoral positions.

CHAPTER ONE

1. All quotations from the five dialogues in this study are based on the translations of West, Nichols, Bartlett, and Pangle, respectively, with occasional revisions of my own to bring the English slightly closer to the Greek.
2. These range from Gregory Vlastos, who considers the irony merely a way of making us think for ourselves, "innocent of intentional deceit" ("Socratic Irony," 84), to Paul Friedländer, who sees in it a biting sarcasm (*Plato*, 2:157–74), to David Leibowitz, who finds it a key to the dialogue (*The Ironic Defense of Socrates*, esp. Chapter 2). My interpretation of the *Apology* is indebted on many points to this last commentary.
3. Leibowitz notes the strangeness of Socrates' statement here and suggests three possible meanings, not mutually exclusive: Socrates' speeches have all been constructed

so as to defend his way of life before the public, or before his most discerning listeners and future readers, or "in his *own* eyes by answering the most powerful challenges to it, human and allegedly divine": *Ironic Defense of Socrates*, 37–38. Cf. Xenophon *Apology of Socrates to the Jury*, section 3.

4. Cf. Plato *Rep* 337a and e, 340d–41b, 487b–c; *Meno* 79e–80b; *Gorgias* 482c–83a.
5. See, for example, Plato *Phaedo* 96a6 ff.; cf. *Theaetetus* 145d1–7.
6. For a good account of the problem of natural science as Socrates first experienced it, see Leibowitz, *Ironic Defense*, 66–69.
7. R. E. Allen stresses this element of skill, arguing that *epistasthai*, like the English *understand* and the German *verstehen*, signifies an active stance with regard to a thing, a taking it up in preparation for acting. Thus, he argues, *epistēmē* means "knowing how" as much as "knowing that," which he says is essential for making sense of the claim that virtue is knowledge (essential, I agree, but not sufficient): "The Socratic Paradox," 256–65.
8. Among those who do not take Socrates to be disavowing all knowledge, there has been considerable debate about the meaning of these disavowals and the status of the knowledge or wisdom that he professes to have—whether the things he claims to know are merely a provisional set of working hypotheses, as George Grote argues in *Plato and the Other Companions of Socrates*, 1:239; whether his professed ignorance is a mere pedagogical feint, as Norman Gulley argues in *The Philosophy of Socrates*; whether Socrates claims to know moral truths for certain but has no ability to say why they are true and hence no wisdom per se, as Thomas Brickhouse and Nicholas Smith argue in *Plato's Socrates*, 30–72 and 123–34; or whether he claims only "subjective certainty" and internal consistency to his assertions, as Terence Irwin argues in *Plato's Ethics*, 27–30. If by "human knowledge" Socrates means such knowledge as is available to us through observation of nature and human nature, self-examination, and rigorous logical analysis, which is provisional only in the sense that he had not ruled out the existence of some radically mysterious god or gods who might render the human understanding of "nature" an illusion, then his wisdom may have been even before the Delphic quest rather more robust than commentators have tended to assume. It may then have become increasingly firm as Socrates confirmed through cross-examinations that neither he nor anyone else knew of any strong reason to doubt human insights into nature, with the ultimate conclusion that he did after all possess human wisdom.
9. Diogenes Laertius' version is "Socrates does injustice by not believing in the gods in whom the city believes, and by introducing other *daimonia* that are novel; he also does injustice by corrupting the young" (2.40; cf. Xenophon *Memorabilia* 1.1.1). Socrates departs from the version of the charge given by Diogenes Laertius not only in reversing the order of the charges but in changing the latter part of the impiety charge from one of "introducing" new *daimonia* to one of "believing in" new *daimonia*. This will allow him to tie the careless Meletus in knots, since the new formulation but not the original charge is incompatible with the atheism Meletus also attributes to him.
10. Leibowitz offers a fascinating suggestion about the deepest meaning of Socrates' involvement with the young and its significance for the theological question in *Ironic Defense*, chapter 4.
11. See, e.g., Plato *Crito* 50–51; *Republic* 520b; *Laws* 631b–d.
12. Plato *Protagoras* 327c–28b; cf. *Gorgias* 459d–60a.
13. Aristotle *NE* 1104b11–13; 1109a24–29.

14. Note that Socrates' awareness of the character of his own ignorance *preceded* this cross-examination (21b); whatever he learned as a result of his famous turn, he was already clear on the problematic character of the "noble and good."
15. Indeed, the craftsmen or manual artisans seem to be the only ones Socrates examines who can not only say many noble or beautiful things (as the poets can), but can make many noble or beautiful things. This passage suggests that Socrates may have gained or solidified what knowledge of the noble or beautiful he had from the artisans, whose works are noble in being beautifully and gracefully suited to their tasks. That he did not need to cross-examine them to learn this is reflected in the fact that while he says here that he examined statesmen, poets, and artisans, and we have examples at least of the first two in Platonic dialogues, we have no examples of dialogues devoted to the third. (Cf., however, Xenophon *Memorabilia* 3.10 for a singular exception).
16. Cf. Leibowitz, *Ironic Defense*, 97n.70, 134, 178–80.
17. Does not Socrates' daimonic voice after all tell him to distance himself from many former associates? See Plato *Theages* 129e.
18. See also *Gorgias* 488a2–3.
19. Leibowitz suggests that the true conclusion of this argument, that all wrongdoing is involuntary, is left unstated here because it is "too radical to pronounce in court" (122).
20. In Leibowitz's provocative formulation, "punitive justice, which seem to be so serious, is in fact comical because it is based on pretense. When men are angry and eager to punish, they do not fully believe what they tend to say, and they do not know what they claim to know" (129).
21. Of course the logical fallacies in Socrates' arguments have occasioned much embarrassed discussion among scholars. Explanations tend to fall into two categories: that logic was not as well developed in Socrates' time as in ours and he or Plato simply failed to notice the problems (e.g. E. R. Dodds, *Plato Gorgias*; Gerasimos Santas, *Socrates: Philosophy in Plato's Early Dialogues*); or that Socrates was interested mainly in showing vain, foolish, or immoral interlocutors how little they knew with a view to improving them, and for this purpose was as happy to use bad arguments as good ones so long as they worked (Richard Robinson, "Plato's Consciousness of Fallacy"; J. P. Sullivan, "The Hedonism in Plato's *Protagoras*"; Roslyn Weiss, *The Socratic Paradox and Its Enemies*).
22. Taking this statement as her pole star, Weiss claims that Socrates is not a eudaimonist at all, let alone a utilitarian, but a "dikaiosunist" or believer in justice as his single principle: *Socratic Paradox*, 7.
23. This last statement is so jarring in its implied utilitarian view of virtue—as well as its evident naïveté—that John Burnet proposes a different reading: "It is goodness that makes money and everything else good for men": *Plato's Euthyphro, Apology of Socrates, and Crito*, 124, a reading critiqued by E. de Strycker in *Plato's Apology of Socrates*, 334 n. 2, but defended as philosophically preferable if linguistically difficult by M. F. Burnyeat in "*Apology* 30b2–4: Socrates, Money, and the Grammar of GIGNESQAI." Granting that Burnet's reading is barely possible Greek and much more commonsensical, the question remains why Socrates, like the Athenian Stranger at *Laws* 631b, should almost go out of his way to give the impression that he trusts that virtue will bring everything good.
24. Two prominent scholars who have taken this strand of Socrates' thought with utmost seriousness are W. K. C. Guthrie, who takes the "utilitarian approach to good-

ness and virtue" to be the core of Socratic ethics: *A History of Greek Philosophy* 3: 462; and Terence Irwin, who argues that the whole of Socrates' ethical theory (as opposed to Plato's) comes down to an instrumental set of calculations about how best to secure one's own happiness—which in fact he reduces to pleasure: *Plato's Ethics*, chapters 3 and 5.

25. Scholars who in various ways read Socrates to say that virtue is an absolute guarantee of happiness include George Grote, *Plato and the Other Companions of Socrates*, 1: 243; Norman Gulley, *The Philosophy of Socrates*, 200; Gerasimos Santas, *Socrates*; and Donald Zeyl, "Socratic Virtue and Happiness." Terence Irwin, despite his reading of Socrates as a hedonist with an instrumentalist view of virtue, also takes this position: *Plato's Ethics*, chapter 4. Irwin denies that Socrates ever presents virtue as requiring a sacrifice of any kind, so that clarity about its dictates would immediately result in a single-minded desire to follow them.

26. Observing such indications in this and other comments of Socrates, Gregory Vlastos concludes that virtue is for him the indispensable core but not the whole of happiness. He rests his argument in no small part on an appeal to common sense: "If happiness were identical with virtue, Job should be as happy after Satan's work has been done as before." But he leaves it less than clear why in every case the value of acting virtuously should outweigh that of goods attainable only through vice. Nor does he explain why Socrates would so habitually speak in exaggerated and misleading ways, although he acknowledges that many passages even in the *Apology* need to be taken as less than completely serious to fit his thesis: *Socrates: Ironist and Moral Philosopher*, chapter 8, esp. 216. Thomas Brickhouse and Nicholas Smith pursue the same approach rather further in *Plato's Socrates*, 103–123. They contend that Socrates' real position is that not the bare possession of virtue but unimpeded virtuous action assures or constitutes happiness, and that by the claim that a worse man cannot harm a better Socrates means not that he cannot deprive him of some good, or even that he cannot deprive him of all hope for happiness in this life, or even that he cannot deprive him of the possibility of happiness altogether, if death is an endless sleep, but only that a worse man cannot inflict on a better man the very worst of all evils, namely a corrupt soul. Again, Brickhouse and Smith offer no suggestions as to why Socrates would choose to speak in such wildly inconsistent ways as to put himself so much in need of their charitable help.

27. Christopher Bruell, *On the Socratic Education*, 152.

28. Cf. Plato *Minos* 318d, where Socrates defends Minos against what he calls Athenian prejudice—yet without adducing any evidence that the traditional Athenian view is in fact wrong.

29. As West and West point out, a variant manuscript reading would translate "is not clear to anyone unless to the god" and would cast doubt not only on Socrates' knowledge of what is best but on the god's as well (*Four Texts on Socrates*, 97n.84).

30. Or indeed, most radically, the *daimonion* that restrains Socrates may be the same wisdom as the erotic yearnings that inspire him, each equally expressible in divine and in wholly human terms, as Socrates suggests in the *Theages* when he calls the *daimonion* "all powerful" in his intercourse with his companions. See *Theages* 129e–30e and Thomas L. Pangle, "On the *Theages*," esp. 170–71.

31. For two examples of moments in Plato's dialogues that may best capture the kind of result that Socrates would have been looking to confirm, see *Republic* 335e, where Polemarchus changes his understanding of what an authoritative poet must have meant by a famous pronouncement about justice, and *Laws* 630c–d.

CHAPTER TWO

1. For further reflections on the connections between the *Apology* and the *Gorgias*, including the significance of Chaerephon's appearance here, see Devin Stauffer, *The Unity of Plato's Gorgias*, 10–13, 17–18. This fine commentary is especially helpful in exploring the flaws in Socrates' argument for the superiority of justice to injustice and the possible rhetorical function of that argument in educating Gorgias about the human attachment to justice. I have tried to supplement Stauffer's commentary by exploring the ways in which the same argument may nonetheless have a serious core and may indeed lead directly into the heart of Socratic thought.
2. Socrates does not say it is specifically Gorgian rhetoric he is critiquing; to the contrary, he makes a point of saying that he does not know whether Gorgias' rhetoric shares the limitations he identifies or not (462e8–63a1). But as Stauffer observes (*Unity of Plato's Gorgias*, 44), it seems to be precisely Gorgian rhetoric that he goes on to discuss, and the point seems to be that Gorgias could and should practice a different sort of rhetoric.
3. Stauffer, *Unity of Plato's Gorgias*, 48.
4. Thucydides, *History of the Peloponnesian War*, 3.37 ff.
5. Xenophon *Anabasis* 2.6.16–20; 5.8.
6. Brickhouse and Smith bring out the boldness and strangeness of Socrates' claim that orators are not even esteemed, as part of Socrates' project not only to show what deserves admiration but to confirm and show what everyone in fact thinks and feels without recognizing it; in this Socrates' frequent profession not to care about the opinions of the many is not the final word on the matter: *Plato's Socrates*, 84–85.
7. The word Socrates uses here, *boulomai*, often translated "desire," is better rendered as "wish," since it refers especially to the ultimate aims of action; to that extent it differs from *epithumeō*, which is used more often for transient desires, especially for pleasure, and hence I translate it as "desire." Daniel Devereux defends well the difference between *epithumeō* and *boulomai* in "Socrates' Kantian Conception of Virtue," 398–403. Socrates makes this difference most clearly in the *Charmides*, where he says that the object of wish is the good, and of desire, pleasure (*Charmides* 167e1–6; cf. *Lysis* 221a7–b3), but he is not absolutely consistent in following this distinction (see, for example, *Lysis* 207d7–e2, where he uses them interchangeably), leading such scholars as Penner, in "Desire and Power in Socrates," and Irwin, in *Plato's Moral Theory*, 310, to deny that there is a significant difference between these terms. I believe Weiss is right: Socrates is at times loose and at other times precise about such distinctions, depending on his purpose (*Socratic Paradox*, 160).
8. Stauffer (*Unity of Plato's Gorgias*, 54–55) makes this point but does not say why Socrates is intent on shaking Polus' confidence in the value of rhetoric. But this first failed attempt to shake Polus' confidence makes sense if Socrates' deeper project is to show him that virtue, not mere external power, is the crucial requisite of happiness, and that at the core of virtue is knowledge or wisdom.
9. What Socrates is not addressing here, but will address in the *Meno* and especially the *Protagoras*, is whether we can still in some sense desire (rather than wish for) anything other than what seems best to us. The fact that he speaks in this passage only of what people wish for and not what they desire means that the whole problem of the phenomenon or apparent phenomenon of *akrasia*, or action that violates one's better judgment, is not on the table.
10. Dodds, *Plato Gorgias*, 236.

11. See especially Xenophon *Memorabilia* 1.6.14; cf. Plato *Lysis* 211d–12b.
12. This view has been taken by Dodds, *Plato Gorgias*, 235–36; M. J. O'Brien, *The Socratic Paradoxes and the Greek Mind*, 217–18; Terry Penner, "Desire and Power in Socrates"; and R. E. Allen, "The Socratic Paradox," 263, who writes: "Everyone begins with a grasp of moral principles; if they did not, Socratic dialectic would have nothing it could say to them. But their grasp is dim and uncertain, and therefore erring, and it was this flaw that dialectic aimed to correct." Norman Gulley, by contrast, argues that wish here is only hypothetically for what is good, designating what we would wish for it if we knew it was good: *The Philosophy of Socrates*, 90.
13. This is the view attributed to Socrates by Robert William Hall in "Techne and Morality in the *Gorgias*," 205–6; and by David Wolfsdorf in "Desire for Good in *Meno* 77B2–78B6." Kevin McTighe takes this position as well, although not as a result of the present argument but because he thinks it sensible; he thinks that in the present argument Socrates is so inconsistent in his use of the words "wish" and "good" that the whole argument is irredeemably flawed and can only have the purpose of baffling and humbling Polus: "Socrates on Desire for the Good and the Involuntariness of Wrongdoing."
14. Anscombe, *Intention*, and Santas, *Socrates*, chapter 6, take a similar position in distinguishing the *actual* (immediate) from the *intended* object of wish, but I do not follow their terminology inasmuch as I think Socrates is saying that the "intended" object is the truer or *more* actual one. Vlastos, concurring with Santas, thinks that Socrates' failure to make these distinctions explicit was just a result of muddleheadedness and that when we do apply them the whole problem of moral responsibility evaporates: one may not have wanted the ultimate results but if one intended the deed, one is responsible (*Socrates: Ironist and Moral Philosopher*, chapter 5). But Penner insists with some force that all such arguments miss Socrates' radical point: the good is not just what we intend to aim at but what we really do seek in everything that we do, so that the particular acts that turn out badly are in the most important respect not what we wanted at all ("Desire and Power in Socrates.")
15. As Stauffer puts it, Archelaus is "both the hero and the villain of Polus' speech" (*Unity of Plato's Gorgias*, 62; cf. notes ad loc). This combination seems so curious that several have sought to deny one side of it or the other. Stauffer is helpful in showing how the two sides may go together and even perhaps necessarily go together in one who is incensed by another's crimes.
16. Socrates' statements here have generated much discussion. Renford Bambrough notes the highly unconventional meaning Socrates here gives to the term "happiness" (like the unconventional meaning he gives to the term "knowledge" in his claim that virtue is knowledge), without quite addressing the key question of whether this usage is just idiosyncratic or whether Socrates can show that it is implicitly held by everyone: "The Socratic Paradox," 289. Stauffer observes this passage's indication of Socrates' equally unconventional understanding of justice in *Unity of Plato's Gorgias*, 59–60. Mark Blitz notes that a pervasive lack of clarity about the meaning Socrates gives to justice may allow him to appear much more conventionally moral than he is: *Plato's Political Philosophy*, 67. Socrates' unqualified attribution of happiness to the virtuous person without any acknowledgment of the role of fortune has also troubled commentators. Taking it literally, we can temper his implicit claim about happiness only as much as Vlastos does, to infer that virtue and happiness must be "interentailing" according to Socrates, even if lesser goods may add something to happiness and their absence take something away: *Socrates:*

Ironist and Moral Philosopher, 214–24. Whether this is adequate or whether we must conclude that Socrates is deliberately, provocatively inconsistent on the question of virtue's sufficiency for happiness remains a question, requiring among other things a careful consideration of his indications at *Gorgias* 512a of the way misfortune can render a life not worth living.

17. Isocrates *Panathenaicus* 117.
18. Stauffer, *Unity of Plato's Gorgias*, 65. Dodds points out as well that these examples illustrate how widely these views are shared among Athenians of different political camps: *Plato Gorgias*, 244.
19. Dodds, *Plato Gorgias*, 249.Vlastos makes this latter argument against Dodds in "Was Polus Refuted?"
20. E.g. Vlastos, "Socrates on Akrasia"; Santas, *Socrates*, chapter 8. After all but despairing over the logic of this argument, Santas adds this important observation, however: "Our praise and admiration for the virtues could not be well founded or reasonable unless the virtues were of some benefit; and our condemnation of the vices could not be well founded and reasonable unless they were in some sense harmful" to the agent himself: Santas, *Socrates*, 233.
21. The sophists and their followers in fact show a fascinating disagreement about who the beneficiaries of beliefs about justice and the noble are. Protagoras in his speech at the beginning of the *Protagoras* presents it as society at large; Thrasymachus in the first book of the *Republic* presents it as the ruling class or the stronger; Glaucon (not a sophist but building on sophistic claims) presents it in the next one as the weaker; and Callicles later in the *Gorgias* seems to see it as all three.
22. Thus Polus would need to bring into dialogue the buried "yearnings" and "hopes" that justice will turn out to be rewarded and injustice punished, which Stauffer so clearly elucidates as the meaning of his love of justice (*Unity of Plato's Gorgias*, 74, 78) with the intuition Polus also has and that Socrates is building on that the just soul is somehow intrinsically healthy and the unjust one "rotting" and "festering."
23. Stauffer, *Unity of Plato's Gorgias*, 77.
24. Dodds, *Plato Gorgias*, 257.

CHAPTER THREE

1. Weiss observes that the paradox "no one does wrong willingly" is featured prominently in the dialogues that have as their interlocutors sophists, rhetoricians, and students of rhetoricians, and she is no doubt right that some of the features of Socrates' arguments for this thesis are shaped by his rhetorical purposes in opposing these famous immoralists. But she carries this thesis so far that her Socrates is *only* a moralist, a fighter, a "man on a mission" for justice; thus the seriousness of Socrates' wrestling with real intellectual problems and the massive challenge he poses to conventional thought disappear from her account. As she puts it, Socrates does not really mean that no one does injustice willingly, or that virtue is knowledge, or that all the virtues are one, or that it is impossible to act contrary to one's knowledge or better judgment; all that he seriously means, his whole innovation in moral and psychological thought, is that virtue is good and therefore "no one who chooses to do wrong is wise." But since she denies the unity of the four cardinal virtues, she cannot logically attribute this claim to Socrates, either. For if, as she claims and claims Socrates acknowledges, cowardice and immoderation and injustice cause people to act against their own knowledge of what is best all the time, she can seriously attribute to Socrates only the claim that no one who chooses to do wrong

has all the virtues—a trivial result, to say the least (*Socratic Paradox* 4–5, 8, 15, 22, 208–13).

2. Xenophon *Anabasis* 2.6.21–29. For hints of Meno's pernicious proclivities in this dialogue, see 78c4–d3 and 86d6–8.
3. Catherine Zuckert suggests that this may be all that Gorgias learned from his encounter with Socrates—to be more modest and therefore consistent in what he claims to teach: *Plato's Philosophers*, 533.
4. Jerome Eckstein notes the irony, if not its serious point, observing further that, in Plato's dialogues, "the degree of sarcasm or illogic in Socrates' responses is in proportion to the degree of arrogance, brashness, hostility, or stupidity in his partner's judgments": *The Platonic Method*, 17.
5. It is such an account of the way the noble comes to sight as sublimely fulfilling that is missing from Robert Bartlett's otherwise highly illuminating "Socratic Political Philosophy and the Problem of Virtue." Bartlett treats the aspects of virtue that are good for us and for others as merely utilitarian or even "mercenary," while (like Stauffer) equating the aspect of virtue that is noble solely with self-sacrifice and the hopes for recompense that accompany it. Were it not for Meno's simultaneous attachment to the noble understood as a simply inspiring perfection of our natures, the self-contradictions Bartlett brings out in Meno's and in all of conventional moral thought would actually be much easier to see.
6. Xenophon *Education of Cyrus*, 1.3–4; Plato *Gorgias* 470d5–71d2; see also Robert Bartlett, "On the *Meno*," 141.
7. For a good discussion of the threefold division in Meno's mind, see Christopher Bruell, *On the Socratic Education*, 171.
8. The verb *poridzesthai* in the middle voice can mean to provide something for oneself, as Bartlett translates it, but it can also be used of cases when one provides things for one's own family, friends, or city.
9. Xenophon *Oeconomicus*; Cicero *Laelius on Friendship*; cf. Aristotle's statement that matters of ethics do not admit of the same precision as scientific questions in *NE* 1.3.
10. Gerasimos Santas calls the claim that all desire good things the first or "prudential" Socratic paradox, the second or "moral" paradox being the claim of the *Gorgias* that no one voluntarily does injustice: Santas, "The Socratic Paradoxes." I agree that this passage emphasizes the prudential argument, but I think that the question of right and wrong is present here in a muted way as well. Socrates invites Meno to make it explicit, but Meno tellingly does not.
11. As R. S. Bluck observes, the premise that good things are beneficial to everyone concerned is assumed without proof: *Plato's "Meno,"* 257–58.
12. Santas brings out well the difference between the first two meanings of desire and makes a strong case that Socrates uses them both for *epithumia* in the present passage. As he interprets it, Socrates' point is that people never desire the bad as bad but sometimes do desire it under the mistaken apprehension that it is good. "What Socrates has tried to show is that in no case are bad things the intended object of people's desires, though in some cases they are the actual objects" ("Socratic Paradoxes," 154). As in the case of wish, I agree with Penner that Santas' categories are not quite Socrates', and that what Santas calls the "intended object" Socrates is suggesting is the truest object. But I disagree with Penner's claim that desire and wish are not importantly different in this respect (see chapter 2, notes 7 and 14 above). In its vivid, immediate attraction to whatever promises pleasure, desire seems more

powerfully focused on immediate objects and less tightly dependent upon thoughts and judgments about our ultimate good than wish is.

13. Devereux makes this point in "Socrates' Kantian Conception of Virtue," 402.

14. Thus Irwin writes that Socrates' view "requires that all desires be rational or good-dependent; if A wants x, he wants it for its contribution to some good y, and ultimately to the final good, and if he ceases to believe that x contributes to the final good, he will cease to want x" (*Plato's Moral Theory*, 78; *Plato's Ethics*, 74–75). Similar views are expressed by Penner, "Desire and Power in Socrates," nn. 3, 5, 6, 26; Penner and Rowe, "The Desire for Good: Is the *Meno* Inconsistent with the *Gorgias*?"; McTighe, "Socrates on Desire for the Good"; and Vlastos, *Socrates*, 148–54. All of them take Socrates to be saying that the true object of desire or wish is the good, which we aim at as well as we can see it, and none makes a sharp distinction between desire and wish. Wolfsdorf, by contrast, maintains that the object of desire and wish is only the apparent good in Socrates' account—a view that leaves him unable to explain, however, Socrates' definition of misery as desiring and possessing what is bad at 78a ("Desire for Good in *Meno* 77B2–78B6").

15. For examples of passages where Socrates speaks of the need to combat fears and desires and pleasures, thus treating them as irrational or not aligned with what is best, see *Laches* 191d6–e1; *Gorgias* 491d10–e1 and 507b4–8; *Protagoras* 352b3–c7; 357c. Citing such passages, Devereux in "Socrates' Kantian Conception of Virtue" argues persuasively against Irwin, Penner, Rowe, and Vlastos that Socrates does recognize the existence of irrational desires that need *enkrateia* or self-control to overcome them. Unfortunately he does not define what he means by "irrational," but in calling these desires "good-independent" (389 n. 15), he suggests, I think without textual evidence, that they need not seem good in any way to have a hold on the soul. This position that passions and judgments bear no necessary connection we may call the "radical misalignment theory."

16. George Nakhnikian argues that when Socrates says that no one wants what is bad, if indeed no one wants to be unhappy, his reasoning is defective, for not wanting to desire what is bad for oneself does not guarantee that one will not do so: "The First Socratic Paradox," 5. Nakhnikian speculates that "Socrates may be confusing an aversion to something with thinking that one ought not to have it." Nakhnikian's argument too suffers from inadequate attention to the difference between desiring and wishing: even if immediate desires can attach to what is on the whole bad, we cannot truly wish to have it.

17. Weiss maintains that at *Meno* 77b–79a Socrates is conceding that human beings not only feel but act upon desires that they know to be bad at the time of acting upon them. Joining this alleged acknowledgment with the observation that at 78e Socrates affirms individuals' ability to limit the pursuit of their own good, she concludes that the *Meno* departs radically from the *Protagoras*' teaching that human beings must do what knowledge or opinion judges best for themselves: *Socratic Paradox*, chapter 5, esp. 148, 159, 163–66. Socrates never concedes, however, that anyone who knows what is best *does* otherwise (even if he is here allowing that he may *feel* some desire for it). Nor does his strong claim for the power of knowledge at *Protagoras* 352b–c depend on egoist premises; it is simply the claim that whatever we know or believe to be best to do at the moment of acting, that we must do. Nothing in the *Meno* contradicts this fundamental and radical claim.

18. Klein, *Commentary on Plato's "Meno,"* 77. I have found this commentary invaluable in illuminating many obscure passages in the dialogue.

19. See Bruell, *On the Socratic Education,* 175.
20. For a rich discussion of all that may be at work in Meno's attraction to this this poetic account, see Bartlett, "On the *Meno,*" 144–45.
21. As Klein points out (*Commentary,* 108), *recollection* when used as a term for learning in Plato is always tied to a "mythical" framework, as in the *Phaedo, Phaedrus,* and *Philebus.* For parallels between this account and other ancient transmigration myths, some attributed to both Empedocles and Pythagoras, see Theodore Ebert, "The Theory of Recollection in Plato's *Meno,*" 187–88.
22. Notwithstanding Socrates' own disclaimer, scholars have traditionally taken the recollection myth quite seriously. See, e.g. E. Thompson, who calls the doctrine of reincarnation and recollection "the very center of Plato's system": *The "Meno" of Plato,* 125; H. F. Cherniss, "The Philosophical Economy of the Theory of Ideas"; and Gregory Vlastos, "*Anamemnesis* in the *Meno.*" At the other extreme are those like Eckstein, *The Platonic Method,* and Theodore Ebert, "The Theory of Recollection in Plato's *Meno.*" Both challenge the seriousness of the whole account but see beneath the flawed surface of the argument little deeper point; Eckstein argues that the only serious lesson is that Meno and Socrates should work hard to become wiser.
23. The question of how the truths that "recollection" discovers are originally present in us has occasioned much debate among those who take the account seriously. Vlastos takes recollection as equivalent to deductive reasoning when it is not simply a matter of recalling the forms one saw before birth: "*Anamemnesis* in the *Meno.*" R. M. Hare argues that what Plato poetically calls recollection is the activity by which we perceive the most basic kind of philosophical truth, grasping through a process of introspection that is neither analytic nor empirical "something which exists before the elucidation begins": "Philosophical Discoveries," 113–14. Julius Moravcsik specifies the objects of recollection as innate ideas: "Learning as Recollection." John Thomas takes recollection to refer broadly to recognition of what we have learned through experience as well as to a recognition of the principles of logic and their proper applications: *Musings on the* Meno, 144–47. His account seems to accord best with the diverse forms of learning that Socrates engages in himself, and especially the learning he expects Meno to undertake in the present scene, beginning from careful observation of the slave's progress.
24. As Bartlett points out, such awareness is one important kind of knowledge that cannot come through recollection, even if the myth is literally true, for according to it we originally had no such ignorance: "Socratic Political Philosophy and the Problem of Virtue," 530.
25. Kathleen Wilkes gives a good account of this juncture of the dialogue and Meno's failure to apply the lesson that true teaching is dialectics in "Conclusions on the *Meno.*"
26. Bluck notes that the problem has eluded the "ingenuity of numerous scholars" (*Plato's "Meno,"* 322). Klein suggests that it may be a hoax (*Commentary,* loc. cit.).
27. Linda Rabieh argues for the first of these alternatives with admirable clarity in *Plato and the Virtue of Courage.*
28. Bartlett, *"Protagoras" and "Meno,"* 120 n. 74; Bluck, *Plato's "Meno,"* 336.
29. This is the suggestion of Craig, in "Strange Misperception," 77.
30. Confirming our hypothesis about the real meaning of recollection, Socrates significantly does not surmise that Anytus must be recollecting any knowledge from before his birth, as Craig observes: "Strange Misperception," 74.
31. Klein, *Commentary,* 236.

32. Bruell observes the irony of Socrates' claim that Themistocles' son's success in learning horsemanship proves that he had a good nature (93d9–10), but also the more serious suggestion of this passage that virtue may well depend on having a good nature in respects not reducible to intelligence (*On the Socratic Education*, 182).
33. Theognis' use of the middle form, *didaxeai*, suggests that there is an element of "teaching oneself" necessary even in the process of learning such noble things as can be acquired from eating and drinking with the great.
34. As Bruell suggests (*On the Socratic Education*, 179), Socrates' reference to a calculation of "cause" or "responsibility" (or even "blame") (*aitia*) points especially to the investigation of moral desert that Meno would need to make to overcome his opinions' instability.
35. I am indebted to Devereux for pointing out the relevance of these questions of *enkrateia* and *akrasia* for the *Meno* and for his good argument that *enkrateia* or vigilant self-control is still needed by the wise, even though *akrasia* in the sense of direct violation of knowledge one has firmly in one's grasp is not possible: "Socrates' Kantian Conception of Virtue," esp. 395–96 n. 28. Where I differ from him is in his claim that Socrates recognizes "nonrational" desires in the sense of desires unaccompanied by beliefs that their objects are good, as well as in the related "Kantian" claim that judgments about what is good can and should operate without accompanying desires or wishes for that good.
36. In Socrates' treatment of Meno here we have an illustration of Xenophon's observation that with those who failed to challenge Socrates' arguments, he refrained from probing the deepest level of the question at hand (*Memorabilia* 4.6.13–15).
37. See Klein, *Commentary*, 253. Bartlett makes the further intriguing suggestion that behind or within the attribution of virtue to divine inspiration is a suggestion that virtue is due to law or *nomos*, which was thought to arise from the gods and on which the dialogue is strikingly silent; he suggests further that divine inspiration and law are the two most powerful possible sources of virtue that Meno unwisely left out of his original question: "Socratic Political Philosophy and the Problem of Virtue," 532.
38. Cf. Wilkes, "Conclusions on the *Meno*."
39. *Memorabilia* 1.2.17–21.

CHAPTER FOUR

1. Diogenes Laertius 9.55–56; Philostratus *Lives of the Sophists* 1.10.3; Sextus Empiricus *Against the Schoolmasters* 9.55–56.
2. See 316c5, where Protagoras shows that he already knows Socrates by name, and 361e2–3. Socrates' criticisms of the sophists are much more often noted by commentators (e.g. J. P. Sullivan, "The Hedonism in Plato's *Protagoras*"; Weiss, *Socratic Paradox*) than the irony surrounding them.
3. Devin Stauffer, "Socrates and the Sophists," 107.
4. The word is *promētheomai*, from which comes the name Prometheus, the hero of the myth that Protagoras will soon tell. He is in effect saying, "You have nobly taken forethought for me, Socrates, but I have anticipated you in taking the best possible forethought for myself."
5. This remark is one of the earliest of a surprisingly large number of statements made by prominent authors down through the centuries to the effect that esoteric writing has been practiced routinely and extensively by great writers of every description. For a comprehensive collection and discussion of such statements, see Arthur

Melzer, "Esoterism and the Critique of Historicism." Socrates, we may note, does not dispute this claim, and a little later will give an example (if a tongue-in-cheek one) of the kind of careful reading he thinks is required to unpack the subtleties of a great writer.

6. For the view that Homer and Hesiod were educators of the Greeks, see Herodotus *Histories* 2.53; Plato *Republic* 595b.

7. Robert Bartlett brings out both the ambiguity of this statement and the fact that an essential element of Protagoras' caution is his persistent evasiveness about what he teaches, as opposed to the fact that he is a teacher: "On the *Protagoras*," 71–72.

8. We have been taught by Socrates himself to think that if one possesses a true art one can teach it, but possibly this is not true of the art of politics, which Socrates claims in the *Gorgias* to have but not to teach.

9. Although the words *mythos* and *logos* were originally synonymous in Greek, by the fifth century they were quite distinct. On the falsity of myth see Plato *Republic* 377a.

10. If Protagoras has modeled his myth on those of the ancient "sophists" Homer and Hesiod as he has understands them, then he evidently thinks they convey some such serious teaching beneath the literal surface of their poems.

11. Or as Bartlett puts it, "The world is fundamentally 'Epimethean': thought follows rather than precedes creation" (*Plato, "Protagoras" and "Meno,"* 73).

12. In beginning his account of human thriving with a crime, Protagoras anticipates Machiavelli, but the difference is also important: Machiavelli makes the crucial act one of political founding while Protagoras puts the arts first and shows even more skepticism about the naturalness and the choiceworthiness of political life.

13. For a gentler expression of the thought that heaven is hostile to the arts, consider the Bible's indication that God prefers herdsmen to farmers and both to city dwellers (Genesis 4:18–19).

14. *Symposium* 203c–d; but cf. *Republic* book 1, in which man in the simplest, most necessary city is a familial but not yet fully erotic being.

15. For even more open statements of Protagoras' conventionalism, see *Theaetetus* 167c, 172a–b, 177c. Protagoras' state of nature has often been compared to that of Hobbes, but it is in fact worse: Protagoras has no teaching about a law of nature or natural right.

16. For a radical argument that the parts of virtue are all just different names for a single motive force or state of the soul, namely knowledge of the good and bad, see Terry Penner, "The Unity of Virtue."

17. Patient classicists helpfully point out the errors that they are sure Plato made unwittingly here, including the "type mistake" of calling justice just and the confusion of the contrary with the contradictory: e.g. Sullivan, "Hedonism in Plato's *Protagoras*," 14; Dodds, *Plato Gorgias*, 336.

18. A major theme of Plato's *Sophist* is the possibility of just such a fundamental opposition between moderation and courage.

19. The demonstration of the unity of wisdom and courage remains and will be taken up at 351b ff. It is perhaps significant that Plato allows Socrates to complete his arguments for the identity of wisdom with moderation and even with courage but not with justice or piety; these identities remain more tenuous.

20. Scholars who have taken Socrates' purpose in the dialogue to be fundamentally or exclusively eristic rather than investigative include Richard Robinson, "Plato's Consciousness of Fallacy"; George Klosko, "Towards a Consistent Interpretation of the *Protagoras*"; Donald Zeyl, "Socrates and Hedonism"; and Weiss, *Socratic Paradox*.

21. Whether Critias' comment in fact came next or whether someone else spoke immediately after Alcibiades Socrates professes not quite to remember. Is his love of Alcibiades momentarily rekindled, just long enough to unsettle his otherwise ironclad attention and memory?
22. This proposal resembles at least superficially the republican principle of ruling and being ruled by turns, as Catherine Zuckert remarks (*Plato's Philosophers*, 224.) But of course Socrates is and knows he is the only one who can control the helm of the ship on such terms.
23. For an example of Simonides' critiques of ancient poetry, see Aristotle *Poetics* 1456b15 ff., where Aristotle reports Simonides' criticism of the opening of Homer's *Iliad* for being overly pious. For an example of Simonides' reputation among the ancients, see Cicero *On the Nature of the Gods* 1.22.
24. Scholars have focused mainly on the outlandishness. Klosko calls Socrates' interpretation little but a string of logical fallacies ("Towards a Consistent Interpretation of the *Protagoras*," 130); Sullivan calls it "blatant sophistry ("The Hedonism in Plato's Protagoras," 26); M. Dyson among others complains especially of Socrates' importation into the poem of "Socratic convictions which it manifestly does not contain" ("Knowledge and Hedonism in Plato's *Protagoras*," 41).
25. Seen in this light, the expression *epi pleiston* at the end of the second stanza (345c3) is perhaps best translated as "for the most part": good for the most part are those whom the gods love, but a few are good in a more autonomous sense.
26. This discussion of the limitations of reading should be compared with Socrates' discussion of the limitations of writing at *Phaedrus* 274b ff.
27. Commentators who hold Socrates or Plato to be seriously espousing hedonism as his own view here include Grote, *Plato and the Other Companions of Socrates* 2:314; T. D. Goodell, "Plato's Hedonism"; Hackforth, "Hedonism in Plato's *Protagoras*," 41; Dodds, *Plato Gorgias*, 21; Irwin, *Plato's Moral Theory*, 93, and *Plato's Ethics*, chapter 6; Martha Nussbaum, *Fragility of Goodness*, 88–121. To the obvious question of how such hedonism fits with all that we see of Socrates elsewhere, Hackforth presents Plato's hedonism as a temporary exploration, soon abandoned; Irwin argues that virtue is critically important but solely a means to pleasure, while Goodell attributes to Socrates a capacious, even noble hedonism by stressing the satisfactions of moral and intellectual pleasures as well as physical ones. But whether Socrates' strong praise of both virtue and knowledge can be shoehorned into such a view, and especially whether he thought the desire to know the truth could ever be reduced to a desire for a certain type of pleasure, is doubtful. The premise that Plato at the time of writing the *Protagoras* espoused hedonism is rejected by Shorey, *Unity of Plato's Thought*, chapter 1; G. M. A. Grube, "The Structural Unity of the *Protagoras*"; J. P. Sullivan, "The Hedonism in Plato's *Protagoras*"; Dyson, "Knowledge and Hedonism in Plato's *Protagoras*"; Zeyl, "Socrates and Hedonism." Shorey and Grube see Socrates as giving ironic exposure to the uncritical hedonism of the sophists. Dyson argues that Socrates espouses a view that is not hedonism but is easily mistaken for hedonism, namely that pleasure is good insofar as it is pleasant, and also that the good life, the life of philosophy, is pleasant, without however holding the good and pleasure to be the same. Zeyl denies that Socrates is even endorsing the view that pleasure as such is good.
28. Cf. Aristotle *NE* 1099a22–31.
29. Of course it may not seem to them to collapse into hedonism; they may voice all sorts of other sentiments. The question Socrates is raising, however, is whether if

pressed hard they would be able to articulate other reasons for the goodness of virtue other than its capacity to bring in this life or the next the pleasures they think everyone wants.

30. For these suggestions about the character of the absurdity the interlocutor is bringing out, I am indebted to M. Dyson, "Knowledge and Hedonism"; Michael Morris, "Akrasia in the *Protagoras* and the *Republic,*" 203.
31. Michael Morris, "Akrasia in the *Protagoras* and the *Republic,*" 203.
32. In rendering this line, I follow the reading of J. L. Stocks, "The Argument of Plato, *Prot.* 351b–356c."
33. Commentators have asked what the force is of this "must," pointing out that it seems descriptive rather than prescriptive, and arguing that if so, Socrates is making an unauthorized assumption about human behavior. Thus David Gallop maintains, in "The Socratic Paradox in the *Protagoras,*" that this argument begs the decisive question of whether *akrasia* is possible. But again, what Plato is offering is neither a complete argument nor a fallacious one but a dialectical engagement with common opinion and a challenge to us to improve upon it if we can. When people allegedly know what is best but do otherwise, how can we account for it? The many can say nothing other than that they were overcome by pleasure, and Socrates has shown that this reduces to saying: "Knowing what was best, I chose what was worse, because it seemed best," which is nonsense. Can we offer another explanation that does not come down to a version of the same nonsense?
34. Bartlett, *Plato, "Protagoras" and "Meno,"* 84–85. Irwin makes a similar argument in *Plato's Ethics*, chapter 4, and Santas in *Socrates*: "Clearly enough, knowledge will not *always* be sufficient for virtue unless virtue *always* brings happiness and vice *always* unhappiness" (218). Along the same lines, Blitz asks: don't we sometimes just run out of strength to resist desires and especially fears, so that we need strength or daring in addition to correct judgment in order to act well? (*Plato's Political Philosophy*, 79).
35. Brickhouse and Smith thus speak of the "false cognitive lens" that makes us aim wrong when we fail to pursue what is best: *Plato's Socrates*, 88; and Devereux observes that desire does not bypass judgment but undermines, flatters, manipulates, and corrupts it when it prevails: "Socrates' Kantian Conception of Virtue," 394–95.
36. For Irwin's and Penner's arguments that it must do so, according to Socrates' argument, see chapter 3 n 14 above. J. J. Walsh concurs in "The Socratic Denial of *Akrasia*": while the many say that men are not governed by reason but by pleasure, he writes, "Socrates has shown them that even if men pursue pleasure alone, they are still governed by reason."
37. Santas presses this question in *Socrates*, 214.
38. Morris, "Akrasia in the *Protagoras* and the *Republic.*"
39. Irvin Yalom captures this experience in his fictional account of Dr. Breuer's struggles with erotic desire: "Insidious fantasies of Bertha seeped in: holding her arm, walking together with her in the warm sun, far from the icy gray slush of Vienna. Soon, however, discordant images intruded: his marriage shattered, his children left behind, as he sailed away forever, to start a new life with Bertha in America. The thoughts haunted him. He hated them: they robbed him of his peace; they were alien, neither possible nor desirable." *When Nietzsche Wept*, 30.
40. This is in fact the conclusion of, among others, Kahn, *Plato and the Socratic Dialogue*, 240; Catherine Zuckert, *Plato's Philosophers*, 227n. 18; and Weiss, who with a reminder of some of Socrates' more dramatic hypermoral statements, writes, "It is

inconceivable that Socrates should subscribe to all he has argued for" in the discussion of human motivation at the end of the *Protagoras* (*Socratic Paradox*, 60–65).

41. Socrates' definition of courage here at 360d4–5 as "wisdom about what is terrible and what is not terrible" is echoed in his diluted, "political" definition of courage in book 4 of the *Republic* as a "power and preservation, through everything, of the right and lawful opinion about what is terrible and what is not" (430b–c). To the extent that the courage sought there is merely political, doggedness becomes more important and love of the truth much less so.

42. On the other hand, if animating the strongest souls is an unusually strong desire for the true good that is available to us, also present in perhaps an unusually high degree, especially at first, would be a desire for the unmixed and unlimited good that is not available, and to that extent the source of their strength would be less than perfectly rational.

CHAPTER FIVE

1. To see how sharply this view departs from the common understanding of even the most serious Greek communities, cf. 626b.
2. Indications that they do not may be found, for example, at 638a–b, 706a and c, 707d, and 742e–43a.
3. Christopher Bobonich offers a lucid and detailed defense of the *Laws'* thesis that everything good depends on virtue in *Plato's Utopia Recast*, chapter 2. He brings out the importance for happiness of understanding what is good and why it is good, but I think without giving sufficient weight to the problem of evident exceptions and conflicting goods that make the Athenian's strongest claims for the unwavering adherence to virtue so problematic. Leo Strauss points to the deepest problem with this claim, the imperfect unity of virtue itself, or the imperfect nobility of justice as ordinarily understood, in *The Argument and the Action of Plato's* Laws, 130. While Strauss seems to take the view that nature points us to a certain rough justice that often falls short of both perfect rationality and perfect nobility, I explore in this chapter the alternative but not incompatible view that Plato is calling on us to take more seriously, whenever we can find it, the perfect justice that *is* thoroughly noble, and not to settle so quickly for its rougher cousin.
4. Further confirmation may found in Xenophon, *Memorabilia* 1.5, 1.6.
5. Here again we see Plato using *phronēsis* and *sophia* almost interchangeably to denote that virtue that consists in a grasp of and inner alignment with the true hierarchy of goods.
6. In my understanding of this complex project I depart decisively from Malcolm Schofield, who views the *Laws* as fundamentally paternalistic: *Plato*, esp. 87, 98n104, 321. Schofield does qualify this claim in comparing the *Laws* with the *Republic* (cf. 283 and 315–19); on the other hand he says that "in the *Laws*, Plato has elected to talk to his readers in language that (unlike the *Republic*) offers no challenge to the conceptual framework with which they are antecedently familiar" (81). In contrast, Bobonich in *Plato's Utopia Recast*, 97–119, makes a good case for the *Laws'* nuanced efforts to take each citizen as far as possible towards virtue based on reason and stresses the crucial fact that the dialogue itself is to serve as a basic educational text. But I think Bobonich goes too far in the other direction, beginning with his denial that virtue for Plato requires philosophic wisdom (90). Throughout Bobonich underestimates the distance the *Laws* leaves even the most serious subphilosophic citizens from perfect rationality.

7. In these ways the polis epitomizes the fraternity that contemporary advocates of restorative justice seek to recreate through their conferences as an antidote to the fragmentation of social connections in the modern world that allows crime to proliferate. The crucial difference is that Plato, unlike advocates of restorative justice, believes that the best community—indeed the only true community—must be built around an agreement that the community's highest purpose is to cultivate the good character that is essential for happiness. For a fuller discussion of the similarities and differences between Plato's approach and modern restorative justice, see my "Moral and Criminal Responsibility in Plato's *Laws*."
8. Morrow, *Plato's Cretan City: A Historical Interpretation of the Laws*, 553.
9. Schofield (*Plato*, 84) makes this point well, and he raises an interesting question as to why the preludes even deserve to be described as entering into a "dialogue" with the citizen at all as the doctor does with a sick patient, since their commands are nonnegotiable. Where is there anything like the respectful give-and-take of dialogue? This discrepancy suggests, I think, that the "patient" addressed by the preludes is as much the law-abiding citizen who needs to ponder the law's reasons as the one on the verge of crime who needs immediate restraint; one need not be a criminal or even seriously drawn to crime to be "sick" and in need of a doctor; anyone who has failed to think through to the bottom what his soul truly needs for happiness is unhealthy and in need of a kind of philosophic inquiry that the preludes can in the best case instigate and help guide.
10. The human inability to accept the temporal limits of our individual lives is also pointed to in the example of poetic speech at 719d–e: this problem is integral to both the need for preludes and the reason these preludes can never be simply rational arguments. Consider further R. F. Stalley's observation on the imperfect match between the marriage law's details and the reason the citizen is given for obeying it: "Persuasion in Plato's *Laws*," 320–21.
11. This passage has occasioned much debate, summarized and joined by E. B. England in *The Laws of Plato* 1:477–78, and by Trevor Saunders, in *Notes on the Laws of Plato*, 18–21. My own reading departs from all of these: I take the word *pathos* in 728c2 to refer to what bad men naturally suffer from one another, mentioned in the previous line (*paschein*). In falling into bad company, one might occasionally escape the quarrels and abuse that naturally occur in such company, but one still is miserable because one is not cured. On the other hand, if one suffers such "natural" retribution to the utmost and is destroyed by one's bad companions, this still is not a just punishment, for its only good effect is that *others* benefit from one's example.
12. So uncomfortable is Stalley with the suggestion that the just response to crime need not be painful that he denies the plain sense of this passage: *An Introduction to Plato's Laws*, 142–43. Saunders grasps clearly what is at stake, commenting, "This passage has a fair claim to be the most radical penological manifesto ever written": *Plato's Penal Code*, 144.
13. Cf. James Booth, "The Unforgotten: Memories of Justice," 779–80.
14. Cf. Aeschylus, *The Libation Bearers*, 37–40. For an eloquent contemporary discussion of the way vengeance is fueled by a desire to keep memory alive (and so in a sense to keep the dead alive), see Booth, "The Unforgotten," 780. Saunders is appropriately troubled by Plato's introduction of such a vengeful element into a law code whose principles abjure retribution: "Penal Law and Family Law in Plato's Magnesia," 118–21. Saunders understands this as the result of a collision between Plato's principles of justice and his decision to give the family a prominent place in

the society of Magnesia; he further tries to bridge the gap by arguing that the relative gain in honor that comes to the dead when their killers suffer retribution is the only "recompense" that can be given them in fulfillment of the criminal law's nonpunitive goal of "redressing the injury" and "restoring friendship" outlined at 862b–c. This may indeed be the only recompense possible, but Plato's recourse to it only serves to highlight the punitive element present in virtually every demand that the law should "take away" from the criminal what he has "gained" so as to restore the proper equilibrium between criminal and victim (cf. Aristotle *NE* 1132a7–14).

15. For a contrasting account that places the significance of the Areopagus not in reason, law, or any constructive civic purpose for punishment that replaces blind fury, but instead in its successful monopoly of authority, see Danielle Allen, *The World of Prometheus*, 18–24. Allen argues persuasively that, on one hand, law was appealed to before this event, and on the other, that revenge remained an important motive to civic punishment after it, but she underrates the importance of the effort to replace anger's pointless destruction with sanctions aimed rationally at social order and peace—and hence misses the significance of the limited success of that effort. In general, following Foucault's emphasis on punishment as an expression of power, Allen focuses on the "who" and "how" of punishment to the neglect of the "why."
16. On the deep connection between Greek notions of shame and honor, see Douglas Cairns's discussion of the meanings of the word *aideomai* in *Aidos*, 1–4, 13, 383–4.
17. Jean Roberts makes an ingenious and often insightful effort to save this whole passage from inconsistency, but she does not face the fact that the Athenian really does begin to speak of voluntary injustices: "Plato on the Causes of Wrongdoing in the *Laws*." Arthur Adkins notes the contradiction but implausibly suggests that Plato never noticed it: *Merit and Responsibility*, 306, 308–9.
18. See Saunders, *Plato's Penal Code*, 143, for a helpful discussion of this paradox. Weiss notes it as well, in *Socratic Paradox*, chapters 1 and 7, although she argues that the Athenian and Plato hold to a conventional view that unjust acts are freely chosen and their agents morally culpable—the very view the Athenian clearly denies but that Kleinias forces him to accommodate. Weiss even claims that Plato holds everyone morally responsible for his ignorance (ibid., 202), and that he departs from the usual view of moral responsibility only in placing a new stress on the importance of character and in insisting on the unenviable state of the unjust man's soul.
19. That the Athenian does not call for execution of the criminally insane is of course an anomaly on his principles. In fact, he calls for execution only in cases where popular outrage and a cool Socratic judgment as to the choiceworthiness of a life *both* support it, as in the case of premeditated murder.
20. Weiss (*Socratic Paradox*, 191–200) denies that the Athenian seriously means this admittedly strange statement that acts based on erroneous opinion should be declared "entirely just." She translates *kan sphalletai ti* at 864a4 not as "even if it is in some way mistaken" but as "even if it does some harm," not seeming to notice the problem this creates for the last line I have quoted. For most people never simply equate acts done out of moral conviction that do some harm with involuntary injustice; if they did they would view all legal punishments as involuntary injustices. The point here is radical: the Athenian is indicating that the city must often declare just what is based on error.
21. Strauss is most helpful in sketching how this civic justice remains distinct from the true justice that is based on true knowledge of what is good, pointing out that only

the latter can be counted upon to do real good: *The Argument and the Action of Plato's* Laws, 132–33.

22. On the inferiority of law to reason, see also 875d.
23. Thomas Pangle suggests that in fact the chief practical effect of the Athenian's reforms in criminal law is to lay the foundation for a new and far less harsh way of dealing with impiety: *The Laws of Plato,* 502.
24. The relation of pollution or miasma to moral responsibility has been much discussed. E. R. Dodds argues that the idea of pollution developed in post-Homeric times out of a new sense of guilt and insecurity that were alien to the "shame culture" depicted by Homer, but he is able to maintain this thesis only by denying the authenticity of significant passages in Homer that do imply clear notions of moral responsibility: *The Greeks and the Irrational,* 44–45; cf. Cairns, *Aidos,* 27–146. Adkins also claims a growing emphasis on pollution in archaic Greece, rooted in a deep sense of foreboding and fear of having transgressed the divine order and often provoked by national disasters that society was able neither to explain nor to cure: *Merit and Responsibility,* 86–108. He observes a tension between the archaic Greek view that any killing incurs pollution and requires expiation, and the code of Draco, the first known Greek homicide law, which distinguishes between willful, accidental, and justifiable homicide and demands no purification in the case of the last. In his account of the archaic world, as in Plato's *Laws,* the notion of pollution seems to blur rather than sharpen the concern with moral responsibility. Morrow, taking a far more rationalist approach than Dodds or Adkins, argues that the concept of pollution was deliberately developed by the Greeks after Homer to ensure that the whole community took a hand in bringing punishment on a murderer, thus putting a stop to cycles of vengeance killing: *Plato's Cretan City,* 120. For a nuanced and I think more persuasive account that argues for the antiquity of the full-blown notion of pollution and its eclipse by formal law, see Robert Parker, *Miasma,* esp. 104–43.
25. As James Booth shows, Germany's difficulty in coming to terms with its Nazi past has caused thoughtful Germans to look beyond simply liberal and individualistic paradigms for ways to understand crime and to expiate a disorder that seems to go to the core of their identity as a nation: "Communities of Memory," 252–58.
26. Morrow, *Plato's Cretan City,* 253–58; Plato *Laws,* 766d–67a and 855c–56a; *Apology* 37a–b.
27. Our own inevitable ambivalence about filling such a punitive function is reflected in the fact that, as Michel Foucault observes and popular modern television shows attest, there is still glory in being the police detective who solves a crime or the district attorney who obtains a conviction, but none at all in carrying out the sentence: *Discipline and Punish,* 9–10.
28. Allen tries to mitigate the problem here by arguing that it is good and even a "cure" for the offender to serve as an example for others (*World of Prometheus,* 279–80), which Plato never says. Nor does she recognize the extent to which nearly all the penal laws in Magnesia in fact make compromises with anger; she claims that *only* in the treatment of incurables does anger come into play (281).
29. The stoic view that anger, being irrational, is never necessary to the good citizen is thus, from Plato's perspective, far too sanguine in its hopes for making political life thoroughly rational: see Seneca *On Anger,* 25–31. Yet Seneca is probably a good illustration of the calming effect that Plato sought to have on high-minded readers. Seneca encourages a proud spirit of independence that rises above all volatile reactivity, but he never grasps the true nerve of the Socratic argument, and hence he con-

tinues to think that retributive punishment—calmly administered—is wholly just. Adkins, M. M. Mackenzie, and Saunders have been more attuned to the problem that the Athenian is compromising his ideal of justice as medicine for sick souls in order to protect the broader community from harm: Adkins, *Merit and Responsibility*, 308–9; Mackenzie, *Plato on Punishment*, 198–204; Saunders, *Plato's Penal Code*.

30. In developing my account of Plato's project for a constructive reform of *thumos* I have built especially upon Thomas Pangle's helpful exposition of the Platonic critique of ordinary *thumos* in "The Political Psychology of Religion in Plato's *Laws*," and in *The Laws of Plato*.

31. Socrates was of course admired for his courage on the battlefield, but his distinction was a calm steadfastness in retreat, not an outstanding boldness in attack. The battles in which he distinguished himself and that he mentions at *Apology* 28d–e were indeed all Athenian defeats.

32. For more intimations of the connection between rage, weakness, and tears, see 935a and 949b; consider also the identification of tragedy as the favored dramatic form of the educated women at 658d.

33. Bacon also observes, "Anger is certainly a kind of baseness, as it appears well in the weakness of those subjects in whom it reigns: children, women, old folks, sick folks": *Essays*, 17–72; cf. Seneca, *On Anger*, 31.

34. Bacon, *Essays*, 170.

35. In this the Dorian training in courage bears a closer resemblance to that advocated by Rousseau, who suggests in *Emile* that courage comes through being continually exposed to new and unfamiliar things. So hopeful does Rousseau profess himself to be on the prospect of overcoming fear, however, that he denies that human beings are by nature afraid of death at all—a fact not unconnected to his attack on swaddling, against Plato: *Emile*, book 1, esp. 55, 60n, 63. This entire discussion forms a fascinating contrast to Plato's discussion of infancy in *Laws*, book 7. By contrast, a certain recognition of the inescapable power of the fear of death and stillness may be found in Rousseau's description of the experience of lying in a rowboat in the fifth walk of the *Reveries*.

36. This passage echoes the Athenian's insistence in book 1 that real courage must make one strong against the lure of pleasures as well as against fears (633e–35d).

37. This proverb was coined or quoted by Simonides in the poem discussed in chapter 4 above.

BIBLIOGRAPHY OF MODERN WORKS AND EDITIONS

Adkins, Arthur W. H. 1960. *Merit and Responsibility: A Study in Greek Values*. Oxford: Clarendon Press.

Ahrensdorf, Peter. 1994. "The Question of Historical Context and the Study of Plato." *Polity* 27: 113–135.

Allen, Danielle S. 2000. *The World of Prometheus: The Politics of Punishing in Democratic Athens*. Princeton: Princeton University Press.

Allen, R. E. 1960. "The Socratic Paradox." *Journal of the History of Ideas* 21: 256–65.

Anscombe, G. E. M. 1957. *Intention*. Cambridge, MA: Harvard University Press.

Bacon, Francis. 1936. *The Essays of Francis Bacon*. Boston: Houghton Mifflin.

Bambrough, Renford. 1960. "The Socratic Paradox." *Philosophical Quarterly* 10: 289–300.

Barker, Ernest. 1950. *Greek Political Theory: Plato and His Predecessors*. London, Methuen.

Bartlett, Robert C., trans. and ed. 2004. *Plato, "Protagoras" and "Meno"* with notes and interpretive essay. Ithaca, NY: Cornell University Press.

———. 2002. "Socratic Political Philosophy and the Problem of Virtue." *American Political Science Review* 96: 525–33.

Blitz, Mark. 2010. *Plato's Political Philosophy*. Baltimore: Johns Hopkins University Press.

Bluck, R. S. 1961. *Plato's "Meno."* Edited with introduction and commentary. Cambridge, UK: Cambridge University Press.

Bobonich, Christopher. 2002. *Plato's Utopia Recast*. Oxford: Clarendon Press.

Bonnette, Amy, trans. 1994. *Xenophon: Memorabilia*. Ithaca: Cornell University Press.

Booth, James. 2001. "The Unforgotten: Memories of Justice." *American Political Science Review* 95: 777–91.

———. 1999. "Communities of Memory: On Identity, Memory, and Debt." *American Political Science Review* 93: 249–63.

Brickhouse, Thomas C., and Nicholas Smith. 1996. *Plato's Socrates*. New York: Oxford University Press.

Bruell, Christopher. 1999. *On the Socratic Education: An Introduction to the Shorter Platonic Dialogues*. Lanham, MD: Rowman and Littlefield.

Burnet, John. 1924a. *Plato's Euthyphro, Apology of Socrates, and Crito*, ed. with notes. Oxford: Oxford University Press.

———. 1924b. *Platonis Opera*. Vol. I. Oxford: Oxford University Press.

———. 1907. *Platonis Opera*. Vol. V. Oxford: Oxford University Press.

———. 1903. *Platonis Opera*. Vol. III. Oxford: Oxford University Press.

———. 1902. *Platonis Opera*. Vol. II. Oxford: Oxford University Press.

Burnyeat, M. F. 2003. "*Apology* 30b2–4: Socrates, Money, and the Grammar of GIGNESQAI." *Journal of Hellenic Studies* 123: 1–25.

Cairns, Douglas L. 2003. *Aidos: The Psychology and Ethics of Honor and Shame in Ancient Greek Literature*. Oxford: Clarendon Press.

Cherniss, H. F. 1965. "The Philosophical Economy of the Theory of Ideas." In R. E. Allen, ed., *Studies in Plato's Metaphysics*, 2: 1–12. London: Routledge & Kegan Paul.

Craig, Leon. 2001. "The Strange Misperception of Plato's *Meno*." In Zdravko Planinc, ed., *Politics, Philosophy, Writing: Plato's Art of Caring for Souls*, 60–79. Columbia: University of Missouri Press.

Devereux, Daniel T. 1995. "Socrates' Kantian Conception of Virtue." *Journal of the History of Philosophy* 33: 381–408.

Diels, Hermann, ed. 1951–52. *Die Fragmente der Vorsokratiker* . 3 vols. 6th ed. by Walter Kranz. Berlin: Weidmann.

Dimas, Panos. 2007. "Teachers of Virtue." *Ancient Philosophy* 27: 1–23.

Dodds, E. R. 1959. *Plato Gorgias: A Revised Text with Introduction and Commentary*. Oxford: Oxford University Press.

———. 1951. *The Greeks and the Irrational*. Berkeley: University of California Press.

Dyson, M. 1976. "Knowledge and Hedonism in Plato's *Protagoras*." *Journal of Hellenic Studies* 96: 32–45.

Ebert, Theodore. 2010. "The Theory of Recollection in Plato's *Meno*: Against a Myth of Platonic Scholarship." In Michael Erler and Luc Brisson, eds., *Gorgias—Meno: Selected Papers from the Seventh Symposium Platonicum*. Sankt Augustin: Academia Verlag.

Eckstein, Jerome. 1968. *The Platonic Method: An Interpretation of the Dramatic-Philosophic Aspects of the Meno*. New York: Greenwood.

England, E. B. 1921. *The Laws of Plato*. 2 vols. Manchester: Manchester University Press.

Foucault, Michel. 1977. *Discipline and Punish*. Translated by Alan Sheridan. New York: Pantheon Books.

Friedländer, Paul. 1964. *Plato*. 2 vols. Translated by Hans Meyerhoff. Princeton, NJ: Princeton University Press.

Gallop, David. 1964. "The Socratic Paradox in the *Protagoras*." *Phronesis* 6: 117–29.

Goodell, T. D. 1921. "Plato's Hedonism." *American Journal of Philology* 42: 25–39.

Grimal, Pierre, ed. 1986. *The Dictionary of Classical Mythology*. Translated by A. R. Maxwell-Hyslop. Oxford: Basil Blackwell.

Grote, George. 1875. *Plato and the Other Companions of Socrates*. 3 vols. London: John Murray.

Grube, G. M. A. 1933. "The Structural Unity of the *Protagoras*." *Classical Quarterly* 27: 203–7.

Gulley, Norman. 1968. *The Philosophy of Socrates*. London: Macmillan.

Guthrie, W. K. C. 1962–81. *A History of Greek Philosophy*. 6 vols. Cambridge, UK: Cambridge University Press.

Hackforth, R. 1928. "Hedonism in Plato's *Protagoras*." *Classical Quarterly* 22: 39–42.

Hall, Robert William. 1971. "Techne and Morality in the *Gorgias*. In J. Anton and G. Kustas, eds. *Essays in Ancient Greek Philosophy*, 202–18. Albany: State University of New York Press.

Hare, R. M. 1965. "Philosophical Discoveries." In Alexander Sesonske and Noel Fleming, eds., *Plato's Meno: Text and Criticism*, 97–114. Belmont, CA: Wadsworth.

Huby, Pamela. 1967. "The First Discovery of the Freewill Problem." *Philosophy* 42: 353–62.

Irwin, Terence. 1995. *Plato's Ethics*. New York: Oxford University Press.

———. 1977. *Plato's Moral Theory*. Oxford: Clarendon Press.

Kahn, Charles. 1996. *Plato and the Socratic Dialogue: The Philosophical Use of a Literary Form*. Cambridge, UK: Cambridge University Press.

Klein, Jacob. 1965. *A Commentary on Plato's* Meno. Chicago: University of Chicago Press.

Klosko, George. 1986. *The Development of Plato's Political Theory*. New York and London: Methuen.

———. 1979. "Towards a Consistent Interpretation of the *Protagoras*." *Archiv für Geschichte der Philosophie* 61: 125–42.

Leibowitz, David. 2010. *The Ironic Defense of Socrates*. Cambridge, UK: Cambridge University Press, 2010.

Lutz, Mark J. 2012. *Divine Law and Political Philosophy in Plato's* Laws. Carbondale: Northern Illinois University Press.

———. 1997. "Civic Virtue and Socratic Virtue." *Polity* 29: 565–592.

Mackenzie, M. M. 1981. *Plato on Punishment*. Berkeley: University of California Press.

McTighe, Kevin. 1984. "Socrates on Desire for the Good and the Involuntariness of Wrongdoing: *Gorgias* 466a–468e." *Phronesis* 29: 193–236. Reprinted in Hugh Benson, ed., *Essays on the Philosophy of Socrates* (New York: Oxford University Press, 1992), 263–97.

Melzer, Arthur. 2006. "Esoterism and the Critique of Historicism." *American Political Science Review*, 100: 279–295.

Moravcsik, Julius. 1971. "Learning as Recollection." In Gregory Vlastos, ed., *Plato: A Collection of Critical Essays. Vol. I: Metaphysics and Epistemology*. New York: Doubleday.

Morris, Michael. 2006. "Akrasia in the *Protagoras* and the *Republic*." *Phronesis* 51: 195–229.

Morrow, Glenn. 1960. *Plato's Cretan City: A Historical Interpretation of the* Laws. Princeton: Princeton University Press.

Nakhnikian, George. 1973. "The First Socratic Paradox." *Journal of the History of Philosophy* 11: 1–17.

Nichols, James H., Jr., trans. and ed. 1998. Plato: *"Gorgias" and "Phaedrus."* Ithaca, NY: Cornell University Press.

Nussbaum, Martha. 2001. *The Fragility of Goodness: Luck and Ethics in Greek Tragedy and Philosophy*. Cambridge, UK: Cambridge University Press.

O'Brien, M. J. 1967. *The Socratic Paradoxes and the Greek Mind*. Chapel Hill: University of North Carolina Press.

Pangle, Lorraine. 2009. "Moral and Criminal Responsibility in Plato's *Laws*," *American Political Science Review*, 103: 456–73.

Pangle, Thomas L. 1987. "On the *Theages*." In Thomas L. Pangle, ed., *The Roots of Political Philosophy: Ten Forgotten Socratic Dialogues*, 147–74. Ithaca, NY: Cornell University Press.

———. 1985. "The Political Defense of Socratic Philosophy: A Study of Xenophon's *Apology of Socrates to the Jury*." *Polity* 18: 98–114.

———. 1980. *The Laws of Plato*. Translation with notes and interpretive essay. New York: Basic Books.

———. 1976. "The Political Psychology of Religion in Plato's *Laws*. *American Political Science Review* 70: 1059–77.

Parker, Robert. 1983. *Miasma: Pollution and Purification in Early Greek Religion*. Oxford: Clarendon Press.

Penner, Terry. 1992. "The Unity of Virtue." In Hugh H. Benson, ed., *Essays on the Philosophy of Socrates*, 162–84. Oxford: Oxford University Press.

———. 1991. "Desire and Power in Socrates: The Argument of *Gorgias* 466a–468e that Orators and Tyrants have no Power in the City." *Apeiron* 24: 147–202.

———. 1973. "Socrates on Virtue and Motivation." In E. N. Lee, A. P. D. Mourelatos, and R. M. Rorty, eds., *Exegesis and Argument*, 133–51. Assen: Van Gorcum.

———. 1971. "Thought and Desire in Plato." In Gregory Vlastos, ed., *Plato: A Collection of Critical Essays*. Vol. II: Ethics, Politics, and Philosophy of Art and Religion, 96–118. New York: Doubleday.

Penner, Terry, and C. J. Rowe. 1994. "The Desire for Good: Is the *Meno* Inconsistent with the *Gorgias*?" *Phronesis* 39: 1–25.

Rabieh, Linda. 2006. *Plato and the Virtue of Courage*. Baltimore, MD: Johns Hopkins University Press.

Roberts, Jean. 1987. "Plato on the Causes of Wrongdoing in the *Laws*." *Ancient Philosophy* 7: 23–37.

Robinson, Richard. 1942. "Plato's Consciousness of Fallacy." *Mind* 51: 97–114.

Rousseau, Jean-Jacques. 1979. *Emile, or On Education*. Translated by Allan Bloom. New York: Basic Books.

Santas, Gerasimos. 1979. *Socrates: Philosophy in Plato's Early Dialogues*. London and Boston: Routledge & Kegan Paul.

———. 1964. "The Socratic Paradoxes." *Philosophical Review* 73: 147–64.

Saunders, Trevor. 2000. *Bibliography on Plato's Laws*. Sankt Augustin: Academia.

———. 1991a. *Plato's Penal Code: Tradition, Controversy, and Reform in Greek Penology*. Oxford: Clarendon Press.

———. 1991b. "Penal Law and Family Law in Plato's Magnesia." In M. Gagarin, ed., *Symposion 1990: Papers on Greek and Hellenistic Legal History*, 115–32. Cologne: Böhlau Verlag.

———. 1972. *Notes on the Laws of Plato*. London: Institute of Classical Studies.

Schofield, Malcolm. 2006. *Plato: Political Philosophy*. Oxford: Oxford University Press.

Seneca. 1995. *On Anger*. In John M. Cooper and J. F. Procopé, eds, *Moral and Political Essays*. Cambridge, UK: Cambridge University Press, 1–116.

Shorey, Paul. 1903. *The Unity of Plato's Thought*. Chicago: University of Chicago Press.

Stalley, R. F. 1994. "Persuasion in Plato's *Laws*." *History of Political Thought*, 15: 157–77.

———. 1983. *An Introduction to Plato's* Laws. Oxford: Blackwell.

Stauffer, Devin. 2010. "Socrates and the Sophists." In Timothy Burns, ed., *Recovering Reason: Essays in Honor of Thomas L. Pangle*, 101–16. Lanham, MD: Lexington Books, 2010.

———. 2006. *The Unity of Plato's Gorgias*. Cambridge, UK: Cambridge University Press.

———. 2001. *Plato's Introduction to the Question of Justice*. Albany: SUNY Press.

Stocks, J. L. 1913. "The Argument of Plato, *Prot.* 351b–356c." *Classical Quarterly* 7: 100–4.

Strauss, Leo. 1975. *The Argument and the Action of Plato's* Laws. Chicago: University of Chicago Press.

Strycker, E. de. 1994. *Plato's Apology of Socrates: A Literary and Philosophical Study with a Running Commentary*. Edited and completed by S. J. Slings. Leiden: E. J. Brill.

Sullivan, J. P. 1961. "The Hedonism in Plato's *Protagoras*." *Phronesis* 6: 9–28.

Thomas, John E. 1980. *Musings on the* Meno: *a New Translation with Commentary*. The Hague: Martinus Nijhoff.

Thompson, E. Seymore. 1901. *The "Meno" of Plato: Edited with Introduction, Notes, and Excursuses*. London: Macmillan.

Tocqueville, Alexis de. 2004. *Democracy in America*. Translated by Arthur Goldhammer. New York: Library of America.

Vlastos, Gregory. 1991. *Socrates: Ironist and Moral Philosopher*. Ithaca, NY: Cornell University Press.

———. 1987. "Socratic Irony." *Classical Quarterly*, n.s. 37: 79–96. Reprinted in Hugh H. Benson, ed., *Essays on the Philosophy of Socrates*. Oxford: Oxford University Press, 66–85.

———. 1985. "Happiness and Virtue in Socrates' Moral Theory." *Topoi* 4: 3–32.

———. 1969. "Socrates on Akrasia." *Phoenix*, suppl. vol. 23: 71–88.

———. 1967. "Was Polus Refuted?" *American Journal of Philology* 88: 454–60.

———. 1965. "*Anamemnesis* in the *Meno*." *Dialogue* 4.

Walsh, J. J. 1971. "The Socratic Denial of *Akrasia*." In Gregory Vlastos, ed., *The Philosophy of Socrates*, 235–63. Notre Dame, IN: University of Notre Dame Press.

Weiss, Roslyn. 2006. *The Socratic Paradox and Its Enemies*. Chicago: University of Chicago Press.

West, Thomas G., and Grace Starry West, trans. 1984. *Four Texts on Socrates: Plato's "Euthyphro," "Apology," and "Crito" and Aristophanes' "Clouds."* Ithaca, NY: Cornell University Press.

Wilkes, Kathleen. 1979. "Conclusions on the *Meno*." *Archiv für Geschichte der Philosophie* 61: 143–53.

Wolfsdorf, David. 2006. "Desire for Good in *Meno* 77B2–78B6." *Classical Quarterly* n.s. 56: 77–92.

Yalom, Irvin. 1992. *When Nietzsche Wept*. New York: Basic Books.

Zeyl, Donald. 1982. "Socratic Virtue and Happiness." *Archiv für Geschichte der Philosophie* 64: 225–38.

———. 1980. "Socrates and Hedonism." *Phronesis* 25: 250–69.

Zuckert, Catherine H. 2009. *Plato's Philosophers: The Coherence of the Dialogues*. Chicago: University of Chicago Press.

INDEX